D1708132

The Best Within Us

The Best Within Us

Positive Psychology Perspectives on Eudaimonia

EDITED BY ALAN S. WATERMAN

AMERICAN PSYCHOLOGICAL ASSOCIATION

WASHINGTON, DC

Copyright © 2013 by the American Psychological Association. All rights reserved. Except as permitted under the United States Copyright Act of 1976, no part of this publication may be reproduced or distributed in any form or by any means, including, but not limited to, the process of scanning and digitization, or stored in a database or retrieval system, without the prior written permission of the publisher.

Published by
American Psychological Association
750 First Street, NE
Washington, DC 20002
www.apa.org

To order
P.O. Box 92984
Washington, DC 20090-2984
Tel: (800) 374-2721; Direct: (202) 336-5510
Fax: (202) 336-5502; TDD/TTY: (202) 336-6123
Online: www.apa.org/pubs/books
E-mail: order@apa.org

In the U.K., Europe, Africa, and the Middle East, copies may be ordered from
American Psychological Association
3 Henrietta Street
Covent Garden, London
WC2E 8LU England

Typeset in Goudy by Circle Graphics, Inc., Columbia, MD

Printer: Maple Press, York, PA
Cover Designer: Berg Design, Albany, NY

The opinions and statements published are the responsibility of the authors, and such opinions and statements do not necessarily represent the policies of the American Psychological Association.

Library of Congress Cataloging-in-Publication Data

The best within us : positive psychology perspectives on eudaimonia /
edited by Alan S. Waterman.
    p. cm.
Includes bibliographical references and index.
ISBN 978-1-4338-1261-3 — ISBN 1-4338-1261-4 1. Positive psychology. 2. Well-being.
3. Happiness. I. Waterman, Alan S.

BF204.6.B477 2013
158—dc23
                              2012030170

British Library Cataloguing-in-Publication Data

A CIP record is available from the British Library.

Printed in the United States of America
First Edition

DOI: 10.1037/14092-000

To David L. Norton (1930–1995) and Erik H. Erikson (1902–1994)

Amid these distractions he is undiverted
from the purpose that is inscribed in his existence—
to become the person he potentially is
and to cultivate the conditions by which others may do likewise.
—David L. Norton, *Personal Destinies*

It is best to do to another
what will strengthen you even as it strengthens him—
that is, what will develop his best potentials
even as it develops your own.
—Erik H. Erikson, *Insight and Responsibility*

CONTENTS

Contributors .... *xi*

Preface .... *xiii*

Introduction: Considering the Nature of a Life Well Lived—
Intersections of Positive Psychology and Eudaimonist Philosophy 3
Alan S. Waterman

Chapter 1.   Recipes for a Good Life: Eudaimonism
     and the Contribution of Philosophy 19
     Valerie Tiberius

Chapter 2.   Feelings, Meanings, and Optimal Functioning:
     Some Distinctions Between Hedonic
     and Eudaimonic Well-Being 39
     Joar Vittersø

Chapter 3.   What Humans Need: Flourishing in Aristotelian
               Philosophy and Self-Determination Theory.................. 57
               Richard M. Ryan, Randall R. Curren,
               and Edward L. Deci

Chapter 4.   Eudaimonic Well-Being and Health: Mapping
               Consequences of Self-Realization................................. 77
               Carol D. Ryff

Chapter 5.   Eudaimonic Identity Theory.. 99
               Alan S. Waterman and Seth J. Schwartz

Chapter 6.   Individual Daimon, Universal Needs, and
               Subjective Well-Being: Happiness as
               the Natural Consequence of a Life Well Lived 119
               Kennon M. Sheldon

Chapter 7.   Pursuing Eudaimonia Versus Hedonia: Distinctions,
               Similarities, and Relationships.................................... 139
               Veronika Huta

Chapter 8.   Is Meaning in Life a Flagship Indicator
               of Well-Being?... 159
               Michael F. Steger, Joo Yeon Shin, Yerin Shim,
               and Arissa Fitch-Martin

Chapter 9.   Passion and Optimal Functioning in Society:
               A Eudaimonic Perspective 183
               Robert J. Vallerand

Chapter 10.   The Importance of Who You Really Are:
               The Role of the True Self in Eudaimonia................... 207
               Rebecca J. Schlegel, Kelly A. Hirsch,
               and Christina M. Smith

Chapter 11.   Cross-Cultural Perceptions of Meaning
               and Goals in Adulthood: Their Roots
               and Relations With Happiness 227
               Antonella Delle Fave, Marié Wissing, Ingrid Brdar,
               Dianne Vella-Brodrick, and Teresa Freire

Chapter 12.   Discovering Positive Lives and Futures:
               Adolescent Eudaimonic Expression Through
               Activity Involvement.. 249
               J. Douglas Coatsworth and Erin Hiley Sharp

Chapter 13.   Human Strengths and Well-Being: Finding
               the Best Within Us at the Intersection
               of Eudaimonic Philosophy, Humanistic
               Psychology, and Positive Psychology 269
               P. Alex Linley

Index 287
About the Editor... 303

CONTRIBUTORS

Ingrid Brdar, PhD, University of Rijeka, Rijeka, Croatia

J. Douglas Coatsworth, PhD, The Pennsylvania State University, University Park

Randall R. Curren, PhD, University of Rochester, Rochester, NY

Edward L. Deci, PhD, University of Rochester, Rochester, NY

Antonella Delle Fave, MD, University of Milano, Milano, Italy

Arissa Fitch-Martin, BA, Colorado State University, Fort Collins

Teresa Freire, PhD, University of Minho, Braga, Portugal

Kelly A. Hirsch, MA, Texas A&M University, College Station

Veronika Huta, PhD, University of Ottawa, Ottawa, Ontario, Canada

P. Alex Linley, PhD, Centre of Applied Positive Psychology, Coventry, United Kingdom

Richard M. Ryan, PhD, University of Rochester, Rochester, NY

Carol D. Ryff, PhD, University of Wisconsin–Madison

Rebecca J. Schlegel, PhD, Texas A&M University, College Station

Seth J. Schwartz, University of Miami, Miami, FL

Erin Hiley Sharp, PhD, University of New Hampshire, Durham, NH

Kennon M. Sheldon, PhD, University of California–Davis

Yerin Shim, MA, Colorado State University, Fort Collins
Joo Yeon Shin, MA, Colorado State University, Fort Collins
Christina M. Smith, BA, BS, Texas A&M University, College Station
Michael F. Steger, PhD, Colorado State University, Fort Collins
Valerie Tiberius, PhD, University of Minnesota, Minneapolis
Robert J. Vallerand, PhD, Université du Québec à Montréal, Montréal, Quebec, Canada
Dianne Vella-Brodrick, PhD, Monash University, Caulfield East, Victoria, Australia
Joar Vittersø, PhD, University of Tromsø, Tromsø, Norway
Alan S. Waterman, PhD, The College of New Jersey, Ewing
Marié Wissing, PhD, North-West University, Potchefstroom Campus, Potchefstroom, South Africa

PREFACE

When approaching a publisher with an idea for a book, an editor needs to be prepared to answer three questions: (a) Why this book? (b) Why now? and (c) Who is it for?

Why this book? I have had a long-standing interest in the philosophical foundations of psychological theories. In my research on identity formation, I have found philosophical writings on eudaimonism of particular benefit to understanding how individuals might make better identity choices. I have followed the work of the contributors to this book for a long time and have seen in their theories and their research a shared eudaimonic foundation for the diverse psychological concepts we have been studying independently. I believe that bringing our work together in a single volume will promote a recognition of the many connections among our research endeavors and promote future efforts to investigate those connections. One goal I have for this book is to advance a broader, more integrated understanding of the best in human functioning, guided in part by our shared philosophical perspective.

Why now? The nature of well-being has been a subject of long-standing concern in psychology. Much of the work on the topic has been directed toward subjective accounts of well-being. The contributors to this volume, in varying ways, have sought to expand the understanding of well-being beyond subjective indices, directing the attention of the field to psychological qualities that are now subsumed under the umbrella of eudaimonic functioning. As part of the growth of positive psychology, the past decade has seen a marked increase in attention paid to distinctions between hedonic and eudaimonic concepts. A book devoted to exploring the breadth of theory and research regarding eudaimonic well-being can help us better understand where this field has been, where it is now, and what may be possible in the future.

Who is it for? This book is intended for a broad audience in the social sciences with an interest in the nature of happiness and well-being and in the empirical research that has been conducted with the goal of better understanding what constitutes a life well lived. The scope of the audience extends beyond those with academic interests. Ideas regarding eudaimonic well-being have much to offer those seeking to advance well-being, whether through education, counseling, clinical interactions, or social policy. The book should be of interest to philosophers seeking to understand how philosophical ideas are influencing work in psychology and other social sciences. It is hoped that the clarity of the presentations offered by the authors here will also make the ideas presented accessible to an even broader general audience with interest in quality of life and looking to learn what the social sciences, guided in part by philosophy, have to contribute.

Another of the goals I had in mind when starting this project was the prospect of increasing dialogue between psychologists and philosophers on themes of mutual interest. On numerous occasions I have had conversations with philosophers on the themes addressed in this book. Most often these conversations have involved a vigorous exchange of ideas that has set my thinking moving in new, and often very productive, directions. There have been instances, rare I am glad to say, when concerns were raised regarding what might be described as the "cherry picking" of ideas from philosophy and their incorporation into psychological theories in ways never envisioned by their originators. My response on these occasions has been that as a psychologist, I am not "doing philosophy" but rather seeking to better understand the best of human functioning and how it may be studied. Philosophical writings can serve as a valuable source of inspiration for advances in psychological theory and empirical investigations. In turn, I believe philosophers can better reflect on what is good for us, both as individuals and as a species, the more they know empirically about human nature and its potentials. It is not that philosophers should seek to be psychologists, nor the reverse, but an ongoing conversation between us can, potentially, serve to advance projects in both our domains.

For a book with the title *The Best Within Us*, exploring as it does eudaimonic themes in psychological functioning and with recurring references to the "true" self, flourishing, self-realization, autonomy, excellence, and well-being, it would be easy to assume that the intent is to focus on self-interest and what benefits the individual. It is, however, an incorrect assumption. A basic premise of my work throughout my career has been that those who have been most successful in achieving the best within themselves have the most to offer to others, have the greatest desire to bring out the best within others, and live lives of greatest mutuality with those they love.

I have dedicated this book to two individuals, one a philosopher, the other a psychologist, whose writings have been sources of continuing inspiration for me. The epigraphs I've chosen to open the book reflect the premise that eudaimonic well-being is both an individual and interdependent value to be pursued. From the perspective of eudaimonic ethics, the benefits to oneself and to others are inseparable.

I am honored that so many scholars whose work I have enjoyed and benefited from over the years have joined me in this project. Their enthusiasm and responsiveness to the vision of this book are deeply appreciated.

I also wish to take this opportunity to express my love and gratitude to my family, my wife, Sally Archer, and our sons and their wives, Aaron and Jessie, and Jeremy and Michelle. Their being who they are has made my life immensely richer.

The Best Within Us

INTRODUCTION: CONSIDERING THE NATURE OF A LIFE WELL LIVED—INTERSECTIONS OF POSITIVE PSYCHOLOGY AND EUDAIMONIST PHILOSOPHY

ALAN S. WATERMAN

The emergence of positive psychology constitutes one of the most important developments in the field of psychology at the start of the 21st century (Seligman & Csikszentmihalyi, 2000). The central premise in positive psychology is that psychological health does not equate with the absence of psychological problems (mental illness), but rather with the ability to lead a fulfilling, meaningful life. The positive psychology perspective did not create an interest in the elements of positive psychological functioning—for example, life satisfaction, self-esteem, intrinsic motivation, psychosocial identity formation—but, instead, brought together disparate lines of research around the more central questions about the nature of a life well lived and what it takes to promote the ability to live such lives. At their core, these are *normative* questions, that is, questions as to how a person ought to live. Such normative questions have traditionally been the province of philosophers. In recognition of the normative implications of the theoretical and research questions positive psychologists are addressing, there has been a growing interest

DOI: 10.1037/14092-001
The Best Within Us: Positive Psychology Perspectives on Eudaimonia, Alan S. Waterman (Editor)
Copyright © 2013 by the American Psychological Association. All rights reserved.

in the philosophical roots of many of the concepts being studied and the potential to use philosophical insights in the development of theory and testable hypotheses. This book brings together the work of a diverse panel of psychologists who are working on the nature of positive psychological functioning and who recognize and draw on the connections of their work to a strand of ethical philosophy termed *eudaimonism*. Our objective is to trace out those connections as they provide a basis for claims that the constructs studied constitute elements in a life well lived.

AN OVERVIEW OF EUDAIMONIST PHILOSOPHY

In an introduction designed to convey the goals for this book and the nature of the material to be covered, it is possible to provide only a brief overview of the nature of eudaimonist philosophy. A more extensive discussion of elements within the philosophy is provided in Chapter 1. Before addressing eudaimonism itself, it will be helpful to say a few words about how a good life was perceived before the concept of *eudaimonia* came to prominence.

Hedonia as the Pursuit of a Life of Pleasure

A commonly held notion in the 4th century BCE was that happiness constituted the key element in a good life. The term *happiness* is generally considered to refer to the subjective condition of hedonic happiness, or *hedonia*. Hedonia includes "the belief that one is getting the important things one wants, as well as certain pleasant affects that normally go along with this belief" (Kraut, 1979, p. 178). The most thorough expression of hedonism as an ethical theory was advanced by Aristippus of Cyrene in the 4th century BCE, who held that "pleasure is the *sole* good, but also that only one's own physical, positive, momentary pleasure is a good, and is so regardless of its cause" (Tatarkiewicz, 1976, p. 317).

It is noteworthy that it is a particular type of subjective experience that is being used as the criteria of a good life and that the source of such experiences is not a factor to be considered. We hear this currently in the expression "Whatever makes you happy." It is the outcome, happiness, that counts, not the process by which that is to be achieved.

Aristotle emphatically rejected the notion that hedonism should be the goal for a good life. In *Nicomachean Ethics*, he wrote the following:

> The many, the most vulgar, seemingly conceive the good and happiness
> as pleasure, and hence they also like the life of gratification. Here they
> appear completely slavish, since the life they decide on is a life fit for
> grazing animals. (Aristotle, trans. 1985, p. 7)

What Aristotle proposed in its stead was eudaimonia, which, like hedonia, has traditionally been translated as *happiness* but which has a very different meaning. For Aristotle, eudaimonia meant "virtue," "excellence," the very "best within us." According to Aristotle, the means by which happiness is brought about is the essential element in a good life, at least as important as the outcome itself, if not more so. This brings us, then, to the various meanings of eudaimonia as the term has evolved within philosophy.

Eudaimonia as Happiness

When social scientists look at terms like *hedonia, pleasure,* and *happiness,* and the contrast of hedonia and eudaimonia with both being translated as happiness, we immediately start thinking in terms of subjective experiences. How does one feel when experiencing happiness, whether in the form of hedonic enjoyment or in the form of eudaimonia involving the pursuit of excellence in what we do? So the first form for a definition of eudaimonia is a subjective definition.

Kraut (1979) and Norton (1976) were explicit in including within their view of eudaimonia a set of distinctive subjective experiences. Norton wrote of eudaimonia as the feeling of "being where one wants to be, doing what one wants to do" (p. 216), where what is wanted is considered something worth doing. Eudaimonia includes a constellation of subjective experiences, including feelings of rightness and centeredness in one's actions, identity, strength of purpose, and competence. May (1969), a psychologist, referred to the intensity that is typical for experiences of eudaimonia as having "the power to take over the whole person" (p. 121).

Telfer (1980) explored the philosophical relationships between subjective experiences of hedonia and eudaimonia, concluding that the latter was a sufficient but not a necessary condition for the former. In other words, activities can result in one of three sets of conditions with respect to subjective experiences of happiness: (a) the simultaneous presence of both hedonia and eudaimonia, (b) the presence of hedonia but not eudaimonia, or (c) neither hedonia nor eudaimonia being present. It is the nature of the activity itself, that is, the source of potential happiness, that makes the difference in what subjective experiences will be present. The pursuit of virtue/excellence gives rise to both eudaimonia and hedonia, whereas the pursuit of gratification can lead only to experiences of hedonia.

Eudaimonia as Flourishing

At this point it is appropriate to point out a famous maxim, originating with Solon, which Aristotle quoted: "Count no man happy (eudaimon) until he is dead." It makes no sense to consider a person to be subjectively happy only after passing on, so we should immediately suspect that Aristotle had something else in mind than subjective happiness, even in the form of how we feel in the pursuit of virtue/excellence. The alternative to a subjective definition of eudaimonia involves determining what objective qualities of human functioning make for a good life, a life well lived, such that when it has ended we can say that this person has lived a quality life. Philosophers such as Rasmussen (1999), Haybron (2008), and others who want to focus on an objective meaning of eudaimonia translate it not as happiness but as flourishing. Flourishing is based on a conception of human nature, with the possibility that such a nature may be expressed well or poorly. For example, the Aristotelian perspective on flourishing includes reason, contemplation, and virtue (Ackrill, 1973). Philosophers have debated whether the focus here should be on a generic consideration of human nature common to everyone (Holma, 2007) or an individualized, agent-relative, self-directed nature specific to each person (Aloni, 2008; Rasmussen, 1999). So now we have a second, objective meaning for the term, one that focuses on the character and characteristics of a life lived well.

Eudaimonia as Self-Realization

There is a third meaning within philosophy attached to the term *eudaimonia*. The word embodies within it the elements *eu* (good or healthy) and *daimon* (true self). The daimon consists of those unique qualities that make each of us not just human, but also an individual different from all those around us. The concept of the daimon was already present in Hellenic philosophy prior to Aristotle. It was conceived of as originating externally to the individual as a kind of guiding spirit or tutelary god provided at birth. But the concept was later internalized, as reflected in the view of Heraclitus that a "man's character is his daimon" (May, 1969, p. 133). The daimon refers to the potentialities of each person, the realization of which represents the greatest fulfillment in living of which each of us is capable. The daimon is an ideal, in the sense of being an excellence and a perfection toward which we can strive, and hence it can provide meaning and direction to our lives. The contemporary eudaimonist philosopher, David Norton (1976), wrote that "each person is obliged to know and live in truth to his *daimon*, thereby progressively actualizing an excellence that is his innately and potentially" (p. ix).

To be consistent with the standards of contemporary psychological theory, the daimon should be interpreted as comprising a number of interrelated psychological processes. If it is accepted that individuals possess certain potentialities (some of which are universal and some of which are unique) by virtue of their physiology and/or experience, then the daimon refs to those processes, both intuitive and reasoned, by which those potentials are discovered and come to attain the status of personally concordant goals that are to be actualized. The concept of *aptitude* embodies the idea that potentials are biologically grounded and is well accepted within psychology. Aptitudes are, however, generally treated as relatively passive qualities that may be identified through psychological testing, rather than as a process with attendant affective and motivational elements. The daimon, in contrast, includes the idea that the subjective experiences accompanying actions consistent with our aptitudes are immediately distinguishable from those experienced when engaged in activities unrelated to our latent talents. Eudaimonia, as a subjective experience, serves to reinforce activity consistent with our aptitudes, promoting similar activity in the future. On the other hand, in the absence of eudaimonia, the reinforcement for continuing efforts regarding a given activity is likely to be dependent on external factors such as encouragement from others, praise, or material rewards for continued performance. Phrased in this way, it is evident that the concept of the daimon is closely allied with the construct of *intrinsic motivation*. (For a more extended discussion of the nature of the daimon, see Waterman, 1990a.)

In contrast to the concept of eudaimonia as *flourishing*, a broad array of qualities that constitute living well, the interpretation of eudaimonia as *self-realization* constitutes a more narrow objective definition of the term. It identifies the expression of a specific element of psychological functioning as most central to a life well lived.

Eudaimonia as a Normative Concept

As mentioned in the opening of this chapter, philosophical consideration as to how individuals ought to live constitutes a normative question. This applies with respect to all three definitions of eudaimonia described here. For example, Aristotle's analysis of eudaimonia—placing excellence and virtue at the center of a life well lived—constitutes a conceptual philosophical claim as to how a person ought to live. The merits of such claims rest entirely on the strength of the logical reasoning advanced to support them. Such claims concern the right ways of acting. Because individuals act in a given way, with particular consequences, does not justify concluding that they ought to act in such a fashion. Thus, empirical data regarding how people actually function with regard to a particular type of behavior, and the consequences that result, cannot serve as a basis for concluding that such are the proper ends of human functioning. Psychology and other social sciences do not have a role to play at this level.

However, Aristotle and contemporary eudaimonist philosophers are making a second type of claim as well. Eudaimonist philosophy includes the proposition that if people act in particular ways—for example, on the basis of the development and expression of their best potentials—this will yield particular types of consequences with respect to happiness and well-being. This is a teleological or consequentialist, rather than conceptual, claim. It pertains to the nature of what is good for human beings rather than what is right. This type of claim is empirically testable and therefore falls within the province of the social sciences as well as philosophy. Do the benefits in terms of happiness and well-being actually accrue to people when acting in ways advocated within eudaimonist philosophy? The psychologists whose work is represented in this volume connect the research questions they are addressing to foundations found within the philosophy. To the extent that they base their views on how people ought to live on conceptual claims, their empirical research addresses questions as to whether the right is also the good. To the extent that their research questions concern the benefits to human flourishing to be derived from particular ways of acting, they are addressing consequentialist claims made within the philosophy. Thus, psychologists and other social scientists have a significant role to play in the evaluating normative questions as to how people ought to live.

POSITIVE PSYCHOLOGICAL PERSPECTIVES ON THE NATURE OF WELL-BEING

Within positive psychology, the concept of well-being constitutes the primary criteria for positive functioning and is generally considered the goal in life to be promoted. It is a term that has been given a variety of meanings, three of which parallel the definitions that have been attached to eudaimonia: (a) subjective well-being, (b) psychological well-being, and (c) eudaimonic well-being. These parallels are explored throughout this volume.

Subjective Well-Being: Well-Being as Happiness

The field of research that has come to be labeled *subjective well-being* (SWB) is centered on the concept of positive psychological functioning as happiness, with the understanding that each person has the right to form a personal judgment as to what makes for happiness (Diener, 2000). Work on SWB predates the development of the positive psychology perspective by several decades. The earliest usage of the term appeared in the 1970s.

Definitions of SWB have focused on the ratio of the presence or frequency of positive and negative emotions over some specified period of time and on a more global, cognitive–affective assessment of life satisfaction. The more positive the ratio of emotions and the higher the level of reported life satisfaction, the greater the level of SWB. It is important to recognize that the widely used methods for assessing SWB do not explicitly take into account the nature of the sources that give rise to the happiness or life satisfaction experienced. High scores on measures of SWB tell us that a person is happy and in that sense is functioning positively, but they do not provide information as to why happiness is being experienced. Thus, high scores may occur because the person is engaging in activities giving rise to subjective experiences of hedonia and eudaimonia simultaneously or in activities the nature of which give rise only to hedonia. Whereas psychologists studying happiness from an SWB perspective recognize that the source of happiness makes a difference in life outcomes (Diener & Biswas-Diener, 2008), to the present, the contributions that source makes to happiness have not been a major focus of investigation in SWB research.

There is, however, a second line of theory and research work on the subjective experiences of happiness that is relevant to making distinctions between eudaimonia and hedonia. Maslow (1968, 1970) drew distinctions between what he labeled *d-cognition* and *b-cognition* (in which *d* and *b* stand for *deficit* and *being*, respectively). *Peak experience* was the alternative term for b-cognition, and the description provided bears a striking resemblance to philosophers' depiction of subjective eudaimonia. Peak experiences are ones transcending our normal experiences of pleasure. They are the most memorable experiences in our lives. We feel more whole, more integrated, more loving and accepting of others, most able to use our talents, in other words, most self-actualizing.

Csikszentmihalyi (1975, 1990) has provided a description of flow experiences, those subjective experiences present when we are intensely engaged in an activity that provides a balance of the challenges posed with the skills we bring to it. We have clear goals, we lose track of time, we forget our personal problems, and we feel we merge with the actions we are performing. These match many of the elements Maslow included as aspects of b-cognition and are compatible with descriptions of eudaimonia.

My own research drawing empirical distinctions between hedonic enjoyment and feelings of personal expressiveness (eudaimonia) follows in this tradition (Waterman, 1993; Waterman, Schwartz, & Conti, 2008). We experience such feelings when we are engaged in activities for which we appear to have a natural affinity or sense of connection. We feel authentic, that "this is who I really am." Such feelings may appear on the very first occasion in which we engage in an activity. We believe they reflect our natural talents. They provide us with a sense of self-realization.

Psychological Well-Being: Well-Being as Flourishing

The focus on positive psychological functioning as flourishing is central to self-determination theory (Deci & Ryan, 1985). Ryan, Huta, and Deci

(2008) presented a model of eudaimonic functioning that is based on four motivational concepts: (a) the pursuit of intrinsic goals and values, that is, objectives valued for their own sake rather than for outcomes unrelated to the activity in itself, such as wealth or admiration; (b) behavior that is self-directed and autonomous rather than based on the preferences of others or their instigation; (c) acting mindfully, that is, with full attention to what is being undertaken; and (d) fulfilling what are seen as being universal, basic psychological needs for competence, relatedness, and autonomy. Acting in eudaimonic ways is posited to promote both psychological and physical well-being.

A similar focus on flourishing is found in the work of Ryff and her colleagues (Ryff, 1989; Ryff & Singer, 2008). Responding to what Ryff considered an overemphasis on affective aspects in the SWB understanding of well-being, she developed an alternative approach that focused on the psychological/behavioral characteristics that can be considered optimal mental health. As with studies on SWB, work on psychological well-being (PWB) was begun before the emergence of the positive psychology perspective. Ryff drew on even earlier work on the nature of mental health (e.g., Jahoda, 1958) and on classical theories of personality that provided descriptions of healthy psychological functioning (e.g., Allport, 1961; Erikson, 1959; Jung, 1933; Rogers, 1961). The six core dimensions she used to describe PWB are (a) autonomy, (b) environmental mastery, (c) personal growth, (d) positive relations with others, (e) purpose in life, and (f) self-acceptance. Ryff (Ryff & Singer, 2008) has been explicit in identifying the philosophical roots of her work in writings of Aristotle on eudaimonia and other philosophers.

Eudaimonic Well-Being: Well-Being as Self-Realization

The term *eudaimonic well-being* (EWB) was first used by Ryan and Deci (2001) in an *Annual Review* article contrasting EWB with hedonic well-being. Under the heading of EWB, Ryan and Deci discussed their own work on self-determination and intrinsic motivation, the work of Ryff on PWB, and my work on personal expressiveness, among other aspects of positive psychological functioning. The theory and research discussed under the heading of hedonic well-being was largely work conducted within the SWB tradition. In contrasting EWB with hedonic well-being, they were bringing into the psychology literature the original Aristotelian counterpointing of eudaimonia and hedonia and were following those philosophers preferring to translate eudaimonia as flourishing rather than as happiness. I will refer to this as the broad conceptualization of eudaimonic well-being. There is, however, a narrower conceptualization of EWB that can be advanced, one building on the translation of eudaimonia as self-realization.

There has been a long-standing concern with self-realization within the field of psychology. Theoretical discussions of self-realization, self-actualization, and related constructs can be found in the work of Goldstein, (1951), Horney (1950), Maslow (1968, 1970), and Rogers (1961). Empirical research on these constructs was particularly active during the 1960s and 1970s but declined dramatically in later decades as the humanistic psychology perspective fell largely out of favor. My efforts to understand identity formation, that is, how individuals come to define themselves in terms of their goals, values, and beliefs (Waterman, 1992, 2004), and to understand the nature of positive human functioning from a eudaimonist perspective (Waterman,1990a, 2008) led me to place self-realization at the center of my current theoretical and empirical research efforts. In doing so, my work is more closely aligned with contemporary eudaimonist philosophers such as Norton (1976) than with Aristotle's classical perspective (Waterman, 1990b).

Conceptualizing EWB as self-realization involves a focus on four elements: (a) the self-discovery of one's aptitudes or latent talents; (b) dedicated effort in the development of those aptitudes into skills and expressed talents; (c) choosing purposes in life through which those talents can be utilized; and (d) finding and using opportunities afforded within one's physical, social, and economic contexts for the ongoing expression of one's skills and talents for one's chosen purposes in life. When engaged in activities related to the self-discovery of the daimon, the development of our talents, and their implementation for meaningful purposes, we experience subjective eudaimonia.

Another view of well-being consistent with this perspective is Sheldon's (2002) theory of self-concordance. *Self-concordance* refers to the feelings of ownership that people experience with respect to the goals they choose to pursue. Self-concordance theory was developed within the framework of self-determination theory and builds on it. Sheldon distinguished between the pursuit of goals consistent with a person's authentic interests and core values and goals chosen for extrinsic considerations or that one is otherwise constrained to act on. In an upward spiral, the pursuit of self-concordant goals is associated with greater sustained effort; a greater likelihood of goal attainment; and, in turn, an increased sense of well-being. This increased well-being promotes still stronger motivation toward the attainment of self-concordant goals, enhancing further successes and still greater well-being (Sheldon & Houser-Marko, 2001). This self-reinforcing cycle is absent for the pursuit of goals not perceived as self-concordant. The theory of self-concordance also stresses the contributions of cross-situational self-consistency and authenticity to experiences of well-being (Sheldon, Ryan, Rawsthorne, & Ilardi, 1997). The concept of the daimon appears an integral component of self-concordance in that well-being is viewed within the theory as a function of the extent to which core or true aspects of the self are finding expression in the goals selected and the activities a person performs.

EWB, conceptualized as self-realization and self-concordance, embodies both objective and subjective components. Self-realization and self-concordance should be seen as objective components of positive psychological functioning in the sense of flourishing. They are singled out for attention within the narrow concept of EWB due both to the special place accorded such concepts within contemporary eudaimonist philosophy and to the possibility that they may serve as the keystone for understanding flourishing. The subjective component is the presence of eudaimonia (as happiness)/ feelings of personal expressiveness typically experienced when engaged in activities associated with self-realization. It is essential to recognize, however, that experiencing eudaimonia/authenticity is not the goal in life being sought; the goal is the full use of our talents for meaningful purposes. Subjective eudaimonia/feelings of personal expressiveness serve as cues that we are on the right track.

When the same term, in this instance EWB, is used with more than one meaning, there is always the potential for confusion. To reduce the likelihood of this occurring, I have asked contributors to this volume when using the term EWB to make clear whether they are using it with the broad (flourishing) or the narrow (self-realization) meaning in mind.

Relationships Among the Three Conceptualizations of Well-Being

As discussed previously, SWB, PWB, and EWB (in the narrow sense) are defined in largely independent ways. SWB (well-being as happiness) is conceptualized in strictly subjective terms, combining both experiences of hedonia and eudaimonia. PWB (well-being as flourishing) is conceptualized in strictly objective terms as elements associated with positive psychological functioning. EWB (well-being as self-realization) involves both subjective and objective components, the subjective focused specifically on eudaimonia rather than hedonia and the objective focused on self-realization, an aspect of positive psychological functioning not given special emphasis within theories of well-being as flourishing.

Despite these largely independent approaches to conceptualizing well-being, there are excellent theoretical grounds for expecting that measures of SWB, PWB, and EWB should be strongly, positively correlated. The presence of the components of positive mental health (PWB) indicates that a person has the capacities to successfully meet the day-to-day life demands likely to be encountered. Under such circumstances it is highly likely that life satisfaction (SWB) will be strongly positive in terms of both hedonia and eudaimonia. This may be tempered, however, by any of a variety of contextual factors, such as a recent setback in the pursuit of some life goal or the loss of some interpersonal relationship. Whereas theories of flourishing have not emphasized the role of self-realization in PWB, the components of mental health they embody constitute an excellent foundation for achieving success with respect to EWB, and success at achieving self-realization will itself further strengthen various other components of flourishing. In addition, high scores on measures of EWB should be positively associated with measures of SWB in that successes with respect to self-realization constitute a source of happiness giving rise to both eudaimonia and hedonia. As mentioned previously, the strength of this relationship may be tempered by contextual variables such as recent setbacks and losses and, of particular relevance here, difficulties encountered in the path of fulfilling one's purposes in life.

Despite minimal item overlap in measures of SWB, PWB, and EWB, it would be predicted that correlations among them would be positive and strong. Findings from one recent study (Schwartz et al., 2011) involving assessment of the three forms of well-being among over 9,000 college students drawn from 30 colleges and universities supported this expectation. The correlations obtained were .60 for SWB–PWB, .65 for PWB–EWB, and .48 for SWB–EWB ($p < .001$ in all instances). Whereas the strength of these correlations is consistent with the hypothesized linkages, they are not of such a magnitude as to indicate that they are a single, unified construct.

THE PLAN FOR THIS BOOK

The chapters in this book are designed to (a) provide an overview of the various conceptual approaches to the understanding of eudaimonism in philosophy and psychology, (b) review theory and research pertaining to various aspects of eudaimonic functioning, and (c) examine contextual factors that affect the expression of such functioning. The opening two chapters provide in-depth discussions of the ways eudaimonia has been conceptualized in philosophy and well-being has been treated in psychology. In Chapter 1, Valerie Tiberius considers the breadth of perspectives advanced within the realm of eudaimonist philosophy as these provide a foundation for the understanding of happiness and well-being. Chapter 2, by Joar Vittersø, contains a presentation of the competing conceptions of well-being addressing the strengths and the problems associated with each of them.

The next four chapters address psychological theories regarding the constituents of eudaimonic functioning. In Chapter 3, Richard M. Ryan, Randall R. Curren, and Edward L. Deci present material with respect to self-determination theory and its contributions to understanding well-being as flourishing. Carol D. Ryff, in Chapter 4, traces the philosophical foundations of psychological well-being and reviews empirical research conducted from this perspective. In Chapter 5, my colleague Seth J. Schwartz and I discuss eudaimonic identity theory and associated research exploring the ways in which the daimon serves as a basis for establishing personal goals, values, and beliefs. Chapter 6, by Kennon M. Sheldon, contains a presentation of self-concordance theory and the research based on this understanding of eudaimonic functioning.

Following these broad theory–based chapters are a series of chapters focusing on theory and research concerning particular constituents of eudaimonic functioning. Chapter 7 by Veronika Huta explores the similarities, differences, and relationships of eudaimonia and hedonia as two conceptions of subjective happiness. In Chapter 8 by Michael F. Steger, Joo Yeon Shin, Yerin Shim, and Arissa Fitch-Martin, the focus is on the concept of meaning in life as a possible flagship indicator of well-being. The nature of passionate involvement in what people do in their lives is the subject of Chapter 9 by Robert J. Vallerand. Chapter 10 by Rebecca J. Schlegel, Kelly A. Hirsch, and Christina M. Smith looks at the psychological importance of the true self-concept.

The next two chapters in the book explore the role of context in eudaimonic functioning and the ways in which it may be promoted. Chapter 11, by Antonella Delle Fave, Marié Wissing, Ingrid Brdar, Dianne Vella-Brodrick, and Teresa Freire reports the findings of a major cross-national study of eudaimonic functioning with a view to identifying cultural generalizations and their limitations. Chapter 12, by J. Douglas Coatsworth and Erin Hiley Sharp, takes a developmental perspective with a specific focus on eudaimonic functioning in adolescence and its implications for positive youth development. The book concludes with a chapter by P. Alex Linley, Chapter 13, which is concerned with interventions for promoting eudaimonic functioning in individuals and communities with an emphasis on the importance of the identification and development of personal strengths.

Given the different conceptualizations of eudaimonia found in philosophical writings (see Chapter 1), I have asked each of the authors here to address how philosophical ideas provide a foundation for their work. In doing so, it is my hope that this volume will promote a greater recognition of the affinities among particular sets of theoretical perspectives on the nature of a life well lived and an appreciation of the breadth of what is meant by eudaimonic functioning.

REFERENCES

Ackrill, J. L. (1973). *Aristotle's ethics*. London, England: Faber and Faber.

Allport, G. W. (1961). *Patterns of growth in personality*. New York, NY: Holt, Rinehart, and Winston.

Aloni, N. (2008). Spinoza as educator: From eudaimonistic ethics to an empowering and liberating pedagogy. *Educational Philosophy and Theory, 40*, 531–544. doi:10.1111/j.1469-5812.2007.00361.x

Aristotle. (1985). *Nicomachean ethics* (T. Irwin, Trans.). Indianapolis, IN: Hackett.

Csikszentmihalyi, M. (1975). *Beyond boredom and anxiety*. San Francisco, CA: Jossey-Bass.

Csikszentmihalyi, M. (1990). *Flow: The psychology of optimal experience*. New York, NY: Harper & Row.

Deci, E. L., & Ryan, R. M. (1985). *Intrinsic motivation and self-determination in human behavior*. New York, NY: Plenum.

Diener, E. (2000). Subjective well-being: The science of happiness and a proposal for a national index. *American Psychologist, 55*, 34–43. doi:10.1037/0003-066X.55.1.34

Diener, E., & Biswas-Diener, R. (2008). *Happiness: Unlocking the mysteries of psychological wealth*. Malden, MA: Blackwell.

Erikson, E. H. (1959). Identity and the life cycle: Selected papers. *Psychological Issues, 1*, 1–171.

Goldstein, K. (1951). On emotions: Considerations from the organismic point of view. *The Journal of Psychology: Interdisciplinary and Applied, 31*, 37–49. doi:10.1080/00223980.1951.9712789

Haybron, D. M. (2008). Happiness, the self, and flourishing. *Utilitas: A Journal of Utilitarian Studies, 20*, 21–49.

Holma, K. (2007). Essentialism regarding human nature in the defence of gender equality in education. *Journal of Philosophy of Education, 41*, 45–57. doi:10.1111/j.1467-9752.2007.00543.x

Horney, K. (1950). *Neurosis and human growth: The struggle toward self-realization*. New York, NY: Norton.

Jahoda, M. (1958). *Current conceptions of positive mental health*. New York, NY: Basic Books. doi:10.1037/11258-000

Jung, C. G. (1933). *Modern man in search of a soul* (W. S. Dell & C. F. Baynes, Trans.). New York, NY: Harcourt, Brace, and World.

Kraut, R. (1979). Two conceptions of happiness. *The Philosophical Review, 88*, 167–196. doi:10.2307/2184505

Maslow, A. H. (1968). *Toward a psychology of being* (2nd ed.). Princeton, NJ: Van Nostrand.

Maslow, A. H. (1970). *Motivation and personality* (2nd ed.). New York, NY: Harper and Row.

May, R. (1969). *Love and will*. New York, NY: Norton.

Norton, D. L. (1976). *Personal destinies*. Princeton, NJ: Princeton University Press.

Rasmussen, D. B. (1999). Human flourishing and the appeal to human nature. *Social Philosophy & Policy, 16*, 1–43. doi:10.1017/S0265052500002235

Rogers, C. (1961). *On becoming a person*. Boston, MA: Houghton Mifflin.

Ryan, R. M., & Deci, E. L. (2001). On happiness and human potentials: A review of research on hedonic and eudaimonic well-being. *Annual Review of Psychology*, *52*, 141–166. doi:10.1146/annurev.psych.52.1.141

Ryan, R. M., Huta, V. A., & Deci, E. L. (2008). Living well: A self-determination theory perspective on eudaimonia. *Journal of Happiness Studies*, *9*, 139–170. doi:10.1007/s10902-006-9023-4

Ryff, C. D. (1989). Happiness is everything, or is it? Explorations of the meaning of psychological well-being. *Journal of Personality and Social Psychology*, *57*, 1069–1081. doi:10.1037/0022-3514.57.6.1069

Ryff, C. D., & Singer, B. H. (2008). Know thyself and become what you are: A eudaimonic approach to psychological well-being. *Journal of Happiness Studies*, *9*, 13–39. doi:10.1007/s10902-006-9019-0

Schwartz, S. J., Waterman, A. S., Vazsonyi, A. T., Zamboanga, B. L., Whitbourne, S. K., Weisskirvh, R. S., . . . Ham, L. S. (2011). The association of well-being with health risk behaviors in college-attending emerging adults. *Applied Developmental Science*, *15*, 20–36. doi:10.1080/10888691.2011.538617

Seligman, M. E. P., & Csikszentmihalyi, M. (2000). Positive psychology: An introduction. *American Psychologist*, *55*, 5–14. doi:10.1037/0003-066X.55.1.5

Sheldon, K. M. (2002). The self-concordance model of healthy goal striving: When personal goals correctly represent the person. In E. L. Deci & R. M. Ryan (Eds.), *Handbook of self-determination research* (pp. 65–86). Rochester, NY: University of Rochester Press.

Sheldon, K. M., & Houser-Marko, L. (2001). Self-concordance, goal attainment, and pursuit of happiness: Can there be an upward spiral? *Journal of Personality and Social Psychology*, *80*, 152–165. doi:10.1037/0022-3514.80.1.152

Sheldon, K. M., Ryan, R. M., Rawsthorne, L. J., & Ilardi, B. (1997). Trait self and true self: Cross-role variation in the Big-Five personality traits and its relations with psychological authenticity and subjective well-being. *Journal of Personality and Social Psychology*, *73*, 1380–1393. doi:10.1037/0022-3514.73.6.1380

Tatarkiewicz, W. (1976). *Analysis of happiness*. The Hague, the Netherlands: Martinus Nijhoff. doi:10.1007/978-94-010-1380-2

Telfer, E. (1980). *Happiness*. New York, NY: St. Martin's Press.

Waterman, A. S. (1990a). Personal expressiveness: Philosophical and psychological foundations. *Journal of Mind and Behavior*, *11*, 47–74.

Waterman, A. S. (1990b). The relevance of Aristotle's conception of eudaimonia for the psychological study of happiness. *Theoretical & Philosophical Psychology*, *10*, 39–44. doi:10.1037/h0091489

Waterman, A. S. (1992). Identity as an aspect of optimal psychological functioning. In G. R. Adams, T. Gullota, & R. Montemayor (Eds.), *Identity formation during adolescence. Advances in adolescent development* (Vol. 4, pp. 50–72). Newbury Park, CA: Sage.

Waterman, A. S. (1993). Two conceptions of happiness: Contrasts of personal expressiveness (eudaimonia) and hedonic enjoyment. *Journal of Personality and Social Psychology, 64*, 678–691. doi:10.1037/0022-3514.64.4.678

Waterman, A. S. (2004). Finding someone to be: Studies on the role of intrinsic motivation in identity formation. *Identity: An International Journal of Theory and Research, 4*, 209–228. doi:10.1207/s1532706xid0403_1

Waterman, A. S. (2008). Reconsidering happiness. A eudaimonist's perspective. *The Journal of Positive Psychology, 3*, 234–252. doi:10.1080/17439760802303002

Waterman, A. S., Schwartz, S. J., & Conti, R. (2008). The implications of two conceptions of happiness (hedonic enjoyment and eudaimonia) for the understanding of intrinsic motivation. *Journal of Happiness Studies, 9*, 41–79. doi:10.1007/s10902-006-9020-7

1

RECIPES FOR A GOOD LIFE: EUDAIMONISM AND THE CONTRIBUTION OF PHILOSOPHY

VALERIE TIBERIUS

Eudaimonia was the word used by the ancient Greek philosophers to describe, in the most general terms, the ultimate goal of life, that at which all human beings aim (Annas, 1993). For the ancients, there was no question about whether eudaimonia was the thing to aim at in life, but there was significant controversy about just what it consisted in. Is the best life for a human being a pleasant or satisfied life? a life in which we develop our capacities to their fullest? a morally virtuous life? This controversy has endured, and it seems to have been inherited by psychology more or less intact.

Attempting to resolve the controversy for good may be a hopeless task. But each of us can aim to articulate our own positions and to understand their advantages and disadvantages. Toward this aim, notice that there are really three different questions we might ask. First, we might ask about the components or ingredients of a well lived or eudaimonic life. If a well lived life is like a cake, then the question is: What goes in the batter? Second, we can ask for a theory that tells us what it is that makes something an ingredient

DOI: 10.1037/14092-002
The Best Within Us: Positive Psychology Perspectives on Eudaimonia, Alan S. Waterman (Editor)
Copyright © 2013 by the American Psychological Association. All rights reserved.

of a well lived life. In other words, we can ask for a recipe that explains why these ingredients are on the list. (The analogy is a little bit strained because cooking recipes do not typically include explanations for the inclusion of ingredients, but they sometimes do; in any case, this explanatory function is a key part of a "recipe" in the sense that I mean.) The important question here, to my mind, is this: What makes this ingredient good for a person? A good philosophical theory of well-being should answer this question. Third, we can ask what makes one theory (or recipe) better than another.

My primary aim in this chapter is to discuss the various theories philosophers have defended and to explain what implications these theories have for eudaimonist ingredients. My focus is, therefore, on the second of my three questions. So, I start with a discussion of theories. Next, I turn to eudaimonist ingredients and consider how the various theories we have surveyed would be applied. Following this, I discuss what difference it makes which theory you choose. Finally, I briefly discuss the remaining question—the question about what makes one theory better than another.

Before getting started, I add a note about terminology. I use the word *well-being* to refer to the most general category of prudential value that is at the center of the above questions. (I also use "x is good for y" to mean that x contributes to y's well-being.) For my purposes, it is important to have a general term that does not presuppose a particular theoretical framework, and this usage comports with the usage of many philosophers and psychologists. So, whether one thinks that a well lived life is hedonistic or eudaimonistic, one is still (in my terms) talking about well-being. I use the term *eudaimonic* in the way that I take psychologists to intend (at least insofar as psychologists are in agreement in their use of the term), that is, as describing ingredients of well-being that go beyond positive affect and life satisfaction. I make no particular assumption about what kind of theory supports claims that eudaimonic ingredients are part of well-being, because as we shall see, such claims can be supported in a variety of ways.

THEORIES OF WELL-BEING

In this section, I survey five different theories of well-being: hedonism, desire-fulfillment, life-satisfaction, nature-fulfillment, and objective-list theory.[1] These philosophical theories of well-being can usefully be distinguished by their presence in one of two camps: subjective theories or objec-

---

[1]Derek Parfit's (1984) oft-cited taxonomy lists three types of theories: hedonism, desire-satisfaction, and objective-list theories. This leaves out some important newer developments (Haybron, 2008).

tive theories. *Subjective* theories hold that whether something counts as contributing to a person's well-being depends on that person's attitudes in some way. *Objective* theories reject this claim; they say that whether something contributes to a person's well-being depends (at least in part) on something else. To put it another way, subjective theories explain why something gets on the list of well-being ingredients by appeal to the attitudes of the well-being subject, whereas objective theories explain what gets on the list by appeal to something beyond the attitudes of the well-being subject.

Discussing some examples will help illustrate this distinction. Let's start with hedonism, which is taken to be a subjective theory because pleasure is a subjective state.[2]

Hedonism

According to hedonism, what is good for a person is pleasure and the absence of pain. Classical utilitarians like Jeremy Bentham (1781) and John Stuart Mill (1861/1979) were hedonists. Both philosophers had what Dan Haybron (2008) and L. W. Sumner (1996) called an *internalist* view of pleasure, sometimes called the *experience account* because it identifies pleasure with a distinctive experience (Moore, 2004). Though Bentham and Mill thought there were distinctions to be made among different kinds of pleasures, they also assumed that all pleasurable experiences had enough in common that they are commensurable (i.e., able to be measured on the same scale).

These assumptions about pleasure are debatable: What exactly do the pleasure of reading a great novel and the pleasure of eating chocolate have in common? Such worries have spurred revised theories of what pleasure is. The main rival to the experiential view of pleasure held by Bentham and (more controversially) Mill has been called an *externalist* or *attitudinal* theory of pleasure. This theory identifies pleasure with an attitude—"being pleased"— taken toward a state of affairs (Feldman, 2004). In this view, what makes an experience or state of affairs pleasurable is that the person having the experience has a certain proattitude toward it: "A person takes attitudinal pleasure in some state of affairs if he enjoys it, is pleased about it, is glad that it is happening, is delighted by it" (Feldman, 2004, p. 56). This solves the problem caused by the fact that different pleasant experiences do not seem to have any common distinctive element, because in this view what they have in

---

[2]Hedonism is actually tricky to classify because people can have different subjective attitudes toward pleasure. (For example, there are masochists who claim to desire pain.) If you're impressed by this fact, you might think that hedonism counts as an objective-list theory with only one item on the list. I leave this complication aside for purposes of our discussion.

common is not something intrinsic to the experience. Rather, pleasures have in common that they are all the object of the proattitude "being pleased by."

Hedonism of all forms as a theory of well-being has been attacked for leaving out something important. A well-known way of putting this objection is Nozick's (1974) "experience machine" thought experiment:

> Suppose there were an experience machine that would give you any experience you desired. Superduper neuropsychologists could stimulate your brain so that you would think and feel you were writing a great novel, or making a friend, or reading an interesting book. All the time you would be floating in a tank, with electrodes attached to your brain. Should you plug into this machine for life, preprogramming your life's experiences? . . . Of course, while in the tank you won't know that you're there; you'll think it's all actually happening. Others can also plug in to have the experiences they want, so there's no need to stay unplugged to serve them. . . . Would you plug in? *What else can matter to us, other than how our lives feel from the inside?* (pp. 42–45; italics in original)

Nozick's answer is that doing and knowing (as opposed to just seeming to do and thinking that we know) can matter to us. He concluded that there are things that matter to us besides pleasure.

Desire-Fulfillment Theories

Objections such as Nozick's led philosophers interested in well-being to *desire-fulfillment* or *preference-satisfaction* theories.[3] According to this type of theory, well-being consists in the attainment of the objects of our desires or preferences. Desire theories have some advantages and are popular in philosophy. First, desire theories can explain what goes wrong in the experience machine: There are things we want (contact with reality, for instance) that we cannot get in the machine. Second, a primary advantage is that desire theories make sense of the individual variability in the particular causes or components of well-being. The quickest survey of the people around us reveals that people are made happy by different things: Jimmy likes physical exertion, Kelly likes intellectual pursuits, and Lou likes to spend time with his family. Desire theory explains how well-being can have so many different causes while at the same time providing a unifying explanation of the phenomena. Third, the explanation offered by this theory explains the special kind of value well-being is supposed to have. Well-being is good for a person; to increase a person's well-being, you must benefit that person. This

---

[3]Though not all philosophers have abandoned hedonism. For those who find the experience machine objection compelling, Feldman (2004, pp. 112–113) offered a version of hedonism that centers on "truth-adjusted" pleasure.

is not necessarily so of moral or aesthetic values, which do not belong to a particular person. Unlike moral value, the value of well-being is a subjective kind of value in at least some important sense, and desire theories explain this by appeal to the fact that it is the subject's own desires that determine his or her well-being. It is because Jimmy wants to exert himself that hiking is good for him; if he wanted to read poetry instead, then hiking would not contribute to his well-being.

Simple preference-satisfaction theories or *present-desire theories*—theories according to which having our actual preferences fulfilled is what is good for us—are favored by economists. This theory of well-being facilitated the construction of economic models that aim to predict and explain behavior in markets. Choices about how to spend money (like all choices, according to this model) express preferences. On the assumption that preference satisfaction is good for us, then, market exchanges track well-being. Few philosophers accept a present-desire theory (but see Heathwood, 2006; Mendola, 2009; Murphy, 1999). Such theories invite myriad counterexamples because of the fact that our desires can be (and often are) misinformed or irrational.

Desire-fulfillment theories have not been abandoned; however, they have been modified to accommodate the fact that our desires can be misdirected. The main form that this modification takes is to idealize the desires whose satisfaction constitutes well-being. In particular, desire-fulfillment theories tend to say that it is only the satisfaction of informed desires that count toward well-being (Griffin, 1986; Railton, 1986). We can see the motivation for this modification with a simple example. Kiry desires French bread, but she is, unbeknownst to her, allergic to gluten. If she were fully informed about her allergy, she would not want French bread because French bread makes her sick. *Informed-desire theory* (sometimes called *full-information theory*) says that getting what she actually wants (bread) is not good for her. Instead, getting what she would want if she were fully informed (gluten-free bread) is good for her. This sort of example is meant to generalize. The thought is that although our actual desires often mislead us, the desires we would have if we really knew everything we needed to know about their objects would not lead us astray.

Informed-desire theory does have its problems. Some critics have argued that the fully informed version of a person might be just as misdirected as her uninformed self, though in different ways (Rosati, 1995; Velleman, 1988). Most of the objections to informed-desire theory have to do with the fact that adding the full information component removes the advantages that desire theories were supposed to have. Desire theories promised to explain the special, subjective value that well-being has. But fully informed desires are not necessarily very closely connected to how people actually feel about things. If Jimmy doesn't want to swim but would if he were fully informed (perhaps about the damage to his joints caused by hiking), then swimming is good for him whether he wants to swim or not. Informed-desire theory may be able to solve these problems by limiting the relevant amount or type of information. Or, there may be a different kind of idealized desire theory that preserves the advantages of informed-desire theory without incurring these costs.

Life-Satisfaction Theory

Life-satisfaction theory is another subjective theory that makes use of idealization. The main proponent of this theory in philosophy, L. W. Sumner (1996), argued that well-being consists in authentic happiness. Happiness, according to Sumner, is life satisfaction, which is "a positive cognitive/affective response on the part of a subject to (some or all of) the conditions or circumstances of her life" (p. 156). Authentic happiness is informed and autonomous life satisfaction. Sumner's motivation for adding these conditions and for not identifying actual life satisfaction with well-being stems from the problem of adaptive preferences, which he takes to be the most fundamental problem for subjective theories. In a nutshell, the problem is that because subjective attitudes can adapt to oppressive circumstances, a subjective theory can have the implication that a person who has adapted to oppression is doing well or achieving well-being. Insofar as well-being is taken to be the target of social policy or the object of beneficent moral action, this implication is problematic. We just don't want to be stuck saying that what we should do for oppressed people is to help them adapt to their limited options and paltry share of resources.

Sumner's (1996) solution to the problem of adaptation is that happiness must be authentic to count as well-being. Because well-being has a special relationship to the subject, life satisfaction only counts as well-being if it expresses an evaluation of one's life that is truly one's own (p. 167). According to Sumner, this means that our life satisfaction (i.e., happiness) only counts as well-being if the assessment of our conditions of life is informed and autonomous. Given this elaboration of the theory, we can see how the problem of adaptation is solved: A person who is satisfied with her life but would not be if she had more information, or if her satisfaction were not warped by oppression, does not count as achieving well-being. Tiberius and colleagues have developed the life-satisfaction theory in a somewhat different way, by arguing that for life satisfaction to count as well-being it must be a response to how well the person is doing in life given her values (Tiberius & Hall, 2010; Tiberius & Plakias, 2010). According to the value-based life-satisfaction theory, your life goes well for you if you achieve what you value and you feel good about your life because of that.

Values do seem important to well-being. Recently, a few philosophers have been developing a subjective theory of well-being according to which well-being is the fulfillment not of our desires or preferences but of our values (Raibley, 2010; Tiberius, 2012). Values, in this view, are stable patterns of affective dispositions that we take to guide our choices and our assessments of how our lives are going. In short, the value fulfillment theory says that living well is a matter of achieving what you care about in a deep and abiding way. This theory might be attractive to psychologists who favor the methodology of distilling components of well-being from trustworthy historical sources. This is the methodology used by Carol Ryff (see Chapter 4, this volume) to arrive at the six key components of eudaimonic well-being. One way we could think about this methodology is that the expert sources have provided us with evidence of what human beings consistently care about when they are being reflective about it. Eudaimonist psychologists, in particular, may find a theory that emphasizes values attractive because of their own emphasis on the importance of aligning one's action with one's values (see Chapter 7, this volume).

Idealizing Conditions in Subjective Well-Being Theories

Both desire theories and life-satisfaction theories in philosophy tend to add idealizing conditions that constrain which subjective states actually contribute to well-being. One explanation for this is that the theories aim to be intuitive, and the idealizing conditions are added to deal with counterexamples. It is not intuitively compelling to think that bread is good for someone with a gluten allergy, for example. But there is a deeper explanation for this move in philosophy. The deeper explanation has to do with two background assumptions: (a) that well-being is a normative notion and (b) that there is a gap between psychological facts and normative claims. In philosophy, to say that a claim (or judgment, or property) is normative is to say that it grounds good reasons for action; *normative* in philosophy is akin to *prescriptive*. Well-being, then, is normative in the sense that when we make claims about something contributing to a person's well-being, we are claiming that there is some reason to secure or promote whatever it is. Claims about well-being are normative in the sense that they have an inherent tie to what we ought to do.

Counterexamples to subjective theories rely on the reason-giving quality of well-being to work. It isn't plausible to think that bread is good for Kiry because it isn't plausible to think that we ought to give her some glutenous bread or that she ought to go and buy some for herself. The idealizing conditions that subjective theories have adopted create distance between the psychological state (desire or life satisfaction) and normative conclusions about what we ought to do. This distance—the gap between *is* and *ought*—may make psychologists think that philosophers' idealized subjective theories are not for them. I don't think this is the right conclusion to draw. Empirical evidence about people's actual psychological states is certainly relevant to what their psychological states would be under ideal conditions. Moreover, idealized subjective theories provide a way for psychologists who want to insist that their work is not value laden to think about how psychological research is nevertheless relevant to normative questions about policy and moral action.

That said, idealized subjective theories are not the only way to go. Indeed, if the goal is to explain the normativity of well-being, one might think that a better solution (better than monkeying around with subjective theories) would be to adopt an objective theory of well-being. Let's turn to these theories now.

Objective-List Theories

The simplest kind of objective theory is an objective-list theory. An *objective-list theory* puts forth a list of objective values that are good for people to achieve (Arneson, 2007; Brink, 1989; Gert, 1998). One proponent stated the following:

> According to the objective list account, a life goes well (for the person whose life it is) to the extent that the individual attains items that occur as entries on a list of objectively intrinsically valuable things. If one gets some item on the list, one's life thereby goes better, independently of one's subjective attitudes or opinions toward getting that thing. (Arneson, 2007, p. 20)

Items on the list tend to be intuitively compelling things such as deep relationships, achievement, and understanding. According to objective-list theory, these things have objective value and contribute to a person's life going well independently of whether she wants them or finds them satisfying.

An objective-list theory accounts for the normativity of well-being by appeal to the value of the items on the list. It therefore has an easy answer to the question of how claims about well-being ground prescriptive or reason-giving conclusions: It is the objective value of the items on the list that secure these conclusions. Some people are sure to find this answer disappointing, however, because it seems to put off the question (or move it to another domain) rather than really answering it. Without a good argument for the objective value of the items on the list, the objective-list theory's solution to the problem of accounting for the value of well-being is empty. Without an accompanying value theory, objective theories are mere lists of ingredients, not recipes that explain the presence of the ingredients on the list.

Nature-Fulfillment Theories

There is another variety of objective theory that provides a more substantial answer: *nature-fulfillment theories*. According to this type of theory, the explanation for how something gets on the list of well-being ingredients has to do with its being essential to our nature. There are two types of nature-fulfillment theory. One takes the relevant sense of nature to be relative to our species: It is fulfilling our human nature that is good for us. The other takes it to be our individual nature the fulfillment of which is good for us.

The human nature-fulfillment theory has its roots in Aristotle. The idea here is that what is good for anything is to function well as the kind of thing that it is. A good knife is a knife that cuts well, a good lioness is one that hunts well and feeds her young, and so on. Along these lines, just as what is good for a lion is to be excellent in the respects that are typical of lions, so too what is good for a person is to excel in the ways that are typical of human beings. Martha Nussbaum's (2000) capabilities approach is a sophisticated development of this basic Aristotelian theory (see also Kraut, 2007).[4] According to Nussbaum, flourishing is to be understood in terms of human functional capabilities such as bodily health, practical reason, and affiliation. A flourishing person is one who develops these capabilities well.

Aristotelian theories of well-being explain what gets on the list of well-being ingredients by appeal to how these items contribute to our functioning where *function* is understood as something we properly attribute to kinds of things (e.g., a species). The normativity of the theory comes from an assumption about the inherent normativity of human nature. The thought is that there is something obviously good about being an exemplary, well-functioning member of one's kind.

One source of concern about such views is that there is no claim about the function of a species that is both empirically respectable and normatively significant. For example, one could argue that ingroup bias is a part of human nature, but surely the fact that our species has evolved with a bias that expresses itself in racism and other forms of prejudice does not mean that it is good for us to be racist. Aristotelians have a response to this challenge: They tend to argue that the project of understanding human nature is not an empirical project but an ethical one (Hursthouse, 1999). But there is another worry about reliance on our human (species) nature, which has to do with individual variability and the thought that well-being has to be good for the person whose well-being it is. If not everyone has the same capacities, why

---

[4]Nussbaum did not take her theory to be a theory of well-being because she associated the term *well-being* with preference satisfaction theories in economics. But in the terms we are using here, where *well-being* and *flourishing* are synonymous, Nussbaum's theory does count as a theory of well-being.

should functioning well as a member of the species be good for everyone? Why should it matter to me if my species is a social one, if I'm not?

This sort of worry about reliance on human nature and species has given rise to a new development in nature-fulfillment theories. Recently, Daniel Haybron (2008) has been developing a nature-fulfillment theory that does not rely on claims about our nature *qua* members of the human species.[5] Instead, Haybron's theory of well-being takes it to consist (at least in part) in the fulfillment of our nature as individuals, particularly in the fulfillment of our "emotional nature," which varies from person to person. Like Sumner (1996), Haybron identified well-being with authentic happiness, but he disagreed with Sumner about what happiness is. Haybron argued for an emotional-state theory of happiness according to which "to be happy is roughly for one's emotional condition to be broadly positive with only minor negatives, embodying a stance of psychic affirmation" (p. 182). Because our emotional dispositions are central to who we are, happiness is a kind of self-fulfillment. Happy people function well with respect to their individual characteristics and tendencies as opposed to their membership in a species. Of course, human beings have a lot in common and are likely to share many characteristics, at least at a general level of description. Haybron's view can accommodate this fact; the important point is that in his view, the order of explanation is different than it is for the Aristotelian.

Haybron's (2008) individual nature-fulfillment theory explains the presence of an item on the list of well-being ingredients by its contribution to our happiness, where what contributes to our happiness is determined by our emotional nature. The normativity of his theory of well-being comes from the intuitive value of happiness and the authenticity constraints on the kind of happiness that can count as well-being. Haybron, following Sumner (1996), thought that happiness must be informed and autonomous to count as well-being. He added that happiness should also be "rich": "the authenticity of one's happiness increases, other things being equal, to the extent that it is grounded in richer, more complex ways of living. For such ways of living more fully express one's nature" (Haybron, 2008, p. 186).

PHILOSOPHICAL THEORIES AND THE ASSUMPTIONS OF PSYCHOLOGICAL RESEARCH

In sum, there are various subjective theories of well-being in philosophy, which will explain why some well-being ingredient is good for a person by reference to that person's attitudes toward it. There are also

---

[5]See also LeBar (2004) for a view that is somewhere in-between the species-fulfillment and individual nature-fulfillment theories.

objective theories that explain why something is good for a person by reference to something other than the subject's attitudes—for example, by reference to an objectively valuable human nature. Looking at the chapters
in this volume from the point of view of a philosopher, it seems to me that
many psychologists, regardless of which well-being ingredients they are
concerned with, implicitly assume a subjective theory in the background.
That is, they presuppose that the explanation for why the things they study
(whether they are subjective feelings or objective modes of functioning)
are good for people is ultimately that people want them, like them, value
them, or think they're important. I think theories like this are on the
right track. In my view, we have to explain the value of ingredients of
well-being by appeal to the attitudes of the very people whose well-being
we're talking about, otherwise we won't succeed in explaining why some
ingredient is good for that person. But I think it is worth acknowledging
that this is a background theory of well-being, and it is one that, historically, was very controversial. No one in the ancient world thought that
what things are good for you would be determined by your own subjective
attitudes. Our subjective feelings can help us discover what's objectively
good for us (in the way that thirst can indicate that you need water), but
our feelings are not, according to the ancients, the foundation of value. In
the modern period, Hobbes had the view that wanting something makes it
good, but he was rather lonely in his support of this kind of subjectivism.
Subjectivism is so much the default now that we don't even see it as a view
in need of any justification; it's like water to us fishes. Nevertheless, it is
a view, and it is of primary concern to philosophers working in this area
whether it is the right view.

   This question about which general theory best explains why some
things are good for us at the most basic level may not be a question that
is of much interest to psychologists. Psychologists can take for granted
that some things are good for us (positive affect or optimal functioning,
for instance) and explain the value of other items by reference to these
uncontroversial goods. If there is to be hope that our two fields can benefit each other in the search for a deeper understanding of well-being and
flourishing, it is important to acknowledge that there are times when we
are actually trying to answer different questions. To be sure, it isn't that
philosophers do not care about the more practical questions about the
actual composition of a good life. But there has been a tendency, especially
in contemporary philosophy, to focus on the abstract and theoretical questions about the general nature or formal structure of well-being. Interestingly, which theory you accept might not make that much difference to
your substantive position on the composition of a good, flourishing life. Or
so I argue in the next section.

THE INGREDIENTS OF A GOOD LIFE

We have considered five different theories of well-being that offer five different explanations for why something counts as an ingredient of well-being. We can now ask whether these different theoretical explanations will tend to give rise to different lists or whether they will turn out to provide different explanations for similar lists of ingredients. I argue that the latter view is closer to the truth: By and large, different theoretical frameworks will end up providing different recipes for the same dish. Before we get to a more detailed discussion of this point, though, it is useful to say a few words about the candidate ingredients.

Psychologists who study subjective well-being, not surprisingly, tend to take the ingredients of well-being to be subjective, psychological states such as life satisfaction or positive affect. In the psychological literature, this position, when it does not incorporate eudaimonic constructs, is often described as hedonic or hedonistic,[6] and as such is contrasted with the eudaimonist position. Eudaimonist psychologists who include subjective psychological states on their list of well-being ingredients frequently incorporate life satisfaction and positive affect along with other subjective variables not on the hedonists' lists—for example, variables such as interest (Rathunde & Csikszentmihalyi, 1993), flow (Csikszentmihalyi, 1990), feelings of personal expressiveness (Waterman, 1993; see also Chapter 5, this volume), vitality (Ryan & Frederick, 1997), engagement (see Chapter 13, this volume), and peak experiences (Maslow, 1968). Moreover, many eudaimonists in psychology put things on the list that are not obviously subjective psychological states, such as integrated functioning toward the satisfaction of basic human needs (see Chapter 3, this volume) or objectively realizing one's potential (see Chapters 5 and 13).

I take it that the reason the second group of psychologists have adopted the eudaimonist label has to do with a perceived affinity to the ancient Greek tradition. There are some affinities. First, the ancients tended to think of well-being as including the kinds of things that eudaimonists in psychology are interested in, and they tended not to think that the kinds of good feelings highlighted by hedonism in psychology have much to do with well-being. There were hedonists in the ancient world, the Epicureans, but the kind of pleasure they favored was more like the kinds of things that eudaimonist psychologists measure (Annas, 1993). *Ataraxia* is a kind of tranquility or contentment that is probably quite different from what Daniel Kahneman (2000) took objective happiness to be. Second, the ancients' reasons for thinking that

---

[6]This terminology is a little misleading for philosophers because in philosophy hedonism is just one example of a subjective theory.

well-being was constituted by this or that had to do with what they took to count as fulfilling one's nature as a human being, as discussed in the previous section. Eudaimonists in psychology who explain the inclusion of ingredients on their lists by reference to human needs or human nature are relying on a similar sort of theory (e.g., Deci & Ryan, 2000; see also Chapter 9, this volume). So, eudaimonism in psychology has affinities to the views of the ancients both in terms of the items on the list and the theoretical explanation for their inclusion.

Indeed, it is not difficult to see how the objectivist theories surveyed here will provide a foundation for the kinds of well-being ingredients that eudaimonist psychologists study. For example, lists in psychology that include close personal relationships, autonomy, and mastery or competence (see Chapter 3, this volume) comport well with Nussbaum's (2000) list of basic human functionings that includes affiliation, practical reason, and control over one's environment. The individual nature-fulfillment theory is also likely to emphasize items that eudaimonists in psychology find to be important, particularly items that have to do with deep emotional responses such as feelings of personal expressiveness or emotional harmony.

Does this mean that eudaimonists in psychology must be philosophical eudaimonists as well? I don't think so. Consider the informed-desire theory. What does this theory tell us about the ingredients on the list of contributors to well-being? In other words, what would an informed desire theorist in philosophy advise a psychologist to study? The answer obviously depends on what it is that people want for its own sake when informed about their options. If the only thing that people wanted for its own sake were pleasure, then eudaimonists in psychology would be on the wrong track. But desire theories are favored in philosophy precisely because they solve the problem for hedonism that pleasure is not the only thing we want for its own sake! Recall Nozick's (1974) experience machine example: He thought we wanted knowledge, interactions with real people, and contact with reality in addition to pleasure. Desire theory, then, lends itself to pluralism about the list of well-being ingredients, and a plausible, desire-based pluralism would likely include eudaimonist ingredients.

Life-satisfaction theories are also likely to provide a foundation for a pluralist view about the ingredients of well-being because there are many causes of life satisfaction. Indeed, as psychologists have demonstrated, many eudaimonist ingredients (e.g., mastery, positive relationships, autonomy) are causes of life satisfaction (see Chapters 3 and 6, this volume). It is important that because the versions of life-satisfaction theory favored by philosophers include idealizing conditions, these causes are not easily replaced or eliminated. We can contrast this with classical hedonism, according to which pleasure caused by taking a drug would be just as good as pleasure caused in some other way. Let me explain why this isn't so for life-satisfaction theories. If it is only authentic life satisfaction that counts, then insofar as a person's satisfaction with one's life would be undermined if she knew that it was caused by a delusion about her relationships and accomplishments, her satisfaction would not count as making her well off. Similarly, if it is value-based life satisfaction that counts, then insofar as a person's satisfaction is caused by a false sense of how her life is going according to these values, her satisfaction does not make her well off.

We have just seen that so-called subjective theories can provide a justification for lists of well-being ingredients that go beyond the subjective components measured by hedonists in psychology. Similarly, nature-fulfillment theories (often called eudaimonist theories in philosophy) could be used to justify lists that include only hedonistic ingredients. If pleasure and life satisfaction are what best fulfill our nature, then these are what would count as well-being according to the theory that philosophical eudaimonists tend to favor. Nature-fulfillment theories do not tend to have this kind of substantive view about what fulfills our nature (though they do typically include hedonistic ingredients like pleasure on their lists). The point here is that neither the ingredients favored by hedonistic psychologists nor the ingredients favored by eudaimonist psychologists get any automatic privilege. Any list needs to be justified by some theory, and theories of different kinds do not necessarily favor one list over the other. Having made this point, it shouldn't be concluded that which theory you accept makes no difference to what's on your list of ingredients. Theories do make a difference (more on this in the next section), but not the kind of difference we might have anticipated: It is not the case that subjective philosophical theories support hedonistic research in psychology and objective philosophical theories support eudaimonist research in psychology. Things are more complicated than this.

One theory I have only briefly mentioned so far is hedonism. Classical hedonism lends itself to the interpretation that there is only one item on the list of well-being ingredients and that is pleasure. Interpreted this way, philosophical hedonism does favor hedonistic psychology, though even here some philosophers (e.g., Epicurus, Mill) might argue that what psychologists measure is not the right kind of pleasure.

HOW PHILOSOPHICAL DISTINCTIONS MATTER TO WELL-BEING RESEARCH

Although it is true that all the going philosophical theories are likely to include some of psychologists' eudaimonist values on the list of ingredients, these theories will not all generate exactly the same lists. Even if there is substantial agreement on many items, some theories will make certain ingredients more central than others. An objective-list theory might hold that knowledge or understanding is as valuable as deep personal relationships, whereas a life-satisfaction theory, which is more tied to subjective experience, would likely place greater value on relationships (as a cause of life satisfaction). Indeed, some theories will take certain values to be built into the very concept of well-being. For example, autonomy is built into Sumner's (1996) authentic happiness theory and Haybron's (2008) individual nature-fulfillment theory as a precondition for our subjective experiences to count as well-being.

It could also be argued that some of the theories we have discussed have a more satisfying answer than others to the charge of elitism that has been leveled at eudaimonists in psychology: "The search for something 'better' than SWB or a better form of happiness connotes a potential elitism, that the Good Life is an experience reserved for individuals who have attained some transcendence from everyday life" (Kashdan, Biswas-Diener, & King, 2008, p. 227).[7]

Subjective theories and individual nature-fulfillment theory have an obvious way to respond to such a charge, because these theories make the subject central to well-being, though in different ways. For example, on the assumption that people would desire meaning in their lives if they were informed, an informed-desire theory will hold that meaning is good for people because it is what they ideally want. In this view, it isn't that meaning has some objective value that psychologists are imposing on people; rather, the value of meaning is grounded in people's desires.

But I do not think that the differences between these philosophical theories are what should be of most interest to psychologists. What is important is something that almost all of these theories have in common: namely, a space between psychological fact and normative conclusion. This is important for two reasons.

First, there are many items on the eudaimonist list that can be interpreted subjectively or objectively.[8] For instance, *purpose* can mean either a subjective sense of purpose or actually having purpose. The same goes for competence, mastery, and meaning. The theories of well-being in philosophy— even most so-called subjective theories—suggest that although the subjective senses of these things matter, the objective attainment of them does too. The gap between psychological fact and conclusions about (normative) well-being allows for the conceptual possibility that well-being isn't guaranteed by our feeling like we are doing well. Granted, it may be impossible to measure

---

[7]A similar criticism is implied in Diener and Suh (2000, p. 4).
[8]Linley, in Chapter 13 of this volume, notes that *eudaimonia* itself can be seen in these two ways.

meaning as opposed to a sense of meaning, but it is surely worth keeping in mind what we actually care about, what we actually want, or what's actually good for us even if we can only measure these indirectly. After all, it may not be impossible to measure something closer to what really matters or to measure something in addition to "a sense of meaning" that complements the subjective measures.

Second, if you accept that the philosophical theories of well-being we have surveyed explain the sense in which well-being is normative (i.e., they explain why the well-being ingredients are good for us), then you have to acknowledge that conclusions about what we ought to do when we help people or construct policy do not follow automatically from empirical facts (about our psychological states, for instance). The case needs to be made for why increasing life satisfaction as measured by the Satisfaction With Life Scale (Diener, Emmons, Larsen, & Griffin, 1985), for example, is a good thing, why "objective happiness" as measured in experience sampling method studies is worth promoting, or why feelings of personal expressiveness might be worth sacrificing something else that is easier to obtain. Sometimes the case is not difficult to make: Positive affect is a good thing no matter what kind of theory you adopt, and so promoting it when there is little cost is not terribly controversial. But any policy has some costs, and the mere idea of government policy designed to promote well-being has been known to provoke controversy.

Finally, there is a general point here in favor of eudaimonist psychological research. Hedonistic psychologists, it seems to me, tend to see their position as the default, deviation from which requires justification. Studying life satisfaction or positive affect is relatively uncontroversial and obvious, whereas studying eudaimonic ingredients like the ones mentioned previously is theoretically suspect. But from the point of view of a philosopher, this is an inaccurate picture. Life satisfaction and positive affect are no more obviously ingredients of well-being than are competence, relationships, and feelings of personal expressiveness. Any ingredient stands in need of some defense, some explanation for its status on the list. In fact, philosophers who take well-being to be normative—that is, to be the kind of thing that informs our moral behavior and gives rise to reasons for action—are likely to think that purely subjective feelings are the more controversial items on the list of well-being ingredients.

WHAT MAKES A BETTER THEORY?

Insofar as there is a division of labor between psychologists and philosophers on the topic of well-being, psychologists have focused on empirical investigations identifying predictors of well-being outcomes, whereas it is the philosophers' job to develop normative theories (theories that aim to explain not just what well-being is but also how it is valuable). Still, psychologists may be interested to know what kinds of arguments we use to decide between competing normative theories. In this last section of the paper, I address this topic very briefly.[9]

Most philosophers working in this area take there to be two basic criteria for an adequate theory of well-being. Sumner (1996) referred to these as the *criterion of descriptive adequacy* and the *criterion of normative adequacy*. Though different philosophers may interpret these criteria as demanding somewhat different things, the current consensus is that both are important. The former is typically taken to require that the theory fit our ordinary experiences and uses of the concept. Sometimes it has been taken to require, further, that the theory make happiness something amenable to empirical investigation and measurement (Griffin, 1986; Tiberius & Plakias, 2010). The criterion of normative adequacy requires that a theory of happiness should justify claims about the value of happiness and explain why we have good reason to pursue it; it may also require that the resulting theory is adequate to playing a particular role in moral theory.[10]

To construct a theory that meets these two criteria, moral philosophers tend to use the method of reflective equilibrium (Daniels, 1979). According to this method, we construct normative theories by bringing into equilibrium ordinary judgments about particular cases (e.g., "Mary lived well, even though she didn't get everything she wanted"), putative normative principles (e.g., well-being is that which is to be promoted by benevolent action), and background theories (e.g., psychological theories about hedonic adaptation). We may not be able to save all of our intuitive judgments, and some of our principles may need to be modified or thrown out altogether, but the goal is to construct a theory that explains and systematizes as much of this large body of information as possible within the relevant theoretical constraints. This methodology has obvious similarities to the scientific method: Empirical theories are based on and aim to explain our observations, but sometimes a theory is well confirmed enough that a conflicting observation must be explained away and discounted. Similarly, when we use reflective equilibrium to defend a normative theory such as a theory of well-being, we aim to systematize our intuitions, but there can be many reasons to discount intuitions when not all of them can be saved.

---

[9]For more, see Tiberius (2013). For a discussion that complicates this neat division of labor, see Tiberius (in press).

[10]For utilitarians, according to whom happiness is the central notion in moral theory, normative adequacy will mean that the theory of happiness should make happiness something that is up to this important job (Griffin, 1986).

This dialectic process has encouraged the development of philosophical theories of well-being into more and more sophisticated forms. In my view, theories become better and more sophisticated as they incorporate insights from other theories. Idealized subjective theories have more in common with objective theories than simple subjective theories do, and Haybron's (2008) individual fulfillment theory has more in common with subjective theories than a simple objective-list theory does. This is progress. The best philosophical theories are likely to have significant overlap in terms of the lists of well-being ingredients they legitimize. But it is worth having some theory in mind so as to keep in mind the ultimate goal of well-being research—that is, something good for us—and the distance between this valuable goal and what we can study empirically.

CONCLUSION

The five major theories of well-being in philosophy—hedonism, desire-fulfillment, life-satisfaction, objective-list, and nature-fulfillment—do not neatly track the division in psychology between hedonistic and eudaimonistic research programs. Rather, we have seen that any of these theories (with the possible exception of hedonism) could be used to argue for a list of well-being ingredients that includes both hedonistic and eudaimonistic elements. Further, I hope to have shown that there is good reason to take seriously philosophical theories that explain the normative dimension of well-being. Though I have not argued for the point explicitly, I also hope that my discussion has indicated some of the value in collaborative efforts between philosophers and psychologists. This might be one area in which having many cooks does not spoil—and may well enrich—the broth.

REFERENCES

Annas, J. (1993). *The morality of happiness.* New York, NY: Oxford University Press.

Arneson, R. (2007). Desire formation and human good. In S. Olsaretti (Ed.), *Preferences and well-being. Royal Institute of Philosophy Supplement, 81*(Suppl. 59), 9–32. Cambridge, England: Cambridge University Press.

Bentham, J. (1781). *An introduction to the principles of morals and legislation.* Retrieved from http://www.utilitarianism.com/jeremy-bentham/index.html

Brink, D. (1989). *Moral realism and the foundations of ethics.* Cambridge, England: Cambridge University Press. doi:10.1017/CBO9780511624612

Csikszentmihalyi, M. (1990). *Flow: The psychology of optimal experience.* New York, NY: Harper & Row.

Daniels, N. (1979). Wide reflective equilibrium and theory acceptance in ethics. *Journal of Philosophy, 76*, 256–282.

Deci, E. L., & Ryan, R. M. (2000). The "what" and "why" of goal pursuits: Human needs and the self-determination of behavior. *Psychological Inquiry, 11*, 227–268. doi:10.1207/S15327965PLI1104_01

Diener, E., Emmons, R. A., Larsen, R. J., & Griffin, S. (1985). The Satisfaction With Life Scale. *Journal of Personality Assessment, 49*, 71–75. doi:10.1207/s15327752jpa4901_13

Diener, E., & Suh, E. (2000). *Culture and subjective well-being*. Cambridge, MA: The MIT Press.

Feldman, F. (2004). *Pleasure and the good life: Concerning the nature, varieties, and plausibility of hedonism*. Oxford, England: Clarendon Press.

Gert, B. (1998). *Morality: Its nature and justification*. Oxford, England: Oxford University Press.

Griffin, J. (1986). *Well-being: Its meaning, measurement and moral importance*. Oxford, England: Clarendon Press.

Haybron, D. (2008). *The pursuit of unhappiness*. Oxford, England: Oxford University Press.

Heathwood, C. (2006). Desire-satisfactionism and hedonism. *Philosophical Studies, 128*, 539–563. doi:10.1007/s11098-004-7817-y

Hursthouse, R. (1999). *On virtue ethics*. Oxford, England: Oxford University Press.

Kahneman, D. (2000). Experienced utility and objective happiness: A moment-based approach. In D. Kahneman & A. Tversky (Eds.), *Choices, values, and frames* (pp. 673–692). Cambridge, England: Cambridge University Press.

Kashdan, T. B., Biswas-Diener, R., & King, L. A. (2008). Reconsidering happiness: The costs of distinguishing between hedonics and eudaimonia. *The Journal of Positive Psychology, 3*, 219–233. doi:10.1080/17439760802303044

Kraut, R. (2007). *What is good and why: The ethics of well-being*. Cambridge, MA: Harvard University Press.

LeBar, M. (2004). Good for you. *Pacific Philosophical Quarterly, 85*, 195–217. doi:10.1111/j.0279-0750.2004.00194.x

Maslow, A. H. (1968). *Toward a psychology of being* (2nd ed.). Princeton, NJ: Van Nostrand.

Mendola, J. (2009). Real desire and well-being. *Nous-Supplement: Philosophical Issues, 19*, 148–165.

Mill, J. S. (1979). *Utilitarianism* (G. Sher, Ed.). Indianapolis, IN: Hackett. (Original work published 1861)

Moore, A. (2004). Hedonism. In E. N. Zalta (Ed.), *Stanford encyclopedia of philosophy*. Retrieved from http://plato.stanford.edu/archives/win2011/entries/hedonism/

Murphy, M. C. (1999). The simple desire-fulfillment theory. *Nous, 33*, 247–272. doi:10.1111/0029-4624.00153

Nozick, R. (1974). *Anarchy, state, and utopia*. New York, NY: Basic Books.

Nussbaum, M. (2000). *Women and human development: The capabilities approach*. Cambridge, England: Cambridge University Press. doi:10.1017/CBO9780511841286

Parfit, D. (1984). *Reasons and persons*. Oxford, England: Oxford University Press.

Raibley, J. (2010). Well-being and the priority of values. *Social Theory and Practice, 36*, 593–620.

Railton, P. (1986). Moral realism. *The Philosophical Review, 95*, 163–207. doi:10.2307/2185589

Rathunde, K. R., & Csikszentmihalyi, M. (1993). Undivided interest and the growth of talent: A longitudinal study of adolescents. *Journal of Youth and Adolescence, 22*, 385–405. doi:10.1007/BF01537720

Rosati, C. (1995). Persons, perspectives, and full information accounts of the good. *Ethics, 105*, 296–325. doi:10.1086/293702

Ryan, R. M., & Frederick, C. (1997). On energy, personality, and health: Subjective vitality as a dynamic reflection of well-being. *Journal of Personality, 65*, 529–565. doi:10.1111/j.1467-6494.1997.tb00326.x

Sumner, L. (1996). *Welfare, happiness and ethics*. Oxford, England: Oxford University Press.

Tiberius, V. (2012). *Well-being for the uninformed: Prudential reasons and the value fulfillment theory*. Unpublished manuscript.

Tiberius, V. (2013). Philosophical methods in happiness research. In S. David, I. Boniwell, and A. C. Ayers (Eds.), *The Oxford handbook of happiness* (pp. 315–325). Oxford, England: Oxford University Press.

Tiberius, V. (in press). Well-being, wisdom, and thick theorizing: On the division of labor between moral philosophy and positive psychology. In S. Kirchin (Ed.), *Thick concepts*. Oxford, England: Oxford University Press.

Tiberius, V., & Hall, A. (2010). Normative theory and psychological research: Hedonism, eudaimonism and why it matters. *The Journal of Positive Psychology, 5*, 212–225. doi:10.1080/17439761003790971

Tiberius, V., & Plakias, A. (2010). Well-being. In J. Doris & The Moral Psychology Research Group (Eds.), *The moral psychology handbook* (pp. 402–432). Oxford, England: Oxford University Press.

Velleman, J. D. (1988). Brandt's definition of good. *The Philosophical Review, 97*, 353–371. doi:10.2307/2185446

Waterman, A. S. (1993). Two conceptions of happiness: Contrasts of personal expressiveness (eudaimonia) and hedonic enjoyment. *Journal of Personality and Social Psychology, 64*, 678–691. doi:10.1037/0022-3514.64.4.678

2

FEELINGS, MEANINGS, AND OPTIMAL FUNCTIONING: SOME DISTINCTIONS BETWEEN HEDONIC AND EUDAIMONIC WELL-BEING

JOAR VITTERSØ

According to mainstream economic theory, spending a thousand dollars for a birthday gift for an aging parent and writing a check for the same amount for a washer and dryer provide the same amount of pleasure (Kagan, 2009). As anyone who has paid for household commodities and given gifts to a beloved one could testify, economists got their belief wrong. According to mainstream hedonic theory, everyone who reports, say, a 7 on a 0–10 pleasantness scale is equally happy. As anyone who has observed the variety of events and life stories that can produce pleasures corresponding to a self-reported 7 could testify, hedonists too, are missing something important.

The qualities of life are multifaceted and complex, and it is unlikely that such variety can be encompassed as a number on a one-dimensional scale. On the other hand, too much complexity does not take us very far either. To paraphrase Albert Einstein, "Everything should be made as simple as possible—but not simpler" ("Albert Einstein," n.d.). In the case of well-being theory, the parsimony of *hedonia*, which in the narrow sense is the idea that happiness

DOI: 10.1037/14092-003
The Best Within Us: Positive Psychology Perspectives on Eudaimonia, Alan S. Waterman (Editor)
Copyright © 2013 by the American Psychological Association. All rights reserved.

consists in the accumulation of momentary experiences of pleasure (and the absence of pain), can hardly be outmaneuvered. But people do not only feel, they also think about their lives (Kahneman & Riis, 2005), and neither feelings nor thinking operates in a series of isolated moments. The moments are chunked together into episodes, and episodes feed into life stories with meanings and normative content (Bruner, 1990; Loewenstein & Ubel, 2008).

There are, in other words, innumerous aspects of a life that might be considered as life qualities, and the challenge for happiness research is thus to establish some criteria in order to constrain the size of the well-being taxonomy. In the present chapter, the notion of functions operates as such a criterion, and the argument to be presented is organized as follows. Theories of pleasures are presented first because the hedonic idea cannot be evaluated without a proper understanding of its core concept. Second, it is pointed out that there are nonhedonic elements in the theory of subjective well-being (SWB), but because these are vaguely articulated and rarely applied in SWB research, SWB is considered to reflect a hedonic approach. Next, two important (but not conclusive) elements in eudaimonic thinking are presented: eudaimonic feelings and optimal functioning. Finally, and to further illustrate why the hedonic approach falls short of covering enough well-being space, evidence regarding a conflict between pleasure and meaning is presented toward the end of the chapter.

HEDONIC WELL-BEING

The term *hedonic* is from the Greek *hêdonê*—their word for pleasure—and the notion of hedonic well-being (HWB) is predominantly taken to mean that happiness can be understood as the greatest attainable surplus of pleasure over pain (Martin, 2008). Classical utilitarians, such as Jeremy Bentham and John Stuart Mill, subscribed to this idea, although Mill thought some pleasures have greater value than others. The view has been defended, more or less, by psychologists as well (Read, 2007). For instance, Kahneman (1999) positioned himself very close to the hedonic ideal, even if he in cautious moments claimed that a pure hedonic concept is not adequate for the psychology of well-being. He nevertheless spent most of his seminal paper from 1999 defending the hedonic idea. Hence, Kahneman acknowledged that hedonism is an oversimplification, but a tolerable one (at least he thought so 10 years ago, but see Kahneman, Schkade, Fischler, Krueger, & Krilla, 2010, for a modified view).

The hedonic approach to well-being is not particularly useful without a proper understanding of the concept of pleasure. But as so often in academia, it has proven difficult to establish common ground. Conceptual confusion and disagreements dominate many scientific debates of hedonia, and in philosophy, for example, pleasure comes in at least two major versions. The difference is between pleasure as a sensation and pleasure as an attitude. The former defines pleasure as a feeling, whereas the latter defines pleasure as an attitude (Sumner, 1996). If you like cold beer and salty peanuts, you are likely to experience sensory pleasure when you eat peanuts and drink beer. By contrast, attitudinal pleasures need not have any feelings attached to them (Feldman, 2010). You can take pleasure in the fact that you live in a democracy without having a pleasant sensation about it.

A parallel distinction exists in psychology. Pleasure may be considered as a sensation or a "raw feeling" that does not involve focal attention on the feeling as such. For instance, as an indication of the experience of a pleasant raw feeling, human newborns who taste something sweet will smack their lips and elicit a rhythmic series of tongue protrusion movements (Berridge, 2003). Similar reactions can also be observed among many nonhuman species, indicating that a kind of "first order" feelings (see Lambie & Marcel, 2002) exists independently of a self than can reflect on and verbally report on the feeling state. Behavior observations have suggested, for instance, that chimpanzees and gorillas have positive and negative affective reactions that are remarkably similar to those of humans (Steiner, Glaser, Hawilo, & Berridge, 2001). Some of these raw feeling states may be defined as pleasure (e.g., Berridge, 2007).

By contrast, Frijda (2005, 2010) reserved the term *pleasure* for something that is added to the feeling itself, something he described as "a gloss of niceness." In this view, pleasure refers to an attribute of a feeling, not a feeling quality in itself. For example, rather than consider the sweetness of a tasty chocolate as pleasantness, the sweetness and the pleasantness can be separated. Enjoying a mouthful of chocolate is normally considered pleasurable, but after having had more than one's fill, a new bite could be distasteful and unpleasant. However, the chocolate still tastes sweet (Small, Zatorre, Dagher, Evans, & Jones-Gotman, 2001).

So, psychological theories of emotions operate with at least two different meanings for the term *pleasure*. It can either indicate a particular feeling quality or it can refer to an attribute that is shared by a series of different positive feeling states. The attribute view in psychological theories is different from the attitude view in philosophy because pleasure as attribute has affective content, whereas pleasure as attitude does not. However, a distinction made within the philosophical feeling approach may account for the difference between pleasure as a homogeneous phenomenological state (the hedonic feeling tone) and pleasure as a proattitude (Moore, 2009). Unlike the philosophical attitude view, philosophical proattitudes are experiential in nature, but they do not assume a common feeling tone. Examples of proattitudes are liking, delight, want, and preference (Moore, 2009).

According to Sumner (1996), Bentham was an internalist, which means that he defended the claim that all pleasures share a common feeling tone. Mill argued differently. As an externalist, preference was to Mill the important attribute of pleasant experiences, and this is how he described the essence of indifferent, pain, and pleasure:

> The first is of such a kind, that I care not whether it is long or short; the second is of such a kind that I would put an end to it instantly if I could; the third is of such a kind that I like it prolonged. To distinguish these feelings I give them names. I call the first Indifferent; the second, Painful; the third, Pleasurable; very often, for shortness, I call the second, Pain, the third, Pleasure. (Mill as cited in Sumner, 1996, p. 90)

The idea of equating pleasure with preferences was adopted by Kahneman (1999), and he went on to proclaim that these were adequate markers of a happy life. For instance, in trying to figure out how happy Helen (an imagined girl) is, Kahneman suggested that

> it makes sense to call Helen "objectively happy" if she spent most of her time engaged in activities that she would rather have continued than stopped, little time in situations she wished to escape, and—very important because life is short—not too much time in a neutral state in which she would not care either way. This is the essence of the approach proposed here. (p. 7)

It appears from this brief review that the term *pleasure* is used in at least three different ways. Two are emotional, and the third is not. First, pleasure sometimes refers to a first-order or "raw" feeling state. Second, pleasure can be defined as a phenomenon separable from the quality of a feeling state itself, and as such it reflects an attribute of a class of feelings. The third meaning of pleasure is attitudinal. Something is pleasant if we judge it to be good or favorable, and the target of the judgment need not be emotional.

The distinction between different kinds of pleasures suggests that several concepts and separate measurements are required to do justice to the idea of HWB. In the next section, I argue that such a plurality is accounted for by the framework of SWB.

SUBJECTIVE WELL-BEING

The term *subjective well-being* became important with the 1984 publication of Diener. Today the concept is staged with two main dimensions: affective/emotional well-being and evaluative/cognitive well-being. Both dimensions can be analyzed at different levels, typically at an overall level (life in general), or at some intermediate level (last week or last month), or at a momentary level ("online" or episodic). I would also argue that both dimensions are essentially judgmental. For example, in a recent consensus document, more than 50 researchers agreed with Diener (2006) that SWB refers to

> all the various types of evaluations, both positive and negative, that people make of their lives. It includes reflective cognitive evaluations, such as life satisfaction and work satisfaction, interest and engagement, and affective reactions to life events, such as joy and sadness. Thus, subjective well-being is an umbrella term for the different valuations people make regarding their lives, the events happening to them, their bodies and minds, and the circumstances in which they live. (pp. 399–400)

Even if life satisfaction is considered to reflect a cognitive evaluation by the stance of this definition, labeling it as *cognitive* is somewhat misleading. When something is evaluated, both cognitive and emotional processes are involved, and basically it seems that the latter override the former (e.g., Albarracín, Johnson, & Zanna, 2005; Bargh, Gollwitzer, & Oettingen, 2010; Zajonc, 2001).

As a striking example of how little variance cognitive computation is able to account for in measures of overall life satisfaction, consider how quickly people respond to the items in a happiness survey. For questions such as "All things considered, how satisfied are you with your life as a whole?" participants typically take no more than a few seconds before they conclude (Vitterso, Oelmann, & Wang, 2009). Such rapidity suggests that "all things" cannot possibly have been considered. Technically speaking, a cognitive algorithm for computing life satisfaction in ways that match the concept's theoretical ambition does not exist, even if it would have been very convenient. And it does not matter whether satisfaction is defined as a rational comparison of everything the respondents have against everything they think they deserve, expect, or may reasonably aspire to (Campbell, Converse, & Rodgers, 1976) or in terms of a broad and integrative judgment about all areas of a person's life since birth (Diener, Scollon, & Lucas, 2009). Humans simply do not have sufficient mental capacity to evaluate "everything" or "all areas" in their lives.

Following this line of reasoning, the variance obtained by self-reported life satisfaction cannot be generated by a cognitive calculation. Rather, a substantial proportion of automaticity must be involved, and the nature of these automatic responses is not accounted for in the theory of SWB. It does, however, seem reasonable to assume that the concept of life satisfaction is strongly influenced by attitudinal processes and that the evaluative component of SWB thus overlaps with attitudinal accounts of HWB.

Pleasure constitutes a central part of the second component of SWB as well, and here is why. Proponents of SWB habitually lump feelings of low arousal (e.g., contentment), moderate arousal (e.g., pleasure), and high arousal (e.g., euphoria) into a broad category of positive affect (e.g., Diener, 2006). A lot of simplicity is gained by this route, but the arrangement can easily reduce the emotional component of SWB into a mere pleasantness component. The reason is that when a variable is composed on the basis of several positive feelings that are sampled across different levels of arousal, such a variable will reflect pleasure more than any other feeling state, and the richness of emotional variety and functionality will thus be lost (see Coombs, 1964, for the principled argument, and Moum, 2007, for a relevant example).

According to the previous account, SWB is basically about pleasant feelings, unpleasant feelings, and pleasant attitudes. Pleasant attitudes are captured in the concepts of life satisfaction and domain satisfaction, whereas pleasant (or unpleasant) feelings are taken care of by the summation of a set of different positive (or negative) affects. This summation can be measured as an average of different feelings across moments or episodes (state level) or as the average of different feelings regarding life in general (trail level).

EUDAIMONIC WELL-BEING

Ancient philosophers disagreed about what eudaimonia is. Epicurus conceived it as pleasure, whereas the Stoic suggested it to be virtue. For Aristotle, eudaimonia was virtue exercised in favorable conditions (Keyes & Annas, 2009). According to Keyes and Annas (2009), then, hedonism is one theory of eudaimonia and Aristotle's theory is another. From a psychological point of view one may argue that to the extent that Aristotle's notion of virtues and/or functioning are important for eudaimonia, the concept of pleasure cannot account for the entire range of human well-being. Hence, Tiberius (see Chapter 1, this volume) suggests that ingredients of well-being that go beyond positive feelings and life satisfaction may be considered eudaimonic in a psychological sense of the term.

In the current section, I present two ingredients of well-being that perform to Tiberius's criterion. The first is emotions that are positive but nonhedonic, and I call these *eudaimonic feelings*. The second ingredient is *optimal functioning*. Together they may help clarify eudaimonic thinking in positive psychology, which should include a psychological conceptualization of the philosophical notion of virtues. The exercise of virtues activities seems to involve a kind of striving toward completeness or excellence (Gewirth, 1998), and in psychological jargon such activities may be referred to as *flourishing* or *self-realization* (see Introduction, this volume) or as *character strengths* (Peterson & Seligman, 2004). They may also be expressed in terms of seeking to use and develop the best in oneself (Huta & Ryan, 2010) or in terms of meaning making (Delle Fave & Bassi, 2009).

Eudaimonic Feelings

The idea of nonhedonic positive emotions is articulated in the functional well-being approach (FWBA; Vitterso, in press; Vitterso, Soholt, Hetland, Thorsen, & Roysamb, 2010). From this perspective, a variety of positive feelings are relevant for a good life, even if they do not belong to the category of pleasure, and the cost of adding an extra layer of complexity to the taxonomy of positive feelings is compensated for by a terminology that fits better with knowledge established in several theories of emotion. Such a differentiated vocabulary also comports with the overarching notion that feelings have functions. The reason why humans are able to discriminate between different kinds of positive feelings, such as interest and engagement on the one hand and pleasure and contentment on the other, is because these feeling states prompt us toward different kinds of actions. (I do, of course, acknowledge that other researchers have made impressive contributions to positive emotions that are not hedonic, including awe [Haidt, 2006] and transcendence [Csikszentmihalyi, 1992], but the emphasis of nonhedonic feelings put forward in the FWBA is somewhat different.)

Mainstream views on emotions hold that the primary function of pleasure is to promote approach behavior, and for pain it is to promote avoidance. But a camp of scholars considers the approach–avoidance dichotomy too simplistic for human beings (e.g., Leyton, 2010; Panksepp, 1998). Their argument is that more than two categories of positive feelings are needed to fully account for the flexibility and complexity of human behavior. Some researchers have even argued that far from providing a typical approach motivation, pleasure instead stimulates behavior that prime movements away from an activated goal (Carver, 2003). The wisdom in this hypothesis is that pleasure typically comes as a result of goal achievement and need fulfillment, and when a dominating goal is reached or a pressing need is satisfied, it is time to move on and look for something else to do. In other words, rather than promoting further approach, the function of pleasure is to afford respite from active involvement in goal striving. Following Carver (2003), pleasure typically leads to coasting, which means putting less effort into the pursuit of the active goal.

Building on these perspectives, the FWBA holds pleasure to be a feeling associated with the return to a state of intrapsychic balance or homeostasis. Evolution has shaped our minds such that we feel distress when we deviate from a "set-point" (or equilibrium) and we feel pleasure when we undertake acts to alleviate disequilibrium. Pleasure is thus typically felt when biological needs are fulfilled; when goals are achieved; or when the current situation is perceived as familiar, trouble free, and safe (see also Winkielman, Schwarz, Fazendeiro, & Reber, 2003).

If pleasure is what we feel when we return to, or operate within the frames of, a "safe haven," other kinds of feelings are needed to prompt behavior that aims for goal striving, exploration, and active involvement in complex problem solving. According to the FWBA, feelings such as interest, inspiration, and engagement fulfill this function. I have proposed that these positive but nonhedonic feeling states (i.e., different from pleasure) may be labeled *eudaimonic feelings*. The role of these feelings is to sustain effort in challenging environments when a quick return to equilibrium is dysfunctional or when a cognitive structure needs to change (accommodate) in order to perceive a stimulus or an event as meaningful.

In an account of why we need eudaimonic feelings (my term, not theirs) in addition to the hedonic ones, Gaver and Mandler (1987) pointed to the process of developing mental representations. Adopting the concept of a schema and Piaget's analysis of cognitive development, these authors argued that simple assimilation requires virtually no mental effort, whereas massive accommodation may demand extensive processing. Using music to illustrate their line of reasoning, Gaver and Mandler claimed that we find music that "fits" an existing schema pleasant, although such music is not interesting. By contrast, great works of music may emerge as interesting, even if they are not considered as pleasant. The reason is that the complexity of great music cannot be easily assimilated, and this is exactly why it appears as interesting. Empirical data reported in the Gaver and Mandler article suggest that interestingness operates as an index of deviation from typicality. This does not mean, of course, that too much deviation cannot produce negative feelings (e.g., Walker, 1981).

Similarly, in a study of how stories with different content affected the feelings of those who read them, Iran-Nejad (1987) found that pleasantness was associated with how much the stories were liked, but not with how interesting they were. Iran-Nejad further observed that the amount of intellectual activity involved in story interpretation predicted feelings of interest, but not how much the participants liked the story.

The difference between hedonic and eudaimonic feelings was also elegantly described by Thagard (2002). He examined the use of emotional words in Jim Watson's (1999) book, *The Double Helix*, and found that happiness was the most frequently mentioned emotion in the book, occurring 65 times. The next most frequently mentioned emotion was interest, with 43 emotional words referring to states such as interest, wonder, and enthusiasm. By dividing the scientific process into three stages—investigation, discovery, and justification—Thagard observed that interest is the most typical emotion for the first context (i.e., investigation), whereas pleasure is more typically experienced in the contexts of discovery and justification. Thagard's message is that interest, curiosity, and wonder arise in contexts in which questions are generated, whereas pleasure, happiness, and beauty arise when answers are found.

Optimal Functioning

Functioning is a word with many meanings. In the context of human well-being, it may refer to elements of well-being that are not captured by HWB, such as psychological well-being and social well-being (Keyes & Annas, 2009). Ryan and Deci (2001) included it in their definition of human well-being, and in this view, the term *functioning* includes concepts such as achievement, creativity, connectedness, resilience, health, and self-endorsed actions congruent with the self-determination theory (Ryan & Huta, 2009). From the perspective of early humanistic psychology, Rogers (1961) proposed that individuals are naturally oriented toward realizing their full potential and that this tendency toward becoming a fully functional person is the only true human motive. More recently, Waterman (1993) suggested that optimal human functioning can be identified as activities that are experienced with feelings of personal expressiveness.

From yet another perspective, functioning may signify what a person manages to do or to be (Sen, 1985). In this view, functioning is a lifestyle, whereas the concept of capabilities reflects a person's ability to achieve a given functioning. In other words, capabilities reflect a person's freedom of choice between possible lifestyles (Clark, 2006).

As the variations in the previous presentation suggest, to carve out a simple conceptualization of optimal functioning is a formidable task. To complicate matters further, I propose a slightly different approach, one that reflects a viewpoint from evolutionary psychology. By looking for universal signs of good functioning and for reasons why these abilities have been critical for survival in our historical past, we may come to fuller grips with the constituents of a eudaimonic concept of optimal functioning.

It turns out that people everywhere describe behavior and functioning in a way that the two converge in a two-dimensional space: Humans can be more or less likable and humans can be more or less competent (Fiske, Cuddy, & Glick, 2006). A respectable line of independent research has identified these two dimensions as the dominant ones in social perception. The dimension of social goodness, which involves characteristics such as warm, happy, popular, helpful, and honest, is relatively independent of the dimension of competence, which involves categories such as skillful, persistent, imaginative, and serious. From a functional point of view, these categories are important because they inform the perceiver first whether the other has good intentions or not, and second whether the other is capable of enacting those intentions. According to Fiske et al. (2006), social goodness (or warmth) and competence promote survival because they provide answers to the important questions about competition and status.

Here is an example of how the distinction between happiness and competence may contribute to understanding the multifaceted nature of optimal functioning. In comparing professional and amateur singers, Grape, Sandgren, Hansson, Ericson, and Theorell (2003) found, not surprisingly, that the professionals were more concentrated and competent during a singing lesson. However, the professionals were also less satisfied. And even if the amateurs seemed to put less effort into the practice, they reported more enjoyment, release of tension, and overall well-being than did the professionals. Hence, in this study the amateurs got higher scores on HWB than the professionals, but it remains unclear to which of the groups one should ascribe the highest level of optimal functioning. Was it the amateurs or the professionals who acted in accordance with the best of their abilities?

Philosophical approaches to self-fulfillment have been reviewed by Gewirth (1998), and examples of definitions of the term include suggestions such as "self-actualization is a fundamental characteristic, inherent in human nature, a potentiality given to all or most human beings at birth"; or "the tendency of the organism to move in the direction of maturation"; or "a person's natural self relentlessly pushes toward health and growth" (p. 9). From these and other conceptualizations, Gewirth arrived at the view that the premise of self-fulfillment is in the reflection of an internally driven development toward optimal functioning, guided by virtuous choices. Building on Aristotle, Gewirth argued that for human beings, the development from potentiality to actuality is not given by nature but is mediated by concepts such as choice, deliberation, and decision. In other words, optimal functioning does not develop by "nature" alone; the idea of moral virtues or deliberate choices plays the important role of a mediator. By practicing virtuous excellence, human beings can be brought to "flourishing completion."

But how should such excellence be developed? Schwartz and Sharpe (2006) suggested that the practical wisdom (the most central of the virtues, as they see it) must be learned but cannot be taught. One can only become wise by "confronting difficult and ambiguous situations, using one's judgment to decide what to do, doing it, and getting feedback" (p. 388).

However, confronting difficult and ambiguous situations is typically not very pleasant, and according to what we now know on how skills are developed beyond habitual use, there is nothing inherently enjoyable in the practice of developing one's potentials to continually higher levels (e.g., Ericsson & Lehmann, 1996). Rather, numerous studies of extraordinary musicians, chess players, scientists, or others who have developed their skills toward the limits reveal that a constant, and typically joyless, push to perform beyond current abilities is needed to achieve excellence. Merely performing the activity is not enough; one must be able to concentrate attention toward a well-defined task with an adequate difficulty level for the particular individual, informative feedback, opportunities for repetition, and corrections of errors (Ericsson, 1996). In terms of feeling states, this way of training, which has been labeled *deliberate practice*, is usually motivated by interest and engagement and not by pleasure or contentment.

When it comes to developing concrete skills and potentials, well-being and well-doing seem to be independent or even negatively correlated (at least when well-being is defined as pleasure). However, the critical question is whether expertise competence in chess, music, science, and so forth counts as optimal functioning. To the extent that these activities are freely chosen and experienced as being a natural and self-expressing part of the actor's identity, they might be eudaimonic (some examples given in the literature on expertise development clearly violate the assumption of free choice, as recently testified by Chua, 2011).

PLEASURE AND MEANING

The ability to ascribe hedonic quality to one's surroundings is essential. Our welfare would be in jeopardy, indeed, if the taste evoked by toxins was good and sugar tasted unpleasant (Johnston, 2003). Pleasures thus assist in organizing preferences and signal whether the current action should be held back or carried on. Moreover, individuals who lack hedonic capacities meet a series of troubles in their lives, and they suffer severely (Meehl, 1975).

But the functional role of pleasure is limited. Pleasant feelings are, for example, silent with regard to cognitive content. Hedonic tone operates independently of the process of categorizing incoming stimuli—what they are and how they relate to cognitive structures and mental models that already are established (or in need of being modified). Hence, the role of pleasure is to inform us about goodness, not about meaning.

One reason why pleasure is unhelpful in the creation of meaning has to do with the step-by-step process by which new information is integrated into the existing cognitive structures. The process of comprehending what a novel or complex object means is almost always a task that is too big a bite to be swallowed whole. As Tomkins (1962) pointed out half a century ago, novel objects must be perceived both in some detail and also as a whole unity. Attention must therefore be held up long enough to appreciate details as well as the unity of the object. To maintain sufficient attention for such a task, Tomkins argued, feelings of interest rather than pleasure are required. Tomkins thus considered interest to be of uttermost importance for learning and personal growth and for mobilizing the attention needed to both understand and be engaged in the world.

More recent evidence from the brain sciences tends to support Tomkins's view. For example, in a popular account of the neuropsychology of personal identities, Greenfield (2009) provided arguments as to why pleasant feelings are not very helpful when it comes to developing personal meanings and creating a sense of self. Basically the reason is that a pleasant mind tends to wipe out the pathways needed to create conceptual frameworks. For new concepts to become meaningful, logical frameworks must be built up gradually. To create such structures, a process of slowly exercising the use of symbols over and over seems necessary. To understand means to see one thing in terms of another, and meaning appears when something is linked to something else. The more connections, the deeper the significance and the greater the understanding (Greenfield, 2009).

For example, to understand something means to connect sequences of content and to use symbols and logic that stretch beyond the immediate here and now. Anatomically, the prefrontal cortex must be active and integrated with other brain structures before something can be perceived as meaningful. But episodes of intense pleasure tend to temporarily shut down the prefrontal cortex, which enables greater focus on the here and now but less on the important step-by-step sequences needed in order to understand and incorporate the moments into a meaningful life story. Episodes of intense pleasure are dominated by the moment and do not prompt a craving or a genuine wish to develop one's potential (Greenfield, 2009).

In addition to the neuropsychological evidence, Greenfield found support for her position in the literature on religious rituals. Referring to Whitehouse (2004), an anthropologist, she pointed out how two contrasting processes are involved in the establishment of religious commitment. The first is a low-arousal, high-frequency kind of behavior that is based on repetition. The second is a high-arousal, low-frequency kind of behavior. It is important that the low-arousal, high-frequency route to commitment seems to elicit a long-term rumination on questions of understanding. The dominant experience during such activities is not pleasure, but a sense of meaning.

CONCLUSION

The promise of HWB is that pleasure—in the sense of feelings, life satisfaction (attitudes), or both—accounts for the essence of a good life. The objection from eudaimonic thinking in psychology is that such a model is too simplistic; some aspects of virtuous activities are necessary in order to supply a full definition of well-being. For some, the eudaimonic elements have nothing to do with different types of mental states but instead represent values and processes through which well-being outcomes are generated (e.g., Ryan & Huta, 2009).

The eudaimonic argument presented in this chapter is different. I have not been concerned with the issue of whether nonmental elements are necessary for a theory of eudaimonic well-being. Rather, my message has been that the concept of pleasure is unable to sustain behavior that is anywhere near the philosophical notion of virtuous activities. Put simply, the role of HWB is to facilitate stability and adaptation, whereas the role of eudaimonic well-being is to facilitate growth and accommodation. Both hedonia and eudaimonia are needed for optimal human functioning, and both have a distinct set of feeling qualities attached to them. This is not to say that elements that go beyond subjective experiences are unimportant for well-being, only that they are not included in the eudaimonic argument presented in the current chapter. My aim has been to show that HWB is not up to the task of accounting for the richness of human experiences and the development of one's best potentials.

If the pleasure reported from, say, reading Tolstoy cannot be discriminated from the pleasure reported from watching a soap opera, the reason, as I see it, is not that reading Tolstoy is more authentic or intrinsic than watching soap operas. Rather, Tolstoy's writing stretches beyond hedonic coverage because the feeling qualities it creates are too complex for the concept of pleasure. And so are many other qualities of human lives.

REFERENCES

Albarracín, D., Johnson, B. T., & Zanna, M. P. (Eds.). (2005). *The handbook of attitudes*. Mahwah, NJ: Erlbaum.

Albert Einstein. (n.d.). In *Wikiquote*. Retrieved August 29, 2012, from http://en.wikiquote.org/wiki/Albert_Einstein

Bargh, J. A., Gollwitzer, P. M., & Oettingen, G. (2010). Motivation. In S. T. Fiske, D. T. Gilbert, & G. Lindzey (Eds.), *Handbook of social psychology* (5th ed., pp. 268–316). Hoboken, NJ: Wiley.

Berridge, K. C. (2003). Pleasures of the brain. *Brain and Cognition, 52*, 106–128. doi:10.1016/S0278-2626(03)00014-9

Berridge, K. C. (2007). The debate over dopamine's role in reward: The case for incentive salience. *Psychopharmacology, 191*, 391–431. doi:10.1007/s00213-006-0578-x

Bruner, J. (1990). *Acts of meaning*. Cambridge, MA: Harvard University Press.

Campbell, A., Converse, P. E., & Rodgers, W. L. (1976). *The quality of American life.* New York, NY: Sage.

Carver, C. S. (2003). Pleasure as a sign you can attend to something else: Placing positive feelings within a general model of affect. *Cognition and Emotion, 17,* 241–261. doi:10.1080/02699930302294

Chua, A. (2011). *Battle hymn of the tiger mother.* London, England: Bloomsbury.

Clark, D. A. (2006). The capability approach: Its development, critiques, and recent advances. In A. E. Clark (Ed.), *The Elgar companion to developmental studies* (pp. 32–44). Cheltenham, England: Edward Elgar.

Coombs, C. H. (1964). *A theory of data.* London, England: Wiley.

Csikszentmihalyi, M. (1992). *Flow. The psychology of happiness.* London, England: Rider.

Delle Fave, A., & Bassi, M. (2009). The contribution of diversity to happiness research. *The Journal of Positive Psychology, 4,* 205–207. doi:10.1080/17439760902844319

Diener, E. (1984). Subjective well-being. *Psychological Bulletin, 95,* 542–575. doi:10.1037/0033-2909.95.3.542

Diener, E. (2006). Guidelines for national indicators of subjective well-being and ill-being. *Journal of Happiness Studies, 7,* 397–404. doi:10.1007/s10902-006-9000-y

Diener, E., Scollon, C. N., & Lucas, R. E. (2009). The evolving concept of subjective well-being: The multifaceted nature of happiness. In E. Diener (Ed.), *Assessing well-being: The collected works of Ed Diener* (pp. 67–100). Dordrecht, the Netherlands: Springer.

Ericsson, K. A. (1996). The acquisition of expert performance: An introduction to some of the issues. In K. A. Ericsson (Ed.), *The road to excellence: The acquisition of expert performance in the arts and sciences, sports, and games* (pp. 1–50). Mahwah, NJ: Erlbaum.

Ericsson, K. A., & Lehmann, A. C. (1996). Expert and exceptional performance: Evidence of maximal adaptation to task constraints. *Annual Review of Psychology, 47,* 273–305. doi:10.1146/annurev.psych.47.1.273

Feldman, F. (2010). *What is this thing called happiness?* Oxford, England: Oxford University Press. doi:10.1093/acprof:oso/9780199571178.001.0001

Fiske, S. T., Cuddy, A. J. C., & Glick, P. (2006). Universal dimensions of social cognition: Warmth and competence. *Trends in Cognitive Sciences, 11,* 77–83. doi:10.1016/j.tics.2006.11.005

Frijda, N. H. (2005). Emotion experience. *Cognition and Emotion, 19,* 473–497. doi:10.1080/02699930441000346

Frijda, N. H. (2010). On the nature and function of pleasure. In M. L. Kringelbach & K. C. Berridge (Eds.), *Pleasures of the brain* (pp. 99–112). Oxford, England: Oxford University Press.

Gaver, W. W., & Mandler, G. (1987). Play it again Sam: On liking music. *Cognition and Emotion, 1,* 259–282. doi:10.1080/02699938708408051

Gewirth, A. (1998). *Self-fulfillment.* Princeton, NJ: Princeton University Press.

Grape, C., Sandgren, M., Hansson, L.-O., Ericson, M., & Theorell, T. (2003). Does singing promote well-being? An empirical study of professional and amateur singers during a singing lesson. *Integrative Physiological and Behavioral Science, 38*, 65–74.

Greenfield, S. (2009). *ID: The quest for meaning in the 21st century*. London, England: Sceptre.

Haidt, J. (2006). *The happiness hypothesis. Putting ancient wisdom and philosophy to the test of modern science*. London, England: Arrow Books.

Huta, V., & Ryan, R. (2010). Pursuing pleasure or virtue: The differential and overlapping well-being benefits of hedonic and eudaimonic motives. *Journal of Happiness Studies, 11*, 735–762. doi:10.1007/s10902-009-9171-4

Iran-Nejad, A. (1987). Cognitive and affective causes of interest and liking. *Journal of Educational Psychology, 79*, 120–130. doi:10.1037/0022-0663.79.2.120

Johnston, V. S. (2003). The origin and function of pleasure. *Cognition and Emotion, 17*, 167–179. doi:10.1080/02699930302290

Kagan, J. (2009). *The three cultures. Natural sciences, social sciences, and the humanities in the 21st century*. Cambridge, England: Cambridge University Press. doi:10.1017/CBO9780511576638

Kahneman, D. (1999). Objective happiness. In D. Kahneman, E. Diener, & N. Schwarz (Eds.), *Well-being: The foundations of hedonic psychology* (pp. 3–25). New York, NY: Russell Sage Foundation.

Kahneman, D., & Riis, J. (2005). Living, and thinking about it: Two perspectives on life. In F. Huppert, N. Baylis, & B. Keverne (Eds.), *The science of well-being* (pp. 285–304). Oxford, England: Oxford University Press. doi:10.1093/acprof:oso/9780198567523.003.0011

Kahneman, D., Schkade, D. A., Fischler, C., Krueger, A. B., & Krilla, A. (2010). The structure of well-being in two cities: Life satisfaction and experienced happiness in Columbus, Ohio; and Rennes, France. In E. Diener, J. F. Helliwell, & D. Kahneman (Eds.), *International differences in well-being* (pp. 16–33). Oxford, England: Oxford University Press. doi:10.1093/acprof:oso/9780199732739.003.0002

Keyes, C. L. M., & Annas, J. (2009). Feeling good and functioning well: Distinctive concepts in ancient philosophy and contemporary science. *The Journal of Positive Psychology, 4*, 197–201. doi:10.1080/17439760902844228

Lambie, J. A., & Marcel, A. (2002). Consciousness and the variety of emotion experience: A theoretical framework. *Psychological Review, 109*, 219–259. doi:10.1037/0033-295X.109.2.219

Leyton, M. (2010). The neurobiology of desire: Dopamine and the regulation of mood and motivational states in humans. In M. L. Kringelbach & K. C. Berridge (Eds.), *Pleasures of the brain* (pp. 222–243). Oxford, England: Oxford University Press.

Loewenstein, G., & Ubel, P. A. (2008). Hedonic adaptation and the role of decision and experience utility in public policy. *Journal of Public Economics, 92*, 1795–1810. doi:10.1016/j.jpubeco.2007.12.011

Martin, L. R. (2008). Paradoxes of happiness. *Journal of Happiness Studies, 9*, 171–184. doi:10.1007/s10902-007-9056-3

Meehl, P. E. (1975). Hedonic capacity: Some conjectures. *Bulletin of the Menninger Clinic, 39*, 295–307.

Moore, A. (2009). Hedonism. In E. N. Zalta (Ed.), *Stanford encyclopedia of philosophy* (Fall ed.). Available from http://plato.stanford.edu/entries/hedonism

Moum, T. (2007). A critique of "Subjective wellbeing as an affective-cognitive construct" by Davern, Cummins and Stokes. *Journal of Happiness Studies, 8*, 451–453. doi:10.1007/s10902-007-9067-0

Panksepp, J. (1998). *Affective neuroscience. The foundations of human and animal emotions.* Oxford, England: Oxford University Press.

Peterson, C., & Seligman, M. E. P. (2004). *Character strengths and virtues: A handbook and classification.* Washington, DC: American Psychological Association.

Read, D. (2007). Experienced utility: Utility theory from Jeremy Bentham to Daniel Kahneman. *Thinking & Reasoning, 13*, 45–61. doi:10.1080/13546780600872627

Rogers, C. (1961). *On becoming a person.* Boston, MA: Houghton Mifflin.

Ryan, R. M., & Deci, E. L. (2001). On happiness and human potentials: A review of research on hedonic and eudaimonic well-being. *Annual Review of Psychology, 52*, 141–166. doi:10.1146/annurev.psych.52.1.141

Ryan, R. M., & Huta, V. (2009). Wellness as healthy functioning or wellness as happiness: The importance of eudaimonic thinking (response to the Kashdan et al. and Waterman discussion). *The Journal of Positive Psychology, 4*, 202–204. doi:10.1080/17439760902844285

Schwartz, B., & Sharpe, K. E. (2006). Practical wisdom: Aristotle meets positive psychology. *Journal of Happiness Studies, 7*, 377–395. doi:10.1007/s10902-005-3651-y

Sen, A. (1985). Well-being, agency, and freedom: The Dewey lectures, 1985. *The Journal of Philosophy, 82*, 169–221. doi:10.2307/2026184

Small, D. M., Zatorre, R. J., Dagher, A., Evans, A. C., & Jones-Gotman, M. (2001). Changes in brain activity related to eating chocolate. From pleasure to aversion. *Brain: A Journal of Neurology, 124*, 1720–1733. doi:10.1093/brain/124.9.1720

Steiner, J. E., Glaser, D., Hawilo, M. E., & Berridge, K. C. (2001). Comparative expression of hedonic impact: Affective reactions to taste by human infants and other primates. *Neuroscience and Biobehavioral Reviews, 25*, 53–74. doi:10.1016/S0149-7634(00)00051-8

Sumner, L. W. (1996). *Welfare, happiness, and ethics.* Oxford, England: Clarendon Press.

Thagard, P. (2002). The passionate scientist: Emotion in scientific cognition. In P. Carruthers, S. Stich, & M. Siegal (Eds.), *The cognitive basis of science* (pp. 235–250). Cambridge, England: Cambridge University Press.

Tomkins, S. S. (1962). *Affect and imagery consciousness: Vol. 1. The positive affects.* New York: Springer.

Vittersø, J. (in press). Functional well-being: Happiness as feelings, evaluations and functioning. In I. Boniwell & S. David (Eds.), *The Oxford handbook of happiness*. Oxford, England: Oxford University Press.

Vittersø, J., Oelmann, H., & Wang, A. L. (2009). Life satisfaction is not a balanced estimator of the good life. Evidence from reaction time measures and self-reported emotions. *Journal of Happiness Studies, 10,* 1–17. doi:10.1007/s10902-007-9058-1

Vittersø, J., Søholt, Y., Hetland, A., Thorsen, I. A., & Røysamb, E. (2010). Was Hercules happy? Some answers from a functional model of human well-being. *Social Indicators Research, 95,* 1–18. doi:10.1007/s11205-009-9447-4

Walker, E. D. (1981). The quest for the inverted U. In H. I. Day (Ed.), *Advances in intrinsic motivation and aesthetics* (pp. 39–70). New York, NY: Plenum Press. doi:10.1007/978-1-4613-3195-7_3

Waterman, A. S. (1993). Two conceptions of happiness: Contrasts of personal expressiveness (eudaimonia) and hedonic enjoyment. *Journal of Personality and Social Psychology, 64,* 678–691. doi:10.1037/0022-3514.64.4.678

Watson, J. (1999). *The double helix: A personal account of the structure of DNA.* London, England: Penguin Books.

Whitehouse, H. (2004). *Modes of religiosity. A cognitive theory of religious transformation.* London, England: Altamira Press.

Winkielman, P., Schwarz, N., Fazendeiro, T. A., & Reber, R. (2003). The hedonic marking of processing fluency: Implications for evaluative judgment. In J. Musch & K. C. Klauer (Eds.), *The psychology of evaluation: Affective processes in cognition and emotion* (pp. 189–217). Mahwah, NJ: Erlbaum.

Zajonc, R. B. (2001). Feeling and thinking: Closing the debate over the independence of affect. In J. P. Forgas (Ed.), *Feeling and thinking: The role of affect in social cognition* (pp. 31–58). Cambridge, England: Cambridge University Press.

3

WHAT HUMANS NEED: FLOURISHING IN ARISTOTELIAN PHILOSOPHY AND SELF-DETERMINATION THEORY

RICHARD M. RYAN, RANDALL R. CURREN, AND EDWARD L. DECI

In this chapter, two psychologists (Ryan and Deci) team up with a philosopher (Curren) to describe an account of human wellness or flourishing that is connected to perennial debates about human nature and what constitutes its most vital and fullest expressions. Specifically, we explore the concept of *eudaimonia*, which derives from neo-Aristotelian perspectives according to which there are human potentialities whose fulfillment is essential to well-being and happiness—potentialities whose fulfillment constitutes "the good" for human beings when it exhibits qualities of goodness and is experienced as meaningful and satisfying (Curren, 2010). We then examine the tenets and findings of self-determination theory (SDT; Deci & Ryan, 2012; Ryan & Deci, 2000) with respect to eudaimonist views and, specifically, evidence derived from SDT that there are universal needs for autonomy, competence, and relatedness whose satisfaction is central to human flourishing. We focus in particular on the importance of autonomy, which plays an essential and

DOI: 10.1037/14092-004
The Best Within Us: Positive Psychology Perspectives on Eudaimonia, Alan S. Waterman (Editor)
Copyright © 2013 by the American Psychological Association. All rights reserved.

instrumental role in allowing persons to realize their individual possibilities, satisfy other basic needs, and thus experience sustained happiness.

What is to be gained by exploring this connection between an ancient philosophical tradition and the empirically based work in SDT? One view is that psychological theorizing can be informed by philosophy, and philosophy by empirical psychological research. This may seem obvious, but it is not without controversy. For example, Kashdan, Biswas-Diener, and King (2008) argued that philosophical perspectives potentially create confusion for behavioral scientists studying happiness because in their view, psychologists can directly study happiness simply by asking people how happy they are and then proceeding to discover what predicts that subjective outcome. Moreover, because people are themselves the best authorities on their own happiness, they expressed concern that eudaimonist thinking, which searches for universal foundations of a good life, is elitist and imposes moral hierarchies and value judgments.

In contrast, we think that differentiations concerning the way in which happiness is pursued, a matter central to eudaimonist thought, have borne, and will continue to bear, significant empirical fruit. In fact, a eudaimonist perspective makes some specific predictions about the good life and flourishing that one would not generate from hedonic theories (Ryan & Huta, 2009). Eudaimonist thinking does indeed posit that there are objective elements in living well, but it is not elitist to hold, as SDT does, that at least some of these elements can be identified empirically, much as nutriments necessary for physical thriving can be identified empirically (Deci & Ryan, 2000; Ryan, 1995). And although living in a eudaimonic way, or in accordance with a neo-Aristotelian conception of flourishing, may indeed involve frequent positive emotions or happiness, wellness is not fully defined by these positive emotions, contrary to what Kahneman, Diener, and Schwarz (1999) once argued. It is also comprised of those aspects of a life that engender such feelings (Niemiec & Ryan, in press; Ryan & Huta, 2009).

Rather than defining happiness as simply having good feelings, the eudaimonist conception of well-being or flourishing rests on the proposition that what is most subjectively satisfying over the course of a life is activity that develops and expresses one's most reflectively valued and well integrated human potentialities. According to this view, pleasure accompanies activities that fulfill human intellectual, social, and productive potentials in good and admirable ways, even though pleasure is not the aim of such activities. As many scholars of ancient ethics have noted, Aristotelian eudaimonism holds that the development of what is best in us is essential to flourishing, and flourishing in turn entails both doing what is objectively good and experiencing subjectively happiness, pleasure, and satisfaction (see Curren, 2000, 2010; Kraut, 1989, 2007). Dorothea Frede (2006) identified this as "Aristotle's principle that what is good *in* a person is also what is good *for* that person and that it should be felt to be so *by* that person" (p. 260). This central tenet of eudaimonistic ethics is resonant not only with SDT (Deci & Ryan, 2000) but also with humanism more generally.

Thus, despite the difficulties of integrating philosophy and empirical-psychological methods, the effort is worthwhile because it is necessary to address the circumstances of human well-being, a topic of wide interest and importance for policy and practice. For example, there are strong global economic and social forces fostering consumptive, materialistic lifestyles and selfishly focused value priorities (Curren, 2009; Kasser, Cohn, Kanner, & Ryan, 2007). Whereas hedonic theories of happiness offer little guidance for public policy and social practices, eudaimonist theorizing suggests that the focus of a good life would be on self-realization consistent with the common good (a moral theoretic norm) and that a fixation on wealth would undermine well-being. Aristotle emphasized this claim, noting that many people confuse limitless accumulation of material goods with living well (Aristotle, trans. 1984b). This can be tested empirically by examining materialistic lifestyles, aspirations, and attainments and their relations to outcomes indicative of well-being (e.g., see Kasser & Ryan, 1996; Niemiec, Ryan, & Deci, 2009). If it is true that people are more satisfied and well when living eudaimonically than when living more materialistically and selfishly, this has significant implications for sustainability and global development and wellness policies.

Aristotle's works address both the nature of "the good" for human beings (eudaimonia) and the characteristics of a society designed to enable its citizens to live well. His view is, indeed, that the proper aim of a society and its institutions is the well-being of all its citizens (Aristotle, trans. 1984b; Curren, 2000; May, 2010). A political community is ideally, in his view, a kind of partnership of citizens in living the best lives human beings are capable of living. Such a partnership is characterized by reciprocity of friendly feeling, trust, goodwill, and cooperation in living well together. Moderation of wealth is not only most conducive to living well but also essential to this ideal of citizenship (Aristotle, trans. 1984b). This ideal is one manifestation of the importance Aristotle attaches to the social potentialities of human beings, potentialities that find their most natural and admirable fulfillment not simply in the pleasures that may draw people together or the usefulness they may have to each other, but in mutual respect, appreciation of the other's goodness, and readiness to act for the other's good (Aristotle, trans. 1984a). The other potentialities emphasized by Aristotle are intellectual, and these are said to find their most admirable and satisfying fulfillment in the exercise of theoretical and practical wisdom. "All men by nature desire to know" and take pleasure in knowing (Aristotle, trans. 1984c, p. 1552), and they are also self-moving beings who take pleasure in self-directed activity (Aristotle, trans.

1984a). Inquiry and deliberation are most successful and satisfying when they are competent or better than competent, they display intellectual virtues such as understanding and good judgment, and they yield knowledge or wise decisions. Although Aristotle regards the exercise of theoretical wisdom in pure inquiry as the most admirable and satisfying use of human intellectual potential and the exercise of practical wisdom or good practical judgment in public service as second best, he also recognizes that human beings have productive potentialities that can be developed and exercised more or less admirably and pleasantly in the competent practice of diverse and more or less intellectually and physically demanding arts or *technai*. Arts make diverse contributions to a society's functionality in enabling its citizens to live well (Aristotle, trans. 1984a), and each requires expertise and the competent mastery of methods. Each provides an avenue, more or less suitable and satisfying to different people, for fulfilling potentialities in accordance with norms of goodness or excellence.

These Aristotelian ideas about well-being and the human good have enjoyed a renaissance in philosophy in recent years (Foot, 2003; Kraut, 1989, 2007; MacIntyre, 1981; Nussbaum, 1993, 2000), and a parallel resurgence has occurred in psychology, as eudaimonist perspectives on well-being have increasingly been contrasted with hedonic views of happiness (Ryan & Deci, 2001; Ryan & Huta, 2009; Ryff & Singer, 2008; Waterman, 1993). These eudaimonist interests and developments in moral philosophy and empirical psychology have so far proceeded largely in isolation from one another, though with some notable exceptions (e.g., see May, 2010).

SDT is a psychological theory of well-being that has drawn on eudaimonist ideas (Deci & Ryan, 1985; Ryan & Deci, 2000). The theory posits three basic universal psychological needs closely associated with the satisfaction of human potentials and describes natural inclinations toward action, exploration, learning, psychological integration, and social connectedness. A central finding that has been replicated transculturally (e.g., Jang, Reeve, Ryan, & Kim, 2009) is that the satisfaction of these basic psychological needs is essential to well-being as assessed by multiple indicators, including subjective assessments of happiness. These findings go a long way toward vindicating the proposition foundational to a eudaimonist view of well-being—namely, that what is most subjectively satisfying is fulfilling certain human potentialities well. They also reveal that subjective satisfaction does not accompany the competent or admirable fulfillment of a potentiality unless potentials for self-determination, good relationships, and competent (intellectual and physical) activity are all fulfilled so that associated needs are satisfied.

Central to our considerations is distinguishing between eudaimonia as a way of living and positive affect as a hedonic outcome (see Ryan, Huta, &

Deci, 2008). Although there are many ways to produce positive affect as a short-term hedonic outcome, we argue that enduring satisfaction and, more generally, fulfilling human functioning are empirically associated with eudaimonic ways of living. The SDT viewpoint on wellness is thus consistent with a eudaimonist perspective in a general sense, yet uses its own specific constructs concerning those processes central to eudaimonic living, namely, acting with autonomy and integrity, pursuing intrinsic goals, and being mindful. Moreover, although the SDT perspective emphasizes eudaimonic living as central to wellness, it also provides a place for hedonically oriented activities within a life of thriving (Huta & Ryan, 2010; Ryan & Deci, 2010).

THE SELF-DETERMINATION THEORY VIEWPOINT ON WELLNESS

SDT is a broad theory of optimal functioning and motivation. The theory's roots lie in organismic thinking—that is, the view that living things have an organizational nature, moving developmentally in a direction of greater autonomy—of greater coherence and integration in functioning. With regard to human psychological development, SDT looks to three fundamental needs as underlying our inherent tendency toward integrated growth and development. To function optimally, an individual must experience competence (efficacy and sense of control), relatedness (social significance and connection), and autonomy (volition and self-endorsement of behavior). Autonomy, competence, and relatedness describe the natural, intrinsic functionalities whose satisfaction predicts both high-quality motivation and well-being—in short, full, thriving functioning. Needs are objectively beneficial, in that their satisfaction or frustration predicts wellness regardless of an individual's explicit values for them. In turn, although flourishing and full functioning are associated with happiness or subjective well-being, they also entail a capacity for experiencing all authentic emotions and for engaging in valued pursuits whether they be hedonically rewarding or not.

The most obvious manifestation of the growth tendency that SDT sees as natural to humans is the phenomenon of intrinsic motivation (Deci & Ryan, 1980). From birth, infants explore, manipulate, and play in interaction with their physical and interpersonal surrounds. Their curiosity is unbounded for those things within their physical and cognitive reach. This natural tendency to engage in play, exploration, and discovery for its own sake is called *intrinsic motivation,* and it has long been a focus of study within SDT. This potentiality for assimilating knowledge and skills out of interest is surely a deep part of human nature whose realization is good and whose dampening or frustration would lead to unhappiness.

Although people have an inherent or evolved propensity to be intrinsically motivated to exercise their physical, cognitive, and social capacities, such motivation is nonetheless based in certain types of satisfactions and requires certain supports. First, intrinsic motivation is by its nature volitional or autonomous—it is characterized by what in attribution theory is labeled an internal perceived locus of causality (IPLOC; de Charms, 1968; Ryan & Connell, 1989). If factors in the social environment detract from autonomy or an IPLOC, intrinsic motivation is undermined (Deci, Koestner, & Ryan, 1999). Intrinsic motivation also is dependent on feelings of competence. Only tasks and challenges within which one can experience some control and mastery are intrinsically motivating, and the negative feedback that comes from being objectively overchallenged or from critical negative evaluative contexts also undermines intrinsic motivation. Thus, we see two basic psychological needs underpinning intrinsic motivation, namely, autonomy and competence. Relatedness is also entailed, but in a less proximal sense, for many intrinsically motivated activities are done in solitude (e.g., reading, playing solitaire). Yet, without relatedness there is less security to explore, a finding not only true in infancy, but throughout the life span. In short, intrinsic motivation is a phenomenon that represents a positive and growth-related strength in human nature, one that is robust when there are supports for autonomy, competence, and relatedness.

A second manifestation of positive human growth and wholeness is the tendency to internalize and integrate social and cultural information. Again, from birth, humans demonstrate not only a propensity to imitate models but also to take interest in and attempt to emulate significant others. Underlying this tendency toward internalization are various needs. Relatedness is fulfilled through internalization, as adopting the values and practices in the ambient social context connects one with the group and enhances a sense of belonging. Competence needs are also satisfied as one gains efficacy and empowerment in a larger social world. Finally, although competence and relatedness could explain modeling and even the active introjection of external regulations and attitudes, integrating regulations and truly making them one's own is a process of identification and autonomy. Thus, with complete internalization a person integrates what was originally external to the self and experiences it as his or her own value and volitional practice.

Hundreds of studies have supported the connection between social supports for autonomy, competence, and relatedness and both more robust intrinsic motivation and fuller internalization (e.g., see the review by Vansteenkiste, Ryan, & Deci, 2008). Yet looking at these studies, there is another clear pattern of findings that concerns the outcome of most importance in this chapter, namely well-being. Using multiple indicators (including hedonically oriented well-being measures, functional measures of mental and physical health, and additional outcomes), people whose basic psychological needs for autonomy, competence, and relatedness are more satisfied experience greater wellness and thriving. This pattern turns out to be reliable across ages, genders, and cultures. Indeed, the three needs explain the preponderance of variance in assessments of well-being, with supports for need satisfaction predicting positive outcomes (e.g., Jang et al., 2009; Miquelon & Vallerand, 2008) and thwarts to any of the needs diminishing well-being (e.g., Bartholomew, Ntoumanis, Ryan, & Thogersen-Ntoumani, 2011).

This pattern of effects is evident not only over aggregate measurements, in which general need satisfaction predicts mental health and happiness, but even on a daily or situational basis. For example, Ryan, Bernstein, and Brown (2010) examined daily wellness indicators in a sample of working adults. They found a large "weekend effect" in which from Friday night through Sunday afternoon there was more happiness, fewer physical symptoms, and more vitality, among other outcomes. This pattern, familiar to most workers, was largely due to within-person changes in psychological need satisfaction—when people were anticipating working or on the job, many felt low autonomy and low relatedness, thus diminishing their mental health. Of course, individuals who were experiencing more autonomy and relatedness at work thrived there as well, demonstrating how flourishing is dependent on need satisfaction within the settings of one's life. Similarly, a plethora of experiments shows how autonomy supports versus thwarts impact moment-to-moment wellness, whether the person is interacting with others (e.g., Weinstein, Hodgins, & Ryan, 2010) or playing a solitary game (Ryan, Rigby, & Przybylski, 2006).

Eudaimonic Living and Need Satisfaction: Detailing the Processes of Actualization

As the SDT empirical literature has demonstrated, the more individuals experience autonomy, competence, and relatedness, the more they are intrinsically motivated and integrated in their regulation of action, and the greater their wellness, broadly assessed. This then suggests that cultures, value systems, and lifestyles that are supportive of basic need satisfactions, including autonomy, will be conducive to well-being. In other words, cultures influence and provide the content for the life goals and projects people internalize, some of which may yield experiences of autonomy, competence, and relatedness, and others of which may frustrate or at best only indirectly conduce to these satisfactions. So, what might these different lifestyles be?

Here we can draw hypotheses from Aristotelian thought. If Aristotle is correct, the good life is one that is volitional, with individuals experiencing both autonomy and ownership of their actions. Thus, lifestyles associated with being controlled by extrinsic rewards and punishments, or which take place within social contexts that are controlling or autonomy thwarting, should be detrimental to wellness. A second Aristotelian hypothesis is that the excellent pursuit of intrinsic goods, especially those that are good for both self and community, will be most compatible with thriving. For example, one could not identify the good in accumulating wealth because it is useful "only for the sake of something else," whereas for the human good, we should turn to those ends that are "valued for themselves" (Aristotle, trans. 1984a, p. 1732). The role of reflective volition in a eudaimonic life also led SDT researchers to examine the attribute of mindfulness (Brown & Ryan, 2003) as a facilitator of the good life. We now address each of these in turn.

Autonomy and Wellness

Eudaimonic living requires thoughtful deliberation and choice of actions and life plans reflecting one's abiding values and beliefs. This would suggest that the relative autonomy of behavioral regulation would be differentially associated with full functioning and indicators of well-being, including subjective happiness. The research evidence supporting this claim is abundant (see, e.g., Deci & Ryan, 2012; Ryan & Deci, 2010), so we describe only a few illustrative examples.

First, it is important to note that around the globe greater personal autonomy is critical for well-being. For example, Diener, Ng, Hartr, and Arora (2010) analyzed data from a worldwide Gallup poll and found that across nations autonomy was one of the strongest predictors of positive affect. That is, being able to exercise autonomy is associated with subjective emotional happiness. This finding supports earlier studies by Chirkov, Ryan, Kim, and Kaplan (2003), Sheldon et al. (2004), and several others who made more specific between-country comparisons and found evidence for the universal importance of autonomy for mental health and wellness.

SDT makes a more specific prediction: Not only are aggregate happiness and wellness dependent on autonomy, autonomy is also important at the levels of domains, situations, and settings. For example, in the work domain, autonomy satisfaction predicts worker wellness (Ryan et al., 2010). Even for unemployed individuals, those with more autonomous self-regulation show higher well-being and greater job-search intensity (Vansteenkiste, Lens, Dewitte, De Witte, & Deci, 2004). In the education domain, elementary students' autonomous self-regulation has been shown to promote greater conceptual learning (Grolnick & Ryan, 1987) and adjustment (Grolnick, Ryan, & Deci, 1991; Yamauchi & Tanaka, 1998). Among college students, autonomous reasons for learning have been related to greater interest and perceived competence, lower anxiety, and higher performance (e.g., Black & Deci, 2000). Indeed, autonomous self-regulation has been associated with myriad positive school-related variables, from lower dropout rates (Vallerand & Bissonnette, 1992), to better classroom attitudes and experiences (Miserandino, 1996), to psychological health (Jang et al., 2009). In the domain of health care, several studies have reported how autonomous self-regulation for working toward smoking cessation has been shown to promote both longer term abstinence and enhanced vitality (e.g., Niemiec, Ryan, Patrick, Deci, & Williams, 2010). Among persons with diabetes, Williams et al. (2009) found that autonomous self-regulation for medication use predicted higher quality of life, greater adherence, and improved health outcomes.

In fact, autonomy has proven critical to full functioning and wellness in multiple contexts, including sport, religion, relationships, work, and leisure (see Ryan & Deci, 2010). The findings from studies across these domains show how greater autonomy facilitates behavioral persistence; task performance; and greater psychological, physical, and social wellness. Thus, the relative autonomy with which behavior is regulated appears to be an important aspect of "the good life."

Life Goals and the Pursuit of Happiness

Aristotle is well known for stating that happiness or living well is every individual's goal. Yet, not everyone chooses the best or most optimal paths to that end, so the eudaimonist tradition has sought to evaluate different conceptions of living well. In this regard, research within SDT on life goals and aspirations has proven particularly relevant. According to Aristotle's conception of eudaimonia, living well entails pursuing ends that are of inherent worth. If so, it follows that the pursuit and attainment of certain types of goals are more likely than others to contribute to well-being.

Within SDT, different types of aspirations have been distinguished according to their association with satisfaction of the basic psychological needs (Ryan, Sheldon, Kasser, & Deci, 1996). Using factor analysis, Kasser and Ryan (1996) found evidence for two categories of life goals. One factor was labeled *extrinsic aspirations* and included valuing of wealth, fame, and an appealing image. The achievement of such goals is contingent on external approval (Aristotle, trans. 1984a) and can thus at best only indirectly satisfy basic psychological needs and at worst may detract from need satisfaction. The second factor was labeled *intrinsic aspirations* and included valuing of personal growth, close relationships, community contribution, and physical health. Such goals are likely to directly support and facilitate need satisfaction. The structural distinction between the intrinsic and extrinsic aspirations has been observed across 15 cultures throughout the world (Grouzet et al., 2005). Therefore, an important question within SDT has concerned whether the felt importance and actual attainment of intrinsic (relative to extrinsic) aspirations differentially predicts full functioning and thriving as need theory would predict.

Kasser and Ryan (1996) found that those who placed strong importance on intrinsic (relative to extrinsic) aspirations reported higher well-being and lower ill-being. Similar results have been obtained in diverse countries (e.g., Ryan et al., 1999) and contexts (Niemiec et al., 2009). In related work, Vansteenkiste et al. (2007) reported that adult employees who reported an intrinsic (relative to extrinsic) work value orientation evidenced greater work-related satisfaction, dedication, and vitality and less work–family conflict, emotional exhaustion, and desire to quit. Further, these positive consequences of holding a relatively more intrinsic orientation in work values were, as predicted, mediated by the individuals' need satisfaction experienced at work. In the exercise domain, Sebire, Standage, and Vansteenkiste (2009) showed that intrinsic (relative to extrinsic) goals predicted cognitive, affective, and behavioral outcomes through their associations with autonomy, competence, and relatedness. In other words, studies are showing that intrinsic versus extrinsic value orientations, even when domain specific, predict wellness outcomes within the domain.

One might ask, however, whether the problem with extrinsic life goals is that they are hard to attain, and therefore as goal-efficacy theories (e.g., Locke & Latham, 1990) would predict, those who succeed at extrinsic life goals would be very happy and well. But SDT predicts to the contrary that, whereas intrinsic goal attainments should reliably enhance wellness and functioning, extrinsic attainments will not reliably do so, because only the former type of goal attainments is likely to fulfill basic psychological needs.

Studies have supported these SDT claims, thus simultaneously providing evidence in support of eudaimonist hypotheses. For example, Kasser and Ryan (2001) found those who attained intrinsic aspirations reported higher psychological health and quality of interpersonal relationships regardless of extrinsic attainments, whereas those who reported high extrinsic attainments were happy and relationally well only if also attaining intrinsic goals. Ryan et al. (1999) obtained similar results in studies of Russian and U.S. college students. In a sample of senior citizens, Van Hiel and Vansteenkiste (2009) reported that attainment of intrinsic aspirations was associated with higher ego integrity and death acceptance, whereas attainment of extrinsic aspirations was associated with more despair. Using a longitudinal design, Niemiec, Ryan, and Deci (2009) examined young adults' life goal attainments as they transition into adult identities and lifestyles, namely from 1 to 2 years post-college. The findings showed that whereas attainments of intrinsic goals promoted psychological health, attainment of extrinsic aspirations was not associated with well-being and instead was actually associated with increases in indicators of ill-being. Furthermore, in line with SDT formulations, the benefits of intrinsic goal attainments were mediated by satisfaction of the basic psychological needs.

One might wonder about the claim that goals associated with overall social good or doing for others would engender happiness. Indeed, such a view is anathema to many economic and behavioral views that assume an inherent selfishness and self-interested calculus to all interactions—views we regard as without foundation in evolutionary science (see, e.g., De Waal, 2009). Human nature is prone toward connectedness and evolved to find inherent satisfactions in helping. In fact, when able to help volitionally, humans derive both need satisfaction and well-being enhancement. As with happiness, the aim of helping is not these hedonic outcomes, but they do, however, accrue. This was demonstrated in a series of studies by Weinstein and Ryan (2010), some of which were experimental and some diary based. Across methods it was shown that when people volitionally engaged in helping others, both they and the recipients of their help gained in well-being. This relation between helping and wellness outcomes was fully mediated by need satisfaction. That is, when people helped others by choice, they, in doing so, experienced autonomy, competence, and relatedness, factors that in turn accounted for the positive outcomes. By contrast, when people were controlled in their helping behavior, they did not experience these need satisfactions to the same degree, nor did the recipients of their help. Thus, need satisfaction was yielded by spontaneous motives, not compelled actions.

Basic need satisfaction can thus easily be obtained as people pursue SDT's intrinsic goals of community service (helping others), personal growth (e.g., learning, experiencing new things), and intimacy (connecting deeply and meaningfully with others). By contrast, extrinsic goals such as the pursuit of wealth, image, or fame often entail forgoing autonomy and relatedness. In fact, much evidence has suggested that as people work to get more money or fame, they often sacrifice relationships and forego abiding interests. Thus when the extrinsic goals become the organizing factor in activities, basic needs are less likely to be ongoingly fulfilled, as Aristotle anticipated.

To summarize, research from SDT has shown that pursuit and attainment of intrinsic (relative to extrinsic) aspirations is associated with enhancement of psychological and relational health. It is important that such associations have been observed in numerous life contexts and across diverse cultures, lending credibility to the postulate that the pursuit and attainment of intrinsic aspirations facilitates optimal functioning and wellness, a finding that appears to be universal. In large part this positive effect of intrinsic life goals, which are oriented toward personal growth and relationship/community values, is attributable to greater basic psychological need satisfaction. As people pursue more intrinsic, eudaimonic goals, they are more likely to feel autonomous, competent, and connected with others, all of which contribute to a sense of wellness.

Awareness and Eudaimonic Living

Thus far we have suggested, and reviewed evidence in support of, the idea that people evidence thriving and flourishing when they are able to act with autonomy and when they embrace lifestyles more oriented toward intrinsic than extrinsic goals, all of which is consistent with eudaimonist thinking. The question of autonomy concerns the "why" of goals—whether one behaves for self-endorsed reasons versus external or internal compulsions. The question of intrinsic versus extrinsic goal orientations concerns the "what" of goals—the content people value and pursue. A further interest in SDT is in the "how" of goals—or the inner processes through which individuals assess and identify what is most important or valuable to pursue in a given moment and then sustain efforts toward such ends. One of the central processes involves awareness.

The importance of self-reflection was a staple of ancient Greek moral thought, and the function of Aristotle's lectures on ethics was largely to promote such reflection. If self-reflection is an important aspect of self-determination and living well, one would expect that being mindful of the quality of one's ongoing experience should facilitate choices more consistent with well-being and intrinsic aspirations and less thoughtlessly reactive in response to threats and momentary pleasures. In other words, if we have intrinsic motives to fulfill our potentialities or actualize them, being aware and mindful will put us more in touch with these inherent propensities and help protect us from being derailed by various pressures or threats.

Brown and Ryan (2003) began a program of research focused on *mindfulness*, defined as receptive attention to present experience. When mindful, people are receptive to experiencing internal and external events without distortion or automatic reactions and thus remain more open to responding in reflectively endorsed, integrated ways. Consistent with this notion, mindfulness has been shown to covary with autonomy and predict well-being (Brown & Ryan, 2003). Also consistent with this formulation, mindfulness is associated with greater valuing of intrinsic (relative to extrinsic) aspirations, engagement in more ecologically responsible behavior (Brown & Kasser, 2005), and more responsive and constructive interactions within relationships (e.g., Barnes, Brown, Krusemark, Campbell, & Rogge, 2007). Furthermore, Weinstein, Brown, and Ryan, (2009) showed in a series of studies that mindfulness was associated with experiencing less stress when challenged and coping better with stress that does accrue.

More recently, Niemiec, Brown, et al. (2010) examined the role of mindfulness in ameliorating commonly displayed defensive responding to existential threats. They found that more mindful individuals responded to mortality salience without engaging in nonconsciously defensive ways. Specifically, they did not engage in worldview defenses or out-group derogations when mortality was made salient, whereas those who were less mindful showed these defensive reactions. To summarize, SDT-based research has shown how mindfulness yields benefits for personal, relational, and broader societal wellness and appears to be an important contributor to living well. Living well requires acting with awareness, which allows the individual to experience greater autonomy and integrity and to more consistently pursue valued goals, resulting in greater happiness.

CONCLUSION: TOWARD A EUDAIMONIC CULTURE

We began this chapter by suggesting that eudaimonia concerns ways of living rather than a particular type of happiness. In fact, eudaimonist thinking is prescriptive, for it suggests that there are objective needs and forms of living that define the good life and yield an array of more positive outcomes. We argued that the search for the necessary elements of a good life is not elitist, but more akin to a nutritionist trying to identify the foods that actually nourish rather than those that just taste good. This search for objective aspects of well-being may be prescriptive, but it is not controlling. The importance of self-determination to a flourishing life rules out any application of eudaimonism that is not autonomy supportive. We were built to self-organize, to take pleasure in effective action, and to connect with others. Fulfilling these human possibilities yields happiness, even though happiness is the direct aim of none of them.

The current zeitgeist in psychology is toward an accretive, atheoretical accumulation of facts. The mainstream nonetheless embraces implicitly a relativistic view, which suggests that efficacy at one's goals, no matter what they are, is what produces pleasure and well-being. In such work there is little by way of hypotheses or guidance because there is little assumed about human nature. By contrast, eudaimonist thinking pushes behavioral scientists to critically evaluate and compare lifestyles, organizations, and cultures in terms of their support for the good life and the outcomes that accompany it. Eudaimonist hypotheses, like hedonic perspectives, are testable and refinable, and those found reliable can be applied in schools, workplaces, and other institutions in which flourishing is (or should be) an organizational goal.

In search of human flourishing, current empirical evidence has strongly sustained the SDT perspective that supports for autonomy, competence, and relatedness, both within specific social settings and in broader cultural contexts, foster human wellness, fuller functioning, and subjective happiness. Need-satisfying settings support human freedom and dignity and put compassion for others in the foreground. It is thus remarkable how the things we perennially refer to as basic or intrinsic values, when available, also make us happy. But then again, that is the point of eudaimonist thought and a central tenet of SDT.

REFERENCES

Aristotle. (1984a). Metaphysics. In J. Barnes (Ed.), *The complete works of Aristotle* (Vol. 2, pp. 1552–1728). Princeton, NJ: Princeton University Press.

Aristotle. (1984b). Nicomachean ethics. In J. Barnes (Ed.), *The complete works of Aristotle* (Vol. 2, pp. 1729–1876). Princeton, NJ: Princeton University Press.

Aristotle. (1984c). Politics. In J. Barnes (Ed.), *The complete works of Aristotle* (Vol. 2, pp. 1988–2129). Princeton, NJ: Princeton University Press.

Barnes, S., Brown, K. W., Krusemark, E., Campbell, W. K., & Rogge, R. D. (2007). The role of mindfulness in romantic relationship satisfaction and responses to relationship stress. *Journal of Marital and Family Therapy, 33,* 482–500. doi:10.1111/j.1752-0606.2007.00033.x

Bartholomew, K. J., Ntoumanis, N., Ryan, R. M., & Thogersen-Ntoumani, C. (2011). Psychological need thwarting on the sport context: Assessing the darker sides of athletic experience. *Journal of Sport & Exercise Psychology, 33,* 75–102.

Black, A. E., & Deci, E. L. (2000). The effects of instructors' autonomy support and students' autonomous motivation on learning organic chemistry: A self-determination theory perspective. *Science Education, 84,* 740–756. doi:10.1002/1098-237X(200011)84:6<740::AID-SCE4>3.0.CO;2-3

Brown, K. W., & Kasser, T. (2005). Are psychological and ecological well-being compatible? The role of values, mindfulness, and lifestyle. *Social Indicators Research, 74,* 349–368. doi:10.1007/s11205-004-8207-8

Brown, K. W., & Ryan, R. M. (2003). The benefits of being present: Mindfulness and its role in psychological well-being. *Journal of Personality and Social Psychology, 84,* 822–848. doi:10.1037/0022-3514.84.4.822

Chirkov, V., Ryan, R. M., Kim, Y., & Kaplan, U. (2003). Differentiating autonomy from individualism and independence: A self-determination theory perspective on internalization of cultural orientations and well-being. *Journal of Personality and Social Psychology, 84,* 97–110. doi:10.1037/0022-3514.84.1.97

Curren, R. (2000). *Aristotle on the necessity of public education.* Lanham, MD: Rowman & Littlefield.

Curren, R. (2009) *Education for sustainable development: A philosophical assessment* (Impact Publication No. 18). London, England: Philosophy of Education Society of Great Britain.

Curren, R. (2010). Aristotle's educational politics and the Aristotelian renaissance in philosophy of education. *Oxford Review of Education, 36,* 543–559.

de Charms, R. (1968). *Personal causation*. New York, NY: Academic Press.

Deci, E. L., Koestner, R., & Ryan, R. M. (1999). A meta-analytic review of experiments examining the effects of extrinsic rewards on intrinsic motivation. *Psychological Bulletin, 125*, 627–668. doi:10.1037/0033-2909.125.6.627

Deci, E. L., & Ryan, R. M. (1980). The empirical exploration of intrinsic motivational processes. In L. Berkowitz (Ed.), *Advances in experimental social psychology* (Vol. 13, pp. 39–80). New York, NY: Academic Press.

Deci, E. L., & Ryan, R. M. (1985). *Intrinsic motivation and self-determination in human behavior*. New York, NY: Plenum.

Deci, E. L., & Ryan, R. M. (2000). The "what" and "why" of goal pursuits: Human needs and the self-determination of behavior. *Psychological Inquiry, 11*, 227–268. doi:10.1207/S15327965PLI1104_01

Deci, E. L., & Ryan, R. M. (2012). Motivation, personality, and development within embedded social contexts: An overview of self-determination theory. In R. M. Ryan (Ed.), *Oxford handbook of human motivation* (pp. 85–107). Oxford, England: Oxford University Press.

De Waal, F. (2009). *The age of empathy: Nature's lessons for a kinder society*. New York, NY: Random House.

Diener, E., Ng, W., Hartr, J., & Arora, R. (2010). Wealth and happiness across the world: Material prosperity predicts life evaluation whereas psychological prosperity predicts positive feeling. *Journal of Personality and Social Psychology, 99*, 52–61. doi:10.1037/a0018066

Foot, P. (2003). *Natural goodness*. New York, NY: Oxford University Press.

Frede, D. (2006). Pleasure and pain in Aristotle's ethics. In R. Kraut (Ed.), *The Blackwell guide to Aristotle's Nichomachean ethics* (pp. 255–275). Malden, MA: Blackwell.

Grolnick, W. S., & Ryan, R. M. (1987). Autonomy in children's learning: An experimental and individual difference investigation. *Journal of Personality and Social Psychology, 52*, 890–898. doi:10.1037/0022-3514.52.5.890

Grolnick, W. S., Ryan, R. M., & Deci, E. L. (1991). Inner resources for school achievement: Motivational mediators of children's perceptions of their parents. *Journal of Educational Psychology, 83*, 508–517. doi:10.1037/0022-0663.83.4.508

Grouzet, F. M. E., Kasser, T., Ahuvia, A., Dols, J. M. F., Kim, Y., Lau, S., . . . Sheldon, K. M. (2005). The structure of goal contents across 15 cultures. *Journal of Personality and Social Psychology, 89*, 800–816. doi:10.1037/0022-3514.89.5.800

Huta, V., & Ryan, R. M. (2010). Pursuing pleasure or virtue: The differential and overlapping well-being benefits of hedonic and eudaimonic motives. *Journal of Happiness Studies, 11*, 735–762. doi:10.1007/s10902-009-9171-4

Jang, H., Reeve, J., Ryan, R. M., & Kim, A. (2009). Can self-determination theory explain what underlies the productive, satisfying learning experiences of collectivistically-oriented Korean students? *Journal of Educational Psychology, 101*, 644–661. doi:10.1037/a0014241

Kahneman, D., Diener, E., & Schwarz, N. (Eds.). (1999). *Well-being: The foundations of hedonic psychology*. New York, NY: Russell Sage Foundation.

Kashdan, T. B., Biswas-Diener, R., & King, L. A. (2008). Reconsidering happiness: The costs of distinguishing between hedonics and eudaimonia. *The Journal of Positive Psychology, 3*, 219–233. doi:10.1080/17439760802303044

Kasser, T., Cohn, S., Kanner, A. D., & Ryan, R. M. (2007). Some costs of American corporate capitalism: A psychological exploration of value and goal conflicts. *Psychological Inquiry, 18*, 1–22. doi:10.1080/10478400701386579

Kasser, T., & Ryan, R. M. (1996). Further examining the American dream: Differential correlates of intrinsic and extrinsic goals. *Personality and Social Psychology Bulletin, 22*, 280–287. doi:10.1177/0146167296223006

Kasser, T., & Ryan, R. M. (2001). Be careful what you wish for: Optimal functioning and the relative attainment of intrinsic and extrinsic goals. In P. Schmuck & K. M. Sheldon (Eds.), *Life goals and well-being: Towards a positive psychology of human striving* (pp. 116–131). Seattle, WA: Hogrefe & Huber.

Kraut, R. (1989). *Aristotle on the human good*. Princeton, NJ: Princeton University Press.

Kraut, R. (2007). *What is good and why: The ethics of well-being*. Cambridge, MA: Harvard University Press.

Locke, E. A., & Latham, G. P. (1990). *A theory of goal setting and task performance*. Englewood Cliffs, NJ: Prentice-Hall.

MacIntyre, A. (1981). *After virtue*. Notre Dame, IN: University of Notre Dame Press.

May, H. (2010). *Aristotle's ethics: Moral development and human nature*. London, England: Continuum International.

Miquelon, P., & Vallerand, R. J. (2008). Goal motives, well-being, and physical health: An integrative model. *Canadian Psychology, 49*, 241–249. doi:10.1037/a0012759

Miserandino, M. (1996). Children who do well in school: Individual differences in perceived competence and autonomy in above average children. *Journal of Educational Psychology, 88*, 203–214. doi:10.1037/0022-0663.88.2.203

Niemiec, C. P., Brown, K. W., Kashdan, T. B., Cozzolino, P. J., Breen, W. E., Levesque-Bristol, C., & Ryan, R. M. (2010). Being present in the face of existential threat: The role of trait mindfulness in reducing defensive responses to mortality salience. *Journal of Personality and Social Psychology, 99*, 344–365. doi:10.1037/a0019388

Niemiec, C. P., & Ryan, R. M. (in press). What makes for a life well lived? Autonomy and its relation to full functioning and organismic wellness. In I. Boniwell & S. David (Eds.), *Oxford handbook of happiness*. Oxford, England: Oxford University Press.

Niemiec, C. P., Ryan, R. M., & Deci, E. L. (2009). The path taken: Consequences of attaining intrinsic and extrinsic aspirations in post-college life. *Journal of Research in Personality, 43*, 291–306. doi:10.1016/j.jrp.2008.09.001

Niemiec, C. P., Ryan, R. M., Patrick, H., Deci, E. L., & Williams, G. C. (2010). The energization of health-behavior change: Examining the associations among autonomous self-regulation, subjective vitality, depressive symptoms, and tobacco abstinence. *The Journal of Positive Psychology, 5*, 122–138. doi:10.1080/17439760903569162

Nussbaum, M. (1993). Non-relative virtues: An Aristotelian approach. In M. Nussbaum & A. Sen (Eds.), *The quality of life* (pp. 242–269). Oxford, England: Clarendon Press. doi:10.1093/0198287976.003.0019

Nussbaum, M. (2000). *Women and human development: The capabilities approach.* Cambridge, England: Cambridge University Press. doi:10.1017/CBO9780511841286

Ryan, R. M. (1995). Psychological needs and the facilitation of integrative processes. *Journal of Personality, 63*, 397–427. doi:10.1111/j.1467-6494.1995.tb00501.x

Ryan, R. M., Bernstein, J. H., & Brown, K. W. (2010). Weekends, work, and well-being: Psychological need satisfactions and day of the week effects on mood, vitality, and physical symptoms. *Journal of Social and Clinical Psychology, 29*, 95–122. doi:10.1521/jscp.2010.29.1.95

Ryan, R. M., Chirkov, V. I., Little, T. D., Sheldon, K. M., Timoshina, E., & Deci, E. L. (1999). The American dream in Russia: Extrinsic aspirations and well-being in two cultures. *Personality and Social Psychology Bulletin, 25*, 1509–1524. doi:10.1177/01461672992510007

Ryan, R. M., & Connell, J. P. (1989). Perceived locus of causality and internalization: Examining reasons for acting in two domains. *Journal of Personality and Social Psychology, 57*, 749–761. doi:10.1037/0022-3514.57.5.749

Ryan, R. M., & Deci, E. L. (2000). Self-determination theory and the facilitation of intrinsic motivation, social development, and well-being. *American Psychologist, 55*, 68–78. doi:10.1037/0003-066X.55.1.68

Ryan, R. M., & Deci, E. L. (2001). On happiness and human potentials: A review of research on hedonic and eudaimonic well-being. In S. T. Fiske, D. L. Schacter, & C. Zahn-Waxler (Eds.), *Annual review of psychology* (Vol. 52, pp. 141–166). Palo Alto, CA: Annual Reviews.

Ryan, R. M., & Deci, E. L. (2010). The SDT perspective on the connections among happiness, well-being, and social, economic, and political supports for autonomy. In V. Chirkov, R. Ryan, & K. Sheldon (Eds.), *Personal autonomy in cultural contexts: Perspectives on the psychology of agency, freedom, and people's well-being* (pp. 45–64). New York, NY: Springer.

Ryan, R. M., & Huta, V. (2009). Wellness as healthy functioning or wellness as happiness: The importance of eudaimonic thinking (response to Kashdan et al. and Waterman discussion). *The Journal of Positive Psychology, 4*, 202–204. doi:10.1080/17439760902844285

Ryan, R. M., Huta, V., & Deci, E. L. (2008). Living well: A self-determination theory perspective on eudaimonia. *Journal of Happiness Studies, 9*, 139–170. doi:10.1007/s10902-006-9023-4

Ryan, R. M., Rigby, C. S., & Przybylski, A. (2006). The motivational pull of video games: A self-determination theory approach. *Motivation and Emotion, 30,* 344–360. doi:10.1007/s11031-006-9051-8

Ryan, R. M., Sheldon, K. M., Kasser, T., & Deci, E. L. (1996). All goals are not created equal: An organismic perspective on the nature of goals and their regulation. In P. M. Gollwitzer & J. A. Bargh (Eds.), *The psychology of action: Linking cognition and motivation to behavior* (pp. 7–26). New York, NY: Guilford.

Ryff, C. D., & Singer, B. H. (2008). Know thyself and become what you are: A eudaimonic approach to psychological well-being. *Journal of Happiness Studies, 9,* 13–39. doi:10.1007/s10902-006-9019-0

Sebire, S. J., Standage, M., & Vansteenkiste, M. (2009). Examining intrinsic versus extrinsic exercise goals: Cognitive, affective, and behavioral outcomes. *Journal of Sport & Exercise Psychology, 31,* 189–210.

Sheldon, K. M., Elliot, A. J., Ryan, R. M., Chirkov, V., Kim, Y., Wu, C., & Meliksah, S. Z. (2004). Self-concordance and subjective well-being in four cultures. *Journal of Cross-Cultural Psychology, 35,* 209–223. doi:10.1177/0022022103262245

Vallerand, R. J., & Bissonnette, R. (1992). Intrinsic, extrinsic, and amotivational styles as predictors of behavior: A prospective study. *Journal of Personality, 60,* 599–620. doi:10.1111/j.1467-6494.1992.tb00922.x

Van Hiel, A., & Vansteenkiste, M. (2009). Ambitions fulfilled? The effects of intrinsic and extrinsic goal attainment on older adults' ego-integrity and death attitudes. *International Journal of Aging and Human Development, 68,* 27–51. doi:10.2190/AG.68.1.b

Vansteenkiste, M., Lens, W., Dewitte, S., De Witte, H., & Deci, E. L. (2004). The "why" and "why not" of job search behaviour: Their relation to searching, unemployment experience, and well-being. *European Journal of Social Psychology, 34,* 345–363. doi:10.1002/ejsp.202

Vansteenkiste, M., Neyrinck, B., Niemiec, C. P., Soenens, B., De Witte, H., & Van den Broeck, A. (2007). On the relations among work value orientations, psychological need satisfaction and job outcomes: A self-determination theory approach. *Journal of Occupational and Organizational Psychology, 80,* 251–277. doi:10.1348/096317906X111024

Vansteenkiste, M., Ryan, R. M., & Deci, E. L. (2008). Self-determination theory and the explanatory role of psychological needs in human well-being. In L. Bruni, F. Comim, & M. Pugno (Eds.), *Capabilities and happiness* (pp. 181–223). Oxford, England: Oxford University Press.

Waterman, A. S. (1993). Two conceptions of happiness: Contrasts of personal expressiveness (eudaimonia) and hedonic enjoyment. *Journal of Personality and Social Psychology, 64,* 678–691. doi:10.1037/0022-3514.64.4.678

Weinstein, N., Brown, K. W., & Ryan, R. M. (2009). A multi-method examination of the effects of mindfulness on stress attribution, coping, and emotional well-being. *Journal of Research in Personality, 43,* 374–385. doi:10.1016/j.jrp.2008.12.008

Weinstein, N., Hodgins, H. S., & Ryan, R. M. (2010). Autonomy and control in dyads: Effects on interaction quality and joint creative performance. *Personality and Social Psychology Bulletin, 36*, 1603–1617. doi:10.1177/0146167210386385

Weinstein, N., & Ryan, R. M. (2010). When helping helps: Autonomous motivation for prosocial behavior and its influence on well-being for the helper and recipient. *Journal of Personality and Social Psychology, 98*, 222–244. doi:10.1037/a0016984

Williams, G. C., Patrick, H., Niemiec, C. P., Williams, L. K., Divine, G., Lafata, J. E., . . . Pladevall, M. (2009). Reducing the health risks of diabetes: How self-determination theory may help improve medication adherence and quality of life. *The Diabetes Educator, 35*, 484–492. doi:10.1177/0145721709333856

Yamauchi, H., & Tanaka, K. (1998). Relations of autonomy, self-referenced beliefs and self-regulated learning among Japanese children. *Psychological Reports, 82*, 803–816. doi:10.2466/pr0.1998.82.3.803

4

EUDAIMONIC WELL-BEING AND HEALTH: MAPPING CONSEQUENCES OF SELF-REALIZATION

CAROL D. RYFF

The purpose of this chapter is to present a multidimensional model of eudaimonic well-being and consider its implications for human health. In the first section, distal philosophical underpinnings of the model are examined, along with conceptual links to existential, humanistic, and developmental psychology. These theoretical foundations predate the recent flurry of interest in positive psychology. Together, they offer uniquely rich conceptions of what constitutes the best within us. Following this historical overview, six key components of eudaimonic well-being are defined and the process of translating them to structured self-report inventories is briefly described. Empirical findings as to who possesses high eudaimonic well-being, depending on one's age, gender, socioeconomic status, race/ethnicity, and culture, are then summarized. Also considered is how aspects of well-being are linked to chronic and acute life events as well as other psychosocial factors.

A central argument is that eudaimonic well-being is not just a matter of psychological flourishing and self-realization, but that it also matters for

DOI: 10.1037/14092-005
The Best Within Us: Positive Psychology Perspectives on Eudaimonia, Alan S. Waterman (Editor)
Copyright © 2013 by the American Psychological Association. All rights reserved.

health. Increasingly, there is recognition that well-being plays a role in offering protection against disease, disability, and early mortality, via optimal regulation of multiple neurological and physiological systems. In support of this perspective, emerging evidence that eudaimonic well-being promotes good health is briefly reviewed. A concluding section addresses how the experience of self-realization might be maximized for ever-greater segments of society, via a focus on intervention programs. Consideration is given to both individual and social structural factors needed to nurture the best within ever-larger segments of society.

Viewed in the context of this edited collection, the formulation advanced in this chapter incorporates ideas of flourishing and self-realization, but not happiness in the hedonic sense. What follows is also a blend of objective and subjective views. The historical overview makes clear that guiding ideas about eudaimonic well-being have emerged from the speculations and observations of individual thinkers, doubtlessly infused with their own subjectivity. Subsequent efforts to develop empirical assessment tools to measure and quantify different components of well-being lend an aura of objectivity to the formulation, in the sense that direct comparisons on the same constructs of well-being can be made across individuals. Still, it is important to recognize that all obtained assessments come from the self-report of individuals about themselves—effectively, their subjective judgments about themselves and their own lives. Thus, where subjectivity ends and objectivity begins, or the reverse, is not a defining feature of the formulation presented in this chapter. Rather, it is a blend of both.

PHILOSOPHICAL AND PSYCHOLOGICAL
UNDERPINNINGS OF EUDAIMONIC WELL-BEING

This section summarizes Hellenic perspectives on eudaimonism, drawing on the writings of Aristotle. Other contributions to the multidimensional model put forth emanate from writings in the middle of the last century related to humanistic, existential, and developmental psychology. These combined perspectives were integrated via convergent themes among them to distill six key components of psychological well-being. Each dimension is defined and anchored to its conceptual precursors.

Aristotle's Highest Good

The *Nichomachean Ethics*, written by Aristotle (trans. 1925) over 2,000 years ago, were put forth not to distill the nature of well-being but to formulate an ethical doctrine providing guidelines for how to live. Aristotle began with the question "What is the highest of all goods achievable by human action?" His query thus situated the *Ethics* squarely on the task of defining the best within us. He answered that for most people, both general run-of-the-mill types as well as those of superior refinement, the highest good is happiness. However, he emphasized that people differ in their views of what constitutes happiness. He then went to great lengths to say that happiness is not about pleasure or satisfying appetites, something he likened to the life of beasts, nor is happiness about wealth or power, or even about amusement and relaxation. Instead, Aristotle claimed that the highest human good was "activity of the soul in accord with virtue" (p. 11).

His answer raised another challenging question: "What is the nature of virtue?" A first key meaning of virtue according to Aristotle is aiming toward that which is intermediate. Whether in confidence or fear, anger or pity, pleasure or pain, his point was that one should strive to experience these feelings at the right time and in the right way, which was fundamentally about the middle ground. So doing meant avoiding excess of either one extreme or the other. Too much honor, for example, leads to vanity, whereas too little honor leads to undue humility. Virtue was thus a state of character concerned with choice in deliberate actions taken to avoid excess or deficiency.

There was, however, more to achieving the highest good than finding the mean in all modes of conduct. The additional part involved reaching for one's highest virtue, which is "the best thing in us" (Aristotle, trans. 1925, p. 263). These words underscored Aristotle's strongly teleological formulation—our highest human good requires achieving the best that is within us. This, in turn, necessitates having goals and objectives, purposes to live for. The essence of his virtue is thus growth toward realization of one's true and best nature.

In sum, Aristotle was strongly opposed to defining the highest of all human goods as hedonic well-being (pleasure, satisfaction of appetites). Rather, he viewed the highest good toward which humans should strive as the task of self-realization, played out individually, each according to personal dispositions and talents. A further point was the recognition that other needs must be met if we are to realize the best within us—for example, we must have healthy bodies, adequate food, and shelter.

Contemporary works, such as David Norton's (1976) *Personal Destinies*, described eudaimonism as an ethical doctrine wherein each individual is obliged to know and live in truth according to his daimon, which is a kind of spirit given to all persons at birth. The focus is on innate potentialities and, particularly, the responsibility of each individual to know himself or herself and strive to realize personal capacities. These tasks were the essence of the two Greek imperatives: Know thyself and become what you are.

Existential, Humanistic, and Developmental Views of Well-Being: Extracting Core Themes

More than 2 millennia after Aristotle wrote the *Nichomachean Ethics*, there has been heightened interest in formulating positive human functioning. Some contend that the devastation of two world wars prompted greater reflection on what constitutes humanity at its best. Ideas from existential and humanistic psychology (Allport, 1961; Frankl & Lasch, 1959/1992; Maslow, 1968; Rogers, 1962) offered useful reminders that meaning and purpose in life could be found in the most difficult of times. Life-span developmental perspectives further elaborated the tasks and opportunities for continued growth at different stages of life (Bühler, 1935; Bühler & Massarik, 1968; Erikson, 1959; Neugarten, 1968, 1973). From clinical psychology, Jahoda (1958) worked to define mental health in positive terms, rather than as the absence of dysfunction. Similarly, Jung (1933) offered a formulation of the fully individuated person.

Input also came from utilitarian philosophy. John Stuart Mill (1893/1989), for example, clarified that happiness will not be achieved if made an end in itself. Instead, it results from keeping our minds fixed on things more noble, such as the happiness of others or the improvement of mankind. Bertrand Russell (1930/1958) further emphasized that happiness does not happen to us effortlessly, like ripened fruit dropping into our mouths, but rather requires hard work; it is a conquest for which we must strive.

The central challenge of working with these many prior perspectives was to find a way to integrate them into a coherent whole. Focusing on recurrent themes or points of convergence among them (Ryff, 1982, 1985, 1989a) offered a way forward. The following section distills key dimensions of well-being that emerged from identifying the primary points of convergence or overlap in the above formulations.

SIX CORE DIMENSIONS OF WELL-BEING

Positive Relations With Others

All of the previous perspectives describe the interpersonal realm as a central feature of a positive, well lived life. Aristotle's *Ethics*, for example, included lengthy sections on friendship and love. Mill's autobiography offered a lengthy account of the great love of his life, and Russell saw affection as one of the two great sources of happiness. Jahoda viewed the ability to love to be a central component of mental health, whereas Maslow described self-actualizers as having strong feelings of empathy and affection for all human beings and the capacity for great love, deep friendship, and close identification with others. Warm relating to others was posed by Allport as a criterion of maturity. Erikson's adult developmental stages emphasized the achievement of close unions with others (intimacy) as well as the guidance and direction of others (generativity). Finally, philosophical accounts of the "criterial goods" of a well lived life (Becker, 1992) underscore the primacy of love, empathy, and affection. From a cultural perspective, there is universal endorsement of the relational well-being as a key feature of fulfilled living.

Personal Growth

Of all the aspects of well-being, it is personal growth that comes closest in meaning to Aristotle's eudaimonia because it is the dimension explicitly concerned with self-realization of the individual. This part of positive functioning is dynamic, involving a continual process of developing one's potential. Self-actualization, as formulated by Maslow and elaborated by Norton, is centrally concerned with realization of personal potentialities, as is Jahoda's conception of mental health. Rogers described the fully functioning person as having openness to experience in which one is continually developing and becoming, rather than achieving a fixed state wherein all problems are solved. Life-span theories (Bühler, Erikson, Neugarten, and Jung) gave explicit emphasis to continued growth and the confronting of new challenges at different periods of life.

Purpose in Life

This dimension of well-being draws heavily on existential perspectives, especially Frankl's search for meaning vis-à-vis adversity. He developed logotherapy, which was directly concerned with helping people find meaning and purpose in the suffering and travails of life. Creating meaning and direction in life is the fundamental challenge of living authentically according to Sartre. Although these views tend to emphasize the will to find meaning in the face of what is awful, difficult, or absurd in life, themes of life purpose are also evident in other, less dark literatures. Russell's emphasis on zest, for example, is fundamentally about actively engaging in and having a reflecting stance toward life. Jahoda's definition of mental health gave explicit emphasis to beliefs that give one a sense of purpose and meaning in life. Allport's definition of maturity included having a clear comprehension of life's purpose, which included a sense of directedness and intentionality. Finally, life-span developmental theories refer to the changing purposes or goals that characterize different life stages, such as being creative or productive in midlife and turning toward emotional integration in later life.

Environmental Mastery

Jahoda defined the individual's ability to choose or create environments suitable to personal psychic conditions as a key characteristic of mental health. Life-span developmental theories also emphasize the importance of being able to manipulate and control complex environments, particularly in midlife, as well as the capacity to act on and change the surrounding world through mental and physical activities. Allport's criteria of maturity included the capacity to "extend the self," by which he meant being able to participate in significant spheres of endeavor that go beyond the self. Together, these views endorsed active participation in and mastery of the environment as important ingredients of an integrated framework on positive psychological functioning. This dimension has parallels with other psychological constructs, such as sense of control and self-efficacy, although the emphasis on finding or creating a surrounding context that suits one's personal needs and capacities is unique to environmental mastery.

Self-Acceptance

The Greeks admonished that we should know ourselves—strive to accurately perceive our own actions, motivations, and feelings. Many of the previously mentioned formulations emphasized something more: namely, positive self-regard. This is a central feature of mental health (Jahoda) as well as a characteristic of self-actualization (Maslow), optimal functioning (Rogers), and maturity (Allport). Life-span theories also emphasized the importance of acceptance of self, including one's past life (Erikson, Neugarten). The process of individuation (Jung) further underscored the need to come to terms with the dark side of one's self (the shadow). Thus, both Erikson's formulation of ego integrity and the Jungian individuation emphasized a kind of self-acceptance that goes beyond usual views of self-esteem. It is a kind of self-evaluation involving long-term awareness and acceptance of both one's personal strengths and weaknesses.

Autonomy

Many of the conceptual frameworks emphasized qualities such as self-determination, independence, and the regulation of behavior from within. Self-actualizers, for example, are described as showing autonomous functioning and a "resistance to enculturation" (Maslow). The fully functioning person described by Rogers has an internal locus of evaluation, whereby one does not look to others for approval, but instead evaluates oneself by personal standards. Individuation is also described as involving a "deliverance from convention" (Jung), in which one no longer belongs to the collective beliefs, fears, and laws of the masses. The existential idea of living in "bad faith" (Sartre, 1956) similarly underscores the importance of self-determination and living authentically, rather than following the dogma or dictates of others. Finally, life-span developmental scholars (Erikson, Neugarten, Jung) wrote about the need to turn inward in the later years of life, which involved gaining a sense of freedom of the norms governing everyday life. From a cultural perspective, this aspect of well-being is the most Western of all of the above dimensions.

How these six dimensions were translated to empirical assessment tools is briefly described in the next section, and initial descriptive findings regarding who does and does not possess high levels of well-being are summarized.

EMPIRICAL TRANSLATION OF EUDAIMONIC CONSTRUCTS AND SCIENTIFIC FINDINGS

This section summarizes the process of constructing measurement instruments for assessing psychological well-being. It is followed by a brief distillation of key findings derived from using the scales in scientific research.

Creating Assessment Tools

Self-report scales were developed to measure the previously mentioned six dimensions of well-being, using the construct-oriented approach to personality assessment (Wiggins, 1980). Of importance at the outset is the presence of psychological theory that specifies the constructs of interest. Thus, the first step in the scale construction process is to define high and low scorers on each of the six dimensions (Ryff, 1989b). Self-descriptive items that fit with these definitions were then generated with large initial item pools (about 80 items per scale). These were then culled on the basis of multiple face validity criteria (i.e., ambiguity or redundancy of item, lack of fit with scale definition, lack of distinctiveness with items from other scales, inability to produce a variable response). Reduced-item pools (32 items per scale divided between positively and negatively worded items) were then administered to the initial research sample of young, middle-aged, and older adults. Item-to-scale correlations were computed, and items failing to correlate more highly with their own rather than another scale were deleted. This process was terminated with 20-item scales, divided equally between positively and negatively scored items. Additional psychometric evaluations (e.g., test–retest reliability, internal consistency) were generated.

Since the original publication (Ryff, 1989b), multiple investigations have examined the factorial validity of the theory-based model of psychological well-being. Five such studies (Cheng & Chan, 2005; Clarke, Marshall, Ryff, & Wheaton, 2001; Ryff & Keyes, 1995; Springer & Hauser, 2006; van Dierendonck, 2004) using confirmatory factor analyses have been conducted. All, including three investigations with nationally representative samples, show that the best-fitting model to the data is the theory-guided, six-factor model.

Empirical Findings: Who Has Eudaimonic Well-Being?

Initial empirical studies examined how the six dimensions of psychological well-being vary by sociodemographic characteristics such as age, gender, or educational status. With regard to age, initial cross-sectional findings (Ryff, 1989b) indicated that some aspects of well-being (e.g., autonomy, environmental mastery) showed incremental profiles with age, whereas others (e.g., purpose in life, personal growth) showed sharply decremental profiles from young adulthood to old age, and still others showed little age variation (e.g., positive relations with others, self-acceptance—only for women). These patterns were replicated with other community samples (Ryff, 1991) and a nationally representative sample of U.S. adults (Ryff & Keyes, 1995), using scales of different length. More recent longitudinal findings have strengthened the evidence that the age differences, especially the downward aging profiles on purpose in life and personal growth, represent actual losses in well-being that many experience as they grow older (Springer, Pudrovska, & Hauser, 2011). Such decline in the two most eudaimonic aspects of well-being may reflect challenges faced by society in providing older persons with meaningful roles and opportunities for continued growth.

Sociologists have referred to this situation as the "structural lag" problem. The idea is that contemporary social institutions lag behind the added years of life that many now experience (Riley, Kahn, & Foner, 1994). Related to such ideas, Greenfield and Marks (2004), using data from the MIDUS (Midlife in the U.S.) national study, found that older persons who occupied few major roles but who also engaged in formal volunteering had higher levels of purpose in life than those lacking both major roles and volunteer experiences. Cultural context may also matter; for example, aging in societies that honor and revere elders may be a different experience than growing old in youth-oriented societies. Our comparative research in Japan (Karasawa et al., 2011) adds some credence to this view. In the comparison of midlife and older adults, we found age increments in personal growth among the Japanese, but age decrements in the United States. Nonetheless, downward trajectories were observed in purpose in life in both cultural contexts.

Whether or not the surrounding context nurtures self-realization is also illuminated by examining how well-being varies depending on one's socioeconomic status, such as level of education, income, or occupational status. We have shown that the six dimensions of well-being are positively linked with educational attainment for both men and women, although the patterns are stronger for women (Ryff & Singer, 2008). The two dimensions that show the greatest increments as a function of educational advancement are personal growth and purpose in life—again, the two pillars of eudaimonia. These findings bring empirical support to Dowd's (1990) observation that the opportunities for self-realization are not equally distributed, but occur via the allocation of resources, which enable some, but not others, to make the most of their talents and capacities.

Aristotle seemed to miss this point. The Greeks lived in a hierarchical society differentiated into subgroups of people. Surprisingly, only some were thought to possess the essential daimon; women and slaves were excluded, for example. In the present era, there is greater awareness of problems of social inequality and greater concern about their implications for health (Adler, Marmot, McEwen, & Stewart, 1999). Our research on educational disparities in psychological well-being (Marmot et al., 1997, 1998) adds to this literature, showing that those at the low end of the socioeconomic hierarchy are not only more likely to succumb to disease and disability but also suffer from diminished opportunities to make the most of their lives. As detailed in the biological section that follows, these patterns are likely to be linked, that is, thwarted self-realization may be a critical part of the interplay of biological and psychosocial processes that contribute to early morbidity and mortality.

Nonetheless, it is important to note variants from these patterns, which show, on average, that higher psychological well-being accompanies higher educational attainment. Our work has, however, also documented remarkable resilience among those who lack socioeconomic advantage and/or have been confronted with significant life challenges (Markus, Ryff, Curhan, & Palmersheim, 2004; Ryff, Singer, & Palmersheim, 2004; Singer & Ryff, 1997, 1999; Singer, Ryff, Carr, & Magee, 1998). We have also found such resilience among racial/ethnic minorities (Ryff, Keyes, & Hughes, 2003). Together, these studies document the meaning-making and growth-producing effects of adversity, thus bringing empirical substance to Frankl's (1959/1992) view that purpose can emerge from the confrontation with difficulty. Such findings challenge the Hellenic view that realization of the highest human good was somehow the exclusive terrain of privileged segments of society.

Apart from investigating age or socioeconomic variants in well-being, other investigators have linked eudaimonic well-being to numerous other psychological constructs, such as identity status (Helson & Srivastava, 2001), self-enhancing cognitions (Taylor et al., 2003a, 2003b), emotion regulation (Gross & John, 2003), personality traits (Lopes, Salovey, & Straus, 2003;

Schmutte & Ryff, 1997), personal goals (Carr, 1997; Riediger & Freund, 2004), values (Sheldon, 2005), coping strategies (Kling, Seltzer, & Ryff, 1997), social comparison processes (Heidrich & Ryff, 1993; Kwan, Love, Ryff, & Essex, 2003), and spirituality (Kirby, Coleman, & Daley, 2004; Wink & Dillon, 2003). Others have examined associations between well-being and chronic and acute life experiences, such as early parental loss or parental divorce (Maier & Lachman, 2000), growing up with an alcoholic parent (Tweed & Ryff, 1991), trauma disclosure (Hemenover, 2003), community relocation (Smider, Essex, & Ryff, 1996), caregiving (Marks, 1998), and change in marital status (Marks & Lambert, 1998). Collectively, these investigations illustrate the diverse interests researchers have brought to the topic of well-being and, in addition, clarify the many factors that may influence, or be influenced by, eudaimonic self-realization.

LINKING EUDAIMONIC WELL-BEING
TO BIOLOGY AND HEALTH

Consequential approaches to moral philosophy focus on outcomes or consequences in determining what constitutes right action. Eudaimonic well-being, as described previously, may be defended as right and worthy of promotion, both at the individual and the societal level, to the extent that it benefits human health. That is, if becoming the best within us is truly the right way to live, it would be expected to lead to other beneficial outcomes, such as greater likelihood of practicing good health behaviors (i.e., the experience of self-realization likely contributes to motivation to take care of oneself). Those living lives of purpose, meaning, and growth may also have better regulation of multiple biological systems because they are better equipped for dealing with stress and challenge when they occur. This combination of motivated self-care and healthy regulation of key systems (neuroendocrine, cardiovascular, inflammatory), in turn, likely contributes to delayed onset of disease and disability and thereby longer and higher quality life. This formulation of health (Ryff & Singer, 1998) constitutes a notable departure from traditional medical models that focus almost exclusively on pathways to illness, disease, and death rather than on the promotion of what keeps people functional, healthy, and well.

An initial test of these ideas involved investigating the neurobiological correlates of psychological well-being, measured with the six dimensions described previously (Ryff, Singer, & Love, 2004). With a sample of older women, we correlated reported well-being with diverse biomarkers (cardiovascular, neuroendocrine, inflammatory). We found that those who reported higher levels of well-being (especially personal growth and purpose in life) had better neuroendocrine regulation, shown in terms of lower levels of salivary cortisol throughout the day. Similarly, higher well-being was linked with lower levels of inflammatory markers, such as interleukin-6 (IL-6) and its soluble receptor (sIL-6r). Higher levels of environmental mastery, positive relations with others, and self-acceptance, in turn, were associated with better glycemic control, measured in terms of glycosylated hemoglobin. Those with higher personal growth and purpose in life also showed higher levels of HDL cholesterol, known as the "good" cholesterol.

Extending these findings with the same older women, we documented the interplay between one aspect of well-being (positive relations with others), sleep, and inflammatory markers (Friedman et al., 2005). The highest levels of IL-6, a precursor to multiple later life diseases, were observed among those who reported both low interpersonal well-being and poor sleep efficiency (defined as the period of REM sleep over total time in bed). However, the findings also underscored various compensatory processes. For example, those experiencing poor sleep were protected against higher IL-6 if they reported better relationships with others; alternatively, those with poor social relations were protected against higher IL-6 if they experienced better sleep. These results were valuable for underscoring the role of well-being as a moderator of other risk factors (e.g., poor sleep) on inflammatory outcomes. A related analysis examined cross-time sleep patterns in these older women and found that those with higher levels of eudaimonic well-being (purpose, growth, mastery, positive relations) at baseline had reduced odds of being in the sleep-disrupted group over time (Phelan, Love, Ryff, Brown, & Heidrich, 2010).

In a separate sample of midlife adults, dimensions of eudaimonic well-being were linked with salubrious brain activation patterns. Specifically, greater left (than right) prefrontal activation was associated with higher levels of multiple aspects of well-being, after adjusting for positive affect and life satisfaction (Urry et al., 2004). This specific brain activation pattern was previously linked to better health outcomes, including increased antibody response to flu vaccine (Rosenkranz et al., 2003). In a more recent study using functional magnetic resonance imaging techniques, van Reekum et al. (2007) found that those with higher eudaimonic well-being showed better regulation of subcortical emotion centers (amygdala) by higher cortical brain regions (anterior cingulate cortex). Individuals with these brain patterns showed reduced emotional responses to negative stimuli.

The more demanding test of whether experienced eudaimonic well-being is biologically protective involves studying the individual under conditions of challenge. Such inquiry brings into high relief the interplay of well-being, biology, and health when faced with adversity. As noted earlier, we have been interested in the experience of eudaimonic well-being vis-à-vis social inequality, measured in terms of educational attainment. Prior health research had repeatedly documented that lower socioeconomic standing contributes to greater risk of illness, disease, and disability, along with earlier mortality (Adler, Marmot, McEwen, & Stewart, 1999; Adler & Rehkopf, 2008; Alwin & Wray, 2005; Kawachi, Kennedy, & Wilkinson, 1999; Matthews & Gallo, 2011). Current inquiries have focused on identifying the biological pathways through which these effects occur, including via heightened cardiovascular risk, elevated neuroendocrine activity, and increased inflammation (e.g., Friedman & Herd, 2010; Karlamangla et al., 2005; Lupien, King, Meaney, & McEwen, 2001; Steptoe, Owen, Kunz-Ebrecht, & Mohamed-Ali, 2002). Limited work has addressed variability within socioeconomic groups, that is, the extent to which some at the low end of the SES hierarchy manage to evade adverse health outcomes.

We have studied this question using psychological well-being as a moderating factor that may offset, or protect against, ill health outcomes among educationally or economically disadvantaged individuals. One longitudinal investigation (Tsenkova, Love, Singer, & Ryff, 2007) based on the above community sample of aging women found, as predicted, that those with higher levels of income had better glycemic control, measured in terms of glycosylated hemoglobin. The effect was, however, moderated by reported levels of well-being (purpose in life, personal growth, positive affect), but the direction of the interaction revealed an exacerbation of biological risk via the lack of well-being. That is, those with low levels of income had worse glycemic control when they also reported compromised levels of well-being.

Recent findings from the MIDUS national sample of American adults document the hypothesized protective effects with a different biological factor, namely, the inflammatory marker IL-6 (Morozink, Friedman, Coe, & Ryff, 2010). Consistent with previous research, the first finding was that those with lower levels of education had higher levels of this inflammatory marker, net of numerous confounds (health behaviors, body mass index, chronic illnesses). However, reported well-being moderated this effect, such that those with higher levels of environmental mastery, positive relations with others, purpose in life, self-acceptance, and positive affect showed less elevated levels of IL-6 compared with their same-education peers who did not report higher levels of well-being. In fact, these individuals with only a high school education or less had IL-6 levels comparable with those in college-educated adults, thus underscoring that the maintenance of high levels of well-being in the face of socioeconomic adversity is linked with better inflammatory profiles. Additional work is needed to examine possible mediating processes, such as better health behaviors (diet, exercise, weight) and better glucocorticoid regulation that may underlie these effects.

A central challenge of aging is maintaining functional capacities, despite the accumulation of chronic conditions; medical comorbidity characterizes the majority of adults over the age of 65 (Friedman & Ryff, in press-b). These normatively experienced health changes also contribute to increased biological risk for subsequent morbidity and mortality. Using the MIDUS sample, we found, for example, that those with increased profiles of chronic conditions had higher levels of IL-6 and C-reactive protein (Friedman & Ryff, in press-a). It is important that these effects were, however, moderated by reported levels of purpose in life and positive relations with others. That is, despite increased burden of disease, those experiencing higher levels of life purpose and quality ties to others showed reduced increments in inflammatory markers compared with those with higher chronic conditions and low well-being.

This summary of well-being and health findings ends with work from other investigators involved with the Rush Memory and Aging Project, a longitudinal study of community-based adults in and around Chicago. Three studies from this group have underscored the protective influence of high purpose in life. Controlling for a variety of confounds and using a prospective design, those with high life purpose showed a significantly reduced risk of mortality 5 years later (Boyle, Barnes, Buchman, & Bennett, 2009) compared with those with lower levels of life purpose. Two subsequent studies found that those with high levels of life purpose were half as likely to develop disability over a 6-year follow up (Boyle, Buchman, & Bennett, 2010) and 2.5 times less likely to develop Alzheimer's disease over a 7-year follow-up compared with those having low levels of life purpose (Boyle, Buchman, Barnes, & Bennett, 2010).

Taken together, this collection of empirical findings offers growing evidence that eudaimonic well-being affords protection against the health challenges of aging as well as those that accompany social inequality. The findings vary with regard to which aspects of well-being convey such protective benefits, although the most consistent patterns were observed for purpose in life, personal growth, and positive relations with others. The protective benefits shown sometimes pertain to better biological regulation (reduced stress hormones, reduced cardiovascular and inflammatory risk factors) and in other cases, to actual disease outcomes (Alzheimer's, disability, mortality). In several instances, the evidence has come from longitudinal inquiries, thereby sharpening causal interpretations. Routinely, such studies have included variables to control for confounding factors. Given the overall pattern of supportive evidence, it is relevant to ask whether and how eudaimonic well-being can be promoted. Of critical importance are interventions that could make it possible for ever-greater numbers of individuals to experience the best within themselves.

CONCLUSION: CAN EUDAIMONIC WELL-BEING BE PROMOTED?

Self-realization not only is desired phenomenologically (a valued subjective experience), but it also appears to be good for biological regulation and health, via brain and biochemical processes that are becoming increasingly understood. Whether more individuals can participate in this salubrious interplay of subjective fulfillment with biology is of critical importance. Fortunately, clinicians treating disorders, such as depression and anxiety, provide encouraging evidence that experiences of well-being are not inherently fixed but can be modified and changed. "Well-being therapy," developed by Fava and colleagues (Fava, 1999; Fava, Rafanelli, Grandi, Conti, & Belluardo, 1998; Fava et al., 2005), is one such intervention offered in combination with cognitive behavior therapy. It has been shown to prevent relapse of major depression over periods of 2 to 6 years. The goal of therapy is to improve patients' experiences of well-being in hopes of preventing relapse during the residual phase of mood and anxiety disorders, when major debilitating symptoms have subsided but the patient remains at risk for falling back into the depressed or anxious condition. It is a short-term therapeutic strategy (8 weeks) that involves the use of structured diaries. Clients are required to record positive experiences from their daily lives, however fleeting. The focus in therapy sessions is on helping clients sustain such experiences rather than prematurely interrupt or curtail them by maladaptive cognitions. The fundamental idea behind the therapy is that recovery from mood and anxiety disorders requires the capacity to experience well-being (Fava, Ruini, & Belaise, 2007), which in treatment is guided by the eudaimonic model of psychological well-being (Ryff, 1989b). Thus, eliminating symptoms of distress is, in and of itself, insufficient to achieve full recovery; one must also be able to participate in positive psychological experience (Fava & Ruini, 2003).

Given the success of well-being therapy in preventing relapse of psychological disorders, it has been adapted for use in preventive contexts as well. Ruini, Belaise, Brombin, Caffo, and Fava (2006), for example, developed an intervention protocol derived from the therapy that has been used with students in school settings. Pilot research demonstrated that the intervention resulted in a reduction of psychological symptoms and an increase in psychological well-being.

Adapting the strategy to other contexts and other age groups, including older adults in the community, is a worthy pursuit. To the extent that individuals can cultivate skills for seeing and savoring the positive in themselves and their lives, much in the same way that people can learn to practice good nutrition, they would have tools at their disposal to draw on in times of distress or adversity. The prior literature on resilience, in both childhood (e.g., Luthar, Cicchetti, & Becker, 2000; Masten, 1999) and adulthood (Klohnen,

1996; Reich, Zautra, & Stuart Hall, 2010; Ryff & Singer, 2003; Staudinger, Marsiske, & Baltes, 1995), has underscored the presence of certain protective factors, such as personality attributes, intellectual abilities, and social supports. The subjective experience of self-realization—that is, the feeling of becoming the best one can be, regardless of age or stage in the life course—may constitute an even greater protective resource. As Aristotle suggested, it is possibly the highest human good, which also appears to be consequential for good health. Taken together, the concluding message is that advanced and enlightened societies are those that promote not the greatest happiness for the greatest number of people, but instead opportunities to realize the best that is with the largest segment of its members.

REFERENCES

Adler, N. E., Marmot, M. G., McEwen, B. S., & Stewart, J. (1999). *Socioeconomic status and health in industrialized nations: Social, psychological, and biological pathways* (Vol. 896). New York, NY: New York Academy of Sciences.

Adler, N. E., & Rehkopf, D. H. (2008). U.S. disparities in health: Descriptions, causes, and mechanisms. *Annual Review of Public Health, 29*, 235–252. doi:10.1146/annurev.publhealth.29.020907.090852

Allport, G. W. (1961). *Pattern and growth in personality*. New York, NY: Holt, Rinehart, & Winston.

Alwin, D. F., & Wray, L. A. (2005). A life-span developmental perspective on social status and health. *The Journals of Gerontology, Series B: Psychological Sciences and Social Sciences, 60B*(Special Issue II), S7–S14. doi:10.1093/geronb/60.Special_Issue_2.S7

Aristotle. (1925). *The Nicomachean ethics* (D. Ross, Trans.). New York, NY: Oxford University Press.

Becker, L. C. (1992). Good lives: Prolegomena. *Social Philosophy & Policy, 9*, 15–37. doi:10.1017/S0265052500001382

Boyle, P. A., Barnes, L. L., Buchman, A. S., & Bennett, D. A. (2009). Purpose in life is associated with mortality among community-dwelling older persons. *Psychosomatic Medicine, 71*, 574–579. doi:10.1097/PSY.0b013e3181a5a7c0

Boyle, P. A., Buchman, A. S., Barnes, L. L., & Bennett, D. A. (2010). Effect of a purpose in life on risk of incident Alzheimer disease and mild cognitive impairment in community-dwelling older persons. *Archives of General Psychiatry, 67*, 304–310. doi:10.1001/archgenpsychiatry.2009.208

Boyle, P. A., Buchman, A. S., & Bennett, D. A. (2010). Purpose in life is associated with a reduced risk of incident disability among community-dwelling older persons. *The American Journal of Geriatric Psychiatry, 18*, 1093–1102.

Bühler, C. (1935). The curve of life as studied in biographies. *Journal of Applied Psychology, 19*, 405–409.

Bühler, C., & Massarik, F. (Eds.). (1968). *The course of human life*. New York, NY: Springer.

Carr, D. (1997). The fulfillment of career dreams at midlife: Does it matter for women's mental health? *Journal of Health and Social Behavior, 38*, 331–344. doi:10.2307/2955429

Cheng, S.-T., & Chan, A. C. M. (2005). The center for epidemiologic studies depression scale in older Chinese: Thresholds for long and short forms. *International Journal of Geriatric Psychiatry, 20*, 465–470. doi:10.1002/gps.1314

Clarke, P. J., Marshall, V. W., Ryff, C. D., & Wheaton, B. (2001). Measuring psychological well-being in the Canadian Study of Health and Aging. *International Psychogeriatrics, 13*, 79–90. doi:10.1017/S1041610202008013

Dowd, J. J. (1990). Ever since Durkheim: The socialization of human development. *Human Development, 33*, 138–159. doi:10.1159/000276507

Erikson, E. H. (1959). Identity and the life cycle: Selected papers [Monograph]. *Psychological Issues, 1*, 1–171.

Fava, G. A. (1999). Well-being therapy: Conceptual and technical issues. *Psychotherapy and Psychosomatics, 68*, 171–179. doi:10.1159/000012329

Fava, G. A., Rafanelli, C., Grandi, S., Conti, S., & Belluardo, P. (1998). Prevention of recurrent depression with cognitive-behavioral therapy. *Archives of General Psychiatry, 55*, 816–820. doi:10.1001/archpsyc.55.9.816

Fava, G. A., & Ruini, C. (2003). Development and characteristics of a well-being enhancing psychotherapeutic strategy: Well-being therapy. *Journal of Behavior Therapy and Experimental Psychiatry, 34*, 45–63. doi:10.1016/S0005-7916(03)00019-3

Fava, G. A., Ruini, C., & Belaise, C. (2007). The concept of recovery in major depression. *Psychological Medicine, 37*, 307–317. doi:10.1017/S0033291706008981

Fava, G. A., Ruini, C., Rafanelli, C., Finos, L., Salmaso, L., Mangelli, L., & Sirigatti, S. (2005). Well-being therapy of generalized anxiety disorder. *Psychotherapy and Psychosomatics, 74*, 26–30. doi:10.1159/000082023

Frankl, V. E., & Lasch, I. (1992). *Man's search for meaning: An introduction to logotherapy*. Boston, MA: Beacon Press. (Original work published 1959)

Friedman, E. M., Hayney, M. S., Love, G. D., Urry, H. L., Rosenkranz, M. A., Davidson, R. J., . . . Ryff, C. D. (2005). Social relationships, sleep quality, and interleukin-6 in aging women. *Proceedings of the National Academy of Sciences, USA, 102*, 18757–18762. doi:10.1073/pnas.0509281102

Friedman, E. M., & Herd, P. (2010). Income, education, and inflammation: Differential associations in a national probability sample (the MIDUS study). *Psychosomatic Medicine, 72*, 290–300. doi:10.1097/PSY.0b013e3181cfe4c2

Friedman, E. M., & Ryff, C. D. (in press-a). A biopsychosocial approach to positive aging. In S. K. Whitbourne & M. J. Sliwinski (Eds.), *Handbook of adult development and aging*. Oxford, England: Blackwell.

Friedman, E. M., & Ryff, C. D. (in press-b). Living well with medical co-morbidities: A biopsychosocial perspective. *The Journals of Gerontology, Series B: Psychological Sciences and Social Sciences*.

Greenfield, E. A., & Marks, N. (2004). Formal volunteering as a protective factor for older adults' psychological well-being. *The Journals of Gerontology, Series B: Psychological Sciences and Social Sciences, 59*(5), S258–S264. doi:10.1093/geronb/59.5.S258

Gross, J. J., & John, O. P. (2003). Individual differences in two emotion regulation processes: Implications for affect, relationships, and well-being. *Journal of Personality and Social Psychology, 85*, 348–362. doi:10.1037/0022-3514.85.2.348

Heidrich, S. M., & Ryff, C. D. (1993). The role of social comparison processes in the psychological adaptation of elderly adults. *The Journals of Gerontology, Series B: Psychological Sciences and Social Sciences, 48*, P127–P136.

Helson, R., & Srivastava, S. (2001). Three paths of adult development: Conservers, seekers, and achievers. *Journal of Personality and Social Psychology, 80*, 995–1010. doi:10.1037/0022-3514.80.6.995

Hemenover, S. H. (2003). The good, the bad, and the healthy: Impacts of emotional disclosure of trauma on resilient self-concept and psychological distress. *Personality and Social Psychology Bulletin, 29*, 1236–1244. doi:10.1177/0146167203255228

Jahoda, M. (1958). *Current concepts of positive mental health.* New York, NY: Basic Books. doi:10.1037/11258-000

Jung, C. G. (1933). *Modern man in search of a soul* (W. S. Dell & C. F. Baynes, Trans.). New York, NY: Harcourt, Brace & World.

Karasawa, M., Curhan, K. B., Markus, H. R., Kitayama, S. S., Love, G. D., Radler, B. T., & Ryff, C. D. (2011). Cultural perspectives on aging and well-being: A comparison between Japan and the U.S. *International Journal of Aging & Human Development, 73*, 73–98.

Karlamangla, A. S., Singer, B. H., Williams, D. R., Schwartz, J. E., Matthews, K., Kiefe, C. I., & Seeman, T. E. (2005). Impact of socioeconomic status on longitudinal accumulation of cardiovascular risk in young adults: The CARDIA study (USA). *Social Science & Medicine, 60*, 999–1015. doi:10.1016/j.socscimed.2004.06.056

Kawachi, I., Kennedy, B. P., & Wilkinson, R. C. (1999). *The society and population health reader: Vol. I. Income inequality and health.* New York, NY: New Press.

Kirby, S. E., Coleman, P. G., & Daley, D. (2004). Spirituality and well-being in frail and nonfrail older adults. *The Journals of Gerontology, Series B: Psychological Sciences and Social Sciences, 59*(3), P123–P129. doi:10.1093/geronb/59.3.P123

Kling, K. C., Seltzer, M. M., & Ryff, C. D. (1997). Distinctive late-life challenges: Implications for coping and well-being. *Psychology and Aging, 12*, 288–295. doi:10.1037/0882-7974.12.2.288

Klohnen, E. C. (1996). Conceptual analysis and measurement of the construct of ego-resiliency. *Journal of Personality and Social Psychology, 70*, 1067–1079. doi:10.1037/0022-3514.70.5.1067

Kwan, C. M. L., Love, G. D., Ryff, C. D., & Essex, M. J. (2003). The role of self-enhancing evaluations in a successful life transition. *Psychology and Aging, 18*, 3–12. doi:10.1037/0882-7974.18.1.3

Lopes, P. N., Salovey, P., & Straus, R. (2003). Emotional intelligence, personality, and the perceived quality of social relationships. *Personality and Individual Differences, 35*, 641–658. doi:10.1016/S0191-8869(02)00242-8

Lupien, S. J., King, S., Meaney, M. J., & McEwen, B. S. (2001). Can poverty get under your skin? Basal cortisol levels and cognitive function in children from low and high socioeconomic status. *Development and Psychopathology, 13*, 653–676. doi:10.1017/S0954579401003133

Luthar, S. S., Cicchetti, D., & Becker, B. (2000). The construct of resilience: A critical evaluation and guidelines for future work. *Child Development, 71*, 543–562. doi:10.1111/1467-8624.00164

Maier, E. H., & Lachman, M. E. (2000). Consequences of early parental loss and separation for health and well-being in midlife. *International Journal of Behavioral Development, 24*, 183–189. doi:10.1080/016502500383304

Marks, N. F. (1998). Does it hurt to care? Caregiving, work-family conflict, and midlife well-being. *Journal of Marriage and the Family, 60*, 951–966. doi:10.2307/353637

Marks, N. F., & Lambert, J. D. (1998). Marital status continuity and change among young and midlife adults: Longitudinal effects on psychological well-being. *Journal of Family Issues, 19*, 652–686. doi:10.1177/019251398019006001

Markus, H. R., Ryff, C. D., Curhan, K. B., & Palmersheim, K. A. (2004). In their own words: Well-being at midlife among high school-educated and college-educated adults. In O. G. Brim, C. D. Ryff, & R. C. Kessler (Eds.), *How healthy are we?: A national study of well-being at midlife* (pp. 273–319). Chicago, IL: The University of Chicago Press.

Marmot, M. G., Fuhrer, R., Ettner, S. L., Marks, N. F., Bumpass, L. L., & Ryff, C. D. (1998). Contribution of psychosocial factors to socioeconomic differences in health. *The Milbank Quarterly, 76*, 403–448. doi:10.1111/1468-0009.00097

Marmot, M. G., Ryff, C. D., Bumpass, L. L., Shipley, M., & Marks, N. F. (1997). Social inequalities in health: Next questions and converging evidence. *Social Science & Medicine, 44*, 901–910. doi:10.1016/S0277-9536(96)00194-3

Maslow, A. H. (1968). *Toward a psychology of being* (2nd ed.). New York, NY: Van Nostrand.

Masten, A. S. (1999). Resilience comes of age: Reflections on the past and outlook for the next generation of research. In M. D. Glantz & J. L. Johnson (Eds.), *Resilience and development: Positive life adaptations* (Vol. 14, pp. 281–296). Dordrecht, the Netherlands: Kluwer Academic.

Matthews, K. A., & Gallo, L. C. (2011). Psychological perspectives on pathways linking socioeconomic status and physical health. *Annual Review of Psychology, 62*, 501–530. doi:10.1146/annurev.psych.031809.130711

Mill, J. S. (1989). *Autobiography*. London, England: Penguin. (Original work published 1893)

Morozink, J. A., Friedman, E. M., Coe, C. L., & Ryff, C. D. (2010). Socioeconomic and psychosocial predictors of interleukin-6 in the MIDUS national sample. *Health Psychology, 29,* 626–635. doi:10.1037/a0021360

Neugarten, B. L. (1968). The awareness of middle age. In B. L. Neugarten (Ed.), *Middle age and aging* (pp. 93–98). Chicago, IL: University of Chicago Press.

Neugarten, B. L. (1973). Personality change in late life: A developmental perspective. In C. Eisodorfer & M. P. Lawton (Eds.), *The psychology of adult development and aging* (pp. 311–335). Washington, DC: American Psychological Association. doi:10.1037/10044-012

Norton, D. L. (1976). *Personal destinies: A philosophy of ethical individualism.* Princeton, NJ: Princeton University Press.

Phelan, C. H., Love, G. D., Ryff, C. D., Brown, R. L., & Heidrich, S. M. (2010). Psychosocial predictors of changing sleep patterns in aging women: A multiple pathway approach. *Psychology and Aging, 25,* 858–866. doi:10.1037/a0019622

Reich, J. W., Zautra, A. J., & Stuart Hall, J. (Eds.). (2010). *Handbook of adult resilience.* New York, NY: Guilford Press.

Riediger, M., & Freund, A. M. (2004). Interference and facilitation among personal goals: Differential associations with subjective well-being and persistent goal pursuit. *Personality and Social Psychology Bulletin, 30,* 1511–1523. doi:10.1177/0146167204271184

Riley, M. W., Kahn, R. L., & Foner, A. (1994). *Age and structural lag.* New York, NY: Wiley.

Rogers, C. R. (1962). The interpersonal relationship: The core of guidance. *Harvard Educational Review, 32,* 416–429.

Rosenkranz, M. A., Jackson, D. C., Dalton, K. M., Dolski, I., Ryff, C. D., Singer, B. H., . . . Davidson, R. J. (2003). Affective style and *in vivo* immune response: Neurobehavioral mechanisms. *Proceedings of the National Academy of Sciences, USA, 100,* 11148–11152. doi:10.1073/pnas.1534743100

Ruini, C., Belaise, C., Brombin, C., Caffo, E., & Fava, G. A. (2006). Well-being therapy in school settings: A pilot study. *Psychotherapy and Psychosomatics, 75,* 331–336. doi:10.1159/000095438

Russell, B. (1930/1958). *The conquest of happiness.* New York, NY: Liveright.

Ryff, C. D. (1982). Successful aging: A developmental approach. *The Gerontologist, 22,* 209–214. doi:10.1093/geront/22.2.209

Ryff, C. D. (1985). Adult personality development and the motivation for personal growth. In D. Kleiber & M. Maehr (Eds.), *Advances in motivation and achievement* (Vol. 4, Motivation and adulthood, pp. 55–92). Greenwich, CT: JAI Press.

Ryff, C. D. (1989a). Beyond Ponce de Leon and life satisfaction: New directions in quest of successful aging. *International Journal of Behavioral Development, 12,* 35–55. doi:10.1177/016502548901200102

Ryff, C. D. (1989b). Happiness is everything, or is it? Explorations on the meaning of psychological well-being. *Journal of Personality and Social Psychology, 57,* 1069–1081. doi:10.1037/0022-3514.57.6.1069

Ryff, C. D. (1991). Possible selves in adulthood and old age: A tale of shifting horizons. *Psychology and Aging, 6,* 286–295. doi:10.1037/0882-7974.6.2.286

Ryff, C. D., & Keyes, C. L. M. (1995). The structure of psychological well-being revisited. *Journal of Personality and Social Psychology, 69,* 719–727. doi:10.1037/0022-3514.69.4.719

Ryff, C. D., Keyes, C. L. M., & Hughes, D. L. (2003). Status inequalities, perceived discrimination, and eudaimonic well-being: Do the challenges of minority life hone purpose and growth? *Journal of Health and Social Behavior, 44,* 275–291. doi:10.2307/1519779

Ryff, C. D., & Singer, B. (2003). Flourishing under fire: Resilience as a prototype of challenged thriving. In C. L. M. Keyes & J. Haidt (Eds.), *Flourishing: Positive psychology and the life well lived* (pp. 15–36). Washington, DC: American Psychological Association. doi:10.1037/10594-001

Ryff, C. D., & Singer, B. H. (1998). The contours of positive human health. *Psychological Inquiry, 9,* 1–28. doi:10.1207/s15327965pli0901_1

Ryff, C. D., & Singer, B. H. (2008). Know thyself and become what you are: A eudaimonic approach to psychological well-being. *Journal of Happiness Studies, 9,* 13–39. doi:10.1007/s10902-006-9019-0

Ryff, C. D., Singer, B. H., & Love, G. D. (2004). Positive health: Connecting well-being with biology. *Philosophical Transactions of the Royal Society of London, Series B: Biological Sciences, 359,* 1383–1394. doi:10.1098/rstb.2004.1521

Ryff, C. D., Singer, B. H., & Palmersheim, K. A. (2004). Social inequalities in health and well-being: The role of relational and religious protective factors. In O. G. Brim, C. D. Ryff, & R. C. Kessler (Eds.), *How healthy are we?: A national study of well-being at midlife* (pp. 90–123). Chicago, IL: University of Chicago Press.

Sartre, J.-P. (1956). *Being and nothingness.* Oxford, England: Philosophical Library.

Schmutte, P. S., & Ryff, C. D. (1997). Personality and well-being: Reexamining methods and meanings. *Journal of Personality and Social Psychology, 73,* 549–559. doi:10.1037/0022-3514.73.3.549

Sheldon, K. M. (2005). Positive value change during college: Normative trends and individual differences. *Journal of Research in Personality, 39,* 209–223. doi:10.1016/j.jrp.2004.02.002

Singer, B. H., & Ryff, C. D. (1997). Racial and ethnic equalities in health: Environmental, psychosocial, and physiological pathways. In B. Devlin, S. E. Feinberg, D. Resnick, & K. Roeder (Eds.), *Intelligence, genes, and success: Scientists respond to* The Bell Curve (pp. 89–122). New York, NY: Springer-Verlag.

Singer, B. H., & Ryff, C. D. (1999). Hierarchies of life histories and associated health risks. In N. E. Adler & M. Marmot (Eds.), *Socioeconomic status and health in industrial nations: Social, psychological, and biological pathways* (Vol. 896, pp. 96–115). New York, NY: New York Academy of Sciences.

Singer, B. H., Ryff, C. D., Carr, D., & Magee, W. J. (1998). Life histories and mental health: A person-centered strategy. In A. Raftery (Ed.), *Sociological methodology* (pp. 1–51). Washington, DC: American Sociological Association.

Smider, N. A., Essex, M. J., & Ryff, C. D. (1996). Adaptation to community relocation: The interactive influence of psychological resources and contextual factors. *Psychology and Aging, 11,* 362–372. doi:10.1037/0882-7974.11.2.362

Springer, K. W., & Hauser, R. M. (2006). An assessment of the construct validity of Ryff's scales of psychological well-being: Method, mode, and measurement effects. *Social Science Research, 35,* 1080–1102. doi:10.1016/j.ssresearch.2005.07.004

Springer, K. W., Pudrovska, T., & Hauser, R. M. (2011). Does psychological well-being change with age? Longitudinal tests of age variations and further exploration of the multidimensionality of Ryff's model of psychological well-being. *Social Science Research, 40,* 392–398. doi:10.1016/j.ssresearch.2010.05.008

Staudinger, U. M., Marsiske, M., & Baltes, P. B. (1995). Resilience and reserve capacity in later adulthood: Potentials and limits of development across the life span. In D. Cicchetti & D. Cohen (Eds.), *Developmental psychopathology: Vol. 2. Risk, disorder and adaptation* (pp. 801–847). New York, NY: Wiley.

Steptoe, A., Owen, N., Kunz-Ebrecht, S., & Mohamed-Ali, V. (2002). Inflammatory cytokines, socioeconomic status, and acute stress responsivity. *Brain, Behavior, and Immunity, 16,* 774–784. doi:10.1016/S0889-1591(02)00030-2

Taylor, S. E., Lerner, J. S., Sherman, D. K., Sage, R. M., & McDowell, N. K. (2003a). Are self-enhancing cognitions associated with healthy or unhealthy biological profiles? *Journal of Personality and Social Psychology, 85,* 605–615. doi:10.1037/0022-3514.85.4.605

Taylor, S. E., Lerner, J. S., Sherman, D. K., Sage, R. M., & McDowell, N. K. (2003b). Portrait of the self-enhancer: Well adjusted and well liked or maladjusted and friendless? *Journal of Personality and Social Psychology, 84,* 165–176. doi:10.1037/0022-3514.84.1.165

Tsenkova, V. K., Love, G. D., Singer, B. H., & Ryff, C. D. (2007). Socioeconomic status and psychological well-being predict cross-time change in glycosylated hemoglobin in older women without diabetes. *Psychosomatic Medicine, 69,* 777–784. doi:10.1097/PSY.0b013e318157466f

Tweed, S. H., & Ryff, C. D. (1991). Adult children of alcoholics: Profiles of wellness amidst distress. *Journal of Studies on Alcohol, 52,* 133–141.

Urry, H. L., Nitschke, J. B., Dolski, I., Jackson, D. C., Dalton, K. M., Mueller, C. J., . . . Davison, R. J. (2004). Making a life worth living: Neural correlates of well-being. *Psychological Science, 15,* 367–372. doi:10.1111/j.0956-7976.2004.00686.x

van Dierendonck, D. (2004). The construct validity of Ryff's Scales of Psychological Well-Being and its extension with spiritual well-being. *Personality and Individual Differences, 36,* 629–643. doi:10.1016/S0191-8869(03)00122-3 van Reekum, C. M., Urry, H. L., Johnstone, T., Thurow, M. E., Frye, C. J., Jackson, C. A., . . . Davidson, R. J. (2007). Individual differences in amygdala and ventromedial prefrontal cortex activity are associated with evaluation speed and psychological well-being. *Journal of Cognitive Neuroscience, 19*, 237–248. doi:10.1162/jocn.2007.19.2.237

Wiggins, J. S. (1980). *Personality and prediction: Principles of personality assessment.* Menlo Park, CA: Addison-Wesley.

Wink, P., & Dillon, M. (2003). Religiousness, spirituality, and psychosocial functioning in late adulthood: Findings from a longitudinal study. *Psychology and Aging, 18*, 916–924. doi:10.1037/0882-7974.18.4.916

5

EUDAIMONIC IDENTITY THEORY

ALAN S. WATERMAN AND SETH J. SCHWARTZ

Central to work in both ethical philosophy and positive psychology is consideration of questions as to how people ought to live. Philosophers often phrase such questions in terms of the proper ends for human functioning and treat this as a matter to be understood analytically. Psychologists working within a positive psychology context begin with the concept of human well-being and address questions as to how such a construct is to be understood theoretically and investigated empirically. Given the similarity of the goals that practitioners within these two disciplines are striving to achieve, it should not be surprising to find extensive correspondences between their efforts. Eudaimonic identity theory reflects one line of confluence between philosophy and positive psychology regarding the nature of human well-being.

Work on eudaimonic identity theory began with two questions central to understanding how individuals form a sense of personal identity during the transition from adolescence to adulthood (Erikson, 1968; Marcia, 1966;

DOI: 10.1037/14092-006
The Best Within Us: Positive Psychology Perspectives on Eudaimonia, Alan S. Waterman (Editor)
Copyright © 2013 by the American Psychological Association. All rights reserved.

Waterman, 1982). *Identity formation* entails establishing goals, values, and beliefs providing direction, purpose, and meaning to life. This task involves deciding what type of person one wishes to become. Given the fact that contemporary societies offer their emerging adults a wealth of alternatives regarding the goals, values, and beliefs that they could potentially adopt, the first of the questions to be considered was: Are some of the identity options available to a person better than others that are equally available? If by *better* we mean likely to result in greater well-being and personal fulfillment, then the answer to this first question is certainly yes. Some options will have a higher likelihood of being successfully implemented, some values and beliefs will receive greater social support than others, and some alternatives will be more consistent with personal potentials and natural inclinations. These outcomes are likely to contribute to higher levels of personal well-being. It should be recognized, however, that the existence of better options does not mean that everyone should be adopting the same set of identity options. Individuals differ with respect to physical endowment, temperament, family and cultural context, developmental events, reinforcement history, and a host of other variables that contribute to differences with respect to what will constitute better options for any given person. So, whereas it can be readily concluded that for each person some available identity alternatives are better than others that are equally available, it is quite another matter to determine which options are likely to be better for a particular person. This is what can make the task of identity formation so difficult and stressful for those adolescents, emerging adults, and others grappling with it. It also gives rise to a second question: Given the variety of identity-related alternative goals, values, and beliefs available, how can the better choices be recognized? Eudaimonic identity theory was developed in an effort to provide answers to the two questions posed here.

A EUDAIMONIC THEORY OF IDENTITY FORMATION

Two Metaphors for Identity Formation

Waterman (1984) described two metaphors that can be applied to understanding identity formation: (a) identity as self-creation/self-construction and (b) identity as self-discovery. Identity as a creation or construction involves bringing into being something that has never previously existed. It entails selecting from among a virtually unlimited set of possibilities and constructing something deemed to be of value from the elements chosen. With respect to philosophy, identity as creation/construction is an existential undertaking. The self, or identity, can be said to emerge from "nothingness" (Sartre, 1943/1956) by an act of personal choice. The range of possibilities is limitless, which represents both an attraction and a problem. From an existential perspective, there are no external or internal standards by which possibilities can be evaluated, such that the choice is ultimately arbitrary. Yet the individual must take personal responsibility for the choice that is made. This is the existential dilemma. The metaphor of self-creation/self-construction provides little assistance for the recognition of "better" identity choices. The person is left to project, to the extent possible, the likelihood of success that is likely to result if any given identity option were adopted. Such projections are likely to be extremely fallible given the number of factors that can affect the outcomes of one's efforts. Further, from an existential perspective, it is inappropriate to rely on the projections or preferences of others as this reflects an abdication of responsibility. Fromm (1941) referred to doing so as an "escape from freedom" and Sartre (1943/1956) as "living in bad faith." So the individuals are left entirely on their own (see Côté, 2000, for a similar perspective).

In contrast, the process of discovery means that we have come to recognize something about the nature of the world or ourselves. That which is found is something that already exists. Now it is recognized and understood. In the identity as self-discovery metaphor, what is discovered pertains to the nature of who we truly are. The philosophical assumptions here are essentialist, presuming not an array of limitless possibilities but an individual human nature with potential strengths and limitations, predispositions, and predilections. This is the perspective expressed within eudaimonist philosophy. The concept of an individual human nature provides an internal standard for distinguishing better identity choices from among the array of possibilities available. That standard is in terms of consistency with one's "true" nature (Waterman, 1990).

The Daimon (the True Self) as a Philosophical and a Psychological Construct

Within eudaimonist philosophy, the concept of an essential human nature is expressed as the daimon or "true self" (Norton, 1976). The *daimon* refers to those potentialities of each person that, when realized, represent the greatest fulfillment in living of which the person is capable. These include both the potentialities that are shared by all humans by virtue of our common specieshood, that is, our generic human nature, as well as those unique potentials that distinguish each individual from all others. The daimon is an ideal in the sense of being an excellence, a perfection toward which one strives, the best within us, and hence it can provide direction and meaning to one's life.

Norton (1976) described the ethics of eudaimonism as follows: "[Each individual] is obliged to know and live in truth to his daimon, thereby progressively actualizing an excellence that is his innately and potentially" (p. ix). This spirit underlies two famous classical Greek injunctions: "Know thyself" and "Become what you are." To choose, in Norton's phrase, "to live freely the life that is one's own" (p. 26) is an affirmation of personal responsibility and a statement of personal integrity. It requires that a commitment be made both to the principles by which one chooses to live and to the goals toward which one's life is to be directed. This commitment involves a conscious recognition and acknowledgment of personal truths already known intuitively.

To speak of the daimon as personal potentialities capable of guiding action in the direction of self-fulfillment seems to invite granting it reified status. In part, this is a carryover of its philosophical origins in Hellenic philosophy in which the daimon was thought of as a guiding spirit provided at birth. However, the Hellenic philosopher Heraclitus observed that "man's character is his daimon" (May, 1969, p. 135), with the inference that the daimon is an internal standard for how one ought to live. To be consistent with the standards of contemporary psychological theories, the daimon should be understood as constituted of a number of interrelated potentialities and psychological processes. These include our latent skills, talents, predispositions, predilections, and response tendencies as well as the intuitive and analytic processes by which such potentialities come to be recognized and become personal goals, values, and beliefs to be actualized (Waterman, 1990).

One of the earliest psychologists to write about the daimon was the neo-analyst Karen Horney. Her term for the daimon was the *real self*, which she distinguished from the *actual self*, that is, the way we think we are, and the *idealized self*, the way we would wish to be, and by implication are not. Horney (1950) defined the real self as

> the central inner force, common to all human beings and yet unique to each, which is the deep source of growth . . . [that is] free, healthy development in accordance with the potentials of one's generic and individual nature. (p. 17)

Like the daimon, the real self should be considered as a "given" for each person, a unique combination of capabilities that, like all capabilities, must be developed over time. Horney made the point that a supportive atmosphere, first within the family and later within the larger community, is essential if those potentialities are to be successfully developed.

The philosophy of eudaimonism, and specifically the concept of the daimon, provides a broad, persuasive answer to the first of the questions posed previously. Better identity choices are those consistent with the nature of our personal daimon, that is, those goals, values, and beliefs that represent the best of both our generic nature and our unique, individual potentialities. This means that the first objective of the task of identity formation must be to recognize the nature of one's personal daimon—one's true self—and to heed the injunction "Know thyself."

The concept of a generic human nature is the foundation of epigenetic theories of development (Erikson, 1963), and psychologists have used concept labels such as *aptitude, temperament,* and *the hereditability of attitudes* to refer to an individual human nature comprising the person's potentials. It is not in serious dispute that each person seems better suited with respect to some abilities in contrast to others. Similarly, there are individual differences in affective expression in the latency, durability, and lability of emotions, and these differences are often evident very early in life. Individual predispositions with respect to attitudes, values, and beliefs are less understood, though it can be readily observed that individuals differ in the ways they resonate more strongly and more intuitively with some perspectives for making sense of the world than with others. One person will find a carefully reasoned and documented analysis of a political or social issue thoroughly persuasive, whereas another will respond to the same argument with indifference. If we are to choose better options among the alternative identity elements we can envision, it behooves us to know ourselves as best we can, including our strengths and limitations, our natural inclinations and response tendencies, and our predispositions to look favorably (or unfavorably) on aspects of the social world we are likely to encounter, presently and in the future.

Eudaimonia, Feelings of Personal Expressiveness, and Recognition of One's Daimon

Given that the potentialities of the daimon are to be used as the criteria for making better identity choices, we return to the question as to how such identity alternatives are to be recognized. Again, eudaimonist philosophy provides guidance, here in the concept of eudaimonia. For Aristotle (trans. 1985), eudaimonia, usually translated as *happiness,* referred to an objective state constituted by activity expressing virtue, in which virtue may be thought to be excellence or the best within us. The contemporary eudaimonist philosopher Norton (1976) described eudaimonia as follows:

> Eudaimonia is both a feeling and a condition. As a feeling it distinguishes right from wrong desire. Moreover it attends right desire, not only upon its gratification, but from its first appearance. Because eudaimonia is fully present to right living at every stage of development, it cannot constitute the aim of such living, but serves instead as merely a mark, a sign. It signals that the present activity of the individual is in harmony with the daimon that is the true self. (p. 5)

Four elements in this quoted statement warrant special attention here:

1. Eudaimonia is conceptualized as a subjective, cognitive–affective condition, a feeling that accompanies right desire, that is, activities consistent with one's best potentials. Right desire and right living entail the pursuit of excellence/virtue in what we do and who we are.

2. Such cognitive–affective experiences are seen as likely to occur on the first occasion on which such activities are engaged in. When someone responds to an activity with statements such as "Where has this been all my life?" or "Why didn't I know about this before?" the experience is one of eudaimonia, in the sense described by Norton. It is important to recognize that such reactions are literally idiosyncratic. It cannot be the activity, in and of itself, that is generating this reaction, because the same activity that is experienced so positively by one person will generate indifference in others, and some may actually find it aversive. Thus, such experiences of connection with particular activities are telling us something about who we are.

3. Experiences of eudaimonia serve as an indicator of those elements that are consistent with our personal functioning and, as such, provide an answer to the question as to how better identity choices are to be recognized. Better identity choices are those with which we feel a special sense of connection, a feeling not experienced with options for which we are less suited.

4. As positive as experiences of eudaimonia are, they are not, in themselves, the criteria for a life well lived. Eudaimonist ethics are based on self-realization, that is, striving for the fulfillment of our best potentials not experiencing particular subjective states. Eudaimonia is merely a signal that our best potentials are being actualized.

It should be recognized that the subjective elements associated with the recognition of one's daimon are considerably broader than an instant connection with certain activities. The constellation of subjective experiences includes feelings of rightness and centeredness in one's actions, strength of purpose, meaningfulness, intrinsic motivation, fulfillment, authenticity, and identity, as in "this is who I really am." When studying such experiences empirically, we have referred to them as "feelings of personal expressiveness," a term used interchangeably with eudaimonia (Waterman, 1993; Waterman, Schwartz, & Conti, 2008; Waterman et al., 2003).

Subjective experiences akin to feelings of personal expressiveness have received extensive research attention within psychology. Expressions of interest in an activity are used as a criterion for the identification of intrinsically motivated activities (Deci & Ryan, 1985; Renninger, Hidi, & Krapp, 1992). Csikszentmihalyi (1990) described the cognitive–affective experience of flow as entailing among other characteristics (a) the presence of clear goals; (b) a merging of action and awareness; (c) the centering of attention on a limited stimulus field with the exclusion of distractions from consciousness; (d) the loss of ego or self-consciousness; and (e) a distortion in the sense of time, with time appearing to move either more quickly or more slowly than in normal consciousness. Csikszentmihalyi found that flow experiences are linked with a balance between the challenges posed by an activity and the skills that the person brings to it. Peak experiences, as described by Maslow (1968, 1970, 1975), represent the most intense form of the type of experience referred to here and were characterized as *acute identity experiences*.

Within eudaimonic identity theory, feelings of personal expressiveness are not to be thought of as infallible indicators of our personal potentials and, therefore, do not provide an unerring basis for making identity decisions. Individuals may experience an initial sense of connection with some activities for such other reasons as particularly successful early experiences or enthusiastic social support. However, feelings of personal expressiveness are likely to be self-correcting when not associated with one's actual potentials. Early successes based on chance are not sustainable. Social support, even when sustained, constitutes an extrinsic reward and in the absence of autonomy and other intrinsic considerations undermines continuing motivation (Deci & Ryan, 1985). In contrast, feelings of personal expressiveness derive from who we really are and serve as a continuing source of reinforcement for activities consistent with our aptitudes and predispositions. Moreover, feelings of personal expressiveness will likely remain self-reinforcing across the fluctuations in outcomes encountered on particular occasions. Thus, eudaimonia can serve to sustain self-defining activities when difficulties are encountered while developing latent talents or predispositions or when our choices are challenged by others.

Eudaimonia and Hedonia as Two Conceptions of Happiness

Eudaimonia and similar subjective states such as interest, flow, and peak experiences are all positive affective conditions, albeit varying in intensity. It is perhaps for this reason that eudaimonia has been traditionally translated from Greek as *happiness*. However, happiness is usually understood as pleasure, and eudaimonist philosophers going back to Aristotle (trans. 1985) have written at length on the importance of distinguishing between eudaimonia and pleasure (hedonia)[1] as two conceptions of happiness (Kraut, 1979).

Within philosophy, happiness in the sense of pleasure or hedonia is generally considered to include "the belief that one is getting the important things one wants, as well as certain pleasant affects that normally go along with this belief" (Kraut, 1979, p. 178). This contrasts with eudaimonia, which embodies the idea, not that one is pleased with one's life or activities, but that one has "what is *worth* desiring and worth having in life" (Telfer, 1980, p. 37) and the feeling of "being where one wants to be, doing what one wants to do" (Norton, 1976, p. 216), where what is wanted is considered to be worth doing. However, the relationship between eudaimonia and hedonia is complex because one of the things people can want, and typically do want, is to engage in personally expressive activities leading to self-realization, and such activities are clearly considered to be worth doing. Telfer (1980) claimed that under most circumstances, experiences of eudaimonia are a sufficient, but not a necessary, condition for experiences of hedonia. Thus, activities can usually be viewed as falling into one of three categories: (a) activities associated with experiences of both eudaimonia and hedonia, that is, activities associated with self-realization; (b) activities associated with experiences of hedonia, but not eudaimonia, that is, activities that are enjoyed for reasons unrelated to self-realization; or (c) activities not associated with either hedonia or eudaimonia, that is, activities that are not enjoyed. Activities that give rise to experiences of eudaimonia but not hedonia can be said to approximate a null category. Because hedonia arises in connection with a far broader range of activities than does eudaimonia, and despite their frequent co-occurrence, it should be possible to distinguish between these two cognitive–affective subjective states.

The Development of Eudaimonic Identity Choices

Waterman (2011) identified four tasks that must be addressed in achieving the eudaimonic goal of realizing one's personal potentials. The first task involves recognizing those personal potentials that represent one's better identity choices. As discussed previously, feelings of personal expressiveness play a key role in this regard. The second task involves investing sustained effort in the development of those latent skills, talents, and values through which such potentials can be expressed. The difficulties and obstacles inevitably encountered must be addressed and overcome. However, to succeed in the development of a skill set or value perspective still does not provide

---

[1]The term *hedonia* was created to have a label for the cognitive–affective subjective state associated with pleasure or enjoyment that would parallel the term *eudaimonia* as a cognitive–affective subjective state.

information on the purposes or goals toward which those skills or values are to be directed. Thus, the third task in this process of achieving eudaimonic identity functioning involves choosing goals worthy of providing direction, purpose, and meaning to life. The fourth task involves finding and using opportunities afforded within one's societal context to implement one's chosen identity commitments. Societies differ widely in the range of opportunities made available to emerging adults and the encouragement they provide for seeking self-realization. There can be no guarantees that individuals will find opportunities through which to pursue eudaimonic goals.

Whereas the process of eudaimonic identity formation just described might seem to suggest an orderly, stagelike progression with a specified outcome to be achieved, such a conceptualization would be misleading. Identity formation and implementation is an ongoing dynamic process throughout life. At any point in time, individuals may find themselves making progress with respect to any of the tasks identified. What is learned in terms of one aspect of the process may trigger the need to reexamine what is thought to be true regarding other elements of identity formation. As one's skills improve, it becomes necessary to identify new challenges that require still further development of these skills. Similarly, it is necessary to identify new goals worthy of pursuing to replace goals that have already been achieved. As Erikson (1963, 1982) observed in his epigenetic description of the life cycle, as individuals age the developmental tasks they undertake change, and thus the nature of self-realization changes as well. Any of these tasks can be returned to at any time.

Eudaimonic Activities and Eudaimonic Well-Being

Eudaimonic identity theory can be used to explore the nature of eudaimonic functioning as both a within-person and between-persons variable. Studying eudaimonic functioning as a within-person variable involves contrasting activities in which individuals engage and that differ in the extent to which they are associated with eudaimonia and hedonia. Such research can promote an understanding of the distinctive nature of eudaimonia and the types of activities that are most likely experienced as personally expressive. Research at the level of activities yields information on the differences between eudaimonia and hedonia as two conceptions of happiness.

Because individuals differ with respect to the extent to which they define themselves in terms of personally expressive activities, eudaimonic functioning can also be studied as a between-persons variable. Some individuals have developed a sense of identity involving commitments to goals, values, and beliefs that are centered on activities associated with eudaimonic experiences. For others, the identity commitments are formed around activities that are motivated by extrinsic considerations. This corresponds to the distinction between better and poorer identity choices. Research at the level of the person entails evaluating aspects of theory involving the quality of identity commitments. Further, research at this level can be used to better understand the relationship of identity functioning to concepts of well-being and the nature of a life well lived.

A PROGRAM OF RESEARCH BASED ON
EUDAIMONIC IDENTITY THEORY

Operational Definitions of Eudaimonic Functioning

The first instrument to be developed for studying eudaimonic identity functioning was the Personally Expressive Activities Questionnaire (PEAQ; Waterman, 1993, 1998). As the name suggests, the PEAQ was designed to study eudaimonic functioning as a within-person variable at the level of activities. The standard form of the PEAQ (PEAQ-S) asks respondents to identify five activities of importance to them that they would use to describe themselves to another person. These instructions are designed to elicit activities that are personally salient, reflecting elements in the respondent's identity. Those activities are then rated for feelings of personal expressiveness, other cognitive–affective experiences, and characteristics of the activities viewed as associated with eudaimonic functioning.

On the PEAQ-S, the scale for feelings of personal expressiveness (eudaimonia) is composed of six items responded to on a 7-point scale, with endpoints anchored from *strongly agree* to *strongly disagree*, as follows:

1. This activity gives me my greatest feeling of really being alive.
2. When I engage in this activity I feel more intensely involved than I do when engaged in most other activities.
3. This activity gives me my strongest feeling that this is who I really am.
4. When I engage in this activity I feel that this is what I was meant to do.
5. I feel more complete or fulfilled when engaging in this activity than I do when engaged in most other activities.
6. I feel a special fit or meshing when engaging in this activity.

Activities are considered to reflect eudaimonic functioning if the average item endorsement scores are at or above 6 on the 7-point response scale for personal expressiveness items.

In addition to (a) feelings of personal expressiveness (eudaimonia), three other scales on the PEAQ-S assess subjective experiences associated with the activities being rated: (b) interest, (c) flow experiences, and (d) hedonic enjoyment (hedonia). Four scales assess characteristics of the manner in which respondents engage in the activities: (e) self-realization values, (f) self-determination, (g) a balance of challenges and skills, and (h) the level of effort expended. Also included are items pertaining to the importance of the activity and the frequency with which it is enacted.

The instrument designed to assess eudaimonic functioning as a between-persons variable is the Questionnaire for Eudaimonic Well-Being (QEWB; Waterman et al., 2010). The QEWB contains items in six interrelated categories with linkages to eudaimonist philosophy: self-discovery, perceived development of one's best potentials, a sense of purpose and meaning in life, investment of significant effort in the pursuit of excellence, intense involvement in activities, and enjoyment of activities as personally expressive. Scores on the QEWB are viewed as an index of the quality of the identity commitments that have been established. Whereas high scores reflect the presence of high-quality commitments, that is, better identity choices, low scores may result either from having established low-quality commitments or from an absence of identity commitments.

Research Findings on Eudaimonic Functioning at the Level of Activities

Hypothesis 1: Feelings of personal expressiveness will be positively correlated with the perception of an activity as involving values associated with self-realization.

Self-realization is assessed on the PEAQ with two items pertaining to extent to which the activity being rated is perceived as associated with the development the one's best potentials and making progress toward one's personal goals. Correlations of eudaimonia with these items (individually or combined) range from .42 to .66, $p < .001$ (Waterman, 1993, 2005; Waterman et al., 2003, 2008). This finding is consistent with the theoretical expectation that eudaimonia, as a subjective state, is a function of recognition and development of one's true self, operationally defined as self-realization.

Hypothesis 2: Feelings of personal expressiveness will be positively correlated with indices of other positive subjective experiences present when engaged in an activity, specifically interest, flow experiences, and hedonic enjoyment (hedonia).

As expected, correlations of feelings of personal expressiveness with interest, flow experiences, and hedonic enjoyments have been found to be strong and statistically significant (Waterman, 1993, 2005; Waterman et al., 2003, 2008).

Hypothesis 3: Feelings of personal expressiveness will be positively correlated with measures of the extent to which the activities rated are characterized by self-determination, the presence of a balance of challenges and skills, the investment of high levels of effort in the activities, and their importance of the activities to the respondent.

The correlations of feelings of personal expressiveness with the activity characteristics of self-determination, a balance of challenges and skills, the investment of sustained effort, and importance were consistently found to be statistically significant, though are not as strong as those observed for the various subjective experience indices (Waterman, 1993, 2005; Waterman et al., 2003, 2008).

Hypothesis 4: Self-realization values for activities, as an indicator of awareness of the daimon, will be positively correlated with measures of the positive cognitive–affective subjective states of interest, flow experiences, and hedonic enjoyment.

All parts of this hypothesis were confirmed, albeit in a somewhat lower set of ranges than the corresponding findings for the relationship of feelings of personal expressiveness with these variables (Waterman et al., 2003, 2008).

Hypothesis 5: The scale for self-realization values will be positively correlated with measures of the extent to which the activities rated are characterized by self-determination, a balance of challenges and skills, the investment of high levels of effort, and importance.

This hypothesis was not supported for self-determination but was supported for both the balance of challenges and skills and the level of effort expended (Waterman et al., 2003, 2008). The anomalous finding for self-determination may be explained in that, for the college student respondents in these studies, a substantial proportion of the activities evaluated pertained to education or work. Those activities were typically characterized as not self-chosen (i.e., low on self-determination) but were, nevertheless, seen as promoting self-realization.

Hypothesis 6: There will be an asymmetry in the relationship of eudaimonia and hedonia in that all activities high on eudaimonia should also be high on hedonia, whereas not all activities high on hedonia would be correspondingly high on eudaimonia.

Analyses of the relative frequencies of activities in the various categories of combinations of high and low scores on scales for feelings of personal expressiveness and hedonic enjoyment have consistently confirmed Hypothesis 6 (Waterman, 1993; Waterman et al., 2008). Across samples, between 81% and 88% of activities high on feelings of personal expressiveness were also rated high on hedonic enjoyment, whereas only between 61% and 71% of activities high on hedonic enjoyment were also rated high on personal expressiveness. In every instance, the difference in proportions was statistically significant.

Hypothesis 7: Despite correlations of eudaimonia and hedonia in the range of .75 to .85, it should be possible to distinguish between them in terms of differences in the strength of the correlations these measures have with other aspects of eudaimonic functioning, including both subjective experiences of interest and flow and the person–activity fit characteristics of self-realization values, self-determination, the balance of challenges and skills, the level of effort invested in the activities, and their importance to the respondent.

This hypothesis was consistently confirmed, with the correlations for eudaimonia with self-realization values, the balance of challenges and skills, the level of effort invested in activities, and their importance to the respondent being significantly stronger than the corresponding correlations with hedonia (Waterman, 1993; Waterman et al., 2008). A similar though less-consistent pattern was found for flow experiences. Contrary to expectations, interest and self-determination had significantly stronger correlations with hedonia than with eudaimonia. Both sets of findings support the premise that eudaimonia and hedonia are distinguishable cognitive–affective subjective states while also suggesting that understanding the differences between them may require some reconceptualization of intrinsic motivation as all of the variables of concern here are positively related to such motivation. Undertaking that reconceptualization is beyond the scope of this chapter.

Research Findings on Eudaimonic Functioning at the Level of the Person

Hypothesis 8a: Respondents who have established identity-defining commitments to specific goals, values, and beliefs, will provide evidence of greater eudaimonic functioning than those who do not have identity commitments.

Hypothesis 8b: Respondents who established commitments through reflective exploration of alternative possibilities will provide evidence of greater eudaimonic functioning than those who have established their commitments through a process of identification with significant others.

To have established identity commitments of high quality (i.e., better identity choices) means, by definition, that identity commitments are present. However, not all commitments are of high quality—some are enacted for extrinsic reasons—suggesting that the strength of the relationship between indices of commitment and commitment quality provide information about the extent to which the commitments formed are of high quality. Regarding Hypothesis 8a, findings from the earliest study to address this hypothesis (Schwartz, Mullis, Waterman, & Dunham, 2000) indicated that college students in the identity achievement status (those who had established identity commitments after exploring a range of possibilities) and in the foreclosure status (those who had established identity commitments primarily through identification with significant others) had higher personal expressiveness scores on the PEAQ than did respondents in the identity diffusion status (those who did not have identity commitments and were not trying to form them) or in the moratorium status (those who were actively exploring alternatives but had yet to form commitments). Subsequently, Waterman (2004) reported that respondents on the PEAQ listing activities that met the criteria for being considered personally expressive scored significantly higher on identity achievement and related scales and significantly lower on scales assessing identity diffusion. Further, Waterman (2007) found significant positive correlations between a scale assessing identity achievement and PEAQ measures indices of personal expressiveness and self-realization values, whereas significant negative correlations were found for identity diffusion. The correlations for the foreclosure and moratorium scales were not significant. In subsequent research using the QEWB, significant positive correlations emerged between measures of identity commitment and eudaimonic well-being, a measure of commitment quality (Waterman et al., 2010). Correlations of QEWB scores with measures of exploration of alternative identity elements were also positive and significant, though of substantially lower strength. Correlations with ruminative exploration, a nonproductive and anxiety-ridden form of exploration, were negative and statistically significant.

As these findings bear on Hypothesis 8b, there is modest support for the view that exploration of identity alternatives promotes the formation of better identity commitments. The substantially stronger association of the PEAQ and QEWB measures with measures of identity commitment than with exploration indicate that, although probabilities are higher for developing high quality through exploration, it is clearly possible for such commitments to develop through a process of identification with significant others.

Hypothesis 9: Identity commitments have been demonstrated to be associated with more favorable levels of psychosocial functioning, but such favorable functioning will be evident only when high-quality, personally expressive commitments have been made. Identity commitments of low quality will yield no benefits and may be associated with poorer psychosocial functioning than is the norm.

There is an extensive body of literature on identity functioning demonstrating that individuals with identity commitments (i.e., those in the identity achievement and foreclosure statuses) evidence more favorable psychosocial functioning than those in the identity diffusion and moratorium status (Kroger & Marcia, 2011). However, from the perspective of eudaimonic identity theory, there are few benefits to be derived from forming and enacting identity commitments that are not experienced as personally expressive. Waterman et al. (2012) found that quality of identity commitment accounted for almost all of the variability in the relationships of identity functioning to a broad range of measures of well-being and other aspects of psychosocial functioning. Similarly, Soenens, Berzonsky, Dunkel, Papini, and Vansteenkiste (2011) reported that identity commitments reflecting intrinsic motivation were associated with more favorable psychosocial functioning than commitments involving extrinsic motivation.

Hypothesis 10: Eudaimonic identity functioning will be positively related to subjective well-being, psychological well-being, and other aspects of positive psychosocial functioning such as self-esteem and an internal locus of control. Eudaimonic functioning will be negatively related to general anxiety, social anxiety, and depression and will be associated with a reduced likelihood of engaging in health-related risk activities.

Data using the QEWB and various measures of well-being and other aspects of psychological functioning provide consistent support for Hypothesis 10 (Waterman et al., 2010). The correlation with the Satisfaction With Life Scale (Diener, Emmons, Larsen, & Griffin, 1985) was significant, demonstrating at the level of the person findings previously reported in research studying eudaimonic functioning at the level of activities. The correlation of QEWB scores with the composite of Ryff's (1989) Scales for Psychological Well-Being was strong. With respect to the individual scales, the strongest correlation emerged for the Self-Acceptance scale; the weakest, though still significant correlation was found for Positive Relations With Others. Similarly, significant correlations with self-esteem and a measure of internal locus of control were both positive, whereas the correlations with general anxiety, social anxiety, and symptoms of depression were all negative. Schwartz et al. (2011) found that high scores on the QEWB were related to reduced risk of engaging in drug-related activities but were not related to risks related to sexual activity or to impaired driving.

Summary of Research Findings

With only minor exceptions, hypotheses drawn from eudaimonic identity theory were supported at the both the level of activities and the level of the person. At the level of activities, eudaimonic functioning, in the form of subjective feelings of personal expressiveness, are associated with perceptions that activities are associated with self-realization in regard to both the development of one's best potentials and furthering one's goals and purposes. For this reason, such activities are deemed to be personally important and worthy of investment of significant effort. In each of these respects, associations were significantly stronger for feelings of personal expressiveness than for hedonic enjoyment. Stronger associations for hedonic enjoyment than feelings of personal expressiveness were found for the variables of interest and self-determination. These results confirm that the subjective states of eudaimonia and hedonia, although strongly correlated, are nevertheless reliably distinguishable.

At the level of the person, eudaimonic functioning is associated with successful identity formation and accounts almost entirely for the relationship of identity commitments with positive psychosocial functioning. Eudaimonic well-being is positively associated with subjective well-being, psychological well-being, self-esteem, and an internal locus of control. It is also associated with lower levels of general anxiety, social anxiety, and symptoms of depression and a reduced likelihood of engaging in some forms of risky behavior.

IMPLICATIONS OF EUDAIMONIC IDENTITY THEORY FOR PARENTING, EDUCATION, AND THERAPY

Given the evidence that eudaimonic functioning is associated with various forms of well-being and positive psychosocial outcomes, it follows that attention should be directed toward understanding how such functioning can be promoted through parenting, education, counseling, and therapy. This is a broad topic and can be addressed only briefly here.

The following guidelines for promoting eudaimonic functioning are applicable across a variety of contexts:

1. The broader the exposure a person has to different types of activities, the greater the likelihood of identifying activities associated with initial experiences of feelings of personal expressiveness. This suggests that parents should try to afford opportunities for varied activities throughout childhood and the adolescent years. The same principle applies to school curricula at the primary and secondary levels. Most such opportunities will result in relatively mild positive or negative reactions or indifference in the developing individual. However, it may take only one strongly positive reaction to set the child or adolescent on the pursuit of a lifelong interest.
2. Parents and teachers can model the discovery of eudaimonic activities and self-realization through talking about the activities they feel passionate about and how they first learned about them.
3. The same principles applying to promoting intrinsic motivation apply to encouraging eudaimonic functioning. Promoting autonomous decision making plays an important role in this regard. Attempts to limit self-determination with respect to activities are likely to trigger psychological reactance (Brehm, 1966) and may well be counterproductive. Encouragement should be provided for continued engagement in activities for which spontaneous interest is expressed. However, excessive rewards promote engaging in activities for controlled (extrinsic),

rather than autonomous, motives and thus undermine intrinsic interest that may be present.

4. Within the contexts of counseling and therapy, it is important to distinguish between clients who have experienced connections with activities earlier in their lives but who have been discouraged from such pursuits by significant others and those who have never made such connections. In the former instance, progress may be made by reconnecting clients with their earlier interests, whereas in the latter instance, it may be necessary to establish the legitimacy of pursuing self-realization before endeavoring to help clients to recognize their personal potentials, predispositions, and inclinations.

5. Whether in parenting, education, counseling, or therapy, focusing on the nature of the task of identity formation is essential in promoting eudaimonic functioning. There is a need for the person to recognize that some identity choices are better than others in terms of their likelihood to promote a fulfilling future. The criteria for better choices have their locus in the fit between the individual's own nature and the opportunities afforded by the community within which one lives. To the extent that identity choices are constrained by external factors, either through having particular choices imposed by one's family or society or through limitations on the range available in the social context, the probability of finding such a fit is reduced.

6. Although maximizing the breadth of choice is considered desirable, it is possible to become overwhelmed by the sheer number of options from which a choice can be made. For this reason, it is important for those seeking to promote eudaimonic identity choices to provide patient support throughout the process, recognizing that there are wide differences among people in the developmental timetable for making identity choices.

A CONCLUDING COMMENT

It should not be expected that forming eudaimonic identity commitments will be one of steady, unidirectional progress from strength to strength. There may be any number of missteps along the way as individuals misjudge their potentials or fail to find opportunities for the expression of valid potentials within their society. However, perseverance in the pursuit of self-realization appears to be a reliable source, very possibly the essential source, of flourishing.

REFERENCES

Aristotle. (1985). *Nicomachean ethics*. (T. Irwin, Trans.). Indianapolis, IN: Hackett.

Brehm, J. W. (1966). *A theory of psychological reactance*. New York, NY: Wiley.

Côté, J. E. (2000). *Arrested adulthood: The changing nature of maturity and identity*. New York, NY: New York University Press.

Csikszentmihalyi, M. (1990). *Flow: The psychology of optimal experience*. New York, NY: Harper & Row.

Deci, E. L., & Ryan, R. M. (1985). *Intrinsic motivation and self-determination in human behavior*. New York, NY: Plenum Press.

Diener, E., Emmons, R. A., Larsen, R. J., & Griffin, S. The Satisfaction With Life Scale. *Journal of Personality Assessment, 49*, 71–75. doi:10.1207/s15327752jpa 4901_13

Erikson, E. H. (1963). *Childhood and society* (2nd ed.). New York, NY: Norton.

Erikson, E. H. (1968). *Identity: Youth and crisis*. New York, NY: Norton.

Erikson, E. H. (1982). *The life cycle completed: A review*. New York, NY: Norton.

Fromm, E. (1941). *Escape from freedom*. New York, NY: Rinehart.

Horney, K. (1950). *Neurosis and human growth: The struggle toward self-realization*. New York, NY: Norton.

Kraut, R. (1979). Two conceptions of happiness. *The Philosophical Review, 88*, 167–196. doi:10.2307/2184505

Kroger, J., & Marcia, J. E. (2011). The identity statuses: Origins, meanings, and interpretations. In S. J. Schwartz, K. Luyckx, & V. L. Vignoles (Eds.), *Handbook of identity theory and research: Vol. 1. Structures and processes* (pp. 31–53). New York, NY: Springer.

Marcia, J. E. (1966). Development and validation of ego identity status. *Journal of Personality and Social Psychology, 3*, 551–558. doi:10.1037/h0023281

Maslow, A. H. (1968). *Toward a psychology of being*. Princeton, NJ: Van Nostrand.

Maslow, A. H. (1970). *Motivation and personality* (2nd ed.). New York, NY: Harper and Row.

Maslow, A. H. (1975). *The farther reaches of human nature*. New York, NY: Viking Compass.

May, R. (1969). *Love and will*. New York, NY: Norton.

Norton, D. L. (1976). *Personal destinies*. Princeton, NJ: Princeton University Press.

Renninger, A., Hidi, S., & Krapp, A. (Eds). (1992). *The role of interest in learning and development*. Hillsdale, NJ: Erlbaum.

Ryff, C. D. (1989). Happiness is everything, or is it? Explorations on the meaning of psychological well-being. *Journal of Personality and Social Psychology, 57*, 1069–1081. doi:10.1037/0022-3514.57.6.1069

Sartre, J.-P. (1956). *Being and nothingness: An essay on phenomenological ontology* (H. E. Barnes, Trans.). New York, NY: Philosophical Library. (Original work published 1943)

Schwartz, S. J., Mullis, R. L., Waterman, A. S., & Dunham, R. M. (2000). Ego identity status, identity styles, and personal expressiveness: An empirical investigation of three convergent constructs. *Journal of Adolescent Research, 15*, 504–521. doi:10.1177/0743558400154005

Schwartz, S. J., Waterman, A. S., Vazsonyi, A. T., Zamboanga, B. L., Whitbourne, S. K., Weisskirch, R. S., . . . Ham, L. S. (2011). The association of well-being with health risk behaviors in college-attending young adults. *Applied Developmental Science, 15*, 20–36. doi:10.1080/10888691.2011.538617

Soenens, B., Berzonsky, M. D., Dunkel, C., Papini, D., & Vansteenkiste, M. (2011). Are all identity commitments created equally? The importance of motives for late adolescents' personal adjustment. *International Journal of Behavioral Development, 35*, 358–369. doi:10.1177/0165025411405954

Telfer, E. (1980). *Happiness.* New York, NY: St. Martin's Press.

Waterman, A. S. (1982). Identity development from adolescence to adulthood: An extension of theory and a review of research. *Developmental Psychology, 18*, 341–358.

Waterman, A. S. (1984). Identity formation: Discovery or creation? *The Journal of Early Adolescence, 4*, 329–341. doi:10.1177/0272431684044004

Waterman, A. S. (1990). Personal expressiveness: Philosophical and psychological foundations. *Journal of Mind and Behavior, 11*, 47–74.

Waterman, A. S. (1993). Two conceptions of happiness: Contrasts of personal expressiveness (eudaimonia) and hedonic enjoyment. *Journal of Personality and Social Psychology, 64*, 678–691. doi:10.1037/0022-3514.64.4.678

Waterman, A. S. (1998). *The Personally Expressive Activities Questionnaire: A manual.* Unpublished manuscript.

Waterman, A. S. (2004). Finding someone to be: Studies on the role of intrinsic motivation in identity formation. *Identity: An International Journal of Theory and Research, 4*, 209–228. doi:10.1207/s1532706xid0403_1

Waterman, A. S. (2005). When effort is enjoyed: Two studies of intrinsic motivation for personally salient activities. *Motivation and Emotion, 29*, 165–188. doi:10.1007/s11031-005-9440-4

Waterman, A. S. (2007). Doing well: The relationship of identity status to three conceptions of well-being. *Identity: An International Journal of Theory and Research, 7*, 289–307. doi:10.1080/15283480701600769

Waterman, A. S. (2011). Eudaimonic identity theory: Identity as self-discovery. In S. J. Schwartz, K. Luyckx, & V. L. Vignoles (Eds.), *Handbook of identity theory and research: Vol. 1. Structures and process* (pp. 357–379). New York, NY: Springer.

Waterman, A. S., Schwartz, S. J., & Conti, R. (2008). The implications of two conceptions of happiness (hedonic enjoyment and eudaimonia) for the understanding of intrinsic motivation. *Journal of Happiness Studies, 9*, 41–79. doi:10.1007/s10902-006-9020-7

Waterman, A. S., Schwartz, S. J., Goldbacher, E., Green, H., Miller, C., & Philip, S. (2003). Predicting the subjective experience of intrinsic motivation: The roles of self-determination, the balance of challenges and skills, and self-realization values. *Personality and Social Psychology Bulletin, 29*, 1447–1458. doi:10.1177/0146167203256907

Waterman, A. S., Schwartz, S. J., Hardy, S. A., Kim, S. U., Lee, R. M., Armenta, B. E., . . . Agocha, V. B. (2012). *Good choices, poor choices: Relationship between the quality of identity commitments and psychosocial functioning.* Manuscript in preparation.

Waterman, A. S., Schwartz, S. J., Zamboanga, B. L., Ravert, R. D., Williams, M. K., Agocha, V. B., . . . Donnellan, M. B. (2010). The Questionnaire for Eudaimonic Well-Being: Psychometric properties, demographic comparisons, and evidence of validity. *The Journal of Positive Psychology, 5*, 41–61. doi:10.1080/17439760903435208

6

INDIVIDUAL DAIMON, UNIVERSAL NEEDS, AND SUBJECTIVE WELL-BEING: HAPPINESS AS THE NATURAL CONSEQUENCE OF A LIFE WELL LIVED

KENNON M. SHELDON

In my research career I have focused on a wide variety of issues relevant to "the best within us," and thus I feel I have much to contribute to the conversation of this book and to the broader question of what eudaimonic functioning is. However, and perhaps surprisingly to some readers, I have been reluctant to use and appropriate the term *eudaimonic* in my work. My first task in this chapter is to explain why. This will allow me to also describe and justify the primary definition of *well-being* that I use, which the editor has asked the chapter authors to do at the beginning of their chapters. As will become apparent, my conception of happiness can be located in Waterman's category of "eudaimonia as happiness." However, by consider-ing the predictors of happiness, my conception also addresses two of the types of happiness theories discussed by Tiberius (Chapter 1, this volume), namely, desire fulfillment and nature fulfillment theories.

DOI: 10.1037/14092-007
The Best Within Us: Positive Psychology Perspectives on Eudaimonia, Alan S. Waterman (Editor)
Copyright © 2013 by the American Psychological Association. All rights reserved.

DEFINING WELL-BEING: THE CASE FOR
A NONEUDAIMONIC MEASURE

An important goal in my research program has been to use a single, relatively content-free measure of subjective well-being (SWB; Diener, 1984, 1994). The use of a single consistent SWB variable across different research programs allows for ready comparisons of different types of predictor in their effects on SWB and for the creation of studies in which different theories and predictors can be tested against each other directly. As is discussed in detail next, the use of a content-free SWB variable also allows us to avoid the potential pitfalls of confusing the predictors of happiness with the outcome of happiness.

Most of my research on the sources and causes of well-being (Sheldon, Cummins, & Khamble, 2010; Sheldon & Elliot, 1998; Sheldon, Gunz, & Schachtman, 2012; Sheldon & Houser-Marko, 2001; Sheldon & Kasser, 1998) has operationally defined SWB as the combination of high positive affect and low negative affect (as measured by the Positive Affect Negative Affect Schedule or PANAS; Watson, Tellegen, & Clark, 1988) and high life satisfaction (as measured by the Satisfaction With Life Scale or SWLS; Diener, Emmons, Larsen, & Griffin, 1985). In this I have followed the pioneering research of Diener and colleagues (Diener, 1984, 1994; Diener & Lucas, 1999) concerning the most basic facets of well-being. Positive affect, negative affect, and life satisfaction typically form a single factor in my data (with negative loadings for negative affect), and thus I aggregate them, although they can certainly be examined separately for many purposes.

According to this operational definition of well-being, a happy person is someone who feels a predominance of the positive moods of interested, strong, alert, inspired, active, proud, determined, excited, enthusiastic, and attentive, relative to the negative moods of scared, irritable, ashamed, nervous, distressed, upset, hostile, jittery, and afraid, and who also makes the global cognitive judgment that "my life is ideal" or "if I could live my life over, I would change almost nothing." Taken together, the three scales provide a broad measure of well-being that includes both biologically grounded (mood, emotion) and cognitively grounded (judgments, evaluations) information. Although this measure is based on subjective reports, such reports have been shown to have important objective effects on people's life outcomes and even life spans (Lyubomirsky, King, & Diener, 2005). The SWB measure is similar to what the philosopher Daniel Haybron (2008) recommended as a definition of *happiness*: that "to be happy is roughly for one's emotional condition to be broadly positive with only minor negatives, embodying a stance of psychic affirmation" (p. 182).

Again, I suggest that an important advantage of this SWB measure is that it is relatively content free. Although it references general emotional tone and abstract life satisfaction, it does not include any items concerning more specific categories of personal or interpersonal experiences, what I call *psychosocial qualities*. I believe that this may be necessary for several reasons. Most important, any measure of happiness that contains specific types of personal or interpersonal experience necessarily presupposes that those psychosocial qualities are part of "happiness itself." Once those particular qualities are rolled into the happiness measure, it is difficult getting them back out in order to test how essential they really are for happiness. Of course, positive affect, negative affect, and life satisfaction, the components of the SWB measure, are not completely "content free"; all words have content, and thus all happiness measures must refer to content. However, I believe that it is important to restrict such content as much as possible (while still producing a defensible measure), in order to avoid introducing conceptual material within the happiness measure that may not belong there. Researchers' intuitions about what happiness is may be mistaken or may be culturally or temporally bound.

For example, Kitayama and Na (2011) speculated that honor, religious purity, and hierarchical social order might be included within a broad eudaimonic conception of well-being. From this vantage point, feeling included within a hierarchical social order might be defined as part of happiness itself. In contrast, I believe that such experiences should be kept on the predictor side, with content-restricted SWB used as the outcome or criterion variable for validation purposes. Perhaps, contrary to Kitayama and Na's speculation, SWB is not positively influenced by feeling securely located within a hierarchical social order. If so, strong hierarchical structure might not be recommendable as a happiness-producing social order. Or perhaps feelings of hierarchical inclusion are indeed salubrious for happiness, but only if you are near the top part of the hierarchy, or perhaps such feelings are salubrious only within collectivist cultures and not within individualist cultures. These are interesting contextual and cultural moderator hypotheses that are more difficult to examine once the focal experience has been rolled into the outcome measure.

Of course, other researchers measure well-being and happiness differently. Indeed, an important contribution of Ryff and Keyes's (1995) seminal "Structure of Psychological Well-Being Revisited" article was to insist that content must be considered as a facet of well-being: A life truly well lived must succeed on other merits beside mere "positive feelings and satisfaction." These researchers provided a measure of six distinct facets of what they called *psychological well-being*: environmental mastery, positive relationships, autonomy, purpose, personal growth, and self-acceptance. Obviously, these are all important phenomena to consider, and Ryff and Keyes are to be commended for bringing them to the attention of well-being researchers. In the 15 years since Ryff and Keyes's article, other researchers have followed their lead in trying to delineate the basic psychosocial components of well-being, including Huppert and So (2009), who proposed three core features and six additional features of flourishing, and Seligman (2011), who proposed the PERMA (positive emotion, engagement, relationships, meaning, and achievement) model of well-being.

However, from the point of view of the SWB arguments outlined previously, there are three possible dangers with multifaceted measures of well-being: (a) By multiplying the number of outcomes, we multiply the number of phenomena to be explained and perhaps overlook more parsimonious phenomena or processes that could explain the whole set of outcomes at once; (b) as discussed previously, by rolling particular psychosocial contents "by definition" into the happiness measure, we run the risk of reifying unseen personal or cultural biases; and (c) by rolling particular psychosocial contents into the happiness measure by definition, we run the risk of accepting a quality as essential for happiness when its "essentialness" was never fully tested. Again, I suggest that all proposed components or predictors of happiness should be empirically tested as such, using a defensible common outcome such as SWB.

One argument against my preference for a single content-restricted happiness measure is that such a measure might not be able to distinguish a lower order, "crass" (hedonic) form of happiness from a higher order, "virtuous" (eudaimonic) form of happiness. The notion that there are two varieties of happiness goes back at least to Aristotle, who distinguished between the happiness of "slavish grazing animals" based on "pleasure" and "gratification" (see Introduction, this volume), and a higher order happiness based on virtue and the realization of one's daimon. The Aristotelian view thus draws a sharp contrast between mere "hedonic pleasure" (implying sloth, greed, and the like) and "eudaimonic virtue" (implying nobility, self-restraint, and the like).

Although it is true that many people fall prey to vices, addictions, and self-gratifying habits, which are maintained because they provide some kind of positive reinforcement but which are bad for people in the long run, I do not believe this fact requires that we expand our measure of happiness or adopt a content-bound measure of happiness. In this context, it is important to notice that none of the items in the SWB measure discussed previously refer to "lower" pleasures and gratifications. For example, the PANAS positive affect items refer to engagement, enthusiasm, pride, and energy—there is a flame burning brightly, with no hint of impurity. What we actually need to do is test the various "pleasures and gratifications" to see whether they predict content-free SWB. When we do such tests, we typically find that addicts, materialists, alcoholics, and people unable to delay gratification tend to be lower in SWB than people who are less extreme on these dimensions. Such findings show that Aristotle was correct: Too much preoccupation with pleasure and short-term gratification is indeed problematic. As we will see next, people are happier, according to the SWB measure, when they have richer varieties of experience; these cause the flame to burn more brightly.

Notably, Waterman (see Introduction, this volume) distinguishes between hedonic and eudaimonic activities, saying that both activities provide hedonic happiness, but only eudaimonic activities also bring eudaimonic happiness, which is what people desire most. Thus, eudaimonic and hedonic activities may be distinguished because the latter do not bring more fulgent forms of happiness. This view is quite similar to mine, but I am advocating that we have only one basic happiness measure and then test directly whether eudaimonic activities are indeed better for obtaining happiness (SWB) than are mere hedonic activities. If a single happiness measure can do the job, and if SWB can already distinguish between higher and lower quality activities, then why add additional, content-bound well-being measures?

The Organismic Perspective

My suggestion that SWB (content-free well-being) is a legitimate single indicator of happiness relies conceptually on an organismic perspective on human nature (Deci & Ryan, 2000; Piaget, 1971; Werner, 1957). *Organismic* approaches, such as evolving systems approaches (Ford & Lerner, 1992), try to understand the integrative and growth-oriented processes that naturally operate at deep levels of the personality. Unfortunately, organismic growth processes do not always hold sway—they may be inhibited or thwarted by nonsupportive contexts and also by people's own mistaken choices (Sheldon, 2004). True thriving depends on doing things that are truly good for us and our deeper organisms and not just on doing things that feel good in the moment. Again, the SWB measure apparently indexes such thriving: Addicts and excessive pleasure-seekers gradually lose the energy, engagement, and curiosity that are measured by the PANAS and gradually become less satisfied with their lives as measured by the SWLS.

What about reporting biases in the measurement of SWB? Of course these exist, because there are many reasons a person might be unable or unwilling to report his or her true state of mind. However, if anything, I believe there are more likely to be biases to endorse socially desirable eudaimonic-type qualities ("I feel purposeful, my life has meaning, I am generous") than there are to be biases to endorse the mood states and abstract satisfactions of the SWB measure. In other words, an excessive hedonist might not be willing to admit that his life has little purpose, but he might be willing to admit that he sometimes feels anxious or fearful or that he is not sure he is satisfied with his life as a whole.

Every new idea struggles for acceptance within its métier. One part of eudaimonia's strategy for acceptance within psychology has been through an insistence that the measurement of happiness be expanded. I would join that call only if what is being expanded is an understanding of the causes of happiness, not the number of different kinds of happiness. I believe my recommendation does not fly in the face of eudaimonist perspectives, but rather can lend greater credence to such perspectives because, as the later review of my own research shows, the predictors of SWB turn out to be exactly the kinds of things eudaimonists think are important. In an important sense, SWB is like a tasty soufflé that results when the right ingredients are brought together and combined in the right way. The soufflé is the result of a life worth living, a reward for the attempt to seek "the best in ourselves."

Three Universal Needs

What are the activities and experiences that people really need? Again, my view relies on an organismic perspective on human nature, which specifies that all humans share in common certain basic needs and propensities and that they will not thrive, no matter what their context or culture, unless these needs are met. In my research I have relied on the propositions of self-determination theory (SDT; Deci & Ryan, 1985, 2000; see also Chapter 3, this volume) concerning basic psychological needs. SDT is an organismic theory of motivation that says that all humans need experiences of autonomy, competence, and relatedness in order to grow, function, and develop to the maximum extent. These three needs are said to be *evolved* because those who sought these experiences, and succeeded in obtaining them, acquired selective advantages compared with those who did not (Deci & Ryan, 2000; Sheldon, 2011). In other words, people who wanted to master new skills, wanted to connect and cooperate with others, and wanted to be self-governing and self-regulating, are likely to have achieved higher fitness on a variety of fronts. And indeed, much research, including much cross-cultural research, now supports the notion that each of these three experiences uniquely predicts positive outcomes of many types, including SWB.

As one example of such research, Sheldon, Elliot, Kim, and Kasser (2001) compared 10 "candidate psychological needs" as predictors of SWB within "most satisfying events," trying to determine which experiences might really be needs. Participants wrote about the most satisfying event they had experienced in the recent past and then rated their SWB during the event and also rated the degree to which the 10 candidate experiences were present during the event. Sheldon et al. (2001) found, as predicted by SDT, that autonomy, competence, and relatedness were most strongly present in the event (i.e., they had the highest means) and also uniquely predicted (despite their higher ceiling) the level of SWB felt within the event, whereas the other candidate needs of popularity, money, meaning, security, health, and pleasure did not. This pattern of findings emerged in both U.S. and South Korean samples, supporting SDT's claim that autonomy, competence, and relatedness are universally important. Thus, the Sheldon et al. (2001) test was precisely the kind I have been recommending in this chapter: comparatively examining different psychosocial qualities as predictors of SWB to determine which experiences are actually most important. Notice that in the Sheldon et al. (2001) studies, the "hedonic" qualities (money, pleasure, popularity) did not pass the test, and the more eudaimonic qualities did. Again, this is what eudaimonic-type theories would predict.

At this point, readers might ask, what is the difference between SDT's three proposed needs that lead to happiness and other researchers' proposals concerning the multiple varieties of happiness? There are two important differences. First, SDT does not conceive of need satisfaction as happiness itself; instead, satisfied needs provide the nutrients so that the psychological system will function in a way that produces happiness, as well as a wide variety of other positive outcomes besides happiness. Second, even if one does not buy into SDT's need-based account, it is still important to test and compare various proposed producers of happiness to see which ones work, or work best. The SDT list of three basic needs has withstood such tests thus far, whereas some other theories addressing multiple components of well-being have not received such testing.

A General Process Model

On the basis of the theory and research previously described, my general approach to the "happiness question" has been to compare various theoretically derived positive psychological conditions and states as predictors of SWB to find out which ones really work. Once such relationships are identified, I then test whether these predictive associations are mediated by (or explained by) psychological need satisfaction (and they almost always are). According to this view, certain activities, goals, values, and identities are salubrious for happiness precisely because they help people to meet their basic psychological needs. People are unique, and they can do a nearly infinite variety of things, but despite this uniqueness, they are all constrained by the need to meet the evolved psychological needs that characterize our species. Thus, both individual choices and directions, and universal needs and human nature, must be considered in tandem to answer the happiness question. The general process model is represented as follows:

High "Quality" Goals/Behavior → Satisfaction of Universal Needs → SWB

RESEARCH SUPPORT

In the second section of this chapter, I describe in some detail my research based on this approach. Then, in the third section, I draw connections between the entire approach I have laid out and various elements of eudaimonist philosophy, showing that my basic approach may help resolve several perennial issues within that branch of philosophy. Finally, in the fourth section of the chapter, I consider some general implications for promoting positive psychological functioning within people.

The Self-Concordance Construct

Waterman (see Introduction, this volume) briefly describes my self-concordance model of optimal functioning, which I now cover in greater detail. The self-concordance model assumes that life is a projective test. Every day, we must make choices about what activities and goals to pursue—that is, how to invest our finite energies. Such choices are vital because pursuing goals is one of the primary ways that we can "bootstrap" ourselves into our own futures, arriving at the futures of our choice (Sheldon & Vansteenkiste, 2005). However, because we lack full information and insight regarding our own nature and personalities (Wilson, 2002), proper goal setting can be a difficult task, requiring considerable skill. Unfortunately, when people lack this skill, they can spend years or even decades pursuing the "wrong" goals for them, to their detriment.

What are the wrong goals? The self-concordance model defines these as goals taken in from the environment that do not represent a person's actual developmental trends; they have little benefit for the person, even if achieved, because they do not succeed in focusing the person's energies in growth-promoting directions. What are the "right" goals? The self-concordance model defines these as goals that accurately represent people's unique developing interests, values, and dispositions. All individuals, as entropy-reducing living systems, have innate growth trends and unique potentials. Such organismic potentials can be importantly forwarded by investing one's energy into goals that well represent those potentials. Again, however, the conscious self that selects and regulates goals may not have the knowledge to recognize these implicit potentials and growth trends or the resources to act on them even if they are recognized.

How do we measure whether a set of goals is self-concordant for a person? In my research I have relied on SDT's perceived locus of causality (PLOC) construct (Deci & Ryan, 2000). PLOC measures of motivation ask people, "Why do you do X?" in terms of four predominant reasons: external motivation ("because I have to, or because I will get some external reward; I wouldn't do it if I didn't have to"), introjected motivation ("because I'd feel guilty if I didn't"), identified motivation ("because I wholeheartedly value what this behavior represents") and intrinsic motivation ("because I enjoy doing this behavior"). According to SDT, these four motives are located on an internalization continuum that ranges (respectively) from not at all internalized, to partially internalized, to completely internalized, to automatically internalized. Truly self-determined behavior is behavior that has an internal PLOC—it is enacted mainly for identified and intrinsic reasons and not for external and introjected reasons (Deci & Ryan, 2000). That is, self-determined behavior feels caused by the self and its values and preferences, rather than by social pressures and obligations.

It is important to realize that this does not mean that people should never oblige others' expectations and values; rather, it means that when they do so, it is better if they can do it with a sense of internal endorsement than with a sense of being controlled. Before they are acted on, external duties, roles, and obligations should be internalized into the self (if possible). This can provide a check on the actual appropriateness of those externalities and prevent mindless conformity to ultimately irrelevant or even harmful externalities.

Prior to my arrival in Rochester as a postdoc in 1992, the PLOC measure was used only to measure why people do experimenter-specified behaviors (e.g., studying, going to church, cleaning one's room). My contribution was to apply the measure to people's open-ended personal goals. Surprisingly, given that I use an idiographic goal-assessment procedure in which participants free-list their own goals on a blank sheet of paper (Emmons, 1989), many people list goals that feel non-self-determined or non-self-concordant. In my work at Rochester I soon discovered that goal self-concordance was a strong predictor of SWB as well as many other positive outcomes, such as greater empathy and vitality (Sheldon & Kasser, 1995), academic performance (Sheldon & Houser-Marko, 2001), and role satisfaction (Sheldon & Elliot, 2000). On the basis of these findings, I suggested that the PLOC measure indeed indexes the "fit" of people's goals with their deeper potentialities and growth trends (Sheldon & Elliot, 2000; Sheldon & Kasser, 1995, 1998), allowing them to invest their motivational energy in personally beneficial ways.

Mediation of Idiographic Goal Effects by Universal Need Satisfaction

Subsequent research began to support the mediational hypothesis discussed previously—the idea that self-concordance predicts SWB because it promotes greater psychological need satisfaction (Sheldon & Elliot, 1999). The general self-concordance model is as follows: Those who manage to select self-concordant goals tap into stable sources of energy that promote sustained effort and achievement; such people try even harder than they expected (Sheldon & Elliot, 1998). Longitudinal goal achievement then interacts with self-concordance to predict accumulated need satisfaction over a period of time (Sheldon & Kasser, 1998). Finally, need satisfaction predicts increased SWB from the beginning to the end of that time (Sheldon & Elliot, 1999; Sheldon & Houser-Marko, 2001). To use an analogy: Pursuing self-concordant goals lets us obtain psychological nutrients (e.g., vitamins) essential to psychological health, just as certain positive dietary behaviors let us obtain essential nutrients for physical health. Stated in terms of the title of this chapter (individual daimon, universal needs, and SWB), self-generated goals provide opportunities to develop one's daimon, that is, one's unique potentialities. Self-concordant goals take best advantage of such opportunities. As a result, self-concordant strivers tend to acquire experiences that all humans need, which in turn tend to produce SWB. Thus, perhaps paradoxically, one may best fulfill one's universal human nature via the maximal expression of one's unique personal goals.

Self-Concordance as Deep Person/Goal Fit

Let us briefly consider a relevant measurement issue. Again, my assumption has been that the self-concordance measure indexes deep person/goal fit, that is, the contact of goals with one's daimon. Because asking people directly about such fit is unlikely to be fruitful ("Does this goal represent your true personality?"), I have used the PLOC measure as a stand-in. The assumption is that feelings of ownership and engagement in one's own goals (in contrast to feelings of pressure and control) are a reasonable index of person/goal fit. Recent data have provided a new type of support for the person/goal fit hypothesis. Sheldon and Cooper (2008) found that people higher in the motive disposition of need for achievement (as measured by both implicit and explicit techniques) rated randomly assigned achievement goals as more self-concordant compared with randomly assigned affiliation goals, with the same pattern holding for the need for affiliation and the rated self-concordance of assigned affiliative versus achievement goals. Sheldon and Schuler (2011) found similar interactions between motive dispositions (needs for achievement and affiliation) and assigned goals (achievement vs. relationship) to predict self-concordance in their data. These findings offer new support for the assumption that high-rated self-concordance (internal PLOC) indicates that one's goals better represent one's deeper personality.

Interestingly, Sheldon and Schuler (2011) found that motive dispositions did not predict listing a greater number of disposition-congruent goals in a free-listing task. This supports the notion that goal selection is a difficult self-perceptual skill; even people high in a particular motive disposition do not necessarily make the "right" goals choices for themselves. Still, when they are assigned the right goals, they are able to recognize such rightness via higher self-concordance ratings.

Other Research Applying the Same General Process Model

Although the self-concordance construct has occupied much of my research attention, I have also studied other eudaimonic-type constructs and issues (i.e., quality of behavior issues), showing many positive effects on SWB that are mediated by psychological need satisfaction. I briefly review these findings now. First, we can consider not just the reasons for pursuing goals (self-concordance) but also the content of goals. Kasser and Ryan (1993, 1996) distinguished between *intrinsic* goal contents (relationships, community, personal growth) and *extrinsic* goal contents (money, appearance, popularity). In numerous ways, they showed that people who prioritize intrinsic over extrinsic goal contents experience greater SWB and thrive to a greater extent (Sheldon & Kasser, 1998). Notice that the intrinsic contents correspond well with eudaimonic concerns, and the extrinsic contents correspond well with hedonic concerns; thus, once again, when eudaimonia and hedonia are tested as predictors of content-free SWB, hedonia loses. Importantly, Niemiec, Ryan, and Deci (2009) showed that goal content effects on SWB are mediated by autonomy, competence, and relatedness need satisfaction, again fitting the general process sequence described previously (individual striving of high quality type → satisfaction of universal needs → SWB).

More recently, I provided a new conceptual and operational definition of *life balance*. Moving away from problematic Likert-based approaches to assessing life balance ("Please rate how balanced your life feels"), Sheldon et al. (2010) assessed people's actual time-use profile and their ideal time-use profile across 10 life domains, showing that having a low computed discrepancy between these two profiles (subjective balance) predicted SWB. Sheldon et al. (2010) also studied people's pattern of apportionment of time across the 10 life domains, finding that a more equal apportionment of time use across the domains (objective balance) also predicted SWB. Thus the data suggest that a balanced life is one in which time is apportioned equitably across many different activities, in a way that is close to one's ideal time-use profile. Again fitting the general process sequence described previously, people can individually apportion their time in a nearly infinite variety of ways; however, certain key qualities of those profiles apparently better satisfy universal needs than others, producing SWB as an outcome. Those characteristics are, once again, the ones we might expect from a eudaimonist perspective—living a life that is balanced across multiple domains and that also expresses how one would ideally like to apportion one's time.

Another recent line of research has examined the issue of optimal self-presentation. Sheldon et al. (2012) introduced a conception of the "social character" that people live in and present to others, and assessed the Big Five traits of the character that people report playing in high-stakes social situations. They also assessed the Big Five traits of the "unguarded self," that is, the person one feels he or she is when he or she is in the comfortable presence of loved ones. Sheldon et al. (2012) showed that having a low discrepancy between these two trait profiles (independent of the particular trait scores composing the profiles) predicted SWB. In other words, those who can be nearly the same person in a self-presentational situation as they are in a nonpresentational situation appear to be happier, regardless of the particular traits involved. Once again, this effect was mediated by psychological need satisfaction, and thus this research shows in yet another way that certain forms or qualities of individuality produce SWB precisely because they help people meet the universal needs within human nature. Incidentally, this research also demonstrated what expressions such as "Just be yourself" or "Get in touch with yourself" really mean; namely, be the person you are when you are feeling comfortable with people you trust. Also, once again, this research supports eudaimonic notions by showing that authentic self-expression is preferable to playing a social character that is overly tailored to the approval of others.

CONNECTIONS WITH EUDAIMONIST PHILOSOPHY

Although I am no expert on eudaimonist philosophy, in this section I consider the relevance of my analysis of optimal functioning to important issues within this branch of philosophy. I rely heavily on the analyses provided by Waterman and Tiberius (Introduction and Chapter 1, respectively) in this volume.

One issue raised by Waterman and Tiberius concerns whether the theorist takes a de-ontological versus a consequentalist approach in conceptualizing eudaimonic well-being. Are some "ingredients" said to be important for well-being by rule or definition (deontological view), or should theorists say that it depends on the effects of those ingredients on the person (consequentalist view)? My own approach combines these two notions. Autonomy, competence, and relatedness are said to be "inherent goods" because of their presumed evolution by natural selection; getting these experiences is, according to SDT, good for SWB (Deci & Ryan, 2000). However, the way that we test this rule is with data illustrating the consequences of obtaining the three experiences. If these three experiences have the consequence of making nearly everybody happy, in all parts of the world, then their status as universal features of personality and inherent constraints on individuality becomes more supportable.

A related issue highlighted in both the Tiberius and Waterman chapters concerns the distinction between subjective eudaimonia (based on positive subjective experiences), objective eudaimonia or flourishing (based on theory-based notions of what objective life accomplishments evidence a life well lived), and a narrower view of objective eudaimonia based on the concept of the daimon and the question of whether people manage to realize their unique and objective potentialities (i.e., do they actualize their individual daimon?). The general process approach to understanding SWB that I have outlined in this chapter addresses all three of these issues by stating that people live distinct lives defined in part by the unique idiographic goals they pursue. If they are able to make self-appropriate, growth-relevant goal choices (i.e., they are able to follow their daimon), then they acquire certain experiences (autonomy, competence, and relatedness) said to be objectively needed by humans because of natural selection. These experiences are of course subjective, but when felt, they in turn promote both the subjective happiness (SWB) as well as the objective thriving (longevity, health) of people. Again, such data can be fed back to help support the claim that these are essential ingredients for human happiness; in this way, the deontologist's arguments can rest on more than mere philosophical reasoning. As the new experimental philosophers are discovering (Knobe & Nichols, 2008), by collecting data, philosophers can sometimes go a long way in resolving perennial controversies within their field.

In discussing the individual daimon in more detail, Waterman and Schwartz (Chapter 5, this volume) identified four aspects of self-realization: discovery of one's latent skills/talents, trying to develop and use them, choosing relevant purposes to do this, and finding opportunities within context to do this. I suggest that all of these are handled by self-concordance construct and research, which concerns the process of trying to select goals relevant to one's latent skills and talents and the subsequent process of trying to take action to achieve these goals within one's life. Again, my definition of eudaimonic activity makes use of both broad (flourishing) and narrow (self-realization) conceptions in that self-realizational striving (narrow) leads to the broad flourishing of evolved human nature (need satisfaction), including SWB (subjective happiness) as one important outcome of such flourishing.

I now consider a few further issues raised by Tiberius (Chapter 1, this volume). She begins by distinguishing between the ingredients (recipe) for happiness, the theory that explains why, and the evidence that this theory is better than other theories. I propose that the general process model I have outlined addresses all three issues: It specifies (based on SDT) the eudaimonic experiences (ingredients) that people need, offers an explanation based on evolutionary reasoning, and appears to be a good theory because it predicts what it should predict (i.e., in the "most satisfying event" studies discussed earlier, only SDT could predict the pattern of findings that resulted, in which autonomy, competence, and relatedness uniquely predicted SWB and other "candidate needs" did not).

Tiberius also calls for a general definition of well-being that does not presuppose a particular theory, just as I do (which is one reason I use the SWB measure). However, in my view she may make a mistake in saying that eudaimonic theories describe ingredients "that go beyond positive affect and life-satisfaction" (p. 20, this volume). If she means that eudaimonic theories (e.g., self-concordance model) specify ingredients for happiness that go beyond hedonic theories, I agree. However, if she means that positive affect and life satisfaction (and low negative affect) are insufficient as indicators of well-being, then I disagree, for the reasons already discussed. These three variables, combined, provide an admirable criterion for studying what produces happiness, in part because they are content free and do not presuppose a particular theory and in part because they really do discriminate between hedonic and eudaimonic activities. In a similar vein, Tiberius states that "psychologists who study subjective well-being . . . take the ingredients of well-being to be subjective, psychological states such as life satisfaction or positive affect" (p. 30). Again, I disagree; I am a psychologist who studies subjective well-being, but I take states of satisfaction and positive affect as the outcome to be predicted by the proper ingredients, not the proper ingredients themselves.

Tiberius also discusses Nozick's (1974) "experience machine" (a variant of Descartes' "evil genius" idea). What if people are getting everything they wanted, but it is all a programmed delusion? Surely, if they find this out, then they won't be happy after all. I suggest that the SDT perspective and the general process model outlined previously can handle this thought experiment. Somebody who finds out he is unknowingly enmeshed in a giant computer program is likely to feel controlled and manipulated (as did Neo in *The Matrix*) and likely to feel that realizing his "daimon" (and fulfilling his organismic potentials) will be compromised. Feeling like a pawn in somebody else's world, that person's autonomy need would no longer be met, and he would suffer. It is interesting to speculate whether people might be able to live fulfilling lives in a virtual reality, even knowing that is what it is. Perhaps they might, as evidenced by the tremendous popularity of online life-simulation games and the popularity of virtual networking technologies such as Facebook. However, whether such modalities can really offer the full richness of face-to-face experience is an open question.

Tiberius (Chapter 1, this volume) also discusses the distinction between *desire-fulfillment theories* of well-being, which say we are happy when we get what we desire, and *informed desire-fulfillment theories*, which say that the desires have to be the right desires, presumably based on full information about what will produce thriving. The self-concordance model (Sheldon & Elliot, 1999) says something very similar: The goals have to be the right goals. However, the self-concordance model also says that we can never have full information because we cannot fully know our own potentialities. Still, we have to choose anyway (thus, the model takes an existentialist perspective as well as an organismic perspective). Personal growth is in part about learning who we are and what we are like, that is, what goals and activities will be most satisfying and self-realizational for us. Consider a premedical student who got straight As her first 3 years in college but was unhappy. In her senior year she finally changes her major to dance, becoming happier as a result. She has moved from fulfilling initial inadequate desires to fulfilling more informed desires by reinvesting her energy into goal choices that better match her own intrinsic nature. In so doing, she has adopted a model for seeking her own happiness that is "nature fulfilling" (Tiberius, Chapter 1, this volume) in both a personal sense and a universal sense—a model that satisfies her basic organismic needs as well as allowing her to express her unique personal nature.

What about a psychopath, who chooses selfish and destructive goals to pursue? In a sense, such goals are concordant with the person's twisted personality. In my view, such people do not get their psychological needs met, and thus their SWB suffers (likely a long-entrenched developmental pattern; Ryan, Kuhl, & Deci, 1997). One point of therapy is to help disordered individuals to regain contact with their "original" nature and potentialities, so that they can get back on a positive growth track. From this perspective, when individuality develops in ways that do not meet people's needs, this means that an earlier or better mode of individuality needs to be found, not that people should try to further develop the distorted individuality they have ended up with. The psychopath should not try to become "the best psychopath possible" as a means of fulfilling his daimon; rather, he should backtrack, to regain the daimon he has lost.

IMPLICATIONS FOR POSITIVE PSYCHOLOGICAL FUNCTIONING: AN EXAMPLE

When Tim Kasser and I were doing our first work on personality integration at Rochester in the early 1990s (Sheldon & Kasser, 1995), we tried to think of people who exemplified the personality characteristics we were finding to be important in our research. Jokingly we referred to "Hillary" as Hillary Clinton was just coming onto the national scene at that time, an evident powerhouse of feminine accomplishment with a seemingly balanced life and perspective. As of this writing, I am still willing to use Ms. Clinton, our secretary of state, as an example! According to the research and theory previously discussed, an integrated, *eudaimonically functioning* person is one who strives to fulfill values and ideals that she feels are deeply important. Hillary fits this bill, and seemingly, she is also able to enjoy most of what she does (e.g., she has self-concordant motivation). In fact, she does exceptionally well in the world, and probably the recognition of others secretly pleases her; however, she keeps her head on straight because she knows that, ultimately, it is not about her. Although her close relationships have certainly been through crises, she has emerged on the other side of those crises with the relationships intact and perhaps even stronger than before. She is as happy as she can imagine being, as happy as she deserves to be. Yet, her happiness is not what her life is about; instead, happiness is the "soufflé," the ultimate reward for a life well lived (Hinckley, 2007).

How can we nourish and support more "Hillarys," that is, people who actualize their potentials while making contributions at the highest levels of society? The research and theoretical perspective outlined previously has several implications. First, help people to internalize the motivations they find in the social surround, so that their behavior becomes more persistent, creative, and effective. According to SDT's organismic perspective, this involves supporting people's autonomy and self-organizational capacities to the greatest extent possible; when this is done, people naturally take in the important values of the surround. But also, according to the self-concordance perspective, it is important to help people develop the skill of self-insight, so that they can better perceive and act on their own developmental potentials. At times such self-insight may lead people to reject what is being promoted by the environment (i.e., the premedical student who defied her father's preferences to become a dancer). Although this can be problematic and uncomfortable for authorities, people's right to make personal choices must be supported—not only because this is one of the most important Western democratic ideals but also because such choices can ultimately lead to enrichment of both individuals and their societies.

Another type of policy implication derivable from the research reviewed in this chapter involves the purported psychological needs (Deci & Ryan, 2000). To the extent possible, social environments should be designed to enable people to move toward greater effectance and mastery (competence), with a sense of being the agent of their own development (autonomy), and with a sense of remaining connected with important others (relatedness). Just as a plant flourishes when it receives optimal levels of the nutrients it requires, people should flourish when they receive support of the basic psychological needs (Ryan, 1995). Programs, interventions, or curricula that do not provide, or that thwart, these needs are unlikely to be successful.

CONCLUSION

In this chapter, I have focused on SWB as an outcome that results naturally from living in a way that expresses our developing potentials, in the process meeting our own core psychological needs. The way that we know which activities and experiences are indeed most fulfilling is that they produce SWB—because true SWB cannot be made from anything but the right ingredients.

REFERENCES

Deci, E. L., & Ryan, R. M. (1985). *Intrinsic motivation and self-determination in human behavior*. New York, NY: Plenum Press.

Deci, E. L., & Ryan, R. M. (2000). The "what" and "why" of goal pursuits: Human needs and the self-determination of behavior. *Psychological Inquiry, 11*, 227–268. doi:10.1207/S15327965PLI1104_01

Diener, E. (1984). Subjective well-being. *Psychological Bulletin, 95*, 542–575. doi:10.1037/0033-2909.95.3.542

Diener, E. (1994). Assessing subjective well-being: Progress and opportunities. *Social Indicators Research, 31*, 103–157. doi:10.1007/BF01207052

Diener, E., Emmons, R., Larsen, R., & Griffin, S. (1985). The Satisfaction With Life Scale. *Journal of Personality Assessment, 49*, 71–75.

Diener, E., & Lucas, R. E. (1999). Personality and subjective well-being. In D. Kahneman, E. Diener, & N. Schwartz (Eds.), *Well-being: The foundations of hedonic psychology* (pp. 213–229). New York, NY: Russell Sage.

Emmons, R. A. (1989). The personal strivings approach to personality. In L. A. Pervin (Ed.), *Goal concepts in personality and social psychology* (pp. 87–126). Hillsdale, NJ: Erlbaum.

Ford, D. H., & Lerner, R. M. (1992). *Developmental systems theory: An integrative approach*. Newbury Park, CA: Sage.

Haybron, D. (2008). *The pursuit of unhappiness*. Oxford, England: Oxford University Press.

Hinckley, D. (2007, October 25). Hillary Clinton looks to her future on her 60th birthday. *New York Daily News*. Retrieved from http://www.nydailynews.com/news/hillary-clinton-future-60th-birthday-article-1.227960

Huppert, F. A., & So, T. T. C. (2009, July). *What percentage of people in Europe are flourishing and what characterizes them?* Paper prepared for the OECD/ISQOLS meeting in Florence, Italy. Cambridge, England: Well-Being Institute, University of Cambridge. Retrieved from http://www.isqols2009.istitutodeglinnocenti.it/Content_en/Huppert.pdf

Kasser, T., & Ryan, R. M. (1993). A dark side of the American dream: Correlates of financial success as a central life aspiration. *Journal of Personality and Social Psychology, 65*, 410–422. doi:10.1037/0022-3514.65.2.410

Kasser, T., & Ryan, R. M. (1996). Further examining the American dream: Differential correlates of intrinsic and extrinsic goals. *Personality and Social Psychology Bulletin, 22*, 280–287. doi:10.1177/0146167296223006

Kitayama, S., & Na, J. (2011). Need, level, and culture: Comments on Sheldon et al. 2011. *Psychological Inquiry, 22*, 26–31. doi:10.1080/1047840X.2011.547984

Knobe, J., & Nichols, S. (Eds.). (2008). *Experimental philosophy*. New York, NY: Oxford University Press.

Lyubomirsky, S., King, L. A., & Diener, E. (2005). The benefits of frequent positive affect: Does happiness lead to success? *Psychological Bulletin, 131*, 803–855. doi:10.1037/0033-2909.131.6.803

Niemiec, C. P., Ryan, R. M., & Deci, E. L. (2009). The path taken: Consequences of attaining intrinsic and extrinsic aspirations in post-college life. *Journal of Research in Personality, 43*, 291–306. doi:10.1016/j.jrp.2008.09.001

Nozick, R. (1974). *Anarchy, state, and utopia*. New York, NY: Basic Books.

Ntoumanis, N., & Standage, M. (2009). Morality in sport: A self-determination theory perspective. *Journal of Applied Sport Psychology, 21*, 365–380. doi:10.1080/10413200903036040

Piaget, J. (1971). *Biology and knowledge: An essay on the relations between organic regulations and cognitive processes*. Chicago, IL: University of Chicago Press.

Ryan, R. M. (1995). Psychological needs and the facilitation of integrative processes. *Journal of Personality, 63*, 397–427.

Ryan, R. M., Kuhl, J., & Deci, E. (1997). Nature and autonomy: An organizational view of social and neurobiological aspects of self-regulation in behavior and development. *Development and Psychopathology, 9*, 701–728. doi:10.1017/S0954579497001405

Ryff, C. D., & Keyes, C. L. M. (1995). The structure of psychological well-being revisited. *Journal of Personality and Social Psychology, 69*, 719–727. doi:10.1037/0022-3514.69.4.719

Seligman, M. E. P. (2011). *Flourish: A visionary new understanding of happiness and well-being*. New York, NY: Free Press.

Sheldon, K. M. (2004). *Optimal human being: An integrated multi-level perspective*. Mahwah, NJ: Erlbaum.

Sheldon, K. M. (2011). Integrating behavioral-motive and experiential-requirement perspectives on psychological needs: A two-process perspective. *Psychological Review, 118*, 552–569.

Sheldon, K. M., & Cooper, M. L. (2008). Goal striving within agentic and communal roles: Functionally independent pathways to enhanced well-being. *Journal of Personality, 76*, 415–448. doi:10.1111/j.1467-6494.2008.00491.x

Sheldon, K. M., Cummins, R., & Khamble, S. (2010). Life-balance and well-being: Testing a two-pronged conceptual and measurement approach. *Journal of Personality, 78*, 1093–1134.

Sheldon, K. M., & Elliot, A. J. (1998). Not all personal goals are personal: Comparing autonomous and controlled reasons as predictors of effort and attainment. *Personality and Social Psychology Bulletin, 24*, 546–557. doi:10.1177/0146167298245010

Sheldon, K. M., & Elliot, A. J. (1999). Goal striving, need-satisfaction, and longitudinal well-being: The self-concordance model. *Journal of Personality and Social Psychology, 76*, 482–497. doi:10.1037/0022-3514.76.3.482

Sheldon, K. M., & Elliot, A. J. (2000). Personal goals in social roles: Divergences and convergences across roles and levels of analysis. *Journal of Personality, 68*, 51–84. doi:10.1111/1467-6494.00091

Sheldon, K. M., Elliot, A. J., Kim, Y., & Kasser, T. (2001). What's satisfying about satisfying events? Comparing ten candidate psychological needs. *Journal of Personality and Social Psychology, 80*, 325–339. doi:10.1037/0022-3514.80.2.325

Sheldon, K. M., Gunz, A., & Schachtman, T. (2012). What does it mean to be in touch with oneself? Testing a social character model of self-congruence. *Self and Identity, 11*, 51–70.

Sheldon, K. M., & Houser-Marko, L. (2001). Self-concordance, goal-attainment, and the pursuit of happiness: Can there be an upward spiral? *Journal of Personality and Social Psychology, 80*, 152–165. doi:10.1037/0022-3514.80.1.152

Sheldon, K. M., & Kasser, T. (1995). Coherence and congruence: Two aspects of personality integration. *Journal of Personality and Social Psychology, 68*, 531–543. doi:10.1037/0022-3514.68.3.531

Sheldon, K. M., & Kasser, T. (1998). Pursuing personal goals: Skills enable progress, but not all progress is beneficial. *Personality and Social Psychology Bulletin, 24*, 1319–1331. doi:10.1177/01461672982412006

Sheldon, K. M., & Schuler, J. (2011). Needing, wanting, and having: Integrating motive disposition theory and self-determination theory. *Journal of Personality and Social Psychology, 101*, 1106–1123. doi:10.1037/a0024952

Sheldon, K. M., & Vansteenkiste, M. (2005). Personal goals and time-travel: How are future places visited, and is it worth it? In A. Strathman & J. Joireman (Eds.), *Understanding behavior in the context of time: Theory, research, and application* (pp. 143–163). Mahwah, NJ: Erlbaum.

Watson, D., Tellegen, A., & Clark, L. (1988). Development and validation of brief measures of positive and negative affect: The PANAS scales. *Journal of Personality and Social Psychology, 54*, 1063–1070. doi:10.1037/0022-3514.54.6.1063

Werner, H. (1957). The concept of development from a comparative and organismic point of view. In D. Harris (Ed.), *The concept of development* (pp. 125–147). Minneapolis, MN: University of Minnesota Press.

Wilson, T. (2002). *Strangers to ourselves: Discovering the adaptive unconscious.* Cambridge, MA: Harvard University Press.

7

PURSUING EUDAIMONIA VERSUS HEDONIA: DISTINCTIONS, SIMILARITIES, AND RELATIONSHIPS

VERONIKA HUTA

This chapter compares eudaimonic motives and hedonic motives in terms of their well-being correlates and consequences, the personality characteristics associated with them, and the behavior of one's parents. A key conclusion is that we need to pursue both eudaimonia and hedonia to achieve the greatest and most well-rounded personal well-being. This is true for several reasons: Eudaimonia and hedonia lead to somewhat different forms of well-being, so that only people with both pursuits have the more comprehensive range of well-being benefits; people who pursue both eudaimonia and hedonia have higher degrees of certain forms of well-being than people with only one of these pursuits; and eudaimonic pursuits may be better at promoting well-being at a later point in time, whereas hedonic pursuits may be better at promoting well-being in the immediate moment, so that eudaimonic and hedonic pursuits may fill different niches over time. Although both eudaimonia and hedonia relate to personal well-being, eudaimonia pursuits appear to contribute more than hedonia pursuits to the well-being of other people.

DOI: 10.1037/14092-008
The Best Within Us: Positive Psychology Perspectives on Eudaimonia, Alan S. Waterman (Editor)
Copyright © 2013 by the American Psychological Association. All rights reserved.

This chapter also provides an initial outline of the differing strengths, personalities, and backgrounds of people who pursue eudaimonia versus hedonia.

HOW EUDAIMONIA AND HEDONIA ARE DEFINED HERE

Different eudaimonia scholars have addressed the topic at different levels of analysis; some have studied eudaimonia as a way of behaving (e.g., a subjective motive, or a more objective set of behaviors), whereas others have studied it as a form of well-being (e.g., a subjective feeling, or a more objective condition or accomplishment like environmental mastery or positive relations with others), or as a mixture of a way of behaving and a form of well-being. More detailed discussions of these issues appear in Huta (in press); Huta and Ryan (2010); and Ryan, Huta, and Deci (2008).

I define both eudaimonia and hedonia as personal motives for activities and thus as ways of behaving that are defined by subjective processes rather than objectively observable criteria. In my view, it is the choices a person makes, and particularly the reasons and aims underlying those choices (i.e., motives), that define a person's eudaimonia and hedonia. What we are responsible for, and what we can control, are our motives and behaviors. It is difficult to change our well-being directly—the most direct point of intervention for bettering our lives is our chosen motives and behaviors, which may in turn produce well-being.

In my work, eudaimonia is specifically defined as seeking to use and develop the best in oneself, in ways that are congruent with one's values and true self. This definition includes both the actualization of the *personal daimon*, also referred to as *individual nature fulfillment*, and *universal nature fulfillment*, such that a desire for excellence and authenticity is assumed to be one of the fundamental tendencies of human nature (along with various other and sometimes competing tendencies). In terms of the distinctions made in the Introduction to this volume among subjective well-being, psychological well-being, and eudaimonic well-being, this conception is most aligned with—though not identical to—the narrow conception of eudaimonic well-being as self-realization. Hedonia is defined as seeking pleasure, enjoyment, and comfort (whether or not this aim is achieved). Eudaimonia and hedonia are assessed as two unipolar dimensions, at either the trait level to characterize a whole person or the state level to characterize a momentary activity or a relatively short period of time. Though much of my research has focused on the well-being correlates and consequences of pursuing eudaimonia, I see eudaimonia as an end in itself rather than a means to some personal benefit. The definition and operationalization of eudaimonia given here is largely but not entirely tied to Aristotle (2001); for example, unlike Aristotle, it permits use of the term *eudaimonia* at the state level, and it does not include objective criteria or good fortune.

HEDONIC AND EUDAIMONIC MOTIVES FOR ACTIVITIES SCALE

The Hedonic and Eudaimonic Motives for Activities (HEMA) Scale (Huta & Ryan, 2010) is the instrument that I developed to study this domain. The instructions for the trait version read as follows: "To what degree do you typically approach your activities with each of the following intentions, whether or not you actually achieve your aim?" The instructions for the state version can be adapted as needed, for example: "To what degree did you approach your [current activity / activities today / activities during the past week] with each of the following intentions, whether or not you actually achieved your aim?" Participants give ratings on various eudaimonic and hedonic motives, which are intermixed. The four eudaimonic motives are "Seeking to pursue excellence or a personal ideal?" "Seeking to use the best in yourself?" "Seeking to develop a skill, learn, or gain insight into something?" and "Seeking to do what you believe in?" The five hedonic motives are "Seeking enjoyment?" "Seeking pleasure?" "Seeking fun?" "Seeking relaxation?" and "Seeking to take it easy?" The items are rated from 1 (*not at all*) to 7 (*very much*). To date, the HEMA has been translated into Polish (Kaczmarek et al., 2011) and Croatian (Anic, 2011), and publications on these versions are forthcoming.

The HEMA (English version) has demonstrated good psychometric properties. The internal consistencies of the eudaimonia and hedonia scales are high (Cronbach αs > .80), and principal components analyses in most studies of the HEMA show precisely two clean factors (though a few studies have suggested a lower order difference between the pursuit of pleasure and the pursuit of relaxation on the hedonia scale, an interesting finding to be explored in future work). Two studies (Studies 3 and 4, as described later) examined relationships between the HEMA and the Orientations to Happiness (OH) scale by Peterson, Park, and Seligman (2005), the only other measure assessing both eudaimonia and hedonia as ways of behaving. There was good convergent and discriminant validity: The mean correlation across the two studies between HEMA eudaimonia and OH eudaimonia was .34 ($p < .05$ in both studies), and between HEMA hedonia and OH hedonia it was .53 ($p < .05$ in both studies); in contrast, the mean correlation between HEMA eudaimonia and OH hedonia was .01, and between HEMA hedonia and OH eudaimonia it was .02. Furthermore, a study currently being prepared for publication (Study 6, as described later) shows that self-reports of eudaimonia are corroborated by friends and family: A person's self-reported eudaimonia score on the HEMA correlates .40 ($p < .01$) with their informant-rated eudaimonia score on the HEMA. Self-reported hedonia correlates .21 ($p < .05$) with informant-rated hedonia. In contrast, serving as discriminant validity, self-reported eudaimonia correlates .10 ($p > .05$) with informant-rated hedonia, and self-reported hedonia correlates .05 ($p > .05$) with informant-rated eudaimonia. The personality correlates of eudaimonia versus hedonia reported next are also consistent with the nature of each pursuit and contribute further evidence of validity.

SOURCES AND PRESENTATION OF THE FINDINGS

The results in this chapter come from a total of nine studies conducted on undergraduates at one of two North American universities. The References section indicates the publication containing each study, labeled Study 1 through Study 9. On occasion, results are added in this chapter that were not included in the published articles. In each table, the mean correlation across studies is provided, along with the median correlation in parentheses if there were three or more studies. Correlations in bold are those that would reach statistical significance at the smallest sample size of the studies summarized (sample sizes for most studies ranged from 102 to 2,094, except for Study 9, in which $n = 34$). If a correlation for one pursuit (eudaimonia or hedonia) is underlined, this indicates that the correlation was significantly greater (at $p < .05$) than the correlation for the other pursuit in at least half of the studies summarized.

RELATIONSHIP BETWEEN EUDAIMONIA AND HEDONIA

One of the most interesting findings, as summarized in Table 7.1, is that the relationship between eudaimonia and hedonia at the trait level differs considerably from the relationship at the state level. Across the eight trait-level data sets, the mean correlation between a person's overall degree of eudaimonia and their overall degree of hedonia is positive .28 ($p < .05$ in all data sets), with a median of .32. At a given moment, however, the degree to which a momentary activity is eudaimonic correlates negatively with the degree to which the activity is hedonic, with a value of $-.28$, $p < .05$ (as found in Study 3, in which participants completed seven experience-sampling forms a day for 7 consecutive days). Studies in which the within-person level is assessed over longer periods show correlations intermediate between these two extremes: When reports summarize a period of on average 90 minutes, the correlation is $-.04$, $p > .05$ (Study 4, in which participants completed a daily report for 10 consecutive days),

TABLE 7.1
How One's Eudaimonia and Hedonia Relate to One's Well-Being

	Trait level			State level		
	Studies	Eudaimonia	Hedonia	Studies	Eudaimonia	Hedonia
Hedonia	1, 2, 3, 4, 5, 6, 7, 8	.28 (.32)		3, 4, 9	−.04 (−.04)	
More related to eudaimonia						
Meaning	1, 2, 3, 4, 5, 6, 7, 8	**.44 (.44)**	.22 (.25)	3, 4, 9	**.48 (.44)**	.10 (.13)
Self-connectedness	1, 2, 3, 4, 5, 6	**.36 (.39)**	.15 (.15)	3, 4, 9	**.44 (.44)**	.19 (.22)
Elevating experience	1, 2, 3, 4, 5, 6, 7, 8	**.44 (.44)**	.14 (.15)	3, 4, 9	**.35 (.42)**	**.23 (.22)**
More related to hedonia						
Carefreeness	1, 2, 3, 4	.04 (.01)	**.28 (.32)**	3, 4, 9	.06 (.06)	**.58 (.58)**
Positive affect	1, 2, 3, 4, 5, 6	.26 (.24)	**.37 (.36)**	3, 4, 9	.15 (.11)	**.63 (.62)**
Negative affect	1, 2, 3, 4, 5, 6	−.03 (−.03)	−.10 (−.12)	3, 4, 9	−.05 (.03)	**−.36 (−.35)**
Equally related to eudaimonia and hedonia						
Life satisfaction	1, 2, 3, 4, 5, 6, 8	.19 (.20)	.19 (.22)			
Vitality	1, 2, 3, 4, 6, 8	.31 (.32)	.26 (.28)	4, 9	**.30 (.23)**	**.40 (.42)**
Self-esteem	1, 2, 3, 4, 5, 6	.19 (.20)	.18 (.17)		.33	.32

Note. In each cell, the mean correlation across studies is provided, along with the median correlation in parentheses if there were three or more studies. Correlations in **bold** would reach significance at the smallest sample size of the studies summarized (sample sizes ranged from 102 to 2,094, except for Study 9, in which $n = 34$). If a correlation for one pursuit (eudaimonia or hedonia) is underlined, the correlation was significantly greater than the correlation for the other pursuit in at least half the studies summarized.

and when reports summarize an entire week, the correlation is .20, $p >$ .05 (Study 9, in which participants completed a weekly diary for 7 consecutive weeks). Thus, at a given moment, a person tends to be oriented toward either eudaimonic or hedonic pursuits but not often both, whereas a person who generally engages in a lot of eudaimonic activity also tends to engage in a lot of hedonic activity.

HOW EUDAIMONIC VERSUS HEDONIC MOTIVATION RELATES TO PERSONAL WELL-BEING

Let us now examine how eudaimonic and hedonic motives relate to various indices of personal well-being. I hypothesize that they serve somewhat different functions in life, filling somewhat different niches in a person's overall well-being. In other words, I believe that both eudaimonic and hedonic pursuits are important.

Below are the specific hypotheses made and the data gathered. (For more details on the hypotheses and findings from four of the studies, see Huta & Ryan, 2010.) In large part, the predictions about the unique well-being niches of eudaimonia and hedonia have been supported, though some have been proven wrong, and the picture regarding some others has proven to be more nuanced, especially when taking into account the difference between trait and state levels of analysis.

Functions of Eudaimonia

Meaning

First and foremost, eudaimonia is likely to be important for building a sense of meaning. This prediction was made because eudaimonia involves striving to align one's actions with one's values and true self, and because the pursuit of excellence often implies concerns beyond the immediate moment or situation. The focus here was on the feeling of meaning that can result from certain ways of living, as distinct from meaning as a way of living (i.e., having a purpose and having a meaning framework for understanding the events of the world). To measure meaning as a feeling at either the trait level or state level, a 13-item measure was developed (Huta & Ryan, 2010). It assesses the degree to which one's activity or activities and experience(s) (a) have had personal significance and really resonated with the individual ("meaningful," "full of significance," "making a lot of sense to me," "I could see how they all added up"), (b) were felt to be valuable ("valuable," "precious," "something I could treasure," "dear to me"), and (c) were believed to have implications for many aspects of the self and the surrounding world ("playing an important role in some broader picture," "I could see where they fit into the bigger picture," "they contributed to various aspects of myself," "they contributed to my community and broader world"). Meaning is a notoriously slippery concept to define, but these are the three facets that make up my current understanding of the feeling of meaning. The 12 items load onto a single factor that is distinct from the other well-being concepts appearing in Table 7.1, and the alpha exceeds .80. Note that in some studies (2, 3, 4, 8, and 9), a shortened version was used, consisting only of "meaningful" and "valuable," or only "meaningful," "full of significance," "valuable," and "precious," with alphas exceeding .75.

As shown in Table 7.1, the prediction regarding meaning was clearly supported. At both the trait level and state level, meaning was significantly more related to the pursuit of eudaimonia than to the pursuit of hedonia.

Meaning is an extremely important aspect of well-being. Certainly, the three components of subjective well-being (Diener, Suh, Lucas, & Smith, 1999)—positive affect, negative affect, and life satisfaction—should be present as part of any well-being assessment. But at the very least, meaning should be added to this list, making a Big Four of well-being assessment. The concept of meaning captures not only affect valence and intensity but also degree of connectedness with different aspects of the self and the world and a feeling that one's experiences and activities not only feel good but matter. I have gone into some detail here on meaning as a feeling because the expansion of well-being assessment has been a major thrust of my research. If the relative benefits of eudaimonia and hedonia are to be assessed adequately, well-being needs to be measured more comprehensively than is usually the case.

Elevating Experience

Another aspect of well-being expected to relate especially to eudaimonia was elevating experience, a combination of three facets that reflect the much neglected "higher" range of well-being: (a) inspiration and moral elevation (Haidt 2000; Thrash & Elliot, 2003), (b) awe (Keltner & Haidt, 2003), and (c) transcendence or sense of connection with a greater whole (Csikszentmihalyi, 1990). Eudaimonia was expected to foster these states because it involves the pursuit of excellence and growth, which should sensitize people to states that elevate them to higher levels of functioning and that stretch them beyond their usual boundaries. No scale was available to measure all three aspects of elevating experience, so a scale was developed to assess them at either the trait or state level (Huta & Ryan, 2010), drawing on the descriptions given by the researchers cited previously. Inspiration and moral elevation were assessed with "inspired," "morally elevated," "enriched," "spiritually uplifted"; awe was assessed with "in awe," "deeply appreciating," "emotionally moved," "in wonder," "profoundly touched by experiences"; and transcendence was assessed with "connected with a greater whole," "part of something greater than myself," "part of some greater entity," and "like I was in the presence of something grand." In most studies, all three concepts cohered into a single factor that was distinct from the other well-being concepts in Table 7.1 (though transcendence occasionally formed a separate factor from a combination of inspiration and awe). The items are therefore used as a single 13-item scale whose alpha exceeds .80. In some studies (2, 3, and 4), a five-item version was used, consisting of "in awe," "deeply appreciating," "morally elevated," "inspired," and "part of something greater than myself," with alpha exceeding .76, or an eight-item version consisting of "in awe," "deeply appreciating," "emotionally move," "morally elevated," "inspired," "enriched," "connected with a greater whole," and "part of something greater than myself," with alpha exceeding .80.

Table 7.1 shows that elevating experience did relate more to eudaimonia than to hedonia at the trait level—that is, people who were generally eudaimonic were also generally likely to experience inspiration, awe, and transcendence. At the state level, elevating experience related to eudaimonia, but no more so than it did to hedonia. Thus, specific activities intended to be enjoyable or relaxing may also increase the likelihood of elevating experience, though habitual pursuit of enjoyment and relaxation does not raise one's general receptivity to this experience.

Of the wide range of variables that might be considered for more frequent inclusion in assessments of well-being, elevating experience may prove to be among the more important ones (as might vitality, which is discussed later). Elevating experiences have been described as particularly transformative (Csikszentmihalyi, 1990; Haidt, 2000; Keltner & Haidt, 2003; Maslow, 1970) and may therefore prove to be among the forms of positive affect that most powerfully promote the broaden-and-build benefits discussed by Fredrickson (2001).

Self-Connectedness

The third aspect of well-being predicted to relate more to eudaimonia than to hedonia was self-connectedness. A five-item scale was created to assess the concept at either the trait level or state level (Huta, 2012) as follows: "connected with myself," "feeling that I know who I am," "having a clear sense of my values," "aware of how I feel," and "aware of what matters to me." The items form a single factor distinct from the other well-being concepts in Table 7.1, and the concept's alpha exceeds .80. Self-connectedness is a concept associated with identity achievement, which Waterman (2007) has shown to relate to the eudaimonic concepts of personal expressiveness and self-realization values; it is part of the congruence component of autonomy in self-determination theory (Weinstein, Przybylski, & Ryan, 2011), and it is prominent in Eastern conceptions of well-being, as well as the ancient Greek aphorism "Know thyself." Self-connectedness was expected to be among the benefits of eudaimonia because eudaimonia involves efforts to identify one's true self and to align one's actions with it.

From Table 7.1, it is clear that the prediction was supported—at both the trait level and the state level, self-connectedness was significantly more related to eudaimonia than to hedonia.

Functions of Hedonia

Positive Affect and Negative Affect

Clearly, the special niche of hedonic pursuits would be the production of pleasure—that is, high positive affect and relief from negative affect. More generally, we have argued that a major function of hedonia is emotional self-regulation, that is, restoring or enhancing one's affect (Huta & Ryan, 2010). Throughout the studies, positive affect and negative affect were assessed using the scales developed by Diener and Emmons (1984).

Table 7.1 shows that hedonia was the pursuit more linked to high positive affect and low negative affect at the state level, that is, at the time of the pursuit or over a relatively short time. The habitual pursuit of pleasure and comfort was also positively linked to high positive affect, but no more so than the habitual pursuit of excellence, and habitual hedonia did not reduce a person's likelihood of negative affect. Together, these findings suggest that the greatest affective benefits of hedonia occur at the momentary or short-term level.

Carefreeness

In addition to high positive affect and low negative affect, it was predicted that hedonia is particularly important for feeling carefree. This concept includes not only an affective component but also a cognitive component representing a release from concerns. Carefreeness was the strongest and most direct benefit expected to arise from hedonia, especially in a life that also includes intense eudaimonic commitments, because it provides respite and time to recharge. The six-item scale created to measure the concept consists of "carefree," "free of concerns," "detached from my troubles," "easygoing," lighthearted," and "happy-go-lucky," with alpha exceeding .80 (Huta & Ryan, 2010). The items load onto a single factor distinct from the other well-being concepts in the top eight of Table 7.1. In the majority of studies (2, 3, and 4), though, a shorter scale was used, consisting of "carefree" and "free of concerns," or alternatively, "carefree," "free of concerns," and "detached from my troubles." Alpha in these studies ranged only from .68 to .69, indicating that the full scale is preferable.

Table 7.1 provides good evidence for the special link of carefreeness with hedonia; it was significantly stronger than its link with eudaimonia at both the state level and the trait levels.

Outcomes Common to Both Eudaimonia and Hedonia

Life Satisfaction

Both eudaimonia and hedonia were expected to relate to life satisfaction because we conceptualized life satisfaction as a global life evaluation that both eudaimonic and hedonic benefits could channel into (Huta & Ryan, 2010; Ryan & Huta, 2009) and also because this is what Peterson et al. (2005) found when using their OH scale. This outcome was assessed using the Satisfaction With Life Scale (Diener, Emmons, Larsen, & Griffin, 1985). Table 7.1 shows that the prediction was supported.

Vitality

Another important outcome is vitality, a positive subjective feeling of aliveness and energy (Ryan & Frederick, 1997). I expect that if people were asked to identify the main feelings that make up their experiences of well-being, feeling alive would be high on the list. In addition, principal components analyses were conducted in each study using the first eight well-being variables in Table 7.1 (when available) and forcing a one-factor solution to determine which variables most directly reflected the higher order concept of well-being. Consistently, the two highest loading variables were vitality (loading highest in four of six studies) and positive affect.

I initially expected vitality to relate more to eudaimonia than to hedonia because vitality is one of the key outcomes used in self-determination theory research and because self-determination theory shares with eudaimonia an emphasis on autonomy and authenticity (Ryan et al., 2008). However, once I completed a second study that failed to support this prediction and instead showed that eudaimonia and hedonia related equally to vitality, I realized the need to develop revised hypotheses (which in retrospect make more sense). At present, I hypothesize that eudaimonia produces vitality because the pursuit of excellence and growth requires active engagement, whereas hedonia produces vitality because relaxation replenishes energy and pleasure-seeking excites the senses. Vitality was assessed using the six-item revision (Bostic, Rubio, & Hood, 2000) of the original seven-item scale by Ryan and Frederick (1997). In all remaining studies, vitality continued to have equal links with eudaimonia and hedonia, at both the trait and state level, as summarized in Table 7.1. It is possible, however, that the vitality scale reflects two subtypes of vitality—eudaimonia might be linked to a quieter feeling of intense aliveness and awareness, whereas hedonia, or at least the pursuit of pleasure, might be linked to a more active feeling of excitement. This would be an interesting question to address in future research.

Self-Esteem

I also initially expected self-esteem to relate more to eudaimonia, on the basis of the assumption that self-esteem arises as the product of acting in congruence with one's values. Self-esteem was measured using the single item by Robins, Hendin, and Trzesniewski (2001). As Table 7.1 shows, self-esteem was about equally related to eudaimonia and hedonia, at both the state level and trait level. My hypothesis at present is that the mechanisms by which eudaimonia and hedonia relate to self-esteem are different. Self-esteem may be a product of eudaimonia, as initially predicted, whereas self-esteem may be both a product and a correlate of hedonia—a product because taking the time to seek enjoyment and comfort implicitly affirms that one is worthy of such self-care and a correlate whereby high self-esteem and hedonic motivation are part of a broader mind-set in which the individual gives priority to personal interests.

Causal Data

Thus far, the findings summarized regarding personal well-being were based on correlational data. It is important to confirm that these correlations exist because it is the pursuit of eudaimonia (or hedonia) that causes well-being. This was the purpose of Study 4, an intervention in which participants were randomized to add either eudaimonic or hedonic activities of their choice to their lives each day for 10 consecutive days. Baseline well-being prior to the intervention was compared with well-being at immediate follow-up (the last 7 days of the intervention, as reported 1 day after the intervention ended) and at 3-month follow-up (inquiring about the previous week).

At immediate follow-up, participants in the eudaimonia condition reported increased meaning and decreased negative affect; participants in the hedonia condition reported increased carefreeness, positive affect, vitality, and life satisfaction and decreased negative affect. At 3-month follow-up, those in the eudaimonia condition reported increased elevating experience, vitality, positive affect, and even carefreeness, and decreased negative affect; those in the hedonia condition reported increased carefreeness and vitality and decreased negative affect. In addition, degree of increase in eudaimonia from baseline to 3-month follow-up was associated with degree of increase in meaning and elevating experience, whereas increase in hedonia was associated with increase in positive affect and life satisfaction and decrease in negative affect. Thus, only eudaimonia promoted meaning and elevating experience, lending support to the prediction that it fulfills unique functions in life.

Different Effects Over Time

In addition to influencing somewhat different forms of well-being, eudaimonia and hedonia may also have different effects over time. Hedonia typically involves the pursuit of fairly immediate gratification and thus should be the stronger source of well-being in the short term. Indeed, within Zimbardo's theory of time perspectives, one subtype is referred to as the present-hedonistic orientation (Zimbardo & Boyd, 1999). Eudaimonic pursuits are often challenging and not necessarily enjoyable at the time they are carried out. Yet they often constitute an investment in the future and thus may produce well-being at a later time, perhaps when the eudaimonic goal is achieved or bears fruit. In addition, repeated eudaimonic activity may gradually build up the resources that produce personal well-being, like greater skills, accomplishments, opportunities, and social connections.

Relatively little data exist on this, but the results thus far are at least congruent with the predictions. As found in the intervention study reported previously, an increase in hedonic activity for 10 days resulted in a greater variety of well-being benefits at immediate follow-up than did an increase in eudaimonic activity. Yet at 3-month follow-up, this pattern was reversed, with participants in the eudaimonia condition experiencing a somewhat greater range of well-being benefits. The results in Table 7.1 also somewhat fit the predicted pattern. In most cases in which trait-level and state-level results differ, it is because hedonia shows stronger benefits at the state level, which represents the short term, whereas eudaimonia shows stronger benefits at the trait level, which may reflect the long-term cumulative effect of repeated eudaimonic activity.

In sum, eudaimonia and hedonia fill somewhat different niches in personal well-being. Eudaimonia relates to cognitive–affective feelings of significance, appreciation, and congruence, whereas hedonia relates more to purely affective outcomes. Eudaimonia relates to feeling more engaged and connected with oneself or a broader whole, whereas hedonia relates to becoming disengaged from concerns. And eudaimonia may relate somewhat more to longer term and person-level outcomes, whereas hedonia relates more to immediate outcomes, suggesting that these pursuits may promote well-being at different time scales.

STUDYING THE COMBINATION OF EUDAIMONIC AND HEDONIC MOTIVES AS IT RELATES TO PERSONAL WELL-BEING

The previous review of personal well-being benefits focused on differences between eudaimonia and hedonia. Yet eudaimonic and hedonic pursuits can also exist in combination. When these pursuits are treated as two unipolar dimensions, it is possible to study whether people high on both pursuits—those living *the full life,* as discussed by Peterson et al. (2005)— experience greater well-being than people who unilaterally pursue only the eudaimonic life or only the hedonic life or people low on both pursuits, which Peterson et al. (2005) termed *the empty life.* This was addressed in the four studies in Huta and Ryan (2010), with the four groups of people created using median splits. In at least two of the studies, we found that the full life showed higher levels than the empty life on elevating experience, meaning, vitality, positive affect, and life satisfaction; the full life showed higher levels than the hedonic life on elevating experience, meaning, and vitality; and the full life showed higher levels than the eudaimonic life on positive affect and carefreeness. Peterson et al. (2005) also found that life satisfaction was highest in people living the full life (though their operationalization included not only eudaimonia and hedonia but also engagement). Together, these findings indicate that people experience the most well-being not when they choose one pursuit at the expense of the other but when they incorporate both eudaimonia and hedonia into their lives.

HOW EUDAIMONIC VERSUS HEDONIC PURSUITS RELATE TO THE WELL-BEING OF OTHER PEOPLE

A natural next step in the study of well-being correlates and consequences is to look beyond personal well-being to the well-being of other people. This step also addresses a major concern in the eudaimonia literature. In both psychology and philosophy, one of the leading criticisms of eudaimonia is the argument that a focus on personal excellence, growth, and actualization implies a lack of concern for the welfare of others. Several decades ago, Waterman (1981, 1984) reviewed the relevant literature and concluded the opposite—that actualization of the self related positively to prosocial behavior, not negatively. Nevertheless, the criticism continues to be made and little research has directly addressed it since.

Several recent studies have addressed this problem. In Huta (2012), we studied the influences that parents have on their children. It was found that highly eudaimonic parents had children who derived a wide range of well-being benefits both from eudaimonic pursuits (meaning, elevating experience, positive affect, low negative affect, self-esteem, vitality, carefreeness, and self-connectedness) and from hedonic pursuits (positive affect, low negative affect, vitality, carefreeness, and self-connectedness). The children of highly hedonic parents had fewer benefits: They derived only positive affect and low negative affect from hedonic pursuits, and only self-esteem from eudaimonic pursuits.

We have also prepared a study for publication (Study 6) on the effects that an individual's self-reported eudaimonia and hedonia have on the way they make their friends and relatives feel, as reported by those friends and relatives (Huta, Pelletier, Baxter, & Thompson, in press). The data for 118 participants and their friends and relatives showed that both eudaimonically and hedonically motivated people promoted feelings of positive affect in close others, but eudaimonically oriented people also benefitted others in several additional ways, by fostering feelings of meaning, self-connectedness, elevating experience, and vitality. These findings are further supplemented by self-report prosocial behavior, which correlated with eudaimonia but not with hedonia. The nine-item prosocial behavior inquired about helping, being unfair, voluntarily doing favors, being manipulative, giving advice, being untruthful, being patient, letting oneself be moody, and really listening (rated 1–7, every other item reverse coded, $\alpha = .70$).

Together, these findings indicate that eudaimonically oriented people are concerned about the welfare of others and have a positive impact on other people's lives.

COMPARING CHARACTERISTICS OF EUDAIMONIC- AND HEDONIC-ORIENTED INDIVIDUALS

Finally, several of the studies summarized here included individual difference measures that could help us develop a feel for the personalities of eudaimonically and hedonically oriented individuals. What emerged are two somewhat distinct profiles, suggesting that the differences between eudaimonia and hedonia run deeper than the domain of well-being.

In Study 3, participants completed the Values In Action Inventory of Strengths (Peterson & Seligman, 2004). Compared with hedonia, eudaimonia had significantly stronger correlations with judgment and wisdom. Hedonia had significantly stronger correlations with playfulness and love, but it also correlated more negatively with humility (eudaimonia was unrelated to humility). Eudaimonia and hedonia correlated about equally with enthusiasm, optimism, curiosity, love of learning, courage, and social skills. In addition, in the U.S. sample of Peterson, Ruch, Beermann, Park, and Seligman (2007), the

OH eudaimonia scale showed significantly and substantially larger correlations with judgment, wisdom, love of learning, curiosity, honesty, spirituality, gratitude, forgiveness, and leadership; the OH hedonia scale showed a significantly larger correlation with playfulness and a significantly more negative correlation with humility (eudaimonia related positively to humility); both pursuits correlated at least .10 with enthusiasm, optimism, appreciation of beauty, courage, creativity, social skills, kindness, and love. Together, these findings suggest that both eudaimonia and hedonia relate to a positive and interested outlook on life, but that eudaimonia relates somewhat more to what Park and Peterson (2010) called strengths of the head, whereas hedonia relates more to the strength of playfulness.

Results from other studies are given in Table 7.2. Eudaimonia was significantly more related to the following: having purpose in life and a framework for interpreting life's events, measured by the Framework subscale of the Life Regard Index Revised (Debats, 1998; original scale by Battista & Almond, 1973) and the Presence of Meaning subscale of the Meaning in Life Questionnaire (Steger, Frazier, Oishi, & Kaler, 2006); integrated motivation, such that one's motives are congruent with one's values, measured by the General Motivation Scale (Pelletier & Huta, 2011); elements of introversion, including an inward orientation (e.g., "I prefer to be alone," "I prefer serenity to liveliness," "I am more focused on thoughts and ideas than people and things"), subjectivity (e.g., "I do things my way"), and introspectiveness (e.g., "I examine my feelings or thoughts"), measured by scales I am developing to assess introversion as an active pursuit in its own right, on the basis of Jung's conceptualization, rather than merely the absence of extraversion (Huta, 2011); and affect valence at work, measured by a single item rated −4 to +4.

Hedonia was significantly more related to materialism, measured by the Material Values Scale by Richins (2004), and to the excitement-seeking and gregariousness components of extraversion, measured by the Extraversion scale of the NEO Personality Inventory Revised Scale (Costa & McCrae, 1992).

The final section of Table 7.2 also provides some initial information on predictors of eudaimonia and hedonia. In Huta (2012), adult participants reported retrospectively on how their parents had raised them. The many aspects of parenting can be summarized by two orthogonal dimensions: demandingness and responsiveness (Baumrind, 1989; Maccoby & Martin, 1983). Demandingness involves imposing of structure and expecting the child to contribute to the family and to mature; responsiveness involves meeting the child's needs and encouraging the child to develop his or her own individuality. Many studies have shown the optimal style of parenting is high on both demandingness and responsiveness (see Huta,

TABLE 7.2
Characteristics of Eudaimonic and Hedonic Individuals

Variable	Studies	Eudaimonia	Hedonia
Meaning framework			
LRI-R Meaning framework	1,2	**.42**	.08
MLQ Having meaning	1	**.47**	.19
MLQ Seeking meaning	1	.03	.07
Motivation			
GMS Amotivation	7,8	−.03	**.12**
GMS External regulation	7,8	**.18**	**.20**
GMS Introjection	7,8	**.15**	.08
GMS Identification	7,8	**.34**	**.24**
GMS Integration	7,8	**.37**	**.16**
GMS Intrinsic motivation	7,8	**.35**	**.23**
Materialism			
Material Values Scale	5	−.19	**.22**
Extraversion			
NEO Extraversion Full Scale	2	**.18**	**.23**
NEO Excitement-seeking	2	.06	**.26**
NEO Gregariousness	2	.00	**.18**
NEO Friendliness	2	**.20**	**.18**
NEO Activity	2	**.21**	**.12**
NEO Assertiveness	2	**.20**	**.11**
NEO Positive affectivity	2	**.19**	**.24**
Introversion			
Inward-orientation, solitariness, and preference for peace and quiet	2	**.13**	−.12
Subjectivity and nonconformism	2	**.29**	.10
Introspectiveness	2	**.36**	.06
Enjoying work versus leisure			
Affect valence at work	2	**.31**	.13
Affect valence during leisure	2	**.14**	**.20**
Characteristics of one's parents			
Parental demandingness	5	**.48**	.09
Parental responsiveness	5	**.27**	.15

Note. In cells with findings from more than one study, the mean correlation is reported. Correlations in **bold** would reach significance at the smallest sample size of the studies summarized (sample sizes ranged from 102 to 2,094). If a correlation for one pursuit (eudaimonia or hedonia) is underlined, the correlation was significantly greater than the correlation for the other pursuit in at least half the studies summarized. LRI-R = Life Regard Index Revised; MLQ = Meaning in Life Questionnaire; GMS = General Motivation Scale; NEO = NEO Personality Inventory Revised Scale.

2012, for a review). Table 7.2 suggests that if parents want their children to pursue eudaimonia, they need to invest the effort to be both demanding and responsive. A child's hedonic pursuits, on the other hand, are unrelated to parenting styles. Perhaps hedonia is more based on innate predispositions, such as those that lead to extraversion, which has been characterized as a seeking of and/or sensitivity toward positive affect (Brebner, 1998; Lucas, Diener, Grob, Suh, & Shao, 2000).

CONCLUSION AND FUTURE DIRECTIONS

The findings in this chapter provide an initial mapping of several important areas: how eudaimonic and hedonic pursuits serve somewhat distinct but complementary functions in personal well-being, how they impact the well-being of other people, and what kinds of personality constellations they are a part of. Methodologically, it is clear that more causal data are needed and that replications should be conducted in a wide range of populations. Conceptually, there are many fruitful avenues. Here are some that I would like to see addressed: whether eudaimonia's benefits extend beyond the well-being of close others to the well-being of the broader community and the environment; whether eudaimonia and hedonia each come in unhealthy forms, perhaps based on extrinsic motives, escapism, or compulsive preoccupations; and what predicts whether one chooses to pursue eudaimonia and/or hedonia in the first place, including the values and life philosophies embedded in one's culture, role models, and biology.

I also think that it will be important for researchers to develop an overview of the points of convergence and divergence in the eudaimonia literature, through meetings, discussions, and initiatives such as this book. Interest in eudaimonia is exploding, but so are its definitions and operationalizations. The diversity of approaches can be confusing and bewildering. And the topic of eudaimonia is so important, so central to the existential questions of life, that we need to take care of it to some degree.

Yet any kind of organization of the field needs to be carried out with caution. There is something very powerful and raw and truthful that emerges when each scholar works as a lone pioneer, having to personally and intimately confront the topic and gradually bring to light his or her particular perspective. With too much organization, there is a risk of making the field tired and bogged down, overly tame, and overly controlled by a single point of view. If we can be vigilant about respecting diversity and maintaining openness to revising our hypotheses, then we can only benefit from a bird's eye view and help the field to flourish.

REFERENCES

Anic, P. (2011). *How to achieve happiness: Adolescents' life goals and free time activities.* (Unpublished doctoral dissertation). University of Ljubljana, Slovenia.

Aristotle. (2001). Nichomachean ethics. In R. McKeon (Ed.), *The basic works of Aristotle* (pp. 928–1112). New York, NY: The Modern Library.

Battista, J., & Almond, R. (1973). The development of meaning in life. *Psychiatry, 36,* 409–427.

Baumrind, D. (1989). Rearing competent children. In W. Damon (Ed.), *Child development today and tomorrow* (pp. 349–378). San Francisco, CA: Jossey-Bass.

Bostic, T. J., Rubio, D. M., & Hood, M. (2000). A validation of the subjective vitality scale using structural equation modeling. *Social Indicators Research, 52,* 313–324. doi:10.1023/A:1007136110218

Brebner, J. (1998). Happiness and personality. *Personality and Individual Differences, 25,* 279–296. doi:10.1016/S0191-8869(98)00041-5

Costa, P. T., & McCrae, R. R. (1992). *Revised NEO Personality Inventory (NEO-PI-R) and NEO Five-Factor inventory (NEO-FFI) professional manual.* Odessa, FL: Psychological Assessment Resources.

Csikszentmihalyi, M. (1990). *Flow: The psychology of optimal experience.* New York, NY: Harper Collins.

Debats, D. L. (1998). Measurements of personal meaning: The psychometric properties of the Life Regard Index (LRI). In P. T. P. Wong & P. S. Fry (Eds.), *Handbook of personal meaning: Theory, research, and application* (pp. 237–259). Mahwah, NJ: Erlbaum.

Diener, E., & Emmons, R. A. (1984). The independence of positive and negative affect. *Journal of Personality and Social Psychology, 47,* 1105–1117. doi:10.1037/0022-3514.47.5.1105

Diener, E., Emmons, R. A., Larsen, R. J., & Griffin, S. (1985). The Satisfaction with Life Scale. *Journal of Personality Assessment, 49,* 71–75. doi:10.1207/s15327752jpa4901_13

Diener, E., Suh, E. M., Lucas, R. E., & Smith, H. L. (1999). Subjective well-being: Three decades of progress. *Psychological Bulletin, 125,* 276–302. doi:10.1037/0033-2909.125.2.276

Fredrickson, B. L. (2001). The role of positive emotions in positive psychology: The broaden-and-build theory of positive emotions. *American Psychologist, 56,* 218–226. doi:10.1037/0003-066X.56.3.218

Haidt, J. (2000). The positive emotion of elevation. *Prevention and Treatment, 3*(1), ArtID3c.

Huta, V. (2011). *Do extraverts always have greater well-being than introverts? It depends on how one measures extraversion, introversion, and well-being.* Manuscript in preparation.

Huta, V. (2012). Linking peoples' pursuit of eudaimonia and hedonia with characteristics of their parents: Parenting styles, verbally endorsed values, and role modeling. *Journal of Happiness Studies, 13,* 47–61. (Contains Study 5) doi:10.1007/s10902-011-9249-7

Huta, V. (in press). Eudaimonia. In I. Boniwell & S. David (Eds.), *Oxford handbook of happiness.* Oxford, England: Oxford University Press.

Huta, V., Pelletier, L. G., Baxter, D., & Thompson, A. (in press). Does an individual's eudaimonia benefit other people? *The Journal of Positive Psychology.* (Contains Study 6)

Huta, V., & Ryan, R. M. (2010). Pursuing pleasure or virtue: The differential and overlapping well-being benefits of hedonic and eudaimonic motives. *Journal of Happiness Studies, 11,* 735–762. (Contains Studies 1, 2, 3, and 4)

Kaczmarek, L. D., Baczkowski, B., Enko, J., Siebers, A., Szaefer, A., & Krol, M. (2011). *Who starts positive life practices? The predictive value of trait curiosity, eudaimonia, and subjective well-being.* Manuscript in preparation.

Keltner, D., & Haidt, J. (2003). Approaching awe, a moral, spiritual, and aesthetic emotion. *Cognition and Emotion, 17,* 297–314. doi:10.1080/02699930302297

Lucas, R. E., Diener, E., Grob, A., Suh, E. M., & Shao, L. (2000). Cross-cultural evidence for the fundamental features of extraversion. *Journal of Personality and Social Psychology, 79,* 452–468. doi:10.1037/0022-3514.79.3.452

Maccoby, E. E., & Martin, J. A. (1983). Socialization in the context of the family: Parent–child interaction. In P. H. Mussen & E. M. Hetherington (Eds.), *Handbook of child psychology: Vol. 4. Socialization, personality, and social development* (4th ed., pp. 1–101). New York, NY: Wiley.

Maslow, A. H. (1970). *Motivation and Personality* (2nd ed.). New York, NY: Harper & Row.

Park, N., & Peterson, C. (2010). Does it matter where we live? The urban psychology of character strengths. *American Psychologist, 65,* 535–547. doi:10.1037/a0019621

Pelletier, L. G., & Huta, V. (2011). *The psychometric properties of the General Motivation Scale.* Manuscript in preparation. (Contains Studies 7 and 8)

Peterson, C., Park, N., & Seligman, M. E. P. (2005). Orientations to happiness and life satisfaction: The full life versus the empty life. *Journal of Happiness Studies, 6,* 25–41. doi:10.1007/s10902-004-1278-z

Peterson, C., Ruch, W., Beermann, U., Park, N., & Seligman, M. E. P. (2007). Strengths of character, orientations to happiness, and life satisfaction. *The Journal of Positive Psychology, 2,* 149–156. doi:10.1080/17439760701228938

Peterson, C., & Seligman, M. E. P. (2004). *Character strengths and virtues: A handbook of classification.* New York, NY: Oxford University Press.

Richins, M. L. (2004). The Material Values Scale: A re-inquiry into its measurement properties and the development of a short form. *Journal of Consumer Research, 31,* 209–219. doi:10.1086/383436

Robins, R. W., Hendin, H. M., & Trzesniewski, K. H. (2001). Measuring global self-esteem: Construct validation of a single-item measure and the Rosenberg Self-Esteem Scale. *Personality and Social Psychology Bulletin*, *27*, 151–161. doi:10.1177/0146167201272002

Ryan, R. M., & Frederick, C. (1997). On energy, personality, and health: Subjective vitality as a dynamic reflection of well-being. *Journal of Personality*, *65*, 529–565. doi:10.1111/j.1467-6494.1997.tb00326.x

Ryan, R. M., & Huta, V. (2009). Wellness as healthy functioning or wellness as happiness: The importance of eudaimonic thinking. *The Journal of Positive Psychology*, *4*, 202–204. doi:10.1080/17439760902844285

Ryan, R. M., Huta, V., & Deci, E. L. (2008). Living well: A self-determination theory perspective on eudaimonia. *Journal of Happiness Studies*, *9*, 139–170. doi:10.1007/s10902-006-9023-4

Steger, M. F., Frazier, P., Oishi, S., & Kaler, M. (2006). The Meaning in Life Questionnaire: Assessing the presence of and search for meaning in life. *Journal of Counseling Psychology*, *53*, 80–93. doi:10.1037/0022-0167.53.1.80

Thrash, T. M., & Elliot, A. J. (2003). Inspiration as a psychological construct. *Journal of Personality and Social Psychology*, *84*, 871–889. doi:10.1037/0022-3514.84.4.871

Waterman, A. S. (1981). Individualism and interdependence. *American Psychologist*, *36*, 762–773. doi:10.1037/0003-066X.36.7.762

Waterman, A. S. (1984). *The psychology of individualism*. New York, NY: Praeger.

Waterman, A. S. (2007). Doing well: The relationship of identity status to three conceptions of well-being. *Identity: An International Journal of Theory and Research*, *7*, 289–307. doi:10.1080/15283480701600769

Weinstein, N., Przybylski, A. K., & Ryan, R. M. (2012). The index of autonomous functioning: Development of a scale of human autonomy. *Journal of Research in Personality*, *46*, 397–413. doi:10.1016/j.jrp.2012.03.007

Zimbardo, P. G., & Boyd, J. N. (1999). Putting time in perspective: A valid, reliable individual-differences metric. *Journal of Personality and Social Psychology*, *77*, 1271–1288. doi:10.1037/0022-3514.77.6.1271

8

IS MEANING IN LIFE A FLAGSHIP INDICATOR OF WELL-BEING?

MICHAEL F. STEGER, JOO YEON SHIN, YERIN SHIM,
AND ARISSA FITCH-MARTIN

Over 50 years ago, *Time* magazine began a story with the question, "What is a chair?" ("Art: Architects' furniture," 1957). To many of us, the answer is so simple that we might suspect a trap. A chair is something one sits on. Perhaps the prototypical chair pops into one's mind: four legs, a back, a flat or subtly contoured surface perpendicular to the legs and back. Perhaps some armrests. Yet, it is also easy to conjure up images of chairs with one, two, three, or no legs; armrests or not; flat seating surface or perhaps webbing, mesh, straps, or a plump cushion for sitting on; a towering back, an enveloping back, an intricately carved back, a rigid slab, a minimalist cantilevered oval, or no back at all. Perhaps there is no form whatsoever, as in a beanbag. Yet we would all agree that we could call each of these objects a *chair*. And of course people can sit on all manner of things, from a snowdrift to a horse. Some things we agree are chairs and some are just other things we sit on. Yet some are chairs museums bid on for their permanent collections. What is special about this kind of chair? In other words, what are the ideal qualities of the perfect chair?

DOI: 10.1037/14092-009
The Best Within Us: Positive Psychology Perspectives on Eudaimonia, Alan S. Waterman (Editor)
Copyright © 2013 by the American Psychological Association. All rights reserved.

In the *Time* article, the famous Bauhaus architect Ludwig Mies van der Rohe is quoted as saying, "A chair is a very difficult object. A skyscraper is almost easier." Considering that one of us (MS) still has a chair he found in a dumpster, this statement seems preposterous. Yet, Mies was an architect first and a chair designer second. He was not referring to the technical and construction demands; rather, he was referring to the design demands. There are several dictionary definitions of *design* and a further profusion of ideas, philosophies, and definitions in industries and fields that design products, projects, and applications (Ralph & Wand, 2009). We adopt the perspective that the heart and soul of the best design is a balancing act between aesthetic expression and functional constraints. Chairs provide a great lens for examining design because the personal scale of a chair essentially places no structural constraints on the final form. Designers have exploited this to create some truly beautiful chairs (as well as some truly kooky ones—see the surreal minimalism collection by David Pompa), expressing a personal aesthetic vision. The perfect chair is not really the most beautiful or idiosyncratically expressive chair, though. Other constraints must be met. The perfect chair is the one that best balances pleasing aesthetic appeal and the designer's personal expressiveness with the constraint of its intended function. Few would be interested in a chair that hurts to sit in, that can never be moved from its spot, or that is gigantic. Thus, the constraints of a chair include conformity to the human body, portability, and size. In essence, the perfect chair must balance subjective ideas like beauty and personal expressiveness with objective constraints like purposefulness and functionality. One could do worse than the chair that Mies and Lily Riech designed, known as the Barcelona chair. You would recognize the steel frame that forms a subtle X form and the hand-sewn leather back and seat (no arms). The Barcelona is captivating to look at, with clean lines, and a juxtaposition of curving and straight lines, soft leather and hard metal, dark seat, and shining frame. And, more important, it is luxurious to sit in, portable, and takes up only as much space as it needs.

WHAT IS A MEANINGFUL LIFE?

Meaning in life is similar to the mundane and familiar object, the lowly chair. People seem to have natural access to ideas about meaning in life, or the meaningful life. It fits a sort of prototype we absorb. Yet, what are the ideal qualities of a meaningful life? Defining it for psychological science is a tougher challenge, and prescribing a path to a meaningful life is even harder. However, we argue that the solutions to the problem of designing the perfect chair are similar to the solutions for designing a meaningful life. As in chair design, a balance needs to be struck between the pure expressiveness and sensory delight of aesthetic appeal and the constraints of the human condition, societal demands, and cultural scripts. We argue that meaning cannot be sustained in a beautiful flourish or pleasing indulgence alone, nor should meaning be built through reflexive obeisance to formulaic platitudes.

In the remainder of this chapter, we first briefly review the venerable conceptualizations of the best to which we aspire: eudaimonia and hedonia. We express our own, simplified understanding of those two concepts. Next, we provide a theoretical overview of meaning in life. Following that, we examine empirical findings about meaning in life that support viewing meaning as being eudaimonic in nature and consider research that casts meaning in a more hedonic light. Finally, we conclude that—in much the same way that the perfect chair is neither a pleasurable object nor a purposeful one—meaning in life is neither hedonic nor eudaimonic. It is derived from the art of balancing both.

WHAT IS THE BEST TO WHICH WE ASPIRE?

Psychologists recently have joined a long-standing debate about the nature of happiness (Tiberus & Hall, 2010). Whereas *eudaimonia* is generally understood as a condition in which one fully realizes his or her own potential (Waterman, 1993), *hedonia* typically refers to maximizing pleasure and minimizing pain (see Chapter 1, this volume). In addition to the debate about which understanding of happiness is most appropriate as a psychological target (Deci & Ryan, 2008), there is also debate about whether the concepts are distinct types of psychological experiences in the first place (Kashdan, Biswas-Diener, & King, 2008). We think that there is value in considering both of these questions, despite the high probability that eudaimonic and hedonic experiences will often overlap. In particular, meaning in life provides an excellent lens for understanding the implications and, we argue, the interplay of the two perspectives. Prior to examining the links between meaning in life and eudaimonia, we briefly review conceptualizations of eudaimonia and hedonia, highlighting differential aspects of the two terms.

Eudaimonia

The search for a term for—and a description of—the best to which humans can aspire has a long history and will probably have a long future. *Eudaimonia* was used by Aristotle to discuss a form of normative, virtue-driven well-being, distinct from pleasure-based happiness (Ryan & Deci, 2001). The term was used to evoke the development of virtues that are morally desirable and thus worth having. In Aristotle's view, there was something toward which all people could strive, a better, "true" happiness, which has the same rough outline for everyone. The form of eudaimonia is not infinitely pliable. Unlike pleasure, which can come from nearly any source depending on the individual, eudaimonia seeks well-being outcomes that are "objectively good" for people because of the inherent nature of being a person. Still, there is some flexibility, and within the range of morally valued attributes people should develop, there is room for individual expression.

More recently, Ryff (1989) developed a model of normatively beneficial qualities that constitute *eudaimonic well-being*—self-acceptance, positive relations with others, autonomy, environmental mastery, purpose in life, and personal growth—and provided a contrast with more subjective or hedonic approaches. Waterman (1993) understood eudaimonia as an experience of personal expressiveness, a condition that is achieved by an effort to live in accordance with one's daimon (i.e., true self) to realize its potentials. Although eudaimonia is linked to beneficial outcomes such as self-realization and personal growth, it is a state that also requires conscious endeavor to achieve. Along these lines, Ryan and Deci (2001) also emphasized the importance of personal volition and autonomy in achieving well-being outcomes, balanced with the recognition of our connectedness to others. A more recent development of this approach resulted in four motivational concepts of eudaimonic living (Ryan, Huta, & Deci, 2008). People are seen to pursue eudaimonic living when they seek to satisfy basic psychological needs (competence, relatedness, and autonomy), pursue intrinsic—not extrinsic—goals and values, behave autonomously, and foster mindfulness and awareness in daily life. The themes of autonomy, intentionality, quality relationships, and meaningful and purposeful activity arise in all of these models. This convergence was supported in a recent empirical study that used an expert panel to rate behaviors that were highly representative of eudaimonic and hedonic conceptualizations of well-being, respectively. "Eudaimonic" behaviors focused on intentional personal development, goal pursuit, and the cultivation and nurturance of interpersonal relationships; "hedonic" behaviors focused on obtaining pleasure and self-gratification, some of an extreme variety (drugs, parties, masturbation), some more mild (seeing a movie, going on a walk in nature; Steger, Kashdan, & Oishi, 2008). This study also found that in multiple samples, engaging in daily hedonic behaviors had no relationship with well-being. In contrast, consistent relationships were found between daily eudaimonic behaviors and several well-being variables; further, the effects of eudaimonic activity appeared to carry over to the next day's well-being. In many ways, eudaimonic models of well-being were developed in contrast to the hedonic models that had become dominant.

Hedonia

Whether because of a bias against "humanistic" or "philosophical" concepts like meaning, autonomy, or personal growth, or because of the excellent rigor and quality of research conducted on emotions and life satisfaction, subjective approaches became the mainstream lens for understanding well-being. Approaches like Diener's (2000) subjective well-being have been characterized as hedonically grounded because of their emphasis on pleasant emotional experience (Deci & Ryan, 2008), although the life satisfaction component of such models is not intended to reflect unstable emotional states. In contrast to eudaimonia, hedonia is framed as maximizing pleasure in life as defined by the individual (see Chapter 1, this volume). In addition, there seems to be a present-centered quality to hedonia that prioritizes the pleasure to be gained in the proximal moment, rather than the distal future. Because of this subjective nature and its focus on immediate pleasure, hedonia has sometimes been devalued by philosophers and researchers. For example, Aristotle considered hedonic happiness as the pursuit of the vulgar, making humans slavish followers of desires (Ryan & Deci, 2001). Ryan et al. (2008) also stated that maximizing pleasure and minimizing pain can be too often associated with dead-end routes to selfishness, materialism, objectified sexuality, and ecological destructiveness.

However, the outcomes of hedonic pursuits are not necessarily, or perhaps even typically, negative. In an empirical study that compared well-being outcomes of eudaimonia and hedonia, it was shown that hedonia and eudaimonia were equally related to vitality and life satisfaction, whereas hedonia was more strongly related to positive affect and carefreeness from concerns and worries (Huta & Ryan, 2010). This research also found that hedonia produced more benefits in the short term, whereas eudaimonia produced more benefits in the long term, consistent with other research (Steger, Frazier, & Zacchanini, 2008). Such results can be interpreted as portraying eudaimonia to be a better, more preferable form of well-being. Yet the positive effect of hedonia should not be ignored, considering the fact that eudaimonia is difficult to achieve and requires effort. Hedonia (in the form of a positive affect balance) seems to both accompany eudaimonic pursuits (Steger, Frazier, & Zacchanini, 2008) and complement them (Huta & Ryan, 2010).

Our View

As our introductory meditation on the perfect chair reveals, our view of hedonism rests on pleasure, uninhibited self-expression, and self-gratification with no particular limits or rules. This pleasure-seeking, uninhibited self-expression differs from Waterman's (1993) eudaimonic personal expressiveness in that it is not directed at growth or goal pursuit; we use it to mean "doing whatever the hell I want to," with a paucity of reflection and consideration of consequences to others. In addition, we do not favor the term *subjective well-being* (SWB) for the kind of fulfillment that can arise from such pursuits. First, life satisfaction, a pillar of SWB, is not of the same stripe as pleasure and affective fulfillment. Second, as Tiberius (see Chapter 1, this volume) and others have pointed out, even the things that appear on "objective" lists and theories of well-being are almost always subjectively measured. The advantage of using hedonia to refer to this emphasis on pleasure, self-expression, and self-gratification is that there is no particular research tradition associated with the term, and it provides a cleaner counterexample to other ways of understanding well-being.

Our view of eudaimonia acknowledges constraints on what should be considered a path to optimal experience. This idea of limits and boundaries is critical to our view of the best to which we aspire. As psychologists, we ultimately have practical concerns. How do we disseminate knowledge of the good life? How do we work with clients toward their fulfillment? How do we build research knowledge about human excellence? An answer that can be boiled down to "do whatever you want as long as it feels good" is ultimately dissatisfying for these purposes. Our view does not completely overlap with Ryff and Singer's (1998) argument for psychological well-being (PWB), although we share their concern of an overemphasis on affect, and we view meaning and purpose in life as being an important part of well-being. We would not make an argument for each of the six factors identified and would see no reason to exclude life satisfaction from metrics of PWB. We also would place a greater emphasis on how the factors perhaps ought to combine to create a unified field of understandings and intentions (which we later argue is what we mean by meaning in life). Our view of eudaimonia fits fairly well with Ryan and Deci's (2001) formulation and Sheldon's (2002) model of self-concordance in that each requires clarification of, and behavior consistent with, people's values and goals, discovered and pursued in an autonomous fashion. Waterman's (see Introduction, this volume) idea of eudaimonic well-being (EWB) is appealing as well in that it requires the intentional development and use of personal talents. What we take from these ideas is the melding of personal expressiveness (which on its own could be hedonistic) with the recognition that other factors (insight and reflection on the self, good relationships, goal pursuit, self-development) should accompany that expressiveness. Thus, our view most closely resembles what Waterman refers to as *eudaimonia as flourishing*, with the recognition that our image of flourishing requires mature self-realization.

As we briefly noted previously, some kinds of self-expressiveness could be considered hedonic rather than eudaimonic. We feel that the difference occurs in the degree to which self-expressiveness arises from an interaction of the other factors we mentioned. In our understanding of eudaimonia, self-expression that nurtures good relationships is preferable to self-expression that does not. Similarly, self-expression that is driven by insight and reflection into the self, that is organized around broad goal setting and pursuit, or that improves the self is better than self-expression that does none of these things. Essentially, we prefer to view many of these variables as being qualities that place constraints on self-expressiveness. Like the constraints that need to be addressed in making a perfect chair, building a "perfect" life needs to recognize and respond to constraints, too. The manner in which we view these constraints fits best with what Tiberius (Chapter 1, this volume) calls *human nature fulfillment theories*, such as the one associated with Aristotle. We feel that to function best, a person needs to hew to the kind of thing a person is (or should be). We feel that meaning in life is a useful crucible for enjoining the momentarily pleasing self-expressiveness of hedonic views with the effortful, autonomous, socially responsive, self-development of eudaimonic views.

MEANING IN LIFE

Meaning in life consistently has been included in eudaimonic psychological models of well-being, broadly speaking. Although meaning is typically measured through subjective means, it is usually held out by proponents as a critical aspect of the best to which we aspire. Essentially, people would not be considered to have attained optimal functioning in the absence of meaningful living (e.g., Ryff & Singer, 1998). Frankl (1963) was the originator of this argument, perceiving that humans are naturally driven to find meaning in their lives. He believed that it is up to the individual to find his or her own meaning and that a lack of meaning in life inevitably leads to psychological distress. This balance of individuality in discernment and pursuit of meaning in life combined with the assertion that meaninglessness undermines well-being illustrates our point about the eudaimonic interplay of personal expressiveness and factors like reflectiveness, acknowledgement of the stakes of others, and self-development.

Although there is broad agreement that meaning in life is an important (though not all feel necessary) attribute for people to have, there is less clarity about how meaning in life is defined. Although some researchers have argued that meaning in life has affective, cognitive, and motivational aspects, as well as additional dimensions of breadth and depth (Reker & Wong, 1988), it is our position that the affective element of meaning-specific fulfillment has not been articulated adequately; therefore, we focus on the cognitive and motivational dimensions. Meaning has been defined as a sense of coherence in life (Battista & Almond, 1973; Reker & Wong, 1988) that accompanies people's understanding of who they are, what the world is like, and how they fit into it (Heine, Proulx, & Vohs, 2006). Meaning has also been defined as goal directedness or purposefulness (e.g., Klinger, 1977; Ryff & Singer, 1998). These two elements—forming a coherent understanding of life and investing in important lifelong aspirations—are the most often used referents for understanding meaning in life (e.g., King, Hicks, Krull, & Del Gaiso, 2006). On the basis of a review of the meaning-in-life literature, Steger (2011, 2012; Steger, Beeby, Garrett, & Kashdan, in press; Steger, Bundick, & Yeager, 2012; Steger, Frazier, Oishi, & Kaler, 2006) provided a conceptual model of meaning in life that integrated both cognitive and motivational dimensions, referred to in this model as comprehension and purpose. Thus, meaning in life is the degree to which people have achieved comprehension (through making sense of their lives and experience, developing a coherent mental model of their selves, the world around them, and their fit and interactions with the world) and have achieved purpose (through discerning, committing to, and pursuing overarching lifelong goals, aims, and aspirations). Steger also has argued that there is a feedback loop between purpose-directed effort and people's comprehension of their lives such that when people are functioning well, they are pursuing purposes that are self-concordant, autonomously chosen, and reinforcing. This loop essentially maintains Frankl's idea that each of us has a purpose (or more than one) that is unique in some ways (see also Battista & Almond, 1973).

Meaning in Life Is a Eudaimonic Well-Being Indicator

The relevance of meaning in life and eudaimonia has appeared in many eudaimonic theories, suggesting meaning in life as an outcome, an indicator, or even a critical component of eudaimonia (Ryff, 1989; Steger, Kashdan, & Oishi, 2008). Meaning and eudaimonia also share several characteristics. First, both are experienced as personally expressive. Second, most eudaimonic theories refer to reciprocally positive relationships (Ryan & Deci, 2001; Ryff, 1989). Relationships also appear as one of the most salient sources of meaning in life (Baumeister, 1991; Debats, 1999; Lambert et al., 2010; Schnell, 2009), and social exclusion appears toxic to meaning in life (Stillman et al., 2009). Third, both views emphasize the importance of pursuit of self-concordant, autonomously chosen goals (McKnight & Kashdan, 2009; Sheldon, 2002; Steger et al., 2006). Fourth, positive self-evaluations are considered important to both sets of theories (Baumeister, 1991; Ryan & Deci, 2001; Ryff, 1989). Finally, although this has not been elaborated particularly well in previous work, there is an assumption about both meaning in life and eudaimonia that emphasizes conscious, deliberate effort rather than automatic reflex (Ryan & Deci, 2001; Steger, Kashdan, & Oishi, 2008; Steger, Kashdan, Sullivan, & Lorentz, 2008; Tiberius & Hall, 2010), particularly when people need to revise their meaning in life in response to life events (Park, 2008; Park & Folkman, 1997).

If eudaimonic theories are correct about meaning in life, then we should see evidence of optimal functioning among people with meaning and deficits among people without it. A sizable body of empirical evidence has drawn consistent links between meaning in life and both psychological and physical well-being. Meaning in life is positively related to happiness (e.g., Debats, 1996; Debats, van der Lubbe, & Wezeman, 1993; Ryff & Keyes, 1995, Steger, Oishi, & Kesebir, 2011), psychological adjustment (Thompson, Coker, Krause, & Henry, 2003), and life satisfaction (Keyes, Shmotkin, & Ryff, 2002; Ryff, 1989; Ryff & Keyes, 1995; Steger, 2006; Steger & Frazier, 2005; Steger & Kashdan, 2007; Steger, Kashdan, & Oishi, 2008; Steger et al., 2006, 2011; Zika & Chamberlain, 1992). Meaning is also positively related to positive self-evaluations, as indicated by self-esteem (Debats, 1996; Ryff, 1989; Steger, 2006; Steger et al., 2006), self-acceptance (Ryff, 1989; Steger, Kashdan, Sullivan, & Lorentz, 2008), self-regard and self-actualization (Phillips, Watkins, & Noll, 1974), and being in touch with one's true self (Schlegel, Hicks, King, & Arndt, 2011). People with greater meaning in life express more positive perceptions of the world (Simon, Arndt, Greenberg, Pyszczynski, & Solomon, 1998) and appear to engage with the world more effectively, as indicated by positive relationships (e.g., Ryff, 1989) and their greater use of effective coping strategies and emotional regulation (e.g., Jim, Richardson, Golden-Kreutz, & Anderson, 2006). Finally, people higher in meaning in life report more positive health (Steger, Mann, Michels, & Cooper, 2009), show less cognitive decline in later life (Boyle, Buchman, Barnes, & Bennett 2010) and less risk of disability (Boyle, Buchman, & Bennett, 2010), and live longer (Boyle, Barnes, Buchman, & Bennett, 2009).

On the flip side of well-being, people with greater meaning in life report lower levels of the personality traits neuroticism (Pearson & Sheffield, 1989; Steger et al., 2006; Steger, Kashdan, Sullivan, & Lorentz, 2008) and psychoticism (Pearson & Sheffield, 1989). Research also shows an inverse relationship between meaning and psychological distress such as PTSD symptom severity (Owens, Steger, Whitesell, & Herrerra, 2009; Steger, Frazier, & Zacchanini, 2008) and depression (e.g., Crumbaugh & Maholick, 1964; Ryff, 1989; Ryff & Keyes, 1995; Steger et al., 2006; Steger & Kashdan, 2009; Zika & Chamberlain, 1992). Those who experience higher meaning in life also report less need for psychotherapy (Battista & Almond, 1973), less substance use (e.g., Newcomb & Harlow, 1986), fewer negative life events (Newcomb & Harlow, 1986), and lower levels of suicidal ideation (e.g., Edwards & Holden, 2001).

Generally, we see that people who feel their lives are meaningful are prospering across a wide range of well-being indicators. In addition, we see some of the successful engagement in the world that would be expected among people achieving eudaimonic well-being. The alignment of what eudaimonic well-being should look like and the psychological profile of someone with abundant meaning in life is often replicated, broad based, and consistent with what one would expect if meaning in life is a primary eudaimonic dimension.

Meaning in Life Is a Hedonic Well-Being Indicator

However, can a competing argument be made that meaning in life is also a hedonic well-being indicator? In this view, meaning in life would be experienced as being pleasant or would occur in the pursuit of pleasure. The strongest evidence that meaning in life has hedonic characteristics comes from a number of studies showing fairly robust inverse relationships between meaning in life and negative affect (e.g., Chamberlain & Zika, 1988; Kennedy, Kanthamani, & Palmer, 1994; Keyes et al., 2002; Schnell & Becker, 2006; Steger, Kashdan, Sullivan, & Lorentz, 2008; Steger et al., 2011; Zika & Chamberlain, 1992), and similar, if not larger, positive relationships between meaning in life and positive affect (Chamberlain & Zika, 1988; Kennedy et al., 1994; Keyes et al., 2002; King et al., 2006; Ryff, 1989; Steger et al., 2006; Steger, Kashdan, Sullivan, & Lorentz, 2008; Steger, Oishi, & Kashdan, 2009; Zika & Chamberlain, 1992). Several studies by Hicks, King, and colleagues have explored the relation between meaning in life and positive affect in greater depth. This research has focused on the information people appear to use in making in-the-moment judgments about how meaningful their lives are. Across this research, there was a clear influence of positive affect, whether assessed in the moment (Hicks, Schlegel, & King, 2010) or induced in the laboratory (King et al., 2006). These researchers theorized that positive affect provides one source of information people may consult in forming judgments of meaningfulness and that positive affect may facilitate the ability to coherently process experience (Hicks & King, 2007; King, Burton, Hicks, & Dragotis, 2007). This perspective is important for understanding meaning in life, as it suggests that the experience of pleasure—at least in terms of pleasant, positive emotions—may not only influence the experience of meaning in life, but may also be a critical aspect of being able to derive meaning from experience. This would have to be considered a hedonistic route to what is most often thought of as a eudaimonic outcome.

Despite this trend in the research, it is not so clear what people should do in order to obtain pleasure as one route toward meaning. In their study of eudaimonic versus hedonic behaviors, Steger and colleagues found that on a day-to-day basis, engaging in hedonic behaviors failed to have a positive relationship with meaning in life, and those who engaged in the greatest number of hedonic behaviors over the course of the study reported the lowest levels of meaning in life (though with a small negative effect size, $r = -22$, $p < .05$; Steger, Frazier, & Zacchanini, 2008). Perhaps trying to identify an objective list of hedonistic behaviors is self-defeating; after all, what is pleasant for one may not be so for another. Taken all together, there appears to be some justification for thinking that meaning in life is useful as an indicator of hedonic well-being.

For psychologists, imagining that meaning in life is both a fine indicator of eudaimonic well-being and a consistent indicator of hedonic well-being is not a particularly sticky intellectual problem. Because, empirically speaking, people who feel their lives are meaningful seem prone to adding desirable qualities to our societies (e.g., Steger, Kashdan, & Oishi, 2008), it does not seem so bad that they enjoy themselves, too. Further, people living self-identified meaningful lives appear to be among the best-functioning members of society (e.g., low drug/alcohol abuse, low levels of mental illness), which complies with Aristotelian ideals about virtue. The central fear about hedonistic paths to fulfillment seems to be that self-gratification can lead to a shallow, trivial, materialistic existence (Ryan et al., 2008). Perhaps that could be so if one used the raw pursuit of pleasure or material goods as the yardstick for measuring hedonic well-being. What is compelling about thinking of meaning in life as an indicator of hedonic well-being is that meaning in life is inversely related to such materialistic pursuits (Kashdan & Breen, 2007).

Meaning in Life Is a Flagship Indicator of Well-Being

From our reading of the literature, we gather the impression that eudaimonic theorists are sympathetic to including meaning in life among the aspects of the best to which we aspire. Hedonistic theorists may argue that meaning in life is fine, as long as it is deemed pleasing, preferable, or desirable by the person whose well-being is being debated. Thus, normatively, people ought to desire meaning in life, and normally speaking, research has confirmed that they do. Yet, the people who report an abundance of meaning seem unlikely to fall into any onanistic, hedonic trap. Meaning in life emphasizes personal expressiveness, and is associated with a pleasant emotional experience of life. At the same time, meaning in life reflects societal expectations regarding relating, contributing, and functioning. Meaning in life seems to occur when people have balanced positive experiences, self-expression, and a reflective, self-knowledgeable pursuit of worthy aims in the context of positive relationships. Meaning, like the perfect chair, balances hedonistic expression and eudaimonic constraint.

Promoting Meaning in Life

Then, how can a person design a balanced life of personal expressiveness with the constraint of his or her self-development, social responsibilities, and unique set of personal circumstances? In this section, we suggest specific paths to promoting meaning in life based on Steger's (2011, 2012; Steger et al., 2006, 2012, in press) conceptual model of meaning in life. As described in an earlier section, the model integrates both cognitive and motivational dimensions, namely comprehension and purpose, respectively, which function reciprocally such that a person's comprehension of life shapes her or his purpose, and her or his purpose is also woven into identity, behavior, and even personality (McKnight & Kashdan, 2009). In sum, Steger's (2011) conceptual model of meaning in life suggests that people are likely to experience a greater sense of meaning in life as they achieve (a) a consistent set of understanding of one's self, the world they live in, and their unique fit in the world (i.e., comprehension side of meaning) and (b) an overarching set of goals or missions they strive to accomplish (i.e., purpose side of meaning), with the close interaction between these two components facilitated by their goal-directed activities.

Promoting Comprehension and Identity Formation

How do people build a comprehensive set of understandings of who they are (e.g., their distinct self-attributes such as abilities, characters and personality, preferences, weaknesses, and strengths), what the world is like to them (e.g., worldview, beliefs, external resources), and where they fit in and how they interact with the world as a person (e.g., one's roles, one's opportunities and limitations)? Literature has suggested that identity formation is the essential in self-understanding (Erikson, 1968) and that people make sense of their lives by making life stories (McAdams, 1993).

Schwartz (2002) proposed two processes of identity formation: affective and cognitive. The first, an affective, discovery-based process, is said to emphasize an intuitive sense of fit between identity alternatives and one's innate, true self. The second, a cognitive, construction-based process, involves problem solving, rational thoughts, decision making, and real-life choice. Emphasizing the first process, eudaimonic identity theory suggests that the best form of identity is achieved when individuals are able to identify their best potentials and engage in activities that move them toward realizing those potentials, which comes from the feelings of personal expressiveness (Waterman, 1992, 2004). The importance of recognizing "true self" and "authenticity" in eudaimonic identity formation is supported by several empirical studies that have shown the relationships between having a greater sense of meaning and higher "true self-concept" accessibility (Schlegel, Hicks, Arndt, & King, 2009), a sense of contact with the self (Debats, Drost, & Hansen, 1995), and people's beliefs that their behavior is authentic (Kernis & Goldman, 2006). Schwartz, Kurtines, and Montgomery (2005) also found that an intervention based on eudaimonic identity theory promoted the identification of, and engagement in, personally expressive activities.

Meanwhile, the second process emphasizes people's rational-thinking process that involves adaptive and realistic problem solving and decision making. This cognitive aspect of identity formation may require an individual to obtain and evaluate information such as what the world is like, how they fit in, and what the resources or barriers are in their external environments. In this sense, this process seems to map onto their understandings of the world and their interactions with the world, which are theorized to be the bases of comprehension along with self-understanding.

As such, the two processes of identity formation appear to highlight how an individual develops a sense of identity from different angles. Thus, combining the cognitively focused and emotionally focused strategies into a single intervention program may effectively enhance people's comprehension of their lives, one of the essential building blocks of promoting meaning in life. Ideally, efforts to promote meaning in life can begin at early stages of life (e.g., early adolescence, if not earlier) because cognitive capacities to narrate and comprehend one's life actively develop in this period (Steger et al., 2012).

Meaning in life has been studied in older people and college students, but there has been relatively less attention paid to meaning development in children and adolescents, let alone to promoting their sense of meaning (Steger et al., 2012). However, developmental literature on cognitive development, identity formation, and life story construction consistently suggests that making sense of oneself and one's life begins at younger ages (Habermas, Ehlert-Lerche, & de Silveira, 2009; Peterson & McCabe, 1983). For example, the capacity of autobiographical reasoning that links events in a life with each other and with individuals' development gradually leads to the construction of a skeletal cognitive "life story schema" that helps them make sense of how various life events have influenced who they are (i.e., the self) and their life trajectories (Habermas & Bluck, 2000; McAdams, 1993; Steger et al., 2012). As such, the bases of leading a meaningful life begin to develop in early life stages, calling for more attention to meaning in life development among the younger population. Autobiographical reasoning abilities also offer another route for increasing meaning in life.

We believe that narrative meaning making may assist people to engage in active exploration of self and the world that may facilitate self-development with insight and understanding. Reflection on self as well as the world around them would be one path to self-expression within constraints, which we argued may lead to achieving a more meaningful life. A substantial body of literature has suggested that cultivating life narratives helps people develop a sense of identity (Erikson, 1968) and create coherent autobiographical themes, self-continuity, and individuality (Singer, 2004). Specifically, life review (Butler, 1974) and life story (McAdams, 1995) give new significance and meaning to an individual's life through the processes of reevaluating prior experience, resolving and integrating past conflict, and reintegrating them into their current life context. In a similar vein, the concept of "self-authorship" (Baxter Magolda, 1992, 2001), referring to one's internal capacities to define one's beliefs and values, identity, and relations with others through "reflective judgments," is also suggested to be central to meaning making. Focusing on life narratives should assist identity formation, in particular, narratives that emphasize growth and development. *Growth narrative* refers to interpreting the individual's life as involving progressive and prosocial development in both the past (e.g., autobiographical memories) and the future (e.g., personal goals; Bauer, McAdams, & Pals, 2008). Research has suggested that life stories with themes of growth are linked to growth-oriented identities that tend to precede increases in meaning making and adaptation (e.g., Bauer & McAdams, 2010; King & Smith, 2004; Pals, 2006), which appears to facilitate eudaimonic resilience that involves personal meaning making (Bauer & Park, in press).

Researchers have suggested that the construction of a life narrative involves social–cognitive processes. For example, Staudinger (2001) argued that reflecting on one's life together with a trusted person may facilitate the life reflection process because striving for new insights about oneself and about life in general is challenging and taxing. Shared family narratives, defined as stories that have been repeatedly told to children and adolescents, comprise younger people's life narratives and self-understanding (Bohanek, Marin, Fivush, & Duke, 2006; Habermas et al., 2009; Hayden, Singer, & Chrisler, 2006), suggesting the role of significant others in their meaning making. Steger et al. (2012) also emphasized the role of social learning and modeling in the development of adolescents' judgments that their lives are meaningful, explaining that people around them (e.g., parents, teachers, and peers) and even media offer various ways of finding and defining meaning. An individual may develop understandings of the constraints of the human condition, societal demands, and cultural scripts through this social learning process, helping balance a desire for unrestrained self-expressiveness and pleasure.

Theory and research have suggested that life stories tend to center on certain themes, needs, and values, from which people tend to derive a sense of meaning in their lives. For example, people tend to use four themes to make sense of their lives, themes that correspond to the four main aspects of the meanings of life (see Baumeister, 1991, for details): (a) *purpose* (i.e., people wish to interpret events as being purposive/desirable ends and outcomes), (b) *efficacy* (i.e., people want to make a difference in external events, autonomy, and control), (c) *value and justification* (i.e., people want to have reliable criteria of right and wrong that can be used to make moral choices and to define one's own actions as good), and (d) *self-worth* (i.e., people seek positive affirmation of the self).

Research has also suggested that meaning is most fully achieved when people actively engage in pursuits that transcend their own immediate interests. Self-transcendence is considered to reflect a more mature form of meaning and is associated with greater experiences of meaning in life (Reker & Wong, 1988) and is a defining feature of purpose in life (Damon et al., 2003). Also, serving some greater good is a core theoretical and empirical feature of calling (Dik & Duffy, 2009) and work that has meaning (Steger & Dik, 2010). In relation to the significance of self-transcendence, Seligman (2002) proposed that meaning comes from the dedication of one's signature talents to some entity beyond one's self, suggesting the importance of recognizing and practicing one's character strengths and positive attributes such as one's core value system. This may lead to self-realization and expressions of virtue, resonating with pursuing a life of virtue or excellence that comprises central tenets of the eudaimonic well-being.

Although some themes—like being a good relationship partner, attaining personal growth, and self-transcendence—seem nearly universal (see Steger, 2012), it appears important for people to shape these and other themes to their idiosyncratic nature and circumstances. Individuals' sources of meaning incorporate modes of conduct and goals in life (Reker, 2000) that reflect the interaction and integration between microlevel and macrolevel life themes (e.g., historically and culturally determined value systems) and further crystallize their perception of who they are and how they see themselves in their social life (Bar-Tur, Savaya, & Prager, 2001). Thus, autonomy support is central to identifying viable sources of meaning, and helping people identify and express their own sources of meaning should facilitate the integrative comprehension of their lives.

In sum, comprehension, a cognitive building block of meaning in life, may be facilitated through engaging in both affective and cognitive identity formation process and making growth-oriented narratives with a particular focus on certain life themes discussed previously. It would be beneficial for this to begin relatively early in development in socially supportive environments, using specific questions, protocols, inventories, and activities that promote self-exploration. Next, let's turn to the motivational components of meaning in life.

Promoting Purpose

Purpose refers to an individual's long-term and overarching goal or mission to which the individual is highly committed and actively engaged (Steger, 2011). The model of purpose specifies that people may cultivate and elaborate their sense of purpose by discerning, committing themselves to, and engaging themselves in their personally meaningful goals. Research has suggested that commitment to personal goals lends a sense of agency, life structure, and personal meaning to people's lives (Cantor & Sanderson, 1999; McGregor & Little, 1998) and serves as an important vehicle for self-discovery and psychological need satisfaction (Sheldon & Elliot, 1999; Sheldon & Kasser, 1998), highlighting the essential role of goal pursuit in achieving a sense of meaning in life. Further, purpose is seen to have the capacity to stimulate goals, manage behaviors, and help people allocate their limited attentional and temporal resources (McKnight & Kashdan, 2009).

Goal pursuit and purpose are tightly associated as the model posits; however, there are two things to be considered in promoting meaning in life. Despite their similarity, purpose and goals are differentiated, in that purpose provides a broader motivational component that stimulates goals and influences behavior, whereas goals are more precise in their influence of proximal behaviors (McKnight & Kashdan, 2009). Also, purpose motivates the person to be goal oriented but does not necessarily lead to goal attainment, nor does it have terminal outcomes (Wilson & Murrell, 2004). Goals may lead the person to obtain terminal outcomes, but those outcomes are not necessarily personally meaningful if not linked to purpose and overarching themes. This suggests that simply having a goal will not indicate a purpose. Understanding the totality of people with respect to what motivates them to do what they do across time and context requires an even higher level construct, that is, purpose. We favor a focus on developing and striving to achieve self-concordant goals (Sheldon, 2002). Because knowledge of the self is a prerequisite for having self-concordant goals, the comprehension-building stages discussed previously are important. Once that is accomplished to some degree, people can begin to develop perspective on the kinds of purposes they would like to pursue by reflecting on the accomplishments they would like to leave behind as their legacy. From these most likely broad and vague desires, people can then proceed to identify specific routes to achieving those aims. For example, if individuals want to be remembered as a great humanitarian, it is likely that some will be better off pursuing that aim by engaging in economic development initiatives in the field, and others will be better off by engaging in social work.

Once a specific route has been found, basic goal-setting techniques can be used to help people identify the specific steps that need to be taken to put one in position to work along that route. Here is another way in which purpose differs from goals. People may not ever accomplish their purposes, and they may strive for them all their lives. Indeed, it is desirable that a purpose lies off in the hazy distance. In contrast, a good goal is concrete and achievable. Like goals, however, it is highly likely that people will feel that they have multiple purposes (e.g., being a good parent, attaining eminence in one's chosen line of work, making the world a better place), and they may need to balance the demands of working toward one purpose versus others.

CONCLUSION

Very few people would invest the time, effort, and occasional sacri-fice required to cultivate a life of meaning if their understandings of their selves, world, and life were grim and pleasureless and their pursuit of pur-pose yielded only tedium and irritation. The meaningful life is, of course, more than an effort to string together an endless succession of pleasures. But the meaningful life—in our view—requires some pleasure, some aes-thetic appeal and beautiful expression (at least in the eyes of the one living the life), within the parameters of autonomous self-development, prolonged effort toward a valued end, and responsibility toward the other stakeholders in our lives. In this view, meaning in life sits comfortably at the merger of the eudaimonic and the hedonic. And perhaps its position there challenges us to consider whether meaning, rather than pleasure, should be considered to be the foundation of well-being.

REFERENCES

Art: Architects' furniture. (1957, February 18). *Time Magazine*. Retrieved from http://www.time.com/time/magazine/article/0,9171,809146,00.html

Bar-Tur, L., Savaya, R., & Prager, E. (2001). Sources of meaning in life for young and old Israeli Jews and Arabs. *Journal of Aging Studies, 15*, 253–269.

Battista, J., & Almond, R. (1973). The development of meaning in life. *Psychiatry, 36*, 409–427.

Bauer, J. J., & McAdams, D. P. (2010). Eudaimonic growth: Narrative growth goals predict increases in ego development and subjective well-being 3 years later. *Developmental Psychology, 46*, 761–772. doi:10.1037/a0019654

Bauer, J. J., McAdams, D. P., & Pals, J. L. (2008). Narrative identity and eudai-monic well-being. *Journal of Happiness Studies, 9*, 81–104. doi:10.1007/s10902-006-9021-6

Bauer, J. J., & Park, S. (in press). Growth isn't just for the young: Growth narratives, eudaimonic resilience, and the aging self. In P. S. Frye and C. L. M. Keyes (Eds.), *Frontiers of resilient aging*. Cambridge, England: Cambridge University Press.

Baumeister, R. F. (1991). *Meanings of life*. New York, NY: Guilford Press.

Baxter Magolda, M. B. (1992). *Knowing and reasoning in college: Gender-related patterns in students' intellectual development*. San Francisco, CA: Jossey Bass.

Baxter Magolda, M. B. (2001). *Making their own way: Narratives for transforming higher education to promote self-development*. Sterling, VA: Stylus.

Bohanek, J. G., Marin, K. A., Fivush, R., & Duke, M. P. (2006). Family narrative interaction and children's sense of self. *Family Process, 45*, 39–54.

Boyle, P. A., Barnes, L. L., Buchman, A. S., & Bennett, D. A. (2009). Purpose in life is associated with mortality among community-dwelling older persons. *Psychosomatic Medicine, 71*, 574–579. doi:10.1097/PSY.0b013e3181a5a7c0

Boyle, P. A., Buchman, A. S., Barnes, L. L., & Bennett, D. A. (2010). Effect of a purpose in life on risk of incident Alzheimer disease and mild cognitive impairment in community-dwelling older persons. *Archives of General Psychiatry, 67*, 304–310. doi:10.1001/archgenpsychiatry.2009.208

Boyle, P. A., Buchman, A. S., & Bennett, D. A. (2010). Purpose in life is associated with a reduced risk of incident disability among community-dwelling older persons. *The American Journal of Geriatric Psychiatry, 18*, 1093–1102. doi:10.1097/JGP.0b013e3181d6c259

Butler, R. N. (1974). Successful aging and the role of the life review. *Journal of the American Geriatrics Society, 22*, 529–535.

Cantor, N., & Sanderson, C. A. (1999). Life task participation and well-being: The importance of taking part in daily life. In D. Kahneman, E. Diener, and N. Schwarz (Eds.), *Well-being: The foundations of hedonic psychology* (230–243). New York, NY: Russell Sage Foundation.

Chamberlain, K., & Zika, S. (1988). Religiosity, life meaning, and well-being: Some relationships in a sample of women. *Journal for the Scientific Study of Religion, 27*, 411–420. doi:10.2307/1387379

Crumbaugh, J. C., & Maholick, L. T. (1964). An experimental study in existentialism: The psychometric approach to Frankl's concept of noogenic neurosis. *Journal of Clinical Psychology, 20*, 200–207. doi:10.1002/1097-4679(196404)20:2<200::AID-JCLP2270200203>3.0.CO;2-U

Damon, W., Menon, J., & Bronk, K. C. (2003). The development of purpose during adolescence. *Applied Developmental Science, 7*, 119–128.

Debats, D. L. (1996). Meaning in life: Clinical relevance and predictive power. *British Journal of Clinical Psychology, 35*, 503–516. doi:10.1111/j.2044-8260.1996.tb01207.x

Debats, D. L. (1999). Sources of meaning: An investigation of significant commitments in life. *Journal of Humanistic Psychology, 39*, 30–57. doi:10.1177/0022167899394003

Debats, D. L., Drost, J., & Hansen, P. (1995). Experiences of meaning in life: A combined qualitative and quantitative approach. *British Journal of Psychology, 86*, 359–375. doi:10.1111/j.2044-8295.1995.tb02758.x

Debats, D. L., van der Lubbe, P. M., & Wezeman, F. R. A. (1993). On the psychometric properties of the Life Regard Index (LRI): A measure of meaningful life. *Personality and Individual Differences, 14*, 337–345. doi:10.1016/0191-8869 (93)90132-M

Deci, E. L., & Ryan, R. M. (2008). Hedonia, eudaimonia, and well-being: An introduction. *Journal of Happiness Studies, 9*, 1–11. doi:10.1007/s10902-006-9018-1

Diener, E. (2000). Subjective well-being: The science of happiness and a proposal for a national index. *American Psychologist, 55*, 34–43. doi:10.1037/ 0003-066X.55.1.34

Dik, B. J., & Duffy, R. D. (2009). Calling and vocation at work: Definitions and prospects for research and practice. *The Counseling Psychologist 37*, 424–450. doi:10.1177/0011000008316430

Edwards, M. J., & Holden, R. R. (2001). Coping, meaning in life, and suicidal manifestations: Examining gender differences. *Journal of Clinical Psychology, 57*, 1517–1534. doi:10.1002/jclp.1114

Erikson, E. H. (1968). *Identity: Youth and crisis.* New York, NY: Norton.

Frankl, V. E. (1963). *Man's search for meaning: An introduction to logotherapy.* New York, NY: Washington Square Press.

Habermas, T., & Bluck, S. (2000). Getting a life: The emergence of the life story in adolescence. *Psychological Bulletin, 126*, 248–269.doi:10.1037/ 0033-2909.126.5.748

Habermas, T., Ehlert-Lerche, S., & de Silveira, C. (2009). The development of the temporal macrostructure of life narratives across adolescence: Beginnings, linear narrative form, and endings. *Journal of Personality, 77*, 527–560. doi:10.1111/ j.1467-6494.2008.00557.x

Hayden, J. M., Singer, J. A., & Chrisler, J. C. (2006). The transmission of birth stories from mother to daughter: Self-esteem and mother-daughter attachment. *Sex Roles, 55*, 373–383. doi:10.1007/s11199-006-9090-3

Heine, S. J., Proulx, T., & Vohs, K. D. (2006). The meaning maintenance model: On the coherence of social motivations. *Personality and Social Psychology Review, 10*, 88–110. doi:10.1207/s15327957pspr1002_1

Hicks, J. A., & King, L. A. (2007). Meaning in life and seeing the big picture: Positive affect and global focus. *Cognition and Emotion, 21*, 1577–1584. doi:10.1080/02699930701347304

Hicks, J. A., Schlegel, R. J., & King, L. A. (2010). Social threats, happiness, and the dynamics of meaning in life judgments. *Personality and Social Psychology Bulletin, 36*, 1305–1317. doi:10.1177/0146167210381650

Huta, V., & Ryan, R. M. (2010). Pursuing pleasure or virtue: The differential and overlapping well-being benefits of hedonic and eudaimonic motives. *Journal of Happiness Studies, 11*, 735–762. doi:10.1007/s10902-009-9171-4

Jim, H. S., Richardson, S. A., Golden-Kreutz, D. M., & Anderson, B. L. (2006). Strategies used in coping with a cancer diagnosis predict meaning in life for survivors. *Health Psychology, 25,* 753–761. doi:10.1037/0278-6133.25.6.753

Kashdan, T. B., Biswas-Diener, R., & King, L. A. (2008). Reconsidering happiness: The costs of distinguishing between hedonics and eudaimonia. *The Journal of Positive Psychology, 3,* 219–233. doi:10.1080/17439760802303044

Kashdan, T. B., & Breen, W. E. (2007). Materialism and diminished well-being: Experiential avoidance as a mediating mechanism. *Journal of Social and Clinical Psychology, 26,* 521–539. doi:10.1521/jscp.2007.26.5.521

Kennedy, J. E., Kanthamani, H., & Palmer, J. (1994). Psychic and spiritual experiences, health, well-being, and meaning in life. *The Journal of Parapsychology, 58,* 353–383.

Kernis, M. H., & Goldman, B. M. (2006). A multi-component conceptualization of authenticity: Theory and research. In M. P. Zanna (Ed.), *Advances in experimental social psychology* (pp. 283–357). New York, NY: Academic Press.

Keyes, C. L. M., Shmotkin, D., & Ryff, C. D. (2002). Optimizing well-being: The empirical encounter of two traditions. *Journal of Personality and Social Psychology, 82,* 1007–1022. doi:10.1037/0022-3514.82.6.1007

King, L. A., Burton, C. B., Hicks, J. A., & Dragotis, S. (2007). Ghosts, UFOs, and magic: Positive affect and the experiential system. *Journal of Personality and Social Psychology, 92,* 905–919. doi:10.1037/0022-3514.92.5.905

King, L. A., Hicks, J. A., Krull, J. L., & Del Gaiso, A. K. (2006). Positive affect and the experience of meaning in life. *Journal of Personality and Social Psychology, 90,* 179–196. doi:10.1037/0022-3514.90.1.179

King, L. A., & Smith, N. G. (2004). Gay and straight possible selves: Goals, identity, subjective well-being, and personality development. *Journal of Personality, 72,* 967–994. doi:10.1111/j.0022-3506.2004.00287.x

Klinger, E. (1977). *Meaning and void.* Minneapolis, MN: University of Minnesota Press.

Lambert, N. M., Stillman, T. F., Baumeister, R. F., Fincham, F. D., Hicks, J. A., & Graham, S. M. (2010). Family as a salient source of meaning in young adulthood. *The Journal of Positive Psychology, 5,* 367–376. doi:10.1080/17439760.2010.516616

McAdams, D. P. (1993). *The stories we live by: Personal myths and the making of the self.* New York, NY: William Morrow.

McAdams, D. P. (1995). What do we know when we know a person? *Journal of Personality, 63,* 365–396. doi:10.1111/j.1467-6494.1995.tb00500.x

McGregor, I., & Little, B. R. (1998). Personal projects, happiness, and meaning: On doing well and being yourself. *Journal of Personality and Social Psychology, 74,* 494–512.

McKnight, P. E., & Kashdan, T. B. (2009). Purpose in life as a system that creates and sustains health and well-being: An integrative, testable theory. *Review of General Psychology, 13,* 242–251. doi:10.1037/a0017152

Newcomb, M. D., & Harlow, L. L. (1986). Life events and substance use among adolescents: Mediating effects of perceived loss of control and meaningless in life. *Journal of Personality and Social Psychology, 51*, 564–577. doi:10.1037/0022-3514.51.3.564

Owens, G. P., Steger, M. F., Whitesell, A. A., & Herrerra, C. J. (2009). Posttraumatic stress disorder, guilt, depression, and meaning in life among military veterans. *Journal of Traumatic Stress, 22*, 654–657.

Pals, J. L. (2006). Narrative identity processing of difficult life experiences: Pathways of personality development and positive self-transformation in adulthood. *Journal of Personality, 74*, 1079–1109. doi:10.1111/j.1467-6494.2006.00403.x

Park, C. L. (2008). Testing the meaning-making model of coping with loss. *Journal of Social and Clinical Psychology, 27*, 970–994. doi:10.1521/jscp.2008.27.9.970

Park, C. L., & Folkman, S. (1997). Meaning in the context of stress and coping. *Review of General Psychology, 1*, 115–144. doi:10.1037/1089-2680.1.2.115

Pearson, P. R., & Sheffield, B. F. (1989). Psychoticism and purpose in life. *Personality and Individual Differences, 10*, 1321–1322. doi:10.1016/0191-8869(89)90245-6

Peterson, C., & McCabe, A. (1983). *Developmental psycholinguistics: Three ways of looking at a child's narratives*. New York, NY: Plenum Press.

Phillips, W. M., Watkins, J. T., & Noll, G. (1974). Self-actualization, self-transcendence, and personal philosophy. *Journal of Humanistic Psychology, 14*, 53–73. doi:10.1177/002216787401400312

Ralph, P., & Wand, Y. (2009). A proposal for a formal definition of the design concept. In K. Lyytinen, P. Loucopoulos, J. Mylopoulos, & W. Robinson, (Eds.), *Design requirements workshop* (LNBIP 14, pp. 103–136). New York, NY: Springer-Verlag.

Reker, G. T. (2000). Theoretical perspective, dimensions, and measurement of existential meaning. In G. T. Reker & K. Chamberlain (Eds.), *Exploring existential meaning: Optimizing human development across the life span* (pp. 39–55). Thousand Oaks, CA: Sage.

Reker, G. T., & Wong, P. T. P. (1988). Aging as an individual process: Toward a theory of personal meaning. In J. E. Birren & V. L. Bengston (Eds.), *Emergent theories of aging* (pp. 214–246). New York, NY: Springer.

Ryan, R. M., & Deci, E. L. (2001). On happiness and human potentials: A review of research on hedonic and eudaimonic well-being. *Annual Review of Psychology, 52*, 141–166. doi:10.1146/annurev.psych.52.1.141

Ryan, R. M., Huta, V., & Deci, E. L. (2008). Living well: A self-determination theory perspective on eudaimonia. *Journal of Happiness Studies, 9*, 139–170. doi:10.1007/s10902-006-9023-4

Ryff, C. D. (1989). Happiness is everything, or is it? Explorations on the meaning of psychological well-being. *Journal of Personality and Social Psychology, 57*, 1069–1081. doi:10.1037/0022-3514.57.6.1069

Ryff, C. D., & Keyes, C. L. M. (1995). The structure of well-being revisited. *Journal of Personality and Social Psychology, 69*, 719–727. doi:10.1037/0022-3514.69.4.719

Ryff, C. D., & Singer, B. H. (1998). The contours of positive human health. *Psychological Inquiry, 9*, 1–28. doi:10.1207/s15327965pli0901_1

Schlegel, R. J., Hicks, J. A., Arndt, J., & King, L. A. (2009). Thine own self: True self-concept accessibility and meaning in life. *Journal of Personality and Social Psychology, 96*, 473–490. doi:10.1037/a0014060

Schlegel, R. J., Hicks, J. A., King, L. A., & Arndt, J. (2011). Feeling like you know who you are: Perceived true self-knowledge and meaning in life. *Personality and Social Psychology Bulletin, 37*, 745–756. doi:10.1177/0146167211400424

Schnell, T. (2009). The Sources of Meaning and Meaning in Life Questionnaire (SoMe): Relations to demographics and well-being. *The Journal of Positive Psychology, 4*, 483–499. doi:10.1080/17439760903271074

Schnell, T., & Becker, P. (2006). Personality and meaning in life. *Personality and Individual Differences, 41*, 117–129. doi:10.1016/j.paid.2005.11.030

Schwartz, S. J. (2002). An examination of change processes in identity: Integrating the constructivist and discovery perspectives on identity. *Identity: International Journal of Theory and Research, 2*, 317–339. doi:10.1207/S1532706XID0204_03

Schwartz, S. J., Kurtines, W. M., & Montgomery, M. J. (2005). A comparison of two approaches for facilitating identity exploration processes in emerging adults: An exploratory study. *Journal of Adolescent Research, 20*, 309–345. doi:10.1177/0743558404273119

Seligman, M. E. P. (2002). *Authentic happiness*. New York, NY: Free Press.

Sheldon, K. M. (2002). The self-concordance model of healthy goal striving: When personal goals correctly represent the person. In E. L. Deci & R. M. Ryan (Eds.), *Handbook of self-determination research* (pp. 65–86). Rochester, NY: University of Rochester Press.

Sheldon, K. M., & Elliot, A. J. (1999). Goal striving, need satisfaction, and longitudinal well-being: The self-concordance model. *Journal of Personality and Social Psychology, 76*, 546–557.

Sheldon, K. M., & Kasser, T. (1998). Pursuing personal goals: Skills enable progress but not all progress is beneficial. *Personality and Social Psychology Bulletin, 24*, 1319–1331.

Simon, L., Arndt, J., Greenberg, J., Pyszczynski, T., & Solomon, S. (1998). Terror management and meaning: Evidence that the opportunity to defend the worldview in response to mortality salience increases the meaningfulness of life in the mildly depressed. *Journal of Personality, 66*, 359–382. doi:10.1111/1467-6494.00016

Singer, J. A. (2004). Narrative identity and meaning-making across the adult lifespan: An introduction. *Journal of Personality, 72*, 437–460. doi:10.1111/j.0022-3506.2004.00268.x

Staudinger, U. M. (2001). Life reflection: A social-cognitive analysis of life review. *Review of General Psychology, 5*, 148–160.

Steger, M. F. (2006). An illustration of issues in factor extraction and identification of dimensionality in psychological assessment data. *Journal of Personality Assessment, 86,* 263–272. doi:10.1207/s15327752jpa8603_03

Steger, M. F. (2011). Meaning in life. In S. J. Lopez & C. R. Snyder (Eds.), *Oxford handbook of positive psychology* (2nd ed., pp. 667–688). New York, NY: Oxford University Press.

Steger, M. F. (2012). Experiencing meaning in life: Optimal functioning at the nexus of spirituality, psychopathology, and well-being. In P. T. P. Wong & P. S. Fry (Eds.), *The human quest for meaning* (2nd ed., pp. 165–184). Mahwah, NJ: Erlbaum.

Steger, M. F., Beeby, A., Garrett, S., & Kashdan, T. B. (in press). Creating a stable architectural framework of existence: Proposing a model of lifelong meaning. In S. David & I. Boniwell (Eds.), *The Oxford handbook of happiness.* Oxford, England: Oxford University Press.

Steger, M. F., Bundick, M., & Yeager, D. (2012). Understanding and promoting meaning in life during adolescence. In R. J. R. Levesque (Ed.), *Encyclopedia of adolescence* (pp. 1666–1677). New York, NY: Springer.

Steger, M. F., & Dik, B. J. (2010). Work as meaning. In P. A. Linley, S. Harrington, & N. Page, (Eds.), *Oxford handbook of positive psychology and work* (pp.131–142). Oxford, England: Oxford University Press.

Steger, M. F., & Frazier, P. (2005). Meaning in life: One link in the chain from religion to wellbeing. *Journal of Counseling Psychology, 52,* 574–582. doi:10.1037/0022-0167.52.4.574

Steger, M. F., Frazier, P., Oishi, S., & Kaler, M. (2006). The Meaning in Life Questionnaire: Assessing the presence of and search for meaning in life. *Journal of Counseling Psychology, 53,* 80–93. doi:10.1037/0022-0167.53.1.80

Steger, M. F., Frazier, P., & Zacchanini, J. L. (2008). Terrorism in two cultures: Traumatization and existential protective factors following the September 11th attacks and the Madrid train bombings. *Journal of Loss and Trauma, 13,* 511–527. doi:10.1080/15325020802173660

Steger, M. F., & Kashdan, T. B. (2007). Stability and specificity of meaning in life and life satisfaction over one year: Implications for outcome assessment. *Journal of Happiness Studies, 8,* 161–179. doi:10.1007/s10902-006-9011-8

Steger, M. F., & Kashdan, T. B. (2009). Depression and everyday social activity, intimacy, and well-being. *Journal of Counseling Psychology, 56,* 289–300. doi:10.1037/a0015416

Steger, M. F., Kashdan, T. B., & Oishi, S. (2008). Being good by doing good: Daily eudaimonic activity and well-being. *Journal of Research in Personality, 42,* 22–42. doi:10.1016/j.jrp.2007.03.004

Steger, M. F., Kashdan, T. B., Sullivan, B. A., & Lorentz, D. (2008). Understanding the search for meaning in life: Personality, cognitive style, and the dynamic between seeking and experiencing meaning. *Journal of Personality, 76,* 199–228. doi:10.1111/j.1467-6494.2007.00484.x

Steger, M. F., Mann, J. R., Michels, P., & Cooper, T. C. (2009). Meaning in life, anxiety, depression, and general health among smoking cessation patients. *Journal of Psychosomatic Research, 67,* 353–358. doi:10.1016/j.jpsychores.2009.02.006

Steger, M. F., Oishi, S., & Kashdan, T. B. (2009). Meaning in life across the life span: Levels and correlates of meaning in life from emerging adulthood to older adulthood. *The Journal of Positive Psychology, 4,* 43–52. doi:10.1080/17439760802303127

Steger, M. F., Oishi, S., & Kesebir, S. (2011). Is a life without meaning satisfying? The moderating role of the search for meaning in satisfaction with life judgments. *The Journal of Positive Psychology, 6,* 173–180. doi:10.1080/17439760.2011.569171

Stillman, T. F., Baumeister, R. F., Lambert, N. M., Crescioni, A. W., DeWall, C. N., & Fincham, F. D. (2009). Alone and without purpose: Life loses meaning following social exclusion. *Journal of Experimental Social Psychology, 45,* 686–694. doi:10.1016/j.jesp.2009.03.007

Thompson, N. J., Coker, J., Krause, J. S., & Henry, E. (2003). Purpose in life as a mediator of adjustment after spinal cord injury. *Rehabilitation Psychology, 48,* 100–108. doi:10.1037/0090-5550.48.2.100

Tiberius, V., & Hall, A. (2010). Normative theory and psychological research: Hedonism, eudaimonism and why it matters. *The Journal of Positive Psychology, 5,* 212–225. doi:10.1080/17439761003790971

Waterman, A. S. (1992). Identity as an aspect of optimal psychological functioning. In G. R. Adams, T. Gullotta, and R. Montemayor (Eds.), *Advances in adolescent development: Vol. 4. Identity formation during adolescence* (pp. 50–72). Newbury Park, CA: Sage.

Waterman, A. S. (1993). Two conceptions of happiness: Contrasts of personal expressiveness (eudaimonia) and hedonic enjoyment. *Journal of Personality and Social Psychology, 64,* 678–691. doi:10.1037/0022-3514.64.4.678

Waterman, A. S. (2004). Finding someone to be: Studies on the role of intrinsic motivation in identity formation. *Identity: An International Journal of Theory and Research, 4,* 209–228. doi:10.1207/s1532706xid0403_1

Wilson, K. G., & Murrell, A. R. (2004). Values work in acceptance and commitment therapy: Setting a course for behavioral treatment. In S. C. Hayes, V. M. Follette, & M. Linehan (Eds.), *Mindfulness and acceptance: Expanding the cognitive-behavioral tradition* (pp. 120–151). New York, NY: Guilford Press.

Zika, S., & Chamberlain, K. (1992). On the relation between meaning in life and psychological well-being. *British Journal of Psychology, 83,* 133–145. doi:10.1111/j.2044-8295.1992.tb02429.x

9

PASSION AND OPTIMAL FUNCTIONING IN SOCIETY: A EUDAIMONIC PERSPECTIVE

ROBERT J. VALLERAND

What is the good life? How can people's lives be most worth living? For centuries, philosophers have pondered these questions with two positions emerging (see Ryan & Deci, 2001; Waterman, 1993). The first approach, referred to as *hedonia*, suggests that the good life entails experiencing positive affect in and of itself. Pleasure, irrespective of its cause, is to be sought as the primary goal of existence. The second position rejects hedonia as being shortsighted and posits that the good life is one wherein the focus is on self-realization and reaching one's potential. This position, called *eudaimonia*, posits that one's happiness is to be found in trying to reach personal fulfillment in accordance with one's true self.

In this chapter, I explore three claims with respect to eudaimonia. First, although self-realization is important in eudaimonia, a eudaimonic position should help document how one can reach personal fulfillment with respect to all aspects of one's life including, but not limited to, achievement. Other aspects that fall under the umbrella of eudaimonia include psychological

DOI: 10.1037/14092-010
The Best Within Us: Positive Psychology Perspectives on Eudaimonia, Alan S. Waterman (Editor)
Copyright © 2013 by the American Psychological Association. All rights reserved.

well-being, physical health, relationships, and contributing to society. This view represents what I term *optimal functioning in society* (OFIS; Vallerand, Forest, et al. 2011). Such a view is in line with Waterman's (see Introduction, this volume) perspective on eudaimonia as happiness, flourishing, and self-realization. Second, I propose that merely seeking to reach one's potential does not ensure high levels of optimal functioning. The energy people put into reaching their potential has a profound effect on the level of optimal functioning that will be reached. In this vein, the concept of passion (Vallerand et al., 2003) deserves a special place. Indeed, when engaging in their passionate activity on a recurrent basis, people seek to reach their potential and are willing to overcome important obstacles. They then should be more likely to persist in their quest for self-realization than nonpassionate individuals. Third, not all types of passion are equal in leading to self-fulfillment. Specifically, harmonious passion is more conducive to optimal functioning than is obsessive passion.

The purpose of this chapter is to document how passion plays a role in leading one to reach high levels of OFIS (Vallerand, Forest, et al., 2011). The first two sections describe the dualistic model of passion (Vallerand et al., 2003) and OFIS, respectively. The third section reviews research dealing with the role of passion in the different elements that make up OFIS. Finally, I offer some conclusions regarding passion and optimal functioning.

ON THE PSYCHOLOGY OF PASSION

Passion has generated considerable attention from philosophers, especially from an emotional perspective. Two positions have emerged (Rony, 1990). The first posits that passion entails a loss of reason and control (Plato, 429–347 BC; Spinoza, 1632–1677). In line with the etymology of the word *passion* (from the Latin *passio* for suffering), people afflicted with passion are seen as experiencing a kind of suffering, as if they were slaves to their passion, because it comes to control them. The second perspective portrays passion in a more positive light. For instance, Descartes (1596–1650) defined passions as strong emotions with inherent behavioral tendencies that can be positive as long as reason underlies the behavior. Similarly, Hegel (1770–1831) argued that passions are necessary to reach the highest levels of achievement. This second view sees passion as yielding positive outcomes when individuals are in control of their passion. Taken together, these two positions highlight the duality of passion.

Until recently, little has been written on the psychology of passion. The few psychologists who have looked at the concept have underscored its motivational aspect. Some authors have noted that people will spend large amounts of time and effort to reach their passionate goals (see Frijda, Mesquita, Sonnemans, & Van Goozen, 1991) or working on an activity that they love (Baum & Locke, 2004). Nearly all empirical work on passion has been conducted in the area of passionate love (e.g., Hatfield & Walster, 1978). This research, however, does not deal with the topic at hand, namely, feeling passionate toward activities. None of this work reflects the inherent duality of passion underscored by philosophers (Vallerand, 2010).

A Dualistic Model of Passion

In line with self-determination theory (Deci & Ryan, 2000), I propose that people engage in various activities throughout life in order to grow as individuals. After a period of trial and error that would appear to start in early adolescence (Erikson, 1968), most people eventually begin to show preferences for some activities, especially those that are perceived as particularly enjoyable and important and that resonate with how they see themselves. These activities can become passionate activities. In line with the above, Vallerand et al. (2003) defined *passion* as a strong inclination toward a self-defining activity that one loves, finds important and meaningful, and in which one invests time and energy. These activities come to be so self-defining that they represent central features of one's identity. For instance, those who have a passion for playing the guitar or jogging do not merely engage in these activities. They see themselves as "guitar players" (or musicians), and "joggers."

Past research has shown that values and regulations concerning noninteresting activities can be internalized in either a controlled or an autonomous fashion (Deci et al., 1994; Vallerand, Fortier, & Guay, 1997). It is posited that activities that people like (or love) will be internalized in the person's identity and self to the extent that these are highly valued and meaningful for the person (Aron, Aron, & Smollan, 1992). Further, it is proposed that the two types of passion, harmonious and obsessive, can be distinguished in terms of how the passionate activity has been internalized. Harmonious passion results from an autonomous internalization of the activity into the person's identity. Such internalization occurs when individuals freely accept the activity as important for them without contingencies attached to it. This type of internalization emanates from the intrinsic and integrative tendencies of the self (Deci & Ryan, 2000; Ryan & Deci, 2003) and produces a motivational force to engage in the activity willingly. It engenders a sense of volition and personal endorsement about pursuing the activity.

When harmonious passion is at play, individuals freely choose to engage in the beloved activity. With this type of passion, the activity occupies a significant but not overpowering space in the person's identity and is in harmony with other aspects of the person's life. In other words, with harmonious passion the authentic integrating self (Deci & Ryan, 2000) is at play, allowing the person to fully partake in the passionate activity with an openness that is conducive to positive experiences (Hodgins & Knee, 2002). Consequently, people with a harmonious passion should be able to fully focus on the task at hand and experience positive outcomes both during task engagement (e.g., positive affect, concentration, flow) and after task engagement (e.g., general positive affect, satisfaction). There should be little or no conflict between the person's passionate activity and other life activities. Further, when prevented from engaging in their passionate activity, people with a harmonious passion should be able to adapt well to the situation and focus their attention and energy on other tasks that need to be done. Finally, with harmonious passion, the person is in control of the activity and can decide when to, and when not to, engage in the activity. People with a harmonious passion are able to forego activity engagement on a given day if needed or even to eventually terminate the relationship with the activity if they decide it has become a permanent negative factor in their life. Behavioral engagement in the passionate activity can be seen as flexible.

Conversely, obsessive passion results from a controlled internalization of the activity into one's identity. At best, it leads to values and regulations associated with the activity being partially internalized in the self and, at worst, to it being internalized completely outside the integrating self (Deci & Ryan, 2000). A controlled internalization originates from intra- and/or inter-personal pressure, typically because contingencies such as feelings of social acceptance or self-esteem have become attached to the activity (Lafrenière, Bélanger, & Sedikides, Vallerand, 2011; Mageau, Carpentier, & Vallerand, 2011) or because the sense of excitement derived from activity engagement is uncontrollable. People with an obsessive passion can thus find themselves in the position of experiencing an uncontrollable urge to partake in the activity they view as important and enjoyable. They cannot help but to engage in the passionate activity. The passion must run its course as it controls the person. Consequently, they risk experiencing conflicts and other negative affective, cognitive, and behavioral consequences during and after activity engagement. It is thus proposed that with obsessive passion, individuals come to display a rigid persistence toward the activity. Ego-invested rather than inte-grative self processes (Hodgins & Knee, 2002) are at play, leading the person to eventually become dependent on the activity. Although rigid persistence may have some benefits (e.g., improved performance), it may also come at a cost for the individual in terms of lack of flexibility and therefore lead to less than optimal functioning. Further, such persistence may lead to experiencing conflicts with other aspects in one's life (e.g., engaging in the passionate activity when one should be doing something else), as well as to frustration and rumination about the activity when prevented from engaging in it.

Initial Research on the Concept of Passion

Initial work on passion (Vallerand et al., 2003) was directed toward (a) determining the prevalence of passion for an activity in one's life, (b) developing the Passion Scale, and (c) testing the validity of elements of the passion constructs. In the initial study, Vallerand et al. (2003) had a large sample of university students complete the Passion Scale with respect to an activity that they loved, valued, and invested time and energy in doing (i.e., the passion definition criteria). A large variety of passionate activities were reported, ranging from physical activities and sports to watching movies, playing a musical instrument, and reading. Participants reported engaging in a specific passionate activity for an average of 8.5 hours per week and had been engaging in that activity for an average of almost 6 years. Clearly passionate activities are meaningful to people and are long lasting in nature. Eighty-four percent of participants indicated that they had at least a moderate level of passion for a given activity in their lives. In a subsequent study, Philippe, Vallerand, and Lavigne (2009), with a large sample ranging in age from 18 to 90 years and using a more stringent criterion for passion, found that 75% of participants had a high level of passion for an activity in their life. Similar results have been obtained in other countries (Liu et al., 2011; Stenseng, 2008). It would thus appear that the prevalence of passion is rather high and not the exclusive experience of the happy few.

The current version of the Passion Scale consists of two subscales of six items each. A sample item for harmonious passion reads: "This activity is in harmony with other activities in my life." A sample item for obsessive passion is: "I almost have an obsessive feeling toward this activity." Internal consistency analyses have shown that both subscales are reliable (typically .75 and above). Test–retest correlations over periods ranging from 4 to 6 weeks revealed moderately high stability values (in the .80s; Rousseau et al., 2002). Exploratory and confirmatory factor analyses of the Passion Scale support the presence of two factors corresponding to the two types of passion (Vallerand et al., 2003), findings that have been replicated in a number of studies with respect to a variety of activities.

With respect to the third purpose of this initial research, partial correlations (controlling for the correlation between the two types of passion) revealed that both harmonious and obsessive passions were positively associated with the passion criteria, providing support for the definition of passion, and both types of passion were found to relate to one's identity. Harmonious passion positively predicted positive affect both during and after engagement in the passionate activity, whereas obsessive passion was unrelated to positive affect but positively related to negative affect, especially after task engagement and when prevented from engaging in the activity. Further, as expected, obsessive passion was found to be more strongly related to conflict with other life activities than was harmonious passion. Since the initial publication, over 100 studies have been conducted on the role of passion in a host of cognitive, affective, behavioral, relational, and performance outcomes experienced within the realms of hundreds of passionate activities (see Vallerand, 2010, for a review).

PASSION AND OFIS

A eudaimonic perspective on well-being should focus on the fully functioning individual. In this vein, several positions have been proposed (e.g., Huppert, 2009; Ryff & Keyes, 1995; Seligman, 2011). What is common to these constructs is their multidimensional perspective. Huppert (2009) posited that psychological well-being refers to feeling good affectively as well as developing one's potential, having a sense of purpose and control, and experiencing positive relationships. Similarly, flourishing, according to Seligman (2011), entails experiencing positive emotions, engagement in valued activities, positive relationships, meaning in life, and accomplishment in one's life. Along these lines, we (Vallerand, in press; Vallerand, Forest, et al., 2011) have recently introduced a new construct, OFIS, which is conceptualized as having five components reflecting high levels of (a) psychological well-being (life satisfaction and meaning in life), (b) physical health, (c) positive relationships, (d) high performance in one's main field of endeavor (e.g., work or studies), and (e) taking to heart the welfare of one's immediate community and that of society at large.

Recent research I conducted with colleagues (Vallerand, Forest, et al., 2011) involved developing and validating an OFIS instrument with subscales corresponding to the five proposed components of OFIS. Exploratory and confirmatory factor analyses supported the presence of a five-factor structure with all items loading moderately to strongly on their respective factor and with few cross-loadings observed. These results suggest that the optimally functioning person is not simply feeling good about himself or herself, but also experiences psychological, physical, and relational wellness; performs at a high level; and contributes more than most to his or her immediate community and society at large.

In the sections that follow, I explore the evidence pertaining to the role of harmonious and obsessive passions in each of the five elements of OFIS. It will be seen that to the extent that one's passion for an activity is harmonious, this sets in motion processes that promote optimal functioning and protect against poor functioning (e.g., Keyes, 2007). However, if one's passion is obsessive, then the positive effects may not be forthcoming on some elements of optimal functioning, and an increase in poor functioning may even take place.

Passion and Psychological Well-Being

An early study evaluating the relationship of passion and psychological well-being involved having senior citizens complete instruments assessing passion, hedonic (e.g., life satisfaction) and eudaimonic (e.g., meaning in life and vitality) psychological well-being, as well as assessments of ill-being (e.g., anxiety and depression; Rousseau & Vallerand, 2003). Having a harmonious passion for an activity was expected to promote psychological well-being and protect against ill-being, whereas being obsessively passionate or nonpassionate would not. Findings supported these hypotheses. The promoting and protective functions of harmonious passion were supported while the less than optimal role of obsessive passion was demonstrated. Subsequent research with teenagers and young and middle-age adults using different measures of psychological well-being has yielded similar findings (e.g., Forest, Mageau, Sarrazin, & Morin, 2011; Vallerand et al., 2007, Studies 1 and 2; Vallerand, Mageau, et al., 2008, Study 2).

In the research discussed previously, the focus was on people who were all passionate for a given activity and how such passion relates to psychological well-being (and ill-being). Such research, however, only compared people differing with respect to types of passion and did not include nonpassionate people. Thus, it is not clear whether harmonious passion actually gives people a psychological boost and obsessive passion a drop in well-being relative to nonpassionate people. In a study looking at this issue (Philippe et al., 2009, Study 1), over 750 men and women between 18 and 90 years of age completed a questionnaire containing the Passion Scale as well as assessing the passion criteria (i.e., loving and valuing the activity, spending regular time on the activity, and the activity being perceived as a "passion") with respect to an activity that was dear to their heart. Participants also completed scales assessing hedonic (life satisfaction) and eudaimonic (self-realization) well-being. Using the passion criteria discussed previously, we distinguished those individuals who were highly passionate (a mean of 5 and more on a 7-point scale on the four passion criteria) from those who were not (below a mean of 5 on the passion criteria). Furthermore, in line with Vallerand and Houlfort (2003), among the passionate individuals we distinguished those who were "harmoniously passionate" (those with a higher z score on the harmonious passion than on the obsessive passion subscale) from those who were "obsessively passionate" (those with a higher z score on the obsessive than on the harmonious passion subscale). We then compared the three groups on the two types of psychological well-being indices.

The results showed that being harmoniously passionate for a given activity leads to higher levels of psychological well-being on both hedonic and eudaimonic psychological well-being relative to being obsessively passionate and nonpassionate. Further, the role of passion in well-being was similar for both men and women across the life span. Another finding of importance was that nonpassionate and obsessively passionate individuals did not differ. A subsequent study (Philippe et al., 2009, Study 2) using a prospective design revealed that people who were harmoniously passionate for a given activity experienced a significant increase in psychological well-being over a 1-year period. Both obsessively passionate and nonpassionate individuals experienced a slight, but significant, decrease in psychological well-being over time. Thus, overall, it would appear that harmonious passion promotes, whereas obsessive passion and being nonpassionate seem to undermine, psychological well-being.

Under which conditions should the promoting and protective functions of harmonious passion operate? Following success, all is well, and thus similar levels of well-being should be experienced by harmoniously and obsessively passionate individuals. However, it is following failure that the major differences between the two types of passionate individuals should take place. Because so much is riding on doing well for obsessively passionate individuals (e.g., maintaining their identity and their sense of self-esteem), failure may have a more devastating psychological impact on their well-being than for those who are harmoniously passionate and who can face the negative information head on, in a mindful and nondefensive manner. We recently tested these hypotheses in two studies (Lafrenière, St-Louis, & Vallerand, in press). In one study, professional painters who had more than 20 years of experience completed the Passion Scale with respect to painting and were then randomly assigned to one of two conditions. They were asked to recollect either a period of their professional life when they were highly creative (success condition) or a period when they were not very creative (failure condition). Participants were asked to recall how satisfied they were with their life at that point in time. As hypothesized, when successful, both types of passion led to equally high levels of life satisfaction. However, when unsuccessful (the failure condition), obsessive passion led to a highly significant reduction in life satisfaction. For harmonious passion, no significant drop in well-being took place. These findings were replicated in a second study (Lafrenière et al., in press, Study 2) using a diary design with passionate hockey fans following wins and losses of their favorite team during the National Hockey League playoffs. These findings indicate that harmonious passion does appear to provide a protective function against negative events with respect to potential drops in psychological well-being, whereas obsessive passion seems to exacerbate such effects.

If passion affects psychological well-being, then what processes mediate such effects? One deals with the repeated experiences of situational (or state) positive affect during the course of engagement of the passionate activity. Research on passion and affect (e.g., Mageau & Vallerand, 2007; Mageau et al., 2005; Vallerand et al., 2003, Study 1) has shown that harmonious passion positively contributes to the experience of positive affect during activity engagement, whereas obsessive passion does not and may even facilitate the experience of negative affect. Similar findings have been found for affect following task engagement (e.g., Mageau & Vallerand, 2007; Vallerand et al., 2003, Studies 1 and 2; Vallerand et al., 2006, Studies 2 and 3). Research has clearly supported the adaptive role of positive affect in a variety of outcomes, including psychological well-being (Lyubomirsky, King, & Diener, 2005; Sedikides, Wildschut, Arndt, & Routledge, 2008). Fredrickson (2001) proposed and found support for her broaden-and-build theory that posits that positive emotions are adaptive because they broaden people's thought-action repertoires and self, leading to better decisions and higher levels of psychological well-being. Thus, such cumulative experience of positive affect may facilitate psychological well-being. In sum, harmonious (but not obsessive) passion facilitates the experience of positive affect that, in turn, has been found to promote psychological well-being.

Rousseau and Vallerand (2008) tested the role of positive affect in the passion–psychological well-being relationship. At Time 1, participants who were passionate toward exercise completed the Passion Scale with respect to physical activity, as well as measures of psychological well-being. A few weeks later (Time 2), immediately following an exercise session, participants completed situational measures of positive and negative affect. Then, 3 weeks later (Time 3), they completed measures of psychological well-being again. A structural equation modeling analysis revealed that harmonious passion positively predicted positive affect that, in turn, led to increases in psychological adjustment from Time 1 to Time 3. On the other hand, obsessive passion was unrelated to positive affect but positively predicted negative affect. The latter did not predict psychological adjustment. However, obsessive passion directly and negatively predicted psychological well-being. These basic findings have been replicated in the work domain (Houlfort, Vallerand, Forest, Lavigne, & Koestner, 2011, Study 3), in which it was found that one's harmonious passion for work led to positive affective experiences at work that in turn predicted increases in psychological well-being over a 6-month period. As in the Rousseau and Vallerand (2008) study, the negative relation between obsessive passion and well-being was direct and was not mediated by affect.

Although the previous research supported the harmonious/positive affect/psychological well-being sequence, it did not address the role of harmonious passion and positive affect in protecting against ill-being or the mediator of the negative effects of obsessive passion on ill-being. Research to address this question was focused on psychological burnout. In line with past research, it was anticipated that harmonious (but not obsessive) passion should be conducive to the affective experience of work satisfaction and should play a protective role in burnout. With respect to obsessive passion, one likely mediator of the contributive effect it should have on burnout may be the psychological conflict experienced between the passionate activity (work) and other life activities (e.g., family activities; Vallerand et al., 2003, Study 1; Vallerand, Ntoumanis, et al., 2008). Because with obsessive passion one experiences an uncontrollable urge to engage in the passionate activity, it becomes very difficult for the person to fully disengage from thoughts about the activity (or from engaging in the activity altogether), leading to conflict with other activities in the person's life. Such conflict can prevent the person from finding replenishment in other life pursuits. The person thus becomes mentally stale, which in turn contributes to ill-being (Garland et al., 2010). Because obsessive passion is typically unrelated to positive affective experiences both during task engagement in the passionate activity (work) and in other life pursuits outside of it (see Carpentier, Mageau, & Vallerand, 2012), obsessive passion does not trigger the protective function against ill-being as harmonious passion does. Conversely, with harmonious passion, the person can let go of the passionate activity after task engagement and more fully immerse in other life pursuits without experiencing conflict between the two.

In line with the above reasoning, two studies (Vallerand, Paquet, Philippe, & Charest, 2010, Studies 1 and 2) were conducted with professional nurses from two cultures (France and Quebec, Canada). In Study 1, scales assessing passion, psychological conflict, work satisfaction, and burnout were completed by 100 nurses from France. Structural equation modeling analyses supported the model, even when controlling for the weekly number of hours worked. Specifically, obsessive passion facilitated the experience of burnout through the psychological conflict it induces between work and other life activities. There was also an absence of relationship between obsessive passion and work satisfaction. On the other hand, harmonious passion prevented the experience of conflict and contributed to the experience of work satisfaction, thereby protecting the person from experiencing burnout. These findings were replicated in a second study using a prospective design with nurses from the Province of Quebec (Vallerand et al., 2010, Study 2), allowing us to predict changes in burnout over a 6-month period.

As a closing note to this section, it should be underscored that the research conducted on passion and outcomes has been largely correlational in nature. Thus, a caveat is in order as pertains to causality issues. However, the results of a recent study (Carbonneau et al., 2008), using a cross-lagged panel design with 500 teachers, revealed that passion for teaching predicted changes in outcomes (life satisfaction and burnout) over a 3-month period, whereas outcomes did not predict changes in passion. Passion, then, would appear involved in producing changes in psychological outcomes, whereas the reverse may not be true. However, clearly future longitudinal research is needed to replicate these findings within the realm of other activities.

Passion and Physical Health

Passion may also affect one's physical health in a number of ways. Having a passion for a sport or physical activity can have both positive and negative effects on one's health. For example, cycling in the spring, summer, and fall can be a lot of fun and can promote one's health. However, ill-advised persistence in cycling in winter is potentially hazardous to health (at least in the Province of Quebec) because of icy road conditions that could lead to falls and injuries. If our hypothesis on the rigid persistence of obsessive passion is correct, then obsessive passion should lead one to engage in risky behaviors such as winter cycling. On the other hand, if we are correct with respect to the flexible persistence of harmonious passion, the latter should not lead a person to engage in such behavior. Vallerand et al. (2003) tested these hypotheses with a group of cyclists who completed the Passion Scale in August and who were contacted again 6 months later to see if they were cycling in midwinter. The 30% of the participants who persisted in their cycling reported higher levels of obsessive passion 6 months earlier than respondents who did not cycle in the winter. No differences were found with respect to harmonious passion.

Vallerand et al. (2003) did not show that obsessive passion led to injuries as such, only that obsessive passion puts people at risk of experiencing injuries. Stephan, Deroche, Brewer, Caudroit, and Le Scanff (2009) studied competitive long-distance runners and found that obsessive passion positively predicted perceived susceptibility to injury while controlling for a number of variables including the number of weekly training sessions and years of experience in running. Harmonious passion was negatively related to susceptibility to injury.

A study with dancers (Rip, Fortin, & Vallerand, 2006) went one step further and examined the passion–injury relation by distinguishing between acute and chronic injuries. Because both types of passion encourage persistence, being passionate should lead one to train regularly, to remain in great shape, and thus to reduce the number of acute injuries. However, when injured, obsessive passion should lead people to continue dancing, because it leads dancers to adopt a rigid persistence toward dancing, where stopping is not an option, thereby leading to chronic injuries. With harmonious passion, the person is in control of the activity, and thus, persistence is expected to be flexible as was seen in the cycling study. As such, the harmoniously passionate dancers can decide to temporarily stop dancing when injured. Thus, they should experience fewer chronic injuries. As hypothesized, results revealed that both types of passion were negatively related to acute injuries (but significantly more so for harmonious passion). The picture was drastically different for chronic injuries for which obsessive passion was positively related to the number of weeks missed because of chronic injuries, whereas harmonious passion was unrelated to chronic injuries.

Would these relationships with respect to passion hold if the activity involved were highly positive? Mere engagement in such activities irrespective of passion may suffice to yield positive outcomes. Although we agree that some activities may be more positive than others in bringing about positive outcomes, it also (perhaps mainly) matters how people engage in a given activity. In addition to leading the person to return to the activity on a regular basis, to the extent that one's passion for a given activity is harmonious, one should be able to reap full benefits from engagement in a "positive" activity. However, if one's passion is obsessive, then less than optimal, and perhaps even negative, outcomes should be experienced even if the activity is highly "positive."

We tested these hypotheses in two studies with an activity widely recognized as being highly positive—yoga. In one study, Carbonneau, Vallerand, and Massicotte (2010, Study 2) had yoga participants complete the Passion Scale for Yoga, as well as measures assessing positive and negative affect and state anxiety while doing yoga, and obtained reports of negative symptoms in general (e.g., rashes, cold symptoms, the flu, muscle aches). It was found 3 months later that harmonious passion predicted decreases in negative emotions, state anxiety, and general (negative) physical symptoms and increases in positive emotions that took place over time during yoga classes. Obsessive passion only predicted a significant increase in negative emotions experienced during yoga classes. These findings were obtained even while controlling for the number of weekly hours and years of involvement in yoga.

These findings are important because they underscore the fact that we need to go beyond mere activity engagement to determine the type of outcomes that will be experienced by the person. The quality of activity engagement matters, with harmonious passion leading to a more positive engagement and consequently to more positive (and less negative) outcomes than obsessive passion.

Passion and Interpersonal Relationships

It appears reasonable to suggest that passion for an activity should influence the quality of interpersonal relationships. Passionate individuals are typically seen as highly engaging and as such should be popular and able to make friends readily. If it is the case, what is the process through which they make friends? Does it make a difference if one's predominant passion is harmonious or obsessive? In line with the work of Fredrickson (2001), the dual model of passion posits that the experience of situational positive affect is conducive to high-quality relationships. This is so because positive affect opens up people's thought–action repertoires, leading to experiencing the world more fully, thereby facilitating smiles, positive sharing of the activity, and connection and openness toward others conducive to positive relationships (Waugh & Fredrickson, 2006). Because harmonious passion leads one to experience positive affect (and protects against negative affect) during engagement in the passionate activity, it would be hypothesized that it should therefore indirectly lead to high quality relationships within the passionate activity. Conversely, because it is typically unrelated to positive affect and at times correlated with negative affect, obsessive passion is expected to negatively affect the quality of relationships that develop within the purview of the passionate activity.

A series of studies conducted in a variety of settings, including the work and sport domains, tested these hypotheses (Philippe, Vallerand, Houlfort, Lavigne, & Donahue, 2010). Consistent with previous research, it was found that among basketball players attending a 1-week summer basketball camp, harmonious passion positively predicted positive affect and negatively predicted negative affect, whereas obsessive passion positively predicted negative affect. In turn, as expected, the positive and negative affect experienced during the week respectively predicted, positively and negatively, both the athletes' and the coach's assessments of the relationships formed by the players. Other research revealed that the positive effects of harmonious passion on the quality of relationships also applies to relationships in which one is a supervisor and the other a subordinate and as assessed by people in both positions (Lafrenière et al., 2008).

Overall, the findings from the Philippe et al. (2010) studies are important for at least three reasons. First, they show that passion does affect the quality of relationships that people develop in the passionate activity, from day one. Second, these studies also reveal the nature of the processes, namely, positive and negative affect, through which harmonious and obsessive passion differentially affect relationships, respectively. Finally, these affective processes are not only experienced by the passionate performers, but are also being picked up by the people with whom they engage in the activity, thereby affecting the relationship for both types of participants.

The dual model of passion posits that there is a second way through which passion can affect our relationships. Specifically, passion toward an activity can also influence our relationships in other areas of our lives through the conflict it might create. Obsessive passion should lead to conflict and problems in other life activities, but this should not be the case for harmonious passion. Vallerand et al. (2003) showed that obsessive (but not harmonious) passion for an activity was positively associated with experiencing conflict between activity engagement and other aspects of one's life. Séguin-Lévesque, Laliberté, Pelletier, Blanchard, and Vallerand (2003) found that controlling for the number of hours that people engaged in the Internet, obsessive passion for the Internet was positively related to conflict with one's spouse, whereas harmonious passion was unrelated to it. Finally, a subsequent study tested more directly the hypothesized sequence in which obsessive passion positively predicts conflict with the relationship with one's spouse that, in turn, predicts the quality of romantic relationship. Vallerand, Ntoumanis, et al. (2008) studied English soccer fans, asking them to complete a questionnaire assessing passion toward soccer, perceptions of conflict between soccer and the loved one, and satisfaction with one's intimate relationship. The results revealed that having an obsessive passion for one's soccer team predicted conflict between soccer and the loved one. Conflict, in turn, negatively predicted satisfaction with the relationship. Although harmonious passion was negatively related to conflict, the effects only approached statistical significance.

Passion and Performance

Years ago, the philosopher Hegel (1770–1831) suggested that "nothing great in this world has ever been accomplished without passion." According to Hegel, passion is essential to high levels of performance. Is it the case? Research in the area of expert performance reveals that to reach international levels in most domains (e.g., sports, music) one must put in roughly 10,000 hours of deliberate practice over a 10-year period (Ericsson, Krampe, & Tesch-Römer, 1993; Starkes & Ericsson, 2003). Mageau et al. (2009) compared one group of musicians who had achieved this level of expertise with another group of young musicians who were nevertheless passionate about music. The results revealed that indeed the expert musicians displayed significantly higher levels of both harmonious and obsessive passion than the younger musicians. Thus, passion seems to matter with respect to performance as initially suggested by Hegel.

So, if passion is involved in expert performance, what is the process through which it affects performance? Deliberate practice entails engaging in the activity with clear goals of improving task components. For instance, a guitarist may work on using a new strumming technique for hours until she successfully masters it. Ericsson and Charness (1994) asked the question, What is the underlying motivational force that leads individuals to spend so much time in perfecting their skills in a given activity in order to achieve high proficiency? We believe that passion represents one answer to that question. Indeed, if one is to engage in the activity for long hours over several years and sometimes a lifetime, one must love the activity dearly and have the desire to persist in the activity, especially when times are rough. Both types of passion (harmonious and obsessive) should lead to engagement in deliberate practice that, in turn, should lead to improved performance. This model was tested in a study with basketball players (Vallerand, Mageau, et al., 2008, Study 1). Male and female basketball players completed scales assessing their passion for basketball as well as deliberate practice (based on Ericsson & Charness, 1994). Coaches independently rated the athletes' performance. Results from a path analysis revealed that both types of passion led to engagement in deliberate practice, which, in turn, led to objective performance.

These findings were replicated in a prospective design with dramatic arts performers (Vallerand et al., 2007, Study 1). In this study, harmonious passion toward dramatic arts was positively and significantly related to life satisfaction, whereas obsessive passion was unrelated to it. This is in line with research reported previously on passion and psychological well-being. It thus appears that both types of passion positively contribute to deliberate practice and thus, indirectly, to performance. However, with harmonious passion, there is a bonus as one may reach high levels of performance while "having a life." This is in line with our position to the effect that harmonious passion contributes to all dimensions of optimal functioning.

The results of the two performance studies presented previously established a direct relationship between passion and deliberate practice and an indirect relationship between passion and performance (through deliberate practice). We conducted an additional study (Vallerand, Mageau, et al., 2008, Study 2) to examine the psychological processes through which passion contributes to deliberate practice and thus indirectly contributes to performance. In line with Elliot (1997), we proposed that achievement goals should represent important mediators between passion and deliberate practice. Elliot and colleagues (Elliot & Church, 1997; Elliot & Harackiewicz, 1996) distinguished between three types of achievement goals: mastery goals (which focus on the development of competence and task mastery), performance-approach goals (which focus on the attainment of personal competence relative to others), and performance-avoidance goals (which focus on avoiding incompetence relative to others). Harmonious passion, being a rather pure autonomous form of regulation, should be positively related to mastery goals but not to performance goals of either type. On the other hand, obsessive passion, being a more pressured, internally controlling, form of regulation should lead the individual to feel compelled to seek any and all forms of success at the activity and may even evoke concerns about doing poorly. As such, obsessive passion should be positively related to mastery and performance-approach goals, as well as performance-avoidance goals.

A study with water-polo and synchronized swimmers was conducted to test the previously mentioned model (Vallerand, Mageau, et al., 2008, Study 2). Early in the season (Time 1), individuals completed the Passion Scale, the Achievement Goals Scale, and scales assessing psychological well-being. They later (Time 2) completed the Deliberate Practice Scale. At the end of the season (Time 3), coaches assessed individuals' performance over the entire season. Results of a path analysis supported the proposed model. Harmonious passion was found to lead to mastery goals that, in turn, led to deliberate practice that positively predicted objective performance. On the other hand, obsessive passion was positively related to all three types of goals. Whereas performance-approach goals did not predict any variables in the model, performance-avoidance goals negatively predicted performance. Finally, harmonious passion was positively associated with psychological adjustment, whereas obsessive passion was unrelated to it. This basic model was replicated in other research involving classical musicians including some of international stature (Bonneville-Roussy, Lavigne, & Vallerand, 2011) and with students who had a passion toward studying psychology as their future profession, with objective exam scores in a psychology course as a measure of performance (Vallerand et al., 2007, Study 2). These findings for performance highlight the fact that there seem to be two roads to excellence, the harmonious and the obsessive roads. The harmonious road is characterized by the sole goal of wanting to improve (i.e., mastery goal), which leads to deliberate practice and high levels of performance. Furthermore, one experiences a happy life in the process. On the other hand, the obsessive path to excellence is paved with both adaptive (i.e., mastery) and maladaptive (i.e. performance-avoidance) goals, and there is no link to psychological well-being. Although both types of passion may lead to high levels of performance, obsessive passion may achieve this at a cost relative to harmonious passion.

Passion and Contributions to Society

Alexis de Tocqueville (1805–1859) suggested that "the health of a democratic society may be measured by the quality of functions performed by private citizens." It does not suffice to display high levels of psychological well-being, physical health, positive relationships, and performance to be considered optimally functioning in society. One must also contribute to society. On the basis of the dual model of passion, those who are passionate about an activity will, through their inspiration and performance, likely contribute something positive to their community and/or society at large. We recently conducted a series of studies to test this hypothesis.

Vallerand, Lafrenière, and St-Louis (2011) looked at individuals who had been selected as "personalities of the week" by a committee of the *La Presse* newspaper (the leading newspaper in the Province of Quebec). The basis for selection was major contributions to Quebec society in any of a variety of areas, including business, music and arts, and sports. We invited over 100 such individuals to complete the Passion Scale as well as to respond to questions related to their area of expertise. Results revealed that the personalities of the week reported higher levels of both harmonious and obsessive passion than did others in corresponding positions. Fully 96% of the personalities indicated being highly passionate for their activity, whereas only 33% of the regular workers did so. Personalities of the week reported working 9 hours more per week (47 hours vs. 38 hours). Interestingly, when statistically controlling for the number hours worked, the differences in passion remained. Passion therefore would appear to play an important role in contributing to society.

If passion leads one to contribute to society, then does the type of passion matter? We have attempted to answer this question in a recent study with humanitarian volunteers working abroad on a 6-month mission (Vallerand, Lafrenière, and St-Louis, 2011, Study 2). On returning from their mission, the volunteers completed a questionnaire assessing their passion for humanitarian work as well as questions assessing their level of perceived success and satisfaction with the mission. Furthermore, they also indicated the level of risk they took regarding themselves and the people under their care during the mission. They also completed a scale measuring posttraumatic stress disorder (PTSD). Results from a canonical correlation analysis revealed the presence of two canonical variates corresponding to harmonious and obsessive passion. Results revealed that harmonious passion positively predicted perceived success and satisfaction with the mission but not risk or posttraumatic stress. Conversely, obsessive passion positively predicted taking risks during the mission and suffering from PTSD. Although obsessive passion was negatively related to both perceived success and satisfaction with the mission, the relationships were nonsignificant.

These findings suggest that harmonious passion may lead one to contribute more positively to society than obsessive passion. Further, in keeping with findings on psychological well-being, obsessive passion may lead one to suffer in the process of trying to contribute to one's cause and thus to society. Of interest is the finding that obsessive passion may lead one to take risks with respect to oneself and others, not unlike the obsessively passionate cyclists in the Vallerand et al. (2003, Study 3) study. It would thus appear that obsessive passion may not be conducive to selecting the most appropriate means for achieving the goal of contributing to society. This hypothesis was supported by research with people passionate for promoting political (Rip,

Vallerand, & Lafrenière, in 2012, Study 1) and environmental (Gousse-Lessard, Vallerand, & Carbonneau, 2011) causes. Results from both studies revealed that obsessive passion leads people to agreeing to engage in a variety of activities including extreme and violent ones (e.g., physically attacking someone polluting the environment). On the other hand, harmonious passion would appear to be conducive to only moderate means to promote the cause (e.g., participating in discussion groups to persuade people of the importance of reaching sovereignty or preserving the environment).

These results suggest harmonious passion is likely to contribute more to society than obsessive passion through the peaceful and moderate behaviors it facilitates. Because it facilitates extreme behaviors that are likely to run against popular opinion, obsessive passion may be detrimental to the very causes it seeks to promote. It is important to point out, however, that these results concern specific behaviors (e.g., humanitarian aid as well as political and environmental causes) taking place in North America. It is possible that obsessive passion, by virtue of the high risk and extreme behaviors it facilitates, may contribute more effectively to society in other contexts (e.g., government overthrow in totalitarian societies). The validity and generality of such ideas need to be empirically tested.

Summary

The research reviewed up to now in this chapter has suggested that harmonious passion is positively and reliably related to each of the five components of OFIS. More specifically, harmonious passion positively predicts psychological well-being, physical health, positive relationships, high-level performance, as well as contributions to society. On the other hand, obsessive passion appears to contribute positively to some outcomes such as high levels of performance and possibly to contributions one may make to society. However, the contribution of obsessive passion to other elements of OFIS, specifically physical health and relationships, would appear to be negative. The results with respect to psychological well-being are mixed.

This summary of findings is based on studies in which various aspects of OFIS were treated separately as outcome measures. Vallerand, Forest, et al. (2011) conducted a study of nurses who completed both the Passion Scale and the OFIS Scale, which measures all five aspects of OFIS. Results indicated the presence of two canonical variates in a pattern consistent with previously reported outcomes. Specifically, harmonious passion was positively related to all five components of OFIS (the relationships with physical health, work performance, and psychological well-being were particularly strong). In contrast, obsessive passion showed mixed findings with the OFIS components. Specifically, obsessive passion positively predicted performance

and contributions to society, was unrelated to psychological well-being, and
negatively predicted health and relationships.

CONCLUSION

The goal of this chapter was to document the role of passion in OFIS.
In so doing, we presented the dualistic model of passion (e.g., Vallerand,
2010; Vallerand et al., 2003) and introduced the construct of OFIS. The
research reviewed leads to a number of conclusions. First, there is convinc-
ing support for the dualistic model of passion. The model defines passion
as a strong inclination toward a self-defining activity that one loves, finds
important, and devotes significant amount of time and energy. Two types
of passion are proposed, varying with respect to how an activity representation is internalized in one's identity. Whereas harmonious passion
entails control of the activity and coexistence of the passionate activity
with other activities in one's life, obsessive passion entails a relative lack
of control over the passionate activity, rigid persistence, and conflict with
other activities.

Second, support was found for the OFIS construct. Consistent with a
eudaimonic perspective, this construct posits that self-realization is multidimensional in nature and includes five elements: psychological well-being,
physical health, meaningful relationships, high levels of performance in one's
main field of endeavor, and contributing to one's immediate community and/
or society at large. The use of the instrument developed for assessing OFIS
will allow researchers to further test both the construct and its relevance for
a eudaimonic perspective.

Finally, passionate engagement on a regular basis in an enjoyable and
meaningful activity matters with respect to OFIS. Merely seeking to reach
one's potential does not ensure high levels of optimal functioning. However, as research has demonstrated, the energy people put into reaching their
potential has a profound effect on the level of optimal functioning experienced. This conclusion needs to be qualified as research shows that harmonious passions are more conducive to optimal functioning overall than
are obsessive passions. Just as there are two roads to high-level performance,
there also seem to be two roads to self-fulfillment, the harmonious and the
obsessive roads. The obsessive road may allow one to reach high levels of one
type of self-realization, namely, performance and making contributions to
society. However, these come at a cost and may prevent one from reaching
self-fulfillment in other areas (psychological, physical, and relational well-
being). In contrast, the harmonious road to self-realization allows people to
reach high levels of all five elements of OFIS. Thus, the harmonious road

to self-fulfillment bridges hedonia and eudaimonia together in experiencing happiness pursuing self-realization goals.

For centuries philosophers have asked the question, How can people's lives be most worth living? Theory and research reveal that one answer to this question is by having in one's life a harmonious passion toward an enjoyable and meaningful activity. Future research in this area would therefore appear to be not only promising but also important.

REFERENCES

Aron, A., Aron, E. N., & Smollan, D. (1992). Inclusion of Other in the Self Scale and the structure of interpersonal closeness. *Journal of Personality and Social Psychology, 63*, 596–612. doi:10.1037/0022-3514.63.4.596

Baum, J. R., & Locke, E. A. (2004). The relationship of entrepreneurial traits, skill, and motivation to subsequent venture growth. *Journal of Applied Psychology, 89*, 587–598. doi:10.1037/0021-9010.89.4.587

Bonneville-Roussy, A., Lavigne, G. L., & Vallerand, R. J. (2011). When passion leads to excellence: The case of musicians. *Psychology of Music, 39*, 123–138. doi:10.1177/0305735609352441

Carbonneau, N., Vallerand, R. J., Fernet, C., & Guay, F. (2008). The role of passion for teaching in intra and interpersonal outcomes. *Journal of Educational Psychology, 100*, 977–988. doi:10.1037/a0012545

Carbonneau, N., Vallerand, R. J., & Massicotte, S. (2010). Is the practice of Yoga associated with positive outcomes? The role of passion. *The Journal of Positive Psychology, 5*, 452–465. doi:10.1080/17439760.2010.534107

Carpentier, J., Mageau, G. & Vallerand, R. J. (2012). Ruminations and flow: Why do people with a more harmonious passion experience higher well-being? *Journal of Happiness Studies, 13*, 501–518. doi:10.1007/s10902-011-9276-4

Deci, E. L., Eghrari, H., Patrick, B. C., & Leone, D. R. (1994). Facilitating internalization: The self-determination perspective. *Journal of Personality, 62*, 119–142. doi:10.1111/j.1467-6494.1994.tb00797.x

Deci, E. L., & Ryan, R. M. (2000). The "what" and "why" of goal pursuits: Human needs and the self-determination of behavior. *Psychological Inquiry, 11*, 227–268. doi:10.1207/S15327965PLI1104_01

Elliot, A. J. (1997). Integrating "classic" and "contemporary" approaches to achievement motivation: A hierarchical model of approach and avoidance achievement motivation. In P. Pintrinch & M. Maehr (Eds.), *Advances in motivation and achievement* (Vol. 10, pp. 143–179). Greenwich, CT: JAI Press.

Elliot, A. J., & Church, M. A. (1997). A hierarchical model of approach and avoidance achievement motivation. *Journal of Personality and Social Psychology, 72*, 218–232. doi:10.1037/0022-3514.72.1.218

Elliot, A. J., & Harackiewicz, J. M. (1996). Approach and avoidance achievement goals and intrinsic motivation: A mediational analysis. *Journal of Personality and Social Psychology, 70*, 461–475. doi:10.1037/0022-3514.70.3.461

Ericsson, K. A., & Charness, N. (1994). Expert performance. *American Psychologist, 49*, 725–747. doi:10.1037/0003-066X.49.8.725

Ericsson, K. A., Krampe, R. T., & Tesch-Römer, C. (1993). The role of deliberate practice in the acquisition of expert performance. *Psychological Review, 100*, 363–406. doi:10.1037/0033-295X.100.3.363

Erikson, E. H. (1968). *Identity: Youth and crisis*. New York, NY: Norton.

Forest, J., Mageau, G. A., Sarrazin, C., & Morin, E. M. (2011). "Work is my passion": The different affective, behavioural, and cognitive consequences of harmonious and obsessive passion toward work. *Canadian Journal of Administrative Sciences, 28*, 27–40. doi:10.1002/cjas.170

Fredrickson, B. L. (2001). The role of positive emotions in positive psychology: The broaden-and-build theory of positive emotions. *American Psychologist, 56*, 218–226. doi:10.1037/0003-066X.56.3.218

Frijda, N. H., Mesquita, B., Sonnemans, J., & Van Goozen, S. (1991). The duration of affective phenomena or emotions, sentiments and passions. In K.T. Strongman (Ed.), *International review of studies on emotion* (Vol. 1, pp. 187–225). New York, NY: Wiley.

Garland, E. L., Fredrickson, B., Kring, A., Johnson, D. P., Meyer, P. S., & Penn, D. L. (2010). Upward spirals of positive emotions counter downward spirals of negativity: Insights from the broaden-and-build theory and affective neuroscience on the treatment of emotion dysfunctions and deficits in psychopathology. *Clinical Psychology Review, 30*, 849–864. doi:10.1016/j.cpr.2010.03.002

Gousse-Lessard, A.-S., Vallerand, R. J., & Carbonneau, N. (2011). *Passion for the environment: On the relative role of harmonious and obsessive passion*. Manuscript submitted for publication.

Hatfield, E., & Walster, G. W. (1978). *A new look at love*. Reading, MA: Addison-Wesley.

Hodgins, H. S., & Knee, R. (2002). The integrating self and conscious experience. In E. L. Deci & R. M. Ryan (Eds.), *Handbook on self-determination research: Theoretical and applied issues* (pp. 87–100). Rochester, NY: University of Rochester Press.

Houlfort, N., Vallerand, R. J., Forest, J., Lavigne, G. L., & Koestner, R. (2011). *On the role of passion for work in psychological well-being*. Manuscript submitted for publication.

Huppert, F. A. (2009). Psychological well-being: Evidence regarding its causes and consequences. *Applied Psychology: Health and Well-Being, 1*, 137–164. doi:10.1111/j.1758-0854.2009.01008.x

Keyes, C. L. M. (2007). Promoting and protecting mental health as flourishing: A complementary strategy for improving national mental health. *American Psychologist, 62*, 95–108. doi:10.1037/0003-066X.62.2.95

Lafrenière, M.-A. K., Bélanger, J. J., Sedikides, C., & Vallerand, R. J. (2011). Self-esteem and passion for activities. *Personality and Individual Differences, 51*, 541–544. doi:10.1016/j.paid.2011.04.017

Lafrenière, M.-A. K., Jowett, S., Vallerand, R. J., Donahue, E. G., & Lorimer, R. (2008). Passion in sport: On the quality of the coach–player relationship. *Journal of Sport & Exercise Psychology, 30,* 541–560.

Lafrenière, M.-A. K., St-Louis, A., & Vallerand, R. J. (in press). The role of passion and success/failure experiences in life satisfaction. *Self and Identity.*

Liu, D., Chen, X.-P., & Yao, X. (2011). From autonomy to creativity: A multilevel investigation of the mediating role of harmonious passion. *Journal of Applied Psychology, 96,* 294–309. doi:10.1037/a0021294

Lyubomirsky, S., King, L., & Diener, E. (2005). The benefits of frequent positive affect: Does happiness lead to success? *Psychological Bulletin, 131,* 803–855. doi:10.1037/0033-2909.131.6.803

Mageau, G., Carpentier, J., & Vallerand, R.J. (2011). The role of self-esteem contingencies in the distinction between obsessive and harmonious passion. *European Journal of Social Psychology, 41,* 720–729. doi:10.1002/ejsp.798

Mageau, G., & Vallerand, R. J. (2007). The moderating effect of passion on the relation between activity engagement and positive affect. *Motivation and Emotion, 31,* 312–321. doi:10.1007/s11031-007-9071-z

Mageau, G. A., Vallerand, R. J., Charest, J., Salvy, S.-J., Lacaille, N., Bouffard, T., & Koestner, R. (2009). On the development of harmonious and obsessive passion: The role of autonomy support, activity valuation, and identity processes. *Journal of Personality, 77,* 601–646. doi:10.1111/j.1467-6494.2009.00559.x

Mageau, G. A., Vallerand, R. J., Rousseau, F. L., Ratelle, C. F., & Provencher, P. J. (2005). Passion and gambling: Investigating the divergent affective and cognitive consequences of gambling. *Journal of Applied Social Psychology, 35,* 100–118. doi:10.1111/j.1559-1816.2005.tb02095.x

Philippe, F. L., Vallerand, R. J., Houlfort, N., Lavigne, G., & Donahue, E. G. (2010). Passion for an activity and quality of interpersonal relationships: The mediating role of positive and negative emotions. *Journal of Personality and Social Psychology, 98,* 917–932. doi:10.1037/a0018017

Philippe, F. L., Vallerand, R. J., & Lavigne, G. (2009). Passion does make a difference in people's lives: A look at well-being in passionate and non-passionate individuals. *Applied Psychology: Health and Well-Being, 1,* 3–22. doi:10.1111/j.1758-0854.2008.01003.x

Rip, B., Fortin, S., & Vallerand, R. J. (2006). The relationship between passion and injury in dance students. *Journal of Dance Medicine & Science, 10,* 14–20.

Rip, B., Vallerand, R. J., & Lafrenière, M.-A. K. (2012). Passion for a cause, passion for a creed: On ideological passion, identity threat, and radicalization. *Journal of Personality, 80,* 573–602.

Rony, J.-A. (1990). *Les passions* [The passions]. Paris, France: Presses Universitaires de France.

Rousseau, F. L., & Vallerand, R. J. (2003). Le rôle de la passion dans le bien-être subjectif des aînés [The role of passion in the subjective well-being of the elderly]. *Revue Québécoise de Psychologie, 24,* 197–211.

Rousseau, F. L., & Vallerand, R. J. (2008). An examination of the relationship between passion and subjective well-being in older adults. *The International Journal of Aging & Human Development, 66,* 195–211. doi:10.2190/AG.66.3.b

Rousseau, F. L., Vallerand, R. J., Ratelle, C. F., Mageau, G. A., & Provencher, P. J. (2002). Passion and gambling: On the validation of the Gambling Passion Scale (GPS). *Journal of Gambling Studies, 18,* 45–66. doi:10.1023/A:1014532229487

Ryan, R. M., & Deci, E. L. (2001). On happiness and human potentials: A review of research on hedonic and eudaimonic well-being. *Annual Review of Psychology, 52,* 141–166. doi:10.1146/annurev.psych.52.1.141

Ryan, R. M., & Deci, E. L. (2003). On assimilating identities of the self: A self-determination theory perspective on internalization and integrity within cultures. In M. R. Leary & J. P. Tangney (Eds.), *Handbook of self and identity* (pp. 253–272). New York, NY: Guilford.

Ryff, C. D., & Keyes, C. L. (1995). The structure of psychological well-being revisited. *Journal of Personality and Social Psychology, 69,* 719–727. doi:10.1037/0022-3514.69.4.719

Sedikides, C., Wildschut, T., Arndt, J., & Routledge, C. (2008). Nostalgia: Past, present, and future. *Current Directions in Psychological Science, 17,* 304–307. doi:10.1111/j.1467-8721.2008.00595.x

Séguin-Lévesque, C., Laliberté, M.-L., Pelletier, L. G., Blanchard, C., & Vallerand, R. J. (2003). Harmonious and obsessive passion for the Internet: Their associations with the couple's relationships. *Journal of Applied Social Psychology, 33,* 197–221. doi:10.1111/j.1559-1816.2003.tb02079.x

Seligman, M. E. P. (2011). *Flourish: A visionary new understanding of happiness and well-being.* New York, NY: Simon & Schuster.

Starkes, J. L., & Ericsson, K. A. (Eds.). (2003). *Expert performance in sports: Advances in research on sport expertise.* Champaign, IL: Human Kinetics.

Stenseng, F. (2008). The two faces of leisure activity engagement: Harmonious and obsessive passion in relation to intrapersonal conflict and life domain outcomes. *Leisure Sciences, 30,* 465–481. doi:10.1080/01490400802353224

Stephan, Y., Deroche, T., Brewer, B. W., Caudroit, J., & Le Scanff, C. (2009). Predictors of perceived susceptibility to sport-related injury among competitive runners: The role of previous experience, neuroticism, and passion for running. *Applied Psychology, 58,* 672–687. doi:10.1111/j.1464-0597.2008.00373.x

Vallerand, R. J. (2010). On passion for life activities: The Dualistic Model of Passion. In M. P. Zanna (Ed.), *Advances in experimental social psychology* (Vol. 42, pp. 97–193). New York, NY: Academic Press.

Vallerand, R. J. (in press). Passion et fonctionnement optimal en société [Passion and optimal functioning in society]. In M. Carlier & P.-Y. Gilles (Eds.), *Perspectives nouvelles en psychologie différentielle.* Marseilles, France: Presses de l'Université de Provence.

Vallerand, R. J., Blanchard, C. M., Mageau, G. A., Koestner, R., Ratelle, C. F., Léonard, M., . . . Marsolais, J. (2003). Les passions de l'âme: On obsessive and harmonious passion. *Journal of Personality and Social Psychology, 85*, 756–767. doi:10.1037/0022-3514.85.4.756

Vallerand, R. J., Forest, J., Houlfort, N., Miquelon, P., Perreault, S., & Rinfret, N. (2011). [Passion and optimal functioning in society]. Unpublished data.

Vallerand, R. J., Fortier, M. S., & Guay, F. (1997). Self-determination and persistence in a real-life setting: Toward a motivational model of high school dropout. *Journal of Personality and Social Psychology, 72*, 1161–1176. doi:10.1037/0022-3514.72.5.1161

Vallerand, R. J., & Houlfort, N. (2003). Passion at work: Toward a new conceptualization. In S. W. Gilliland, D. D. Steiner, & D. P. Skarlicki (Eds.), *Emerging perspectives on values in organizations* (pp. 175–204). Greenwich, CT: Information Age.

Vallerand, R. J., Lafrenière, M.-A. K., & St-Louis, A. (2011). *Passion for a cause.* Manuscript in preparation.

Vallerand, R. J., Mageau, G. A., Elliot, A., Dumais, A., Demers, M.-A., & Rousseau, F. L. (2008). Passion and performance attainment in sport. *Psychology of Sport and Exercise, 9*, 373–392. doi:10.1016/j.psychsport.2007.05.003

Vallerand, R. J., Ntoumanis, N., Philippe, F., Lavigne, G. L., Carbonneau, C., Bonneville, A., . . . Maliha, G. (2008). On passion and sports fans: A look at football. *Journal of Sports Sciences, 26*, 1279–1293. doi:10.1080/02640410802123185

Vallerand, R. J., Paquet, Y., Philippe, F. L., & Charest, J. (2010). On the role of passion in burnout: A process model. *Journal of Personality, 78*, 289–312. doi:10.1111/j.1467-6494.2009.00616.x

Vallerand, R. J., Rousseau, F. L., Grouzet, F. M. E., Dumais, A., & Grenier, S. (2006). Passion in sport: A look at determinants and affective experiences. *Journal of Sport & Exercise Psychology, 28*, 454–478.

Vallerand, R. J., Salvy, S. J., Mageau, G. A., Elliot, A. J., Denis, P., Grouzet, F. M. E., & Blanchard, C. B. (2007). On the role of passion in performance. *Journal of Personality, 75*, 505–534. doi:10.1111/j.1467-6494.2007.00447.x

Waterman, A. S. (1993). Two conceptions of happiness: Contrasts of personal expressiveness (eudaimonia) and hedonic enjoyment. *Journal of Personality and Social Psychology, 64*, 678–691. doi:10.1037/0022-3514.64.4.678

Waugh, C. E., & Fredrickson, B. L. (2006). Nice to know you: Positive emotions, self-other overlap, and complex understanding in the formation of new relationships. *The Journal of Positive Psychology, 1*, 93–106. doi:10.1080/17439760500510569

10

THE IMPORTANCE OF WHO YOU REALLY ARE: THE ROLE OF THE TRUE SELF IN EUDAIMONIA

REBECCA J. SCHLEGEL, KELLY A. HIRSCH, AND CHRISTINA M. SMITH

As Tiberius notes—philosophers and psychologists alike have long searched for the "ingredients" of a eudaimonic life (see Chapter 1, this volume). This search is akin to the way a baker may search for the perfect list of ingredients for a cake. If eudaimonia was a cake, it could be argued that the true self is as essential as the flour. Indeed, the idea of the *daimon* in eudaimonia has been understood by some to mean "true self" (e.g., May, 1969; Norton, 1976), and scholars have argued that eudaimonic well-being can be separated from hedonic well-being precisely because of its association with authentic self-expression (Keyes & Haidt, 2003; Ryan & Deci, 2001; Waterman, 1984). Just as flour serves as the foundation for a cake, the true self may be the foundation of a life well lived.

The idea that the true self is critical to the good life has a rich tradition in psychological theorizing and has been touted by the likes of Carl Rogers (1961) and Abraham Maslow (1968). It is also consistent with the nature-fulfillment perspective described by Tiberius (Chapter 1, this volume) and

DOI: 10.1037/14092-011
The Best Within Us: Positive Psychology Perspectives on Eudaimonia, Alan S. Waterman (Editor)
Copyright © 2013 by the American Psychological Association. All rights reserved.

the self-realization perspective described by Waterman (Introduction, this volume). Empirical researchers are beginning to turn their attention to this idea and are examining the specific ways in which the true self might enrich the "cake" of people's psychological lives. Specifically, this growing area of research has demonstrated that people hold lay theories about the importance of the true self to a life well lived and that the possession of these lay theories has a variety of observable consequences. In this chapter, we review the existing theory and empirical research for the importance of the idea of a true self as well as review our own growing program of research that specifically examines the meaning-making function of the true self-concept.

DEFINING THE TRUE SELF

Before examining the importance of the true self in a life well lived, it is useful to ask what the true self is. Classic theorists (Horney, 1950; Miller, 1979; Rogers, 1959) tended to view the true self as a set of innate characteristics that each person is born with, arguing that the true self is something that each person must discover within his or her self. This idea is echoed in essentialist views of personality (e.g., Costa & McCrae, 1992; McGregor et al., 2006) that argue that "who a person is" is a function of the traits that he or she is born with (Bouchard, 2004; McCrae & Costa, 1994).

Other contemporary psychological theorists have taken a more fluid approach to defining the true self. For example, self-determination theory (SDT) recognizes that the true self may be quite elaborate and complex and may even include contradictory characteristics (Kernis & Goldman, 2006; see also Harter, 1999, 2002). According to SDT, the true self is not a static set of traits or tendencies we are born with; rather, it is any aspect of personality that feels autonomous, internally caused, personally meaningful, and self-determined (deCharms, 1968; Deci, 1980; Deci & Ryan, 1985, 1991; Ryan, 1993). Waterman (1990) offered a somewhat similar view of the daimon, which he argued includes a person's potentialities (both those one is born with and those that arise from experience) as well as the subjective experience of activities consistent with those potentialities.

Interestingly, people's lay beliefs about the true self seem to correspond more with the essentialist conception of the true self as a static set of traits than with the more fluid definitions. Indeed, Gergen (1991) argued that the very idea of a true self is a reflection of the Western view that there is something inside each person that is inherent and unchanging (vs. a more Eastern view of the self as consisting of dialectical traits). Consistent with this, our own data suggests that people are more likely to believe that the true self is discovered within themselves rather than created (Schlegel, Vess, & Arndt,

2012) and that even after writing about a significant change in either them-selves or a close friend, people tend to agree with statements that the true self is "something very basic about them" and that "it can't really be changed" (Bench, Schlegel, & Davis, 2012).

Regardless of whether it's viewed as something static or something fluid, the true self is defined by its private, internal nature. That is, the true self is the authentic or "real" version of who a person is inside when they are stripped of their outward social masks (e.g., Jung, 1953; Kernis & Goldman, 2006; Rogers, 1959; Winnicott, 1960). This idea is reflected in adolescents' lay theories, as they report believing that the true self is "the real me inside" and that only they and their close friends have access to the contents of their true selves (Harter, 2002; Rosenberg, 1979). Several studies similarly suggest that people believe that private aspects of the self (i.e., thoughts and feelings) are more diagnostic of the true self than public behaviors (Andersen, 1984; Andersen, Lazowski, & Donisi, 1986; Andersen & Ross, 1984; Andersen & Williams, 1985; Johnson, Robinson, & Mitchell, 2004).

In sum, the true self may best be defined as the version of the self that rep-resents who a person really is, regardless of that person's outward behavior. It is the part of the self that is genuine and uninfluenced by context or outside factors (e.g., social norms, pressures, societal demands). Of course, operationalizing this part of the self for the purposes of empirical research is a thorny issue. Indeed, Waterman (1984) suggested that the true self is an abstraction that can never be observed or measured directly. Thus, most empirical research has focused on people's subjective beliefs about who their true selves are, what we have termed their *true self-concepts*. A variety of empirical approaches in psychology have argued for the importance of these beliefs in psychological functioning.

THE TRUE SELF AND PSYCHOLOGICAL FUNCTIONING

Before turning to the specific importance of the true self in meaning mak-ing (a critical component of eudaimonia, in our opinion), we review the past theory and research on the importance of the true self in more general psy-chological functioning. This work may best be summarized by examining the importance of the true self in three life domains: self-knowledge, behavior, and close relationships. Though not all of these perspectives emphasize eudaimonia specifically, they certainly speak to the importance of the true self to a happy life.

Self-Knowledge

The notion that the true self should be discovered dates back to at least Socrates and the ancient Greeks who inscribed "know thyself" on the temple of Apollo (Norton, 1976; Pojman, 2006). Similar messages pervade contemporary novels and movies that frequently tell the story of someone who is searching for his or her true self. Once the protagonists of these stories come to learn and accept the "truth" about themselves, their lives are suddenly imbued with happiness. Psychologists have also argued that true self-discovery should facilitate a number of aspects of healthy functioning including maturity (Erikson, 1963), self-esteem (Miller, 1979), growth (Jung, 1953; Maslow, 1968; May, 1983; Rogers, 1959), and the lack of depression and neuroses (Horney, 1945; Miller, 1979).

Though it is difficult, if not impossible, to empirically assess whether a person actually knows his or her true self, research has suggested that subjective feelings of true self-knowledge are important. For example, Kernis and Goldman (2006) addressed this issue with a measure of true self-awareness (a subscale of their more general measure of authentic functioning) that includes items such as "For better or for worse I am aware of who I truly am" and "I am able to distinguish those self-aspects that are important to my core or true self from those that are unimportant." They find that greater feelings of true self-awareness predict self-actualization, vitality, mindfulness, self-esteem, active coping, and decreased defensiveness (Kernis & Goldman, 2006; Lakey, Kernis, Heppner, & Lance, 2008).

In a related vein, true self-knowledge is beneficial to the extent that simply reflecting on one's true self makes people feel good. In a study conducted by Andersen and Williams (1985), participants were asked to reflect on positive aspects of their true self (i.e., private thoughts and cognitions) or positive aspects of their actual self (i.e., public behaviors). Thinking about one's true self led to increased self-esteem, whereas thinking about one's actual self did not influence self-esteem. Similarly, a series of studies by Arndt, Schimel, and colleagues (Arndt & Schimel, 2003; Arndt, Schimel, Greenberg, & Pyszcynski, 2002; Schimel, Arndt, Banko, & Cook, 2004; Schimel, Arndt, Pyszcynski, & Greenberg, 2001) have suggested that activating the "intrinsic self," or beliefs about who you really are, leads to less general defensiveness, conformity, and self-handicapping. Thus, the action of thinking about one's true self may be valuable in and of itself (see also Debats, Drost, & Hansen, 1995).

Behavior

Behaviors can be classified as either reflective of the true self (authentic) or reflective of external demands (inauthentic, e.g., Heidegger, 1927/1962; Kernis & Goldman, 2006). Philosophers (Hiedegger, 1927/1962; Kierkegaard 1849/1983; Sartre, 1943/1956) and psychologists (Erikson, 1963; Miller, 1979; Rogers, 1951) alike have long argued that behaving authentically is a critical ingredient of positive psychological functioning. As Kierkegaard once succinctly wrote, "to will to be that self which one truly is, is indeed the opposite of despair" (1849/1983, p. 3). Similar points have been made by self-determination theorists who have stressed the importance of "true self-esteem" or self-esteem based on simply being who one is rather than one's ability to live up to expectations (Deci & Ryan, 1995; Ryan, 1993; see Fleeson & Wilt, 2010, for an alternative conceptualization of authenticity).

Kernis and Goldman (2006) cited behavior as one of the four key components of authentic functioning. Studies using their measure of authenticity have found that, similar to the awareness subscale, the authentic behavior subscale predicts self-actualization, mindfulness, and self-esteem, as well as decreased psychological stress, substance use, and physical symptomology (Kernis & Goldman, 2005, 2006). Similarly, other studies of authentic expression have shown that self-reported levels of authentic behavior are positively related to subjective well-being, self-esteem, affect, creativity, and hope and are negatively related to depressive symptoms, physical symptoms, stress, and verbal defensiveness (Bettencourt & Sheldon, 2001; Harter, 2002; Harter et al., 1996; Heppner et al., 2008; Kernis, 2003; Lakey et al., 2008; Ryan, LaGuardia, & Rawsthorne, 2005; Sheldon, Ryan, Rawsthorne, & Ilardi, 1997). Using a slightly different methodology to address the issue of authentic behavior, Sheldon, Gunz, and Schachtman (2012) measured discrepancies between people's social character and their true self. The amount of discrepancy between these two self-concepts was negatively related to subjective well-being, happiness, and basic psychological need satisfaction and positively related to neuroticism.

Personal Relationships

The true self is also important to relationship quality because it influences the ways in which we think about others and how close we feel to them. That is, people appear not only to be motivated to reveal their true self to others through authentic behavior, but also to hope and expect others to do the same. Liking, intimacy, and relationship quality are all influenced by how much the relationship partners believe they know about each other's true self and the extent to which the partners behave authentically around each other.

This desire to know others' inner experiences is evidenced in the way people try to get to know each other. As Turner (1976) noted, people seek to learn about each other through learning about their feelings, attitudes, and desires rather than by learning about their social roles or the social categories they may fall into and that these types of true self-disclosures play an important role in liking (e.g., Collins & Miller, 1994). For example, a study by Andersen and Ross (1984) found that participants thought they would like a person better if they knew more about that person's true self than about their overt behaviors. In a second study, these intuitions were supported when participants actually listened to interviews of other participants that focused on either their inner thoughts or behavior. Similarly, it has been suggested that true self-disclosures are important for the development of intimacy (Andersen, 1984; Jourard, 1964; McAdams, 1988; Morton, 1978; Reis & Patrick, 1996; Reis & Shaver, 1988; Sullivan, 1953; Van den Broucke, Vendereycken, & Vertommen, 1995). Revealing private information about the self communicates that one trusts, likes, and is committed to developing intimacy with a partner (Altman & Taylor, 1973; Collins & Miller, 1994; Derlega, Metts, Petronio, & Margulis, 1993).

Finally, although we have already established that authenticity plays an important role in psychological health, there might be reason to suspect that mutual authenticity plays a particularly important role in close relationships. Perhaps close relationships become a venue where authenticity is not only beneficial, but expected. Although no research to date has directly examined whether norms for authenticity exist in close relationships, a variety of research findings have suggested their existence. Indeed, mutual self-disclosure and the freedom to be one's self have been identified as the most defining and cherished components of close relationships by participants (Argyle & Henderson, 1984; DePaulo & Kashy, 1998; Maxwell, 1985; Parks & Floyd, 1996) and theorists alike (Aron, 2003; Deci & Ryan, 1991; Hazan & Shaver, 1994; Reis & Shaver, 1988; Rogers, 1961). Evidence has also suggested that felt authenticity in romantic relationships is an important predictor of relationship quality and durability as well as general well-being (Argyle & Henderson, 1984; Harter, Marold, & Whitesell, 1992; Harter et al., 1998; Hendrick, 1981; Leak & Cooney, 2001; Lopez & Rice, 2006; Neff & Harter, 2002a, 2002b; Neff & Suzio, 2006). Dispositional authenticity also predicts the extent to which people engage in healthy relationship behaviors such as accommodation and trust and can even elicit the same behaviors from their partners (Brunell et al., 2010).

Although we have focused on the importance of the true self to relationships, it is worth noting that, of course, the converse is also true: Relationships are important for the true self. Indeed, secure and supportive relationships, in particular, are an important vehicle for both self-discovery and authentic behavior (Didonato & Krueger, 2010; Gillath, Sesko, Shaver, & Chun, 2010; Leak & Cooney, 2001; Rogers, 1961).

THE TRUE SELF AND EUDAIMONIA

We now turn specifically to the role of the true self in eudaimonic functioning. Though there are a variety of ways in which one may operationalize eudaimonic functioning, we focus specifically on one subjective process: the perception of meaning in one's life. By assessing the perception of meaning in life, we are taking a subjective approach to the study of eudaimonia (see Waterman, 2008, for a discussion of the subjective assessment of eudaimonia). Feelings of meaning are important to eudaimonia in that they should be the flagship indicator that one is pursuing activities that are worthwhile and that one's life has purpose. Indeed, we know almost intuitively the importance that meaning has in our lives, and many people are familiar with the experience of feeling that they are searching for meaning. Consistent with these intuitions, a person's subjective experience of meaningfulness is associated with many important noneudaimonic outcomes such as life satisfaction (Steger & Kashdan, 2007; Zika & Chamberlain, 1992), quality of life (e.g., Krause, 2007), depression (e.g., Mascaro & Rosen, 2005), alcohol and drug use (e.g., Lecci, MacLean, & Croteau, 2002), and suicidal ideation (e.g., Heisel & Flett, 2004).

However, achieving this feeling of meaning can be challenging in a world in which people often make choices between options that, at least objectively, are of equal value. For example, imagine someone trying to choose whether to go to law or business school. Clearly, this is a major life decision. People devote huge amounts of time and effort into their careers and want to believe that this time is well spent. However, it isn't clear which of these two choices will ultimately give the person a greater sense of meaning in their lives. Neither seems to be explicitly more or less valued by society, suggesting there is no universal agreement about which is more meaningful, so how does one make such a choice? This is a situation in which the true self is able to serve as a foundation for meaning. Like Carl Rogers (1961) and others (e.g., Horney, 1945; Laing, 1960; Waterman, 1993), we argue that it is the choice that is more consistent with one's true self that leads to a greater feeling of meaning.

Why would the true self be linked to the personal experience of meaning? The experiences associated with intrinsic motivation (e.g., Deci & Ryan, 1985) or feelings of personal expressiveness (Waterman, 2008) should foster the relationship between the true self and meaning. That is, when one engages in pursuits for intrinsic reasons (i.e., reasons that originate within the self), those pursuits are deemed valuable for that very reason (i.e., that there is no outside/extrinsic motivation for engaging in them). Thus, when we engage in these types of activities, we feel a natural sense of connection to what we are doing and a sense of ownership over our lives. This connection to what we are doing should promote the eudaimonic feeling that one is "being where one wants to be, doing what one wants to do" (Norton, 1976, p. 216).

A wealth of empirical studies supports the importance of such intrinsic activities for meaning making. For example, the extent to which older adults believe they participate in activities that express their unique talents and abilities predicts an increased ability to extract meaning from and to feel grateful for one's life (Krause, 2007). Similarly, the extent to which people rate their personal projects as reflective of core aspects of their self predicts their experience of meaning in life (McGregor & Little, 1998). Sheldon's (2002; Sheldon & Houser-Marko, 2001) work on self-concordance similarly suggested that engaging in goal pursuit that is concordant with who you really are promotes a feeling of ownership over your goals that can increase your well-being.

THE TRUE SELF-CONCEPT AND MEANING IN LIFE

In line with these perspectives, we argue that the true self can provide each person with a unique "life philosophy" (Schlegel & Hicks, 2011; Schlegel, Hicks, Arndt, & King, 2009) that can be used to help make decisions about which relationships, behaviors, and goals are valuable, as well as the relative importance of these domains to each other, thus imbuing life activities and pursuits with meaning and value. Consistent with this idea, Bellah, Madsen, Sullivan, Swidler, and Tipton (1985) found that when people are asked to justify their life decisions, many people make reference to the self, leading these researchers to conclude that "each self constitutes its own moral universe" (p. 76). Baumeister (1991) made similar points, stating that

> the self exports a considerable amount of value, for personal relationships and work and other activities depend on the self for their justification. Thus, the self provides legitimacy and justification to other things without itself needing a higher source of value. (p. 107)

We aim to explore these ideas by directly investigating the role of the true self in meaning making. To do so, we rely on methodologies that move away from the exclusive use of self-reports and instead focus on the cognitive accessibility (Bargh & Chartrand, 2000) or the metacognitive ease of thinking about one's true self-concept (Schwarz, 1998). In a typical study, we ask participants to freely generate or to pick from a list words that they believe describe their true self and/or their actual self (i.e., how they behave in their daily life; cf. Bargh, McKenna, & Fitzsimmons, 2002). We then compare the effects of either the cognitive accessibility or ease of retrieval of these two self-concepts on a meaning relevant outcome. Using this basic paradigm, we have examined how the true self relates to global judgments of meaning in life and decision satisfaction. We have also examined how specific true self beliefs might influence these relationships.

Global Judgments of Life's Meaning

If people are using their true self-concepts to imbue life with meaning, we reasoned that one area in which this process should be observable is at the level of global judgments of meaning (e.g., indicating agreement with statements such as "I understand my life's meaning"; Steger, Frazier, Oishi, & Kaler, 2006).

In a set of five studies, we examined how the cognitive accessibility of the true self-concept relates to these types of judgments. Using the basic methodology previously described, we asked participants to provide words that they felt best described both their true and actual selves (Schlegel et al., 2009) and then used either reaction times on a Me/Not Me task to measure (or priming techniques to manipulate) the cognitive accessibility of one's true self-concept (e.g., Bargh & Chartrand, 2000). In each study, true self-concept accessibility predicted people's global meaning in life judgments such that the more accessible one's true self-concept, the greater one's perception that his or her life was meaningful. In contrast, actual self-concept accessibility had no relationship with meaning in life, suggesting that the true self has a unique relationship with the experience of meaning over and above the self-concept more generally. These findings are consistent with previous work that has suggested that the accessibility of other meaning sources (e.g., religion, personal relationships) predicts meaning judgments (e.g., Hicks & King, 2008, 2009a, 2009b; Hicks, Schlegel, & King, 2010; King, Hicks, Krull, & Del Gaiso, 2006). In these studies, we also controlled for the potentially related influences of positive and negative affect, authenticity, self-esteem, and the valence of the self-concepts, suggesting that it is indeed the true self that is a particularly potent source of meaning.

Next, we examined how perceived true self-knowledge might mirror the observed effects of true self-concept accessibility (Schlegel, Hicks, King, & Arndt, 2011). Studying the effects of accessibility required the use of relatively nonconscious and difficult to control measures and manipulations (i.e., very quick reaction times or subliminal priming). Although this has the appeal of decreasing the chance of response biases, we also wanted to examine how other true self processes, particular those that participants were more aware of, might influence meaning. In this way, we wanted to more directly examine the subjective experiences that people are more likely to encounter in their daily lives. Thus, we used the metacognitive experience of ease/difficulty (Schwarz, 1998; Schwarz & Clore, 1996) in a true self-description task. Because people use the metacognitive experience of ease (or difficulty) as a cue to how much they know about a topic (Schwarz, 2004), experiencing true self description as easy (vs. difficult) should influence the perception of possessing (or not possessing) true self-knowledge. People who experience true self description as easy should feel confident in their level of true self-knowledge, whereas those who experience it as difficult should question their level of true self-knowledge. Across three studies, we asked participants to generate lists of words that described their true and/or actual selves and either measured perceived self-knowledge by asking participants how easy it was to complete the task or manipulated perceived self-knowledge by explicitly making the task easy or difficult by asking participants to generate either a few words (8) or many words (15; adapted from Schwarz et al., 1991). Consistent with the findings for true self-concept accessibility, we found that perceived true self-knowledge positively predicted global judgments of meaning in life and that perceived actual self-knowledge was unrelated to those judgments. These studies also controlled for positive and negative affect as well as self-esteem, further supporting the strong influence of the true self-concept in meaning.

Taken together, these studies on the relationship between the true self-concept and global judgments of meaning provide compelling evidence for the role of the true self in eudaimonic functioning in general and meaning making specifically.

Decision Satisfaction

Encouraged by the findings for global judgments, we endeavored to look more specifically at what we believed was ultimately driving our effects: the use of the true self as a "guide" to decision making (Schlegel, Hicks, Davis, Hirsch, & Smith, 2012). We reasoned that if people are using the true self as a guide in their decision making, then people must be confident in their true self-knowledge in order to also feel confident in their decisions. We again used metacognitive ease as a means of measuring and manipulating perceived self-knowledge and asked participants to either reflect on major decisions they had recently made in their lives (e.g., the university they chose to attend, the choice of their current major) or to complete a simulated career choice task in which they were asked to quickly choose which career they would prefer from a number of paired choices (adapted from Nakao et al., 2010). Consistent with predictions, perceived true self-knowledge was related to satisfaction with both real life and simulated decisions, whereas perceived actual self-knowledge was unrelated to decision satisfaction. These findings suggest that perceived true self-knowledge is an important contributor to the experience of confidence both in one's past decisions and in one's ability to make future decisions, both of which could have potentially important implications for one's ability to find meaning in his or her life.

True Self Beliefs

Tiberius (Chapter 1, this volume) notes that philosophers have separated theories of well-being into two camps: objective and subjective. Whereas objective theories suggest that the ingredients of well-being are universal, subjective theories suggest that the ingredients depend on a person's attitudes. All of the research review thus far is based on the assumption that the true self is an objective ingredient of eudaimonia. Recently, however, we have begun to take a more subjective approach and investigated the possibility that the true self is not an equally important meaning-maker for all people (Schlegel, Vess, & Ardnt, 2012). Specifically, we argue that the use of the true self as a meaning-maker depends on the perceived validity of the true self. In other words, people only use the true self to create meaning if they see it as something that is inherently "real." Because we cannot directly observe the true self, it's reasonable to think that some people may be skeptical of its existence, much like Baumeister (1995), who wrote that the true self is "an appealing idea with heuristic or didactic value but, in the final analysis, a falsehood" (p. 60). People who do not perceive the true self as something that is ontologically real should then also be unlikely to use it as a justification for their life decisions.

One factor we identified that influences this perceived legitimacy of the true self is the use of discovery metaphors for identity development (Waterman, 1984). The belief that the self is discovered is important to the perceived validity of the true self because it implies that an underlying true self exists and is simply waiting to be found. By comparison, the alternative belief (that the self is created) lacks this validating implication. Guided by this analysis, we hypothesized that believing the self is discovered should influence the perceived validity of the true self, which should, in turn, influence the relationship between true self-knowledge and meaning.

Across three studies, we found that individual differences in discovery beliefs positively correlate with the belief that the true self is "real" (whereas creation beliefs are uncorrelated). Further, we found that individual differences in the discovery beliefs interact with true self-knowledge to predict meaning. That is, true self-knowledge is a strong predictor of meaning for individuals with relatively strong discovery beliefs, whereas this relationship is attenuated among individuals with relatively weak discovery beliefs. Creation beliefs had no influence on the relationship between true self-knowledge and meaning in life (Schlegel, Vess, & Arndt, 2012).

Taken together, these studies are the first to suggest that true self may be a subjective, rather than objective, ingredient to the eudaimonia "cake." Considering that the discovery metaphor may be a predominantly Western idea (e.g., Gergen, 1991), these findings also yield a promising avenue for future research on the role of culture in these processes.

CONCLUDING COMMENTS

Returning to the cake analogy that opened this chapter, we hope that we have helped earn the true self a place in the recipe for "the good life." By serving as a wellspring for meaning and value, we believe that the true self-concept is an important component of eudaimonic functioning, particularly for those who believe it is real. Although the research cannot (yet) speak to whether the true self literally exists or to the potential importance of accuracy in true self-knowledge if it does exist, we think this research nonetheless suggests that people who are searching for meaning should look inward. After all, it appears that the feeling that you know what's inside yourself may be just as important as what is actually in there.

REFERENCES

Altman, I., & Taylor, D. A. (1973). *Social penetration: The development of interpersonal relationships*. New York, NY: Holt, Rinehart & Winston.

Andersen, S. M. (1984). Self-knowledge and social inference: II. The diagnosticity of cognitive/affective and behavioral data. *Journal of Personality and Social Psychology, 46*, 294–307. doi:10.1037/0022-3514.46.2.294

Andersen, S. M., Lazowski, L. E., & Donisi, M. (1986). Salience and self-inference: The role of biased recollections in self-inference processes. *Social Cognition, 4*, 75–95. doi:10.1521/soco.1986.4.1.75

Andersen, S. M., & Ross, L. (1984). Self-knowledge and social inference: I. The impact of cognitive/affective and behavioral data. *Journal of Personality and Social Psychology, 46*, 280–293. doi:10.1037/0022-3514.46.2.280

Andersen, S. M., & Williams, M. (1985). Cognitive/affective reactions in the improvement of self-esteem: When thoughts and feelings make a difference. *Journal of Personality and Social Psychology, 49*, 1086–1097. doi:10.1037/0022-3514.49.4.1086

Argyle, M., & Henderson, M. (1984). The rules of friendship. *Journal of Social and Personal Relationships, 1*, 211–237. doi:10.1177/0265407584012005

Arndt, J., & Schimel, J. (2003). Will the real self-esteem please stand up? Toward an optimal understanding of the nature, functions, and sources of self-esteem. *Psychological Inquiry, 14*, 27–31.

Arndt, J., Schimel, J., Greenberg, J., & Pyszcynski, T. (2002). The intrinsic self and defensiveness: Evidence that activating the intrinsic self reduces self-handicapping and conformity. *Personality and Social Psychology Bulletin, 28*, 671–683. doi:10.1177/0146167202288011

Aron, A. (2003). Self and close relationships. In M. Leary & J. Tangney (Eds.), *Handbook of self and identity* (pp. 442–461). New York, NY: Guilford Press.

Bargh, J. A., & Chartrand, T. L. (2000). A practical guide to priming and automaticity research. In H. Reiss & C. Judd (Eds.), *Handbook of research methods in social psychology* (pp. 253–285). New York, NY: Cambridge University Press.

Bargh, J. A., McKenna, K. Y., & Fitzsimmons, G. M. (2002). Can you see the real me? Activation and expression of the "true self" on the internet. *Journal of Social Issues, 58*, 33–48. doi:10.1111/1540-4560.00247

Baumeister, R. F. (1991). *Meanings of life*. New York, NY: Guilford Press.

Baumeister, R. F. (1995). Self and identity. In A. Tesser (Ed.), *Advanced social psychology* (pp. 51–99). Boston, MA: McGraw Hill.

Bellah, R. N., Madsen, R., Sullivan, W. M., Swidler, A., & Tipton, S. M. (1985). *Habits of the heart: Individualism and commitment in American life*. Berkeley, CA: University of California Press.

Bench, S. W., Schlegel, R. J., & Davis, W. E. (2012). *Perceived legitimacy in changes in the self vs. others*. Manuscript in preparation.

Bettencourt, B. A., & Sheldon, K. (2001). Social roles as mechanisms for psychological need satisfaction within social groups. *Journal of Personality and Social Psychology, 81*, 1131–1143. doi:10.1037/0022-3514.81.6.1131

Bouchard, T. J. (2004). Genetic influence on human psychological traits: A survey. *Current Directions in Psychological Science, 13*, 148–151. doi:10.1111/j.0963-7214.2004.00295.x

Brunell, A. B., Kernis, M. H., Goldman, B. M., Heppner, W., Davis, P., Cascio, E. V., & Webster, G. D. (2010). Dispositional authenticity and romantic relationship functioning. *Personality and Individual Differences, 48*, 900–905. doi:10.1016/j.paid.2010.02.018

Collins, N. L., & Miller, L. C. (1994). Self-disclosure and liking: A meta-analytic review. *Psychological Bulletin, 116*, 457–475. doi:10.1037/0033-2909.116.3.457

Costa, P. T., & McCrae, R. R. (1992). *Revised NEO Personality Inventory (NEO-PI-R) and NEO-Five Factor Inventory professional manual*. Odessa, FL: Psychological Assessment Resources.

Debats, D. L., Drost, J., & Hansen, P. (1995). Experiences of meaning in life: A combined qualitative and quantitative approach. *British Journal of Psychology, 86*, 359–375. doi:10.1111/j.2044-8295.1995.tb02758.x

deCharms, R. (1968). *Personal causation*. New York, NY: Academic Press.

Deci, E. L. (1980). *The psychology of self-determination*. Lexington, MA: D.C. Health.

Deci, E. L., & Ryan, R. M. (1985). *Intrinsic motivation and self-determination in human behavior*. New York, NY: Plenum.

Deci, E. L., & Ryan, R. M. (1991). A motivational approach to self: Integration in personality. In R. Dienstbier (Ed.), *Nebraska Symposium on Motivation: Vol. 38. Perspectives on motivation* (pp. 237–288). Lincoln, NE: University of Nebraska Press.

Deci, E. L., & Ryan, R. M. (1995). Human autonomy: The basis for true self-esteem. In M. H. Kernis (Ed.), *Efficacy, agency and self-esteem* (pp. 31–49). New York, NY: Plenum Press.

DePaulo, B. M., & Kashy, D. A. (1998). Everyday lies in close and casual relationships. *Journal of Personality and Social Psychology, 74*, 63–79. doi:10.1037/0022-3514.74.1.63

Derlega, V. J., Metts, S., Petronio, S., & Margulis, S. T. (1993). *Self-disclosure*. Newbury Park, CA: Sage.

Didonato, T. E., & Krueger, J. I. (2010). Interpersonal affirmation and self-authenticity: A test of Rogers's self-growth hypothesis. *Self and Identity, 9*, 322–336. doi:10.1080/15298860903135008

Erikson, E. (1963). *Childhood and society* (2nd ed.). New York, NY: Norton.

Fleeson, W., & Wilt, J. (2010). The relevance of Big Five trait content in behavior to subjective authenticity: Do high levels of within-person behavioral variability undermine or enable authenticity achievement? *Journal of Personality, 78*, 1353–1382.

Gergen, K. J. (1991). *The saturated self: Dilemmas of identity in contemporary life*. New York, NY: Basic Books.

Gillath, O., Sesko, A. K., Shaver, P. R., & Chun, D. S. (2010). Attachment, authenticity, and honesty: Dispositional and experimentally induced security can reduce self- and other-deception. *Journal of Personality and Social Psychology, 98*, 841–855. doi:10.1037/a0019206

Harter, S. (1999). *The construction of the self: A developmental perspective*. New York, NY: Guilford Press.

Harter, S. (2002). Authenticity. In C. R. Snyder & S. J. Lopez (Eds.), *Handbook of positive psychology* (pp. 382–394). Oxford, England: Oxford University Press.

Harter, S., Marold, D. B., & Whitesell, N. R. (1992). Model of psychosocial risk factors leading to suicidal ideation in young adolescents. *Development and Psychopathology, 4*, 167–188. doi:10.1017/S0954579400005629

Harter, S., Marold, D. B., Whitesell, N. R., & Cobbs, G. (1996). A model of the effects of parent and peer support on adolescent false self-behavior. *Child Development, 67*, 360–374. doi:10.2307/1131819

Harter, S., Waters, P., Whitesell, N. R., & Kastelic, D. (1998). Level of voice among female and male high school students: Relational context, support, and gender orientation. *Developmental Psychology, 34*, 892–901. doi:10.1037/0012-1649.34.5.892

Hazan, C., & Shaver, P. R. (1994). Attachment as an organizational framework for research on close relationships. *Psychological Inquiry, 5*, 1–22. doi:10.1207/s15327965pli0501_1

Heidegger, M. (1962). *Being and time* (J. Macquarrie & E. Robinson, Trans.). New York, NY: Harper & Row. (Original work published 1927)

Heisel, M. J., & Flett, G. L. (2004). Purpose in life, satisfaction with life, and suicide ideation in a clinical sample. *Journal of Psychopathology and Behavioral Assessment, 26*, 127–135. doi:10.1023/B:JOBA.0000013660.22413.e0

Hendrick, S. S. (1981). Self-disclosure and marital satisfaction. *Journal of Personality and Social Psychology, 40*, 1150–1159. doi:10.1037/0022-3514.40.6.1150

Heppner, W. L., Kernis, M. H., Nezlek, J. B., Foster, J., Lakey, C. E., & Goldman, B. M. (2008). Within-person relationships among daily self-esteem, need satisfaction, and authenticity. *Psychological Science, 19*, 1140–1145. doi:10.1111/j.1467-9280.2008.02215.x

Hicks, J. A., & King, L. A. (2008). Religious commitment and positive mood as information about meaning in life. *Journal of Research in Personality, 42*, 43–57. doi:10.1016/j.jrp.2007.04.003

Hicks, J. A., & King, L. A. (2009a). Meaning in life as a subjective judgment and lived experience. *Social and Personality Psychology Compass, 3*, 638–653. doi:10.1111/j.1751-9004.2009.00193.x

Hicks, J. A., & King, L. A. (2009b). Positive mood and social relatedness as information about meaning in life. *The Journal of Positive Psychology, 4*, 471–482. doi:10.1080/17439760903271108

Hicks, J. A., Schlegel, R. J., & King, L. A. (2010). Social threats, happiness, and the dynamics of meaning in life judgments. *Personality and Social Psychology Bulletin, 36*, 1305–1317. doi:10.1177/0146167210381650

Horney, K. (1945). *Our inner conflicts*. New York, NY: Norton.

Horney, K. (1950). *Neurosis and human growth: The struggle toward self-realization*. Oxford, England: Norton.

Johnson, J. T., Robinson, M. D., & Mitchell, E. B. (2004). Inferences about the authentic self: When do actions say more than mental states? *Journal of Personality and Social Psychology, 87*, 615–630. doi:10.1037/0022-3514.87.5.615

Jourard, S. M. (1964). *The transparent self*. New York, NY: Van Nostrand.

Jung, C. G. (1953). *Two essays in analytical psychology* (R. F. Hull, Trans.). New York, NY: Pantheon.

Kernis, M. H. (2003). Toward a conceptualization of optimal self-esteem. *Psychological Inquiry, 14*, 1–26. doi:10.1207/S15327965PLI1401_01

Kernis, M. H., & Goldman, B. M. (2005). Authenticity, social motivation and psychological adjustment. In J. P. Forgas, K. D., Williams, & S. Laham (Eds.), *Social motivation: Conscious and unconscious processes* (pp. 210–227). Cambridge, England: Cambridge University Press.

Kernis, M. H., & Goldman, B. M. (2006). A multi-component conceptualization of authenticity: Theory and research. In M. P. Zanna (Ed.), *Advances in experimental social psychology* (Vol. 38, pp. 283–357). New York, NY: Academic Press.

Keyes, C. L. M., & Haidt, J. (2003). Human flourishing—The study of that which makes life worthwhile. In C. L. M. Keyes & J. Haidt (Eds.), *Flourishing: Positive psychology and the life well lived* (pp. 3–12). Washington, DC: American Psychological Association. doi:10.1037/10594-000

Kierkegaard, S. (1983). *The sickness unto death* (H. F. Hong & E. H. Hong, Trans.). Princeton, NJ: Princeton University Press. (Original work published 1849)

King, L. A., Hicks, J. A., Krull, J., & Del Gaiso, A. (2006). Positive affect and the experience of meaning in life. *Journal of Personality and Social Psychology, 90*, 179–196. doi:10.1037/0022-3514.90.1.179

Krause, N. (2007). Self-expression and depressive symptoms in late life. *Research on Aging, 29*, 187–206. doi:10.1177/0164027506298226

Laing, R. D. (1960). *The divided self*. New York, NY: Pantheon.

Lakey, C. E., Kernis, M. H., Heppner, W. L., & Lance, C. E. (2008). Individual differences in authenticity and mindfulness as predictors of verbal defensiveness. *Journal of Research in Personality, 42*, 230–238. doi:10.1016/j.jrp.2007.05.002

Leak, G. K., & Cooney, R. R. (2001). Self-determination, attachment styles, and well-being in adult romantic relationships. *Representative Research in Social Psychology, 25*, 55–62.

Lecci, L., MacLean, M. G., & Croteau, N. (2002). Personal goals of predictors of college student drinking motives, alcohol use and related problems. *Journal of Studies on Alcohol, 63*, 620–630.

Lopez, F. G., & Rice, K. G. (2006). Preliminary development and validation of a measure of relationship authenticity. *Journal of Counseling Psychology, 53*, 362–371. doi:10.1037/0022-0167.53.3.362

Mascaro, N., & Rosen, D. H. (2005). Existential meaning's role in the enhancement of hope and prevention of depressive symptoms. *Journal of Personality, 73*, 985–1014. doi:10.1111/j.1467-6494.2005.00336.x

Maslow, A. H. (1968). *Toward a psychology of being* (2nd ed.). New York, NY: Van Nostrand Reinhold.

May, R. (1969). *Love and will*. New York, NY: Norton.

May, R. (1983). *The discovery of being: Writings in existential psychology*. New York, NY: Norton.

Maxwell, G. M. (1985). Behaviour of lovers: Measuring the closeness of relationships. *Journal of Social and Personal Relationships, 2*, 215–238. doi:10.1177/0265407585022007

McAdams, D. P. (1988). Personal needs and personal relationships. In S. Duck (Ed.), *Handbook of personal relationships: Theory, research and interventions* (pp. 7–22). New York, NY: Wiley.

McCrae, R. R., & Costa, P. T. (1994). The stability of personality: Observation and evaluations. *Current Directions in Psychological Science, 3*, 173–175. doi:10.1111/1467-8721.ep10770693

McGregor, I., & Little, B. R. (1998). Personal projects, happiness, and meaning: On doing well and being yourself. *Journal of Personality and Social Psychology, 74*, 494–512. doi:10.1037/0022-3514.74.2.494

McGregor, I., McAdams, D. P., & Little, B. R. (2006). Personal projects, life stories, and happiness: On being true to traits. *Journal of Research in Personality, 40*, 551–572. doi:10.1016/j.jrp.2005.05.002

Miller, A. (1979). *The drama of the gifted child: The search for the true self*. New York, NY: Basic Books.

Morton, T. L. (1978). Intimacy and reciprocity of exchange: A comparison of spouses and strangers. *Journal of Personality and Social Psychology, 36*, 72–81. doi:10.1037/0022-3514.36.1.72

Nakao, T., Mitsumoto, M., Nashiwa, H., Takamura, M., Tokunaga, S., Miyatani, M., . . . Watanabe, Y. (2010). Self-knowledge reduces conflict by biasing one of plural possible answers. *Personality and Social Psychology Bulletin, 36,* 455–469. doi:10.1177/0146167210363403

Neff, K. D., & Harter, S. (2002a). The authenticity of conflict resolutions among adult couples: Does women's other-oriented behavior reflect their true selves? *Sex Roles, 47,* 403–417. doi:10.1023/A:1021692109040

Neff, K. D., & Harter, S. (2002b). The role of power and authenticity in relationship styles emphasizing autonomy, connectedness, or mutuality among adult couples. *Journal of Social and Personal Relationships, 19,* 835–857. doi:10.1177/0265407502196006

Neff, K. D., & Suzio, M. A. (2006). Culture, power, authenticity and psychological well-being within romantic relationships: A comparison of European American and Mexican Americans. *Cognitive Development, 21,* 441–457. doi:10.1016/j.cogdev.2006.06.008

Norton, D. L. (1976). *Personal destinies: A philosophy of ethical individualism.* Princeton, NJ: Princeton University Press.

Parks, M. R., & Floyd, K. (1996). Meanings for closeness and intimacy in friendship. *Journal of Social and Personal Relationships, 13,* 85–107. doi:10.1177/0265407596131005

Pojman, L. (2006). *Who are we? Theories of human nature.* New York, NY: Oxford University Press.

Reis, H. T., & Patrick, B. C. (1996). Attachment and intimacy: Component processes. In E. T. Higgins & A. W. Kruglanski (Eds.), *Social psychology: Handbook of basic principles* (pp. 523–563). New York, NY: Guilford Press.

Reis, H. T., & Shaver, P. (1988). Intimacy as an interpersonal process. In S. W. Duck (Ed.), *Handbook of personal relationships* (pp. 367–389). Chichester, England: Wiley.

Rogers, C. (1961). *On becoming a person.* Boston, MA: Houghton Mifflin.

Rogers, C. R. (1951). *Client-centered therapy: Its current practice, implications and theory.* Oxford, England: Houghton Mifflin.

Rogers, C. R. (1959). A theory of therapy, personality and interpersonal relationships, as developed in the client-centered framework. In S. Koch (Ed.), *Psychology: A study of science* (pp. 184–256). New York, NY: McGraw Hill.

Rosenberg, M. (1979). *Conceiving the self.* New York, NY: Basic Books.

Ryan, R. M. (1993). Agency and organization: Intrinsic motivation, autonomy and the self in psychological development. In J. Jacobs (Ed.), *Nebraska Symposium on Motivation: Vol. 40. Developmental perspectives on motivation* (pp. 1–56). Lincoln, NE: University of Nebraska Press.

Ryan, R. M., & Deci, E. L. (2001). On happiness and human potentials: A review of research on hedonic and eudaimonic well-being. *Annual Review of Psychology, 52,* 141–166. doi:10.1146/annurev.psych.52.1.141

Ryan, R. M., LaGuardia, J. G., & Rawsthorne, L. J. (2005). Self-complexity and the authenticity of self-aspects on well-being and resilience to stressful events. *North American Journal of Psychology, 7,* 431–448.

Sartre, J.-P. (1956). *Being and nothingness: An essay on phenomenological ontology* (H. Barnes, Trans.). New York, NY: Philosophical Library. (Original work published 1943)

Schimel, J., Arndt, J., Banko, K. M., & Cook, A. (2004). Not all self-affirmations were created equal: The cognitive and social benefits of affirming the intrinsic (vs. extrinsic) self. *Social Cognition, 22,* 75–99. doi:10.1521/soco.22.1.75.30984

Schimel, J., Arndt, J., Pyszcynski, T., & Greenberg, J. (2001). Being accepted for who we are: Evidence that social validation of the intrinsic self reduces generaldefensiveness. *Journal of Personality and Social Psychology, 80,* 35–52. doi:10.1037/0022-3514.80.1.35

Schlegel, R. J., & Hicks, J. A. (2011). The true self and psychological health: Emerging evidence and future directions. *Social and Personality Psychology Compass, 5,* 989–1003. doi:10.1111/j.1751-9004.2011.00401.x

Schlegel, R. J., Hicks, J. A., Arndt, J., & King, L. A. (2009). Thine own self: True self-concept accessibility and meaning in life. *Journal of Personality and Social Psychology, 96,* 473–490. doi:10.1037/a0014060

Schlegel, R. J., Hicks, J. A., Davis, W. E., Hirsch, K. A., & Smith, C. M. (2012). *Self relevant metacognition and decision satisfaction.* Manuscript submitted for publication.

Schlegel, R. J., Hicks, J. A., King, L. A., & Arndt, J. (2011). Knowing who you are: Perceived true self-knowledge and meaning in life. *Personality and Social Psychology Bulletin, 37,* 745–756. doi:10.1177/0146167211400424

Schlegel, R. J., Vess, M. K., & Arndt, J. A. (2012). To discover or to create: Metaphors and the true self. *Journal of Personality, 80,* 969–993.

Schwarz, N. (1998). Accessible content and accessibility experiences: The interplay of declarative and experiential information in judgment. *Personality and Social Psychology Review, 2,* 87–99. doi:10.1207/s15327957pspr0202_2

Schwarz, N. (2004). Metacognitive experiences in consumer judgment and decision making. *Journal of Consumer Psychology, 14,* 332–348. doi:10.1207/s15327663jcp1404_2

Schwarz, N., Bless, H., Strack, F., Klumpp, G., Rittenauer-Schatka, H., & Simons, A. (1991). Ease of retrieval as information: Another look at the availability heuristic. *Journal of Personality and Social Psychology, 61,* 195–202. doi:10.1037/0022-3514.61.2.195

Schwarz, N., & Clore, G. L. (1996). Feelings as phenomenal experiences. In E. T. Higgins & A. Kruglanski (Eds.), *Social psychology: Handbook of basic principles* (pp. 433–465). New York, NY: Guilford Press.

Sheldon, K. M. (2002). The self-concordance model of healthy goal-striving: When personal goals correctly represent the person. In E. L. Deci & R. M. Ryan (Eds.), *Handbook of self-determination research* (pp. 65–86). Rochester, NY: University of Rochester Press.

Sheldon, K. M., Gunz, A., & Schachtman, T. R. (2012). What does it mean to be in touch with oneself? Testing a social character model of self-congruence. *Self and Identity, 11*, 51–70.

Sheldon, K. M., & Houser-Marko, L. (2001). Self-concordance, goal-attainment, and the pursuit of happiness: Can there be an upward spiral? *Journal of Personality and Social Psychology, 80*, 152–165. doi:10.1037/0022-3514.80.1.152

Sheldon, K. M., Ryan, R. M., Rawsthorne, L., & Ilardi, B. (1997). "True" self and "trait" self: Cross-role variation in the Big-Five personality traits and its relations with authenticity and well-being. *Journal of Personality and Social Psychology, 73*, 1380–1393. doi:10.1037/0022-3514.73.6.1380

Steger, M. F., Frazier, P., Oishi, S., & Kaler, M. (2006). The Meaning in Life Questionnaire: Assessing the presence of and search for meaning in life. *Journal of Counseling Psychology, 53*, 80–93. doi:10.1037/0022-0167.53.1.80

Steger, M. F., & Kashdan, T. B. (2007). Stability and specificity of meaning in life and life satisfaction over one year. *Journal of Happiness Studies, 8*, 161–179. doi:10.1007/s10902-006-9011-8

Sullivan, H. S. (1953). *The interpersonal theory of psychiatry*. New York, NY: Norton.

Turner, R. H. (1976). The real self: From institution to impulse. *American Journal of Sociology, 81*, 989–1016. doi:10.1086/226183

Van den Broucke, S., Vandereycken, W., & Vertommen, H. (1995). Marital intimacy: Conceptualization and assessment. *Clinical Psychology Review, 15*, 217–233. doi:10.1016/0272-7358(95)00007-C

Waterman, A. S. (1984). Identity formation: Discovery or creation? *The Journal of Early Adolescence, 4*, 329–341. doi:10.1177/0272431684044004

Waterman, A. S. (1990). Personal expressiveness: Philosophical and psychological foundations. *Journal of Mind and Behavior, 11*, 47–74.

Waterman, A. S. (1993). Two conceptions of happiness: Contrasts of personal expressiveness (eudaimonia) and hedonic enjoyment. *Journal of Personality and Social Psychology, 64*, 678–691. doi:10.1037/0022-3514.64.4.678

Waterman, A. S. (2008). Reconsidering happiness: A eudaimonist's perspective. *The Journal of Positive Psychology, 3*, 234–252. doi:10.1080/17439760802303002

Winnicott, D. W. (1960). *The maturational processes and the facilitating environment: Studies in the theory of emotional development*. New York, NY: International Universities Press.

Zika, S., & Chamberlain, K. (1992). On the relation between meaning in life and psychological well-being. *British Journal of Psychology, 83*, 133–145. doi:10.1111/j.2044-8295.1992.tb02429.x

11

CROSS-CULTURAL PERCEPTIONS OF MEANING AND GOALS IN ADULTHOOD: THEIR ROOTS AND RELATIONS WITH HAPPINESS

ANTONELLA DELLE FAVE, MARIÉ WISSING, INGRID BRDAR, DIANNE VELLA-BRODRICK, AND TERESA FREIRE

Positive psychology is gaining increasing popularity within the social sciences. This is due largely to its emphasis on individual strengths and resources and its strong focus on designing interventions aimed at promoting people's well-being. However, much of the related research has overlooked the interplay between individuals and their social and cultural environment. The human capacity for culture led to the development of stable communities, to the setting of social norms and rules, and to the interpretation of reality according to symbolic meanings (Jablonka & Lamb, 2005). From this perspective, culture shapes individuals' behavior and conceptions of a good and just life, both providing a meaning-making system and fostering or limiting opportunities for personal growth and self-expression (Delle Fave & Bassi, 2009; see also Chapters 3 and 4, this volume).

In this chapter, we provide empirical evidence about how individuals conceptualize and contextualize happiness, life goals, and meaning across seven Western countries. We analyze these aspects through the findings

DOI: 10.1037/14092-012
The Best Within Us: Positive Psychology Perspectives on Eudaimonia, Alan S. Waterman (Editor)
Copyright © 2013 by the American Psychological Association. All rights reserved.

obtained from the Eudaimonic and Hedonic Happiness Investigation (EHHI) project (Delle Fave, Brdar, Freire, Vella-Brodrick, & Wissing, 2011). We outline our theoretical reference framework, present findings, and explore connections and differences between our perspective and some philosophical and psychological conceptualizations of well-being referred to in this book. Although we acknowledge the importance of collaboration across disciplines when dealing with any aspect of human life, in our opinion there are still several issues that should be clarified in order to develop solid connections between the psychological and philosophical theories currently dealing with well-being.

INDIVIDUAL WELL-BEING IN CONTEXT

In general, contextual factors such as culture are neglected in Western psychology, which primarily focuses on the subjective dimension of meaning making and on the level of autonomy individuals experience in determining which goals, values, and meanings they want to endorse in their lives. Contextual factors are considered only to the extent that they are incorporated into the individuals' definition of themselves, thus becoming isolated from the environment as components of stable and well-defined personal identities in spite of the changes that both the environment and the individual ceaselessly undergo (Slife & Richardson, 2008). This approach ignores the very fact that cultural differences in value systems affect the weight and the meaning individuals attribute to collective norms, daily activities, and social roles (Berry, Segall, & Kagitçibasi, 1997; Triandis, 1994).

Positive psychology is not immune from this bias (Richardson & Guignon, 2008). Scholars adopting a constructivist point of view, which emphasizes the ceaseless interplay of individuals and contexts in reciprocally shaping each other, have argued that positive psychology treats individuals as basically "fixed and essential selves" who autonomously shape their inner reality and their relationship with the environment (Christopher & Hickinbottom, 2008). According to these scholars, the Western individualistic background (Smith & Bond, 1999) in which positive psychology was developed leads researchers to neglect the impact of cultural norms and beliefs on the subjective interpretation of happiness, well-being, and quality of life (Becker & Marecek, 2008).

Cultural, economic, and collective rules and norms can indeed expand or restrict the opportunities for action, development, and flourishing available to individuals and groups within a society. For example, members of socially stratified communities have access to a limited variety of jobs, according to the class or caste to which they belong. However, they are not necessarily aware of the wider range of opportunities for action and self-expression that they could experience in more egalitarian societies, and subsequently they can perceive well-being in their daily life in spite of constraints and limitations (Delle Fave & Massimini, 2005; Prilleltensky, 1994).

Within positive psychology, the individualistic and abstractionist approach is, in fact, molded by theories and models that highlight the prominent role of social connections in promoting quality of life, meaning making, and happiness. For example, positive relations are part of Ryff's (1989; see also Chapter 4, this volume) psychological well-being model; relatedness is a basic psychological need in Deci and Ryan's (2002) self-determination theory (see also Chapter 3, this volume); Keyes (1998, 2007) conceptualized social well-being and included it in his mental health continuum theory; Peterson and Seligman (2004) identified the virtues of humanity and justice; and relationships are one of the well-being components in the PERMA (positive emotions, engagement, relationships, meaning, achievement) model (Forgeard, Jayawickreme, Kern, & Seligman, 2011). The contextual perspective is also endorsed by research addressing the role of spirituality and religiousness in promoting well-being, both directly through the connection with a universal or supernatural reality transcending the individual and indirectly through the support derived from belonging to a community sharing values, rituals, and social events (Emmons, 2005; WHOQOL SRPB Group, 2006).

Research in positive psychology also includes efforts to contextualize subjective evaluations of well-being using cultural and socioeconomic dimensions as objective indicators of quality of life. From the hedonic perspective, the relationship between satisfaction with life and objective well-being indicators was widely explored (Diener, Oishi, & Lucas, 2003). Within the eudaimonic perspective, the influence of age, socioeconomic conditions, ethnicity, and level of education were taken into account in various studies (Chirkov, Ryan, & Sheldon, 2011; Keyes et al., 2008; Park, Peterson, & Seligman, 2006; see also Chapter 4, this volume). However, many of these studies are correlational and not causal in nature; more targeted studies are still needed to examine cultural and social issues as core dimensions and not just as lateral factors. In addition, these studies rely heavily on quantitative data, gathered through scales containing questions about abstract and general concepts. The way participants contextualize their scaled answers and the meaning they attribute to such concepts are seldom considered. For example, what do Indian and German participants think about when they rate their family relations as highly positive? Do people in Greece and Iran refer to the same standard and value system when invited to rate their levels of freedom to express feeling and ideas? To better disentangle the role of the context in shaping individual evaluations of well-being, more culture-fair models and studies are needed as well as more qualitative research, possibly combining the collection of qualitative and quantitative findings through a mixed-method approach.

THE INDIVIDUAL PURSUIT OF WELL-BEING

Besides being influenced by their environment, individuals play an active role in shaping their own developmental pathway and ultimately in contributing to the changes of the culture they live in (Laland, Odling-Smee, & Feldman, 2000). A process of active psychological selection (Csikszentmihalyi & Massimini, 1985) takes place at the individual level, promoting the differential reproduction of cultural information units—in terms of activities, beliefs, habits, behavioral norms. Several cross-cultural studies (summarized in Delle Fave, Massimini & Bassi, 2011) showed that two core components of eudaimonic well-being play a key role in guiding this process of selection. The first component is the association of specific cultural information units with optimal experience, or flow (Csikszentmihalyi, 2000), characterized by engagement, skill mobilization, involvement, and enjoyment. The second component is the long-term meaning individuals attribute to the cultural information units available to them in their daily environment.

In positive psychology, growing attention is paid to meaning, its measurement, and its relationship with happiness, purpose in life, goal pursuit and achievement, and development of personal potentials (Hart & Sasso, 2011; Linley et al., 2009; Waterman et al., 2010; see also Chapters 6, 8–10, this volume). Through the attribution of meaning to specific life activities and domains, individuals pursue goals deemed relevant and meaningful as well as consistent with social values and others' needs, even when these goals undermine their quality of life in the short run in hedonic terms of positive emotions and pleasure. For example, they can choose to volunteer as ambulance rescuers during their free time instead of more relaxing leisure activities or material comforts (Sen, 1992).

THE EUDAIMONIC AND HEDONIC HAPPINESS INVESTIGATION STUDY

On the basis of these premises, we report findings obtained from an international study using both qualitative and quantitative methods. In particular, we aim to (a) investigate what happiness is to people; (b) explore the main goals and meaningful things people report in their life, in terms of their contents (the "what") and the motives that support their pursuit and relevance (the "why"); and (c) look for connections between participants' answers and the cultural and social context in which they live. We pay attention to both the eudaimonic and hedonic dimensions emerging from our findings, considering that, as stated by Waterman (see Introduction, this volume), positive correlations between subjective well-being (SWB), psychological well-being (PWB), and eudaimonic well-being (EWB) were detected across several studies. Previous studies have clearly shown that SWB and PWB contribute to well-being in different ways and can operate independently of each other (Delle Fave, Brdar, et al., 2011; Huta & Ryan, 2010).

As psychologists involved in empirical research, we are well aware that meta-theoretical assumptions influence the theories we refer to and that guide our work. However, we also believe that research findings can help us modify or develop theories, which in their turn may contribute to metatheoretical philosophical assumptions about human nature and the substance of "the good life" (see Chapter 1, this volume). We use both top-down and bottom-up processes in our efforts to come to new understandings. Our potential contribution to this book is predominantly at a subjective level rather than at a normative level, as we focus on individuals' evaluations of what is good for them. Our data may contribute to the understanding of well-being by empirically establishing what people think makes life go best for them, as reflected in the content and motives for goals and most meaningful things, and by identifying cultural differences and similarities in these evaluations.

Participants and Procedures

The study sample consisted of 666 participants from seven countries: Australia ($n = 99$), Croatia ($n = 104$), Germany ($n = 85$), Italy ($n = 104$), Portugal ($n = 78$), Spain ($n = 92$), and South Africa ($n = 104$). The participants ranged in age from 30 to 51 (mean age, 39.9) and were living in urban areas. The subsamples from each country were approximately equally distributed by gender and education level (high school diploma or a university degree). Participants provided their informed consent to researchers, completed the Eudaimonic and Hedonic Happiness Investigation (EHHI) at a time and place convenient to them, and handed in their responses or sent them via mail or e-mail.

Following a linguistic/cultural criterion based on the different use and meaning of the word *happiness*, participants were divided into the following three groups:

1. Participants from Germany, Australia, and South Africa speaking languages within the Anglo-Saxon heritage (German, English, and Afrikaans, and Enlish, respectively) belonged to the Germanic group. All Australian and South African participants

were Caucasian, and the latter group spoke English or Afrikaans as their mother tongue.

2. Italian, Spanish and Portuguese participants, speaking neo-Latin languages, belonged to the Romance group.
3. The third group included only Croatian participants, speaking a Slavic language.

In English, *happiness* is related to *happen*—event, chance, luck (good or bad). Similarly, in German the term *Glück*, which identifies happiness, also means luck, fortune. In Afrikaans *happiness* is translated as *gelukkig*, which on the one hand refers to the experience of luck or fortune but on the other hand may also refer to being filled with contentment. It is also linked to the Dutch word *lukken*, which refers to being successful. In all the three Romance languages the term for happiness derives from the Latin word *Felicitas*, evolved from the Indo-european root *fe*—related to terms underlying a process of development, such as foetus, faith, flourishing, fruitful. Finally, in Croatian the term *sreća* stems from the Old Slavic word *sretja*, which means happening, event, or encounter.

This partition is also consistent with some differences in historical traditions of value systems and social organization. The Germanic group includes countries with a substantially egalitarian structure whose historical background is partially related to the Protestant ethic, which emphasizes individual initiative and achievement, pragmatism, and autonomy support (Bruce, 2004; Weber, 1958). The Romance group comprises countries historically characterized by the religious and institutional influence of the Catholic Church and by a tradition of feudal and hierarchical structure, implying a higher power distance (Hofstede, 1994) and a higher social control on individual initiative (House, Hanges, Javidan, Dorfman, & Gupta, 2004; Veenhoven, 2010). Finally, Croatia was historically exposed to both Germanic and Romance cultures because of its relationships with Venice and the Austrian empire; however, during the 20th century, the country underwent deep political changes and socioeconomic transitions that were not shared by the other two groups of countries.

Data were collected through the EHHI (Delle Fave, Brdar, et al., 2011). Participants were asked to define happiness in their own words, to list their three main goals and explain why each goal is important, and to list the three most meaningful things in their life and then explain why they are meaningful. They also rated their levels of happiness and of meaningfulness in different life domains on 1–7 point scales. The reliability in the coding process for open-ended questions was established by independent ratings followed by discussion involving at least two researchers in each country, and the remaining doubts were discussed within the international team.

Results

In this section, we show findings derived from the EHHI administration. The findings obtained from each group of participants (Germanic, Romance, and Croatian) are presented separately to allow for group comparisons.

Happiness *Definition*

Participants were invited to define *happiness* in their own words, without specific constraints. Complex and multifaceted descriptions were often provided, referring to different aspects of happiness. Each aspect was coded separately, and up to six answers were retained for each participant. Some answers referred to situations occurring within specific life domains (e.g., "playing with my children"), whereas others represented descriptions of psychological states (e.g., "fulfillment" or "a positive emotion"). Table 11.1 shows the percentage distribution of participants who provided answers across the different categories that were identified within each type of definition.

Major similarities were detected across groups. Participants providing psychological definitions of happiness referred to eudaimonic dimensions such as balance, meaning, and development more often than they did to hedonic dimensions such as satisfaction and positive emotions. Among situational, domain-related definitions, family and interpersonal relations were prominent, whereas few participants referred to spirituality/religion and community/society issues.

Cultural differences were also identified. In general, the percentage of participants providing psychological definitions of happiness was significantly higher for the Romance group than for the Germanic group, and the opposite was true of domain-related definitions. Within the domain-related definitions, the percentage of participants reporting family was lowest for the Romance group, whereas a significantly higher percentage of Croatian participants referred to health.

Goals and Meaningful Things

Participants were then asked to list the three most important goals and the three most meaningful things in their lives. Table 11.2 depicts the percentage distribution of participants in each group who provided answers related to the various life domains.

Cultural similarities were detected for the domains of family and work, regularly quoted in relation to both goals and meaningful things. Social relationships were associated with meaning by about one third of participants across groups, whereas a lower percentage of participants identified them as goals to be pursued. Community and society issues ranked lowest for both

TABLE 11.1

Percentage Distribution of Participants Reporting Psychological and
Domain-Related Definitions of Happiness in Each Cultural Group

	n answers	% Germanic	% Romance	% Croatian	χ^2
Psychological definitions	916	68.7	82.2	75.0	13.5**
Harmony/ balance	233	26.7	32.5	17.3	8.9*
Positive emotion	152	23.3	16.8	22.1	3.8
Meaning	33	13.9	7.7	8.7	6.2 *
Engagement/ growth	43	10.8	4.4	—	17.8**
Achievement	80	9.7	9.5	14.4	2.2
Satisfaction	66	11.5	4.0	20.2	24.1**
Well-being	108	5.9	27.0	11.5	49.3**
Freedom/ autonomy	43	7.6	1.8	7.7	11.0**
Optimism	57	11.1	5.1	4.8	8.6*
Gratification	14	1.7	1.1	—	2.0
Fulfillment	43	5.2	6.6	9.6	2.5
Domain-related definitions	931	73.6	51.1	69.2	32.4**
Family	270	36.5	16.8	42.3	36.3**
Relations	250	31.9	26.6	29.8	1.9
Health	113	17.4	10.6	30.8	22.3**
Life in general	97	14.2	11.7	23.1	7.9*
Work	58	10.4	5.5	10.6	5.2
Standard of living	59	9.0	6.2	11.5	3.2
Spirituality	38	6.3	4.7	1.0	4.7
Community/ society	23	4.5	2.9	1.9	1.9

*$p < .05$. **$p < .01$

answers. As for cultural differences, a significantly higher percentage of Croatian participants rated health as an important goal, whereas spirituality emerged as both a goal and meaningful thing in the Germanic group because of the almost exclusive contributions of South African participants.

Because work and family were the domains most strongly related to happiness, meaning, and goals, participants' answers were classified within subcategories according to their specific contents. Contents prominently referred to core constructs in positive psychology, such as development and expression of competences, self-actualization, satisfaction, and meaning.

In the domain of work, participants' goals and meaningful things mainly referred to personal growth, development, and achievement (e.g., "To improve knowledge/skills at work," "Goal achievement at work," "Passion for work"). A limited percentage of participants referred to the extrinsic value of

TABLE 11.2
Goals and Meaningful Things in Life Domains: Percentage
of Participants in Each Cultural Group

	n answers	Germanic	Romance	Croatian	χ^2
Goals					
Family	630	68.6	72.6	81.7	6.5*
Work	354	43.8	57.3	59.6	13.3**
Health	196	31.9	21.5	40.4	15.2**
Standard of living	231	30.2	32.1	38.5	2.4
Personal life	196	23.6	24.1	23.1	0.1
Leisure	126	18.7	19.1	11.5	3.2
Relationships	46	10.8	2.6	6.7	15.0**
Spirituality	28	7.6	1.5	1.9	14.9**
Community	37	6.6	4.7	1.0	5.1
Meaningful things					
Family	778	83.0	86.5	79.8	2.8
Work	299	36.5	48.9	53.9	13.4**
Relationships	205	27.8	31.0	29.8	0.7
Health	173	20.5	28.4	34.6	9.4**
Personal life	132	18.8	17.1	18.3	0.7
Standard of living	100	14.9	12.4	17.3	1.7
Spirituality	84	21.5	4.4	8.7	39.5**
Leisure	78	10.8	12.8	5.8	3.8
Community/society	38	8.7	3.7	1.0	11.7**

*$p < .05$. **$p < .01$

work (e.g., "Stability/security in job"; "Minimum work, maximum income").
With regard to goals, job satisfaction was quoted by the highest percentage
of participants across cultures. Group differences were detected for competence (reported by a significantly higher share of Romance participants) and
self-actualization (emphasized by Germanic participants). As for meaningful
things, the majority of participants in the three groups referred to the domain
of work as a whole. However, a significantly higher percentage of Romance
and Croatian participants provided answers referring to the intrinsic value
and meaning of work, whereas Germanic participants quoted satisfaction
with work in a significantly higher percentage.

Within the family domain, participants from all groups prominently
referred to the intrinsic relevance of having a family and to the relational
aspects of sharing and reciprocity (because of space limitations, data are
not shown). Only a limited percentage of participants quoted pursuit of
personal rewards from family as a goal or meaningful thing. As for family-
related goals, a significantly higher percentage of Germanic participants
emphasized their personal contribution and support to family, whereas a
significantly higher percentage of Croatian participants referred to family
well-being as a goal, without any specification about a personal role in it.

With regard to meaningful things, almost all Romance participants (92.4%) referred to family as a meaningful thing per se, whereas Germanic participants referred to sharing experiences and to providing a personal contribution to the family in a significantly higher percentage compared with the other two groups.

Motives Underlying Goals and Meaningful Things

Figure 11.1 summarizes participants' answers to the questions "why the goal is important" and "why the meaningful thing is meaningful." Differently from the previous analyses, cumulative findings are presented, because no relevant group differences were detected. As Figure 11.1 shows, the percentage distribution of the answers to the two questions across categories is very similar. Personal life clearly emerged as the prominent motive supporting both goal setting and meaning. Family, standard of living, life in general, and work followed in rank as motives supporting goals. Life in general and relations followed in rank among motives for meaningful things.

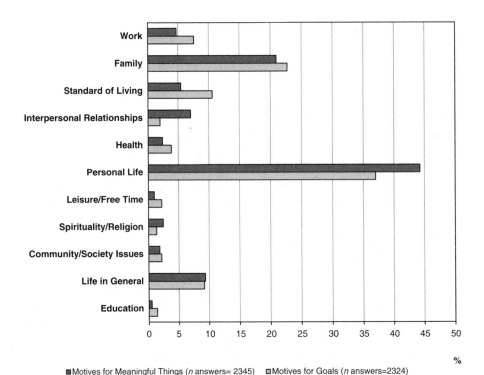

■Motives for Meaningful Things (*n* answers= 2345)   ☐Motives for Goals (*n* answers=2324)

Figure 11.1. Motives underlying meaningful things and goals. Overall percentage distribution of the answers across life domains for the global sample.

Because of the relevance of personal life among motives for pursuing goals and attributing meaning, the related answers were analyzed with greater detail and divided into subcategories. In sum, satisfaction, value, and personal growth were prominent as the main motives supporting goal setting and pursuit. Optimism ranked least, with only Germanic participants referring to it. As for meaningful things, participants across groups quoted value as the prominent motive underlying them. It is worth specifying that within the subcategory "value," participants referred to the intrinsic relevance and essential role of the things they rated as meaningful. Deriving satisfaction, support, harmony/balance, and personal growth were other motives similarly quoted across groups.

Some differences emerged as well. Regarding the motives underlying goals, a significantly lower percentage of Romance participants reported positive emotions; self-actualization was quoted by a significantly lower percentage of Croatian participants; and happiness/well-being (described as a general inner state, without specifications) was indicated by a significantly lower percentage of Germanic participants. In relation to meaning, Germanic participants reported positive emotions and optimism more often and happiness/well-being less often than did the other two groups.

Ratings of Happiness and Meaningfulness

Table 11.3 shows the mean ratings of happiness, meaningfulness, and satisfaction with life across cultures. This comparative analysis substantially reflects the cumulative findings reported in Delle Fave, Brdar, et al. (2011) for the international sample. Participants across countries reported the highest levels of happiness and meaningfulness in four main domains: family, health, interpersonal relations and personal growth (with slight variations in their order across groups). In contrast, spirituality and society issues were associated with the lowest levels of happiness and meaningfulness.

DISCUSSION

The findings illustrated previously partially confirmed previous studies, but they also provided some new contributions to the investigation of meanings and goals as crucial components of well-being.

The Prominence of Family

A substantial congruence across groups was evident between qualitative and quantitative findings referring to family, which ranked first among

TABLE 11.3
Mean Levels of Happiness, Meaningfulness, and Life Satisfaction Across Cultural Groupings

	Germanic (G)		Romance (R)		Croatian (C)			
	M	SD	M	SD	M	SD	$F(2,661)$	Post hoc[a]
Happiness								
Family	5.95	1.15	5.82	1.29	5.98	1.27	1.03	
Relations	5.60	1.16	5.38	1.16	5.24	1.12	4.81**	G > C
Health	5.55	1.21	5.73	1.21	5.80	1.21	2.22	
Life in general	5.45	1.03	5.29	1.02	5.33	1.14	1.54	
Personal growth	5.31	1.08	5.39	1.21	5.22	1.26	0.84	
Standard of living	5.19	1.13	4.96	1.09	4.87	1.22	4.60**	G > R, C
Leisure/free time	4.99	1.24	4.68	1.42	4.50	1.60	5.43**	G > R, C
Spirituality/religion	4.88	1.64	4.06	1.78	4.32	1.72	14.87**	G > R, C
Work	4.86	1.28	4.56	1.44	4.72	1.44	3.30*	G > R
Community issues	4.41	1.14	4.21	1.42	4.94	1.21	12.46**	C > G, R
Society issues	4.10	1.20	4.11	1.41	4.17	1.35	0.11	
Meaningfulness								
Family	6.40	0.91	6.57	0.87	6.85	0.43	15.11**	C > G, R
Relations	6.03	0.91	5.82	1.13	5.97	1.04	2.90	
Health	6.27	0.89	6.54	0.92	6.78	0.54	19.24**	C > R > G
Life in general	5.87	0.99	5.96	1.18	6.18	0.86	3.11*	C > G, R
Personal growth	5.80	1.09	6.00	1.07	5.97	0.88	2.81	
Standard of living	5.33	1.03	5.21	1.20	5.52	1.06	3.12*	C > R
Leisure/free time	5.44	1.02	5.33	1.26	5.19	1.09	1.86	
Spirituality/religion	4.86	1.97	3.92	1.95	4.55	1.74	16.70**	G, C > R
Work	5.38	1.21	5.50	1.12	5.65	1.08	2.31	C > G
Community issues	4.62	1.31	4.55	1.46	5.52	1.11	23.08**	C > G, R
Society issues	4.46	1.41	4.58	1.50	4.67	1.27	1.02	
Life satisfaction	5.07	1.09	4.68	1.12	4.66	1.22	10.20**	G > R, C

[a]Duncan's post hoc test.
*$p < .05$. **$p < .01$.

domain-related definitions of happiness, goals, and meaningful things and scored highest in the ratings of happiness and meaningfulness. The prominent motives for quoting family as a goal and a meaningful thing were also shared by participants across groups, who valued family in its own right, and as a context promoting personal growth, providing support, and fostering hedonic and eudaimonic well-being. These findings are consistent with the literature on relationships and support facets of other theoretical perspectives (see Chapters 3 and 4, this volume), but they also specify in more detail what interpersonal relationships mean to laypeople. Throughout life, social and family relationships contribute to personal growth and individual self-actualization by providing trust, self-esteem, support, and well-being (An & Cooney, 2006; Ryff & Keyes, 1995).

The developmental phase and age cohort of the participants involved in this study may have specifically contributed to the prominence of family throughout the EHHI answers. The majority of participants (65%) had children and were engaged in parenting and child-rearing tasks. A different emphasis on family may be found in data obtained from younger and older groups.

Only one major difference was detected across groups in the evaluation of the family: A significantly lower percentage of Romance participants quoted family as a domain related to happiness. This finding apparently runs against the stereotypical assumptions of family centeredness in Mediterranean societies. However, in these societies the family presence and influence are almost taken for granted, and they entail a certain amount of constraints as well. Previous cross-cultural studies with both adults and adolescents (Delle Fave, Massimini, & Bassi, 2011) supported this interpretation.

The Peculiarity of Work

Across groups, the percentage of participants reporting work as a goal and a meaningful thing was second only to the percentage of those reporting family. Job-related goals and meaningful things referred primarily to work as a value per se and to its role in promoting individual well-being in both hedonic (satisfaction) and eudaimonic terms (competence development, self-actualization). The analysis of motives underlying work goals and meaning were in line with these findings: personal growth, job-related satisfaction, and competence development prevailed. As suggested by studies on self-concordance and self-determination in goal orientation (Gong & Chang, 2007; Sheldon et al., 2004), these motives are intrinsic. In addition, personal growth and competence development are connected to the eudaimonic perspective, because they entail personal resource mobilization and commitment, as well as meaning making. This is also consistent with eudaimonic identity theory (see Chapter 5, this volume). Work enables one to develop latent talents and to find opportunities to act on personal potentials, thus giving rise to feelings of personal expressiveness.

A discrepancy was, however, detected between qualitative and quantitative findings in relation to work, as across groups this domain ranked only seventh in level of happiness and fifth in level of meaningfulness. This discrepancy can be at least partially clarified by comparing the levels of happiness and meaningfulness at work between participants who quoted work as a goal (345; 51.8%) and as a meaningful thing (295, 44.3%) and participants who did not. In particular, participants who quoted work as a goal reported significantly higher levels of work meaningfulness ($M = 4.80$, $SD = 1.29$, $t = 2.81$, $p < .01$) than participants who did not ($M = 4.47$, $SD = 1.44$). Participants who quoted work as meaningful reported significantly higher levels of work happiness ($M = 4.94$, $SD = 1.25$, $t = 4.06$, $p < .001$) and meaningfulness ($M = 5.79$, $SD = 0.96$, $t = 6.72$, $p < .001$), compared with participants who did not ($M = 4.5$, $SD = 1.45$, and $M = 5.21$, $SD = 1.23$, respectively).

Theoretical, Methodological, and Practical Implications

The findings presented here confirm previous evidence of the conceptual and evaluative differences between happiness and meaningfulness (Delle Fave, Brdar, et al., 2011), which can be generally extended to the hedonic and eudaimonic dimensions of well-being. In particular, the identification of goals and meanings and the level of meaningfulness in a given life domain are distinctly related to eudaimonic dimensions such as its intrinsic value, competence development, and personal growth. Such a relation emerged from the motives underlying participants' pursuit of goals and their perception of meaningfulness in the various life domains. More specifically, the prominent motive underlying meaningful things was their intrinsic value and relevance in participants' life, as also indirectly suggested by Ryan and colleagues (see Chapter 3, this volume). This apparently recursive outcome suggests that things perceived as meaningful are intrinsically valuable, thus suggesting the importance of meaning and the process of meaning making as substantial dimensions of well-being, strongly connected to individual and collective values.

These findings also support the theoretical view according to which meaning can be perceived and pursued in domains that do not provide hedonic happiness. Other empirical works confirm the plausibility of a condition in which high levels of eudaimonic well-being are combined with low levels of hedonic well-being (Keyes, 2007; see also Chapter 7, this volume).

The results presented here point to an additional crucial aspect, too often neglected in well-being research: the usefulness of qualitative information for contextualizing the quantitative one. The findings provided some hints on the interplay between individuals and their daily context, specifically with regard to their active psychological selection of opportunities for action and long-term commitment on the basis of the perception of happiness, meaningfulness, and future worthiness.

Cultural comparisons revealed more similarities than differences, considering that all participants belonged to Western countries or ethnic groups. In line with most psychological studies in the eudaimonic literature (inter alia Chapters 3 and 4, this volume), our findings suggest that the relevance of an activity for both the individual and the cultural context represents a core ingredient to promote development and well-being, even when the pursuit of complex goals and meanings entails a purposeful reduction of hedonic happiness (see Chapter 2, this volume). Although there are life domains in which this condition is more frequent (e.g., work), in other domains the sustained personal commitment is matched with emotional well-being, as happens with family.

This statement is partially contradicted by the low levels of happiness and meaningfulness participants associated with community and society issues, which could represent a sign of disengagement from the collective needs (Delle Fave, Brdar, et al., 2011). Participants, however, were found to invest the best within them in socially relevant domains, such as family and work, though primarily on the basis of personal motives rather than altruistic or collective ones. These two prominent domains of commitment represent important dimensions of the value system shared by countries involved in this research. This is evident when looking at their constitutions and normative codes. For example, the Italian constitution claims that Italy is a democratic republic based on work, and it defines family as a form of natural society, acknowledging its rights and establishing provisions to support it. In addition, further in-depth analyses conducted on these participants (Delle Fave, Brdar, Wissing, & Vella-Brodrick, 2012) highlighted that the personal motives associated with their commitment to family and work prominently referred to broader value-laden dimensions, such as meaning of life, virtues, and ethical evaluations, that enable the individual to live a more "full life" that extends beyond the self (Peterson, Park, & Seligman, 2005).

These findings also suggest that it can be useful to distinguish between short-term and long-term well-being and between proximal versus distant domains. Work and relationships (with family and friends) are usually both long-term and proximal commitments, and to derive optimal benefits from this association, individuals are incorporating eudaimonic criteria when determining their level of well-being in these domains (Delle Fave & Massimini, 2005). Moreover, as concerns relationships, emotional and meaning-related factors are inextricably linked. In both domains, nevertheless, our finding highlighted the prominence of resource mobilization in the pursuit of goals that are meaningful for the person, for significant others, and for the society.

Some cultural differences emerging from our study could be related to contingent socioeconomic aspects. For example, a significantly higher percentage of Croatian participants referred to health in relation with happiness and goals. In the past 2 decades, economic and political transitions and the independence war took place in Croatia. The related stress negatively affected people's health. Moreover, because health services are no longer available as they were before, people are more concerned about their health. These findings are consistent with studies highlighting the relationship between stress and health, and between health and general well-being (Idler & Benyamini, 1997; Kaplan & Baron-Epel, 2003; see also Chapter 4, this volume).

Other differences can partially be explained from a broader cultural perspective. In particular, the higher percentage of Romance participants providing psychological definitions of happiness and the emphasis on domain-related definitions among Germanic ones can be related to the different meaning of the word *happiness* in the two linguistic areas, as an inner process versus an event respectively. The high percentage of South African participants quoting spirituality as a goal and a meaningful thing can be partly related to the fact that the data were collected in the vicinity of a previously Christian university but is probably an expression of a more widespread phenomenon. Spirituality and religiosity as devotional or life orientations as well as coping mechanisms are relatively strong in all cultural groups and in various contexts in South Africa (Mpedi, 2008; Temane & Wissing, 2006). Other differences emerged in domains quoted by low percentages of participants across groups, thus not allowing for any general consideration.

Strengths and Limitations

Our research includes samples from seven different countries across three continents, and this diversity is a key strength of our study. We grouped the countries on the basis of a linguistic and historical criterion, which we assume is wide enough to encompass the most relevant sources of the differences detected across groups. However, the countries could have been grouped according to other criteria, and the results would probably have been different. We also acknowledge that countries may differ in many ways—some cultural, others not. Many noncultural factors could be sources of between-country differences, such as affluence and socioeconomic status or educational practices. In addition, it is difficult to separate intracultural variations (within-cultural differences) from intercultural variations (culture-level differences).

The samples were balanced according to age, education, gender, and residence, thus controlling for possible differences caused by these variables. However, this feature also limits the possibility of generalization. The restricted age range may be considered both as a strength and as a limitation. On the one hand, most cross-cultural research uses student samples, while neglecting the adult stage of life. On the other hand, generalization to other age groups is not possible. Another limitation is that samples are relatively small, though acceptable for qualitative analyses.

CONCLUSION: CONNECTIONS TO PHILOSOPHY AND ETHICS

Our study moved from the implicit assumptions that philosophical accounts of the good life might influence our preferred theories and empirical focus, but also that empirical findings may inform theories of well-being and speak to philosophical projects. On the basis of our previous findings, we assumed that both hedonic and eudaimonic accounts of well-being are relevant and therefore linked with both subjective and objective theories as described by Tiberius (see Chapter 1, this volume). We collected empirical data on lay people's perceptions and selection of the components of well-being, deriving findings that may inform psychological theories as well as metatheoretical assumptions, in particular substantive philosophical accounts (Tiberius, 2004). On the level of psychological theories and hypotheses, our findings showed that self-advantaged, more hedonic and utilitarian choices and explanations are interconnected with eudaimonic, focus-on-the-greater-good, value-driven, and virtue perspectives. This result points to a rich and complex picture of ingredients of well-being—skewed to the eudaimonic side—not yet captured and explained satisfactorily in existing psychological theories and suggesting links with teleological, deontological, and virtue-based metatheoretical assumptions.

Considering the philosophical theories outlined by Tiberius (see Chapter 1, this volume), the emphasis on emotions, affect, and life satisfaction as the core dimensions of human nature proposed by hedonist, desire, and life-satisfaction theories is not entirely consistent with our findings. Norton's concept of self-realization (Norton, 1976) as the progressive actualization of potentialities that gives direction and meaning to life appears closer to our empirical evidence. Our findings also support Sumner's consideration that well-being, when evaluated through its emotional and strictly subjective dimensions, is constrained by contextual information and autonomy (Sumner, 1996). Haybron's (2008) assumption that authentic happiness is grounded in rich and complex ways of living is also consistent with our results, which suggest a lay conception of well-being characterized by the integration between positive but also complex subjective experiences on the one hand and socially constructed dimensions, values, and meanings on the other.

Nevertheless, in the attempt to link our findings with philosophical theories of well-being, we encountered several challenges. First, the same labels are used to refer to theories and constructs developed within different disciplines. To exemplify, life satisfaction and subjective well-being are described and operationalized in psychology, but they are also proposed as philosophical theories/perspectives (see Chapter 1, this volume). The connotations and denotations of these constructs differ across disciplines, and therefore no direct or single link should be made between psychological findings and philosophical ethical perspectives on the relationship between values and behavior. The same discrepancy applies to the constructs *hedonism* and *eudaimonism* used in psychology as higher order categories, including various specific theoretical perspectives but characterized by different connotations and denotations on the normative philosophical level. This discrepancy specifically applies to the link between eudaimonic ingredients found on an empirical level and eudaimonist theories on a philosophical level. There is thus a gap between psychological findings and normative perspectives, as remarked by Tiberius (see Chapter 1, this volume). More collaboration between psychologists and philosophers is necessary to bridge the gap and build a coherent paradigm of well-being.

The second challenge we encountered relates to the etic/emic debate in psychology (Triandis, 2007), grounded in the contrast between researchers emphasizing universal human commonalities beyond cultural differences and scholars claiming the impossibility to understand individual behavior and psychological functioning separately from the specific cultural contexts in which they unfold. Whereas philosophical theories aim at developing general and potentially universalistic models, as psychologists we are aware of the risks entailed in generalization of findings gathered in a specific context. We do not refer only to culture but also to sociodemographic factors such as gender, age, and level of education. Although a dynamic systems approach integrating contextualist and organismic perspectives (Witherington, 2007) may serve as a metatheory to integrate etic and emic views on a psychological level, the links to eudaimonist philosophical theories of well-being are not clarified as yet. However, our empirical findings on cultural similarities and differences may inform substantive philosophical accounts of well-being (Tiberius, 2004) or at least pose a challenge to the philosophical projects, underlining the possible value of cooperation between disciplines.

Ultimately, we think that a multimethod, multidisciplinary perspective is needed, blending theory-driven and evidence-based approaches to reach a full understanding of the human experience of well-being, overcoming semantics and scholarly dichotomizations.

REFERENCES

An, J. S., & Cooney, T. M. (2006). Psychological well-being in mid to late life: The role of generativity development and parent-child relationships across the lifespan. *International Journal of Behavioral Development, 30,* 410—421. doi:10.1177/0165025406071489

Becker, D., & Marecek, J. (2008). Positive psychology: History in the remaking? *Theory & Psychology, 18,* 591–604. doi:10.1177/0959354308093397

Berry, J. W., Segall, M. H., & Kagitçibasi, C. (Eds.). (1997). *Handbook of cross-cultural psychology: Vol. 3. Social behavior and applications.* Needam Heights, MA: Allyn & Bacon.

Bruce, S. (2004). Did Protestantism create democracy? *Democratization, 11,* 3–20. doi:10.1080/1351034042000234503

Chirkov, V., Ryan, R. M., & Sheldon, K. M. (Eds.). (2011). *Personal autonomy in cultural contexts: Global perspectives on the psychology of agency, freedom, and people's well-being*. Dordrecht, the Netherlands: Springer.

Christopher, J. C., & Hickinbottom, S. (2008). Positive psychology, ethnocentrism, and the disguised ideology of individualism. *Theory & Psychology, 18*, 563–589. doi:10.1177/0959354308093396

Csikszentmihalyi, M. (2000). *Beyond boredom and anxiety: Experiencing flow in work and play*. San Francisco, CA: Jossey-Bass.

Csikszentmihalyi, M., & Massimini, F. (1985). On the psychological selection of bio-cultural information. *New Ideas in Psychology, 3*, 115–138. doi:10.1016/0732-118X(85)90002-9

Deci, E., & Ryan, R. (Eds.). (2002). *Handbook of self-determination research*. Rochester, NY: University of Rochester Press.

Delle Fave, A., & Bassi, M. (2009). Sharing optimal experiences and promoting good community life in a multicultural society. *The Journal of Positive Psychology, 4*, 280–289. doi:10.1080/17439760902933716

Delle Fave, A., Brdar, I., Freire, T., Vella-Brodrick, D., & Wissing, M. (2011). The eudaimonic and hedonic components of happiness: Qualitative and quantitative findings. *Social Indicators Research, 100*, 185–207. doi:10.1007/s11205-010-9632-5

Delle Fave, A., Brdar, I., Wissing, M. P. & Vella-Brodrick, D. A. (2012). *Sources and motives for personal meaning in adulthood*. Manuscript submitted for publication.

Delle Fave, A., & Massimini, F. (2005). The investigation of optimal experience and apathy: Developmental and psychosocial implications. *European Psychologist, 10*, 264–274. doi:10.1027/1016-9040.10.4.264

Delle Fave, A., Massimini, F., & Bassi, M. (2011). *Psychological selection and optimal experience across cultures: Social empowerment through personal growth*. Dordrecht, the Netherlands: Springer.

Diener, E., Oishi, S., & Lucas, R. E. (2003). Personality, culture, and subjective well-being: Emotional and cognitive evaluations of life. *Annual Review of Psychology, 54*, 403–425. doi:10.1146/annurev.psych.54.101601.145056

Emmons, R. A. (2005). Striving for the sacred: Personal goals, life meaning, and religion. *Journal of Social Issues, 61*, 731–745. doi:10.1111/j.1540-4560.2005.00429.x

Forgeard, M. J. C., Jayawickreme, E., Kern, M. L., & Seligman, M. E. P. (2011). Doing the right thing: Measuring wellbeing for public policy. *International Journal of Wellbeing, 1*, 79–106.

Gong, Y., & Chang, S. (2007). The relationships of cross-cultural adjustment with dispositional learning orientation and goal setting. *Journal of Cross-Cultural Psychology, 38*, 19–25.

Hart, K. H., & Sasso, T. (2011). Mapping the contours of contemporary positive psychology. *Canadian Psychology, 52*, 82–92. doi:10.1037/a0023118

Haybron, D. (2008). *The pursuit of unhappiness*. New York, NY: Oxford University Press.

Hofstede, G. (1994). *Uncommon sense about organizations: Cases, studies and field observations*. Thousand Oaks, CA: Sage.

House, R. J., Hanges, P. J., Javidan, M., Dorfman, P. W., & Gupta, V. (Eds.). (2004). *Culture, leadership, and organizations: The GLOBE study of 62 societies*. Thousand Oaks, CA: Sage.

Huta, V., & Ryan, R. M. (2010). Pursuing pleasure or virtue: The differential and overlapping well-being benefits of hedonic and eudaimonic motives. *Journal of Happiness Studies, 11*, 735–762. doi:10.1007/s10902-009-9171-4

Idler, E. L., & Benyamini, Y. (1997). Self-rated health and mortality: A review of twenty-seven community studies. *Journal of Health and Social Behavior, 38*, 21–37. doi:10.2307/2955359

Jablonka, E., & Lamb, M. (2005). *Evolution in four dimensions: Genetic, epigenetic, behavioral, and symbolic variation in the history of life*. Cambridge, MA: MIT Press.

Kaplan, G., & Baron-Epel, O. (2003). What lies behind the subjective evaluation of health status? *Social Science & Medicine, 56*, 1669–1676. doi:10.1016/S0277-9536(02)00179-X

Keyes, C. L. M. (1998). Social well-being. *Social Psychology Quarterly, 61*, 121–140. doi:10.2307/2787065

Keyes, C. L. M. (2007). Promoting and protecting mental health as flourishing: A complementary strategy for improving national mental health. *American Psychologist, 62*, 95–108. doi:10.1037/0003-066X.62.2.95

Keyes, C. L. M., Wissing, M. P., Potgieter, J., Temane, Q. M., Kruger, A., & Van Rooy, S. (2008). Evaluation of the Mental Health Continuum Short Form (MHC-SF) in Setswana speaking South Africans. *Clinical Psychology & Psychotherapy, 15*, 181–192. doi:10.1002/cpp.572

Laland, K. N., Odling-Smee, J., & Feldman, M. W. (2000). Niche construction, biological evolution, and cultural change. *Behavioral and Brain Sciences, 23*, 131–146. doi:10.1017/S0140525X00002417

Linley, P. A., Maltby, J., Wood, A. M., Osbourne, G., & Hurling, R. (2009). Measuring happiness: The higher order factor structure of subjective of psychological well-being measures. *Personality and Individual Differences, 47*, 878–884. doi:10.1016/j.paid.2009.07.010

Mpedi, L. G. (2008). The role of religious values in extending social protection: A South African perspective. *Acta Theologica, 28*, 105–125.

Norton, D. L. (1976). *Personal destinies*. Princeton, NJ: Princeton University Press.

Park, N., Peterson, C., & Seligman, M. E. P. (2006). Character strengths in fifty-four nations and the fifty U.S. states. *The Journal of Positive Psychology, 1*, 118–129. doi:10.1080/17439760600619567

Peterson, C., Park, N., & Seligman, M. E. P. (2005). Orientations to happiness and life satisfaction: The full life versus the empty life. *Journal of Happiness Studies, 6*, 25–41. doi:10.1007/s10902-004-1278-z

Peterson, C., & Seligman, M. E. P. (2004). *Character strengths and virtues: A handbook and classification*. Washington, DC: American Psychological Association.

Prilleltensky, I. (1994). *The morals and politics of psychology: Psychological discourse and the status quo*. Albany, NY: State University of New York Press.

Richardson, F. C., & Guignon, C. B. (2008). Positive psychology and philosophy of social science. *Theory & Psychology, 18*, 605–627. doi:10.1177/0959354308093398

Ryff, C. D. (1989). Happiness is everything, or is it? Explorations on the meaning of psychological well-being. *Journal of Personality and Social Psychology, 57*, 1069–1081. doi:10.1037/0022-3514.57.6.1069

Ryff, C. D., & Keyes, C. L. M. (1995). The structure of psychological well-being revisited. *Journal of Personality and Social Psychology, 69*, 719–727. doi:10.1037/0022-3514.69.4.719

Sen, A. K. (1992). *Inequality re-examined.* Oxford, England: Clarendon Press.

Sheldon, K. M., Elliot, A. J., Ryan, R. M., Chirkov, V., Kim, Y., Wu, C., . . . Sun, Z. (2004). Self-concordance and subjective well-being in four cultures. *Journal of Cross-Cultural Psychology, 35*, 209–223. doi:10.1177/0022022103262245

Slife, B. D., & Richardson, F. C. (2008). Problematic ontological underpinnings of positive psychology. *Theory & Psychology, 18*, 699–723. doi:10.1177/0959354308093403

Smith, P. B., & Bond, M. H. (1999). *Social psychology across cultures.* Boston, MA: Allyn & Bacon.

Sumner, L. (1996). *Welfare, happiness and ethics.* New York, NY: Oxford University Press.

Temane, Q. M., & Wissing, M. P. (2006). The role of spirituality as a mediator for psychological well-being across different contexts. *South African Journal of Psychology, 36*, 582–597.

Tiberius, V. (2004). Cultural differences and philosophical accounts of well-being. *Journal of Happiness Studies, 5*, 293–314. doi:10.1007/s10902-004-8791-y

Triandis, H. C. (1994). *Culture and social behavior.* New York, NY: McGraw-Hill.

Triandis, H. C. (2007). Culture and psychology: A history of the study of their relationships. In S. Kitayama & D. Cohen (Eds.), *Handbook of cultural psychology* (pp. 59–76). New York, NY: Guilford Press.

Veenhoven, R. (2010). *World Database of Happiness, collection Happiness in Nations.* Erasmus University, Rotterdam. Retrieved from: http://www1.eur.nl/few/happiness/hap_nat/nat_fp.php?mode=1

Waterman, A. S., Schwartz, S. J., Zamboanga, B. L., Ravert, R. D., Williams, M. K., Agocha, V., . . . Donnellang, M. B. (2010). The Questionnaire for Eudaimonic Well-Being: Psychometric properties, demographic comparisons, and evidence of validity. *The Journal of Positive Psychology, 5*, 41–61. doi:10.1080/17439760903435208

Weber, M. (1958). *The Protestant ethic and the spirit of capitalism.* New York, NY: Scribner's Press.

WHOQOL SRPB Group. (2006). A cross-cultural study of spirituality, religion, and personal beliefs as components of quality of life. *Social Science & Medicine, 62*, 1486–1497. doi:10.1016/j.socscimed.2005.08.001

Witherington, D. C. (2007). The Dynamic Systems Approach as metatheory for developmental psychology. *Human Development, 50*, 127–153. doi:10.1159/000100943

12

DISCOVERING POSITIVE LIVES AND FUTURES: ADOLESCENT EUDAIMONIC EXPRESSION THROUGH ACTIVITY INVOLVEMENT

J. DOUGLAS COATSWORTH AND ERIN HILEY SHARP

The science of well-being has made substantial gains over the past few decades. Yet, defining well-being has been a consistent challenge to philosophers and psychologists alike, and clearly articulated theoretical models that are able to describe, explain, predict, and guide both the study and implementation of activities to promote well-being across developmental phases of the life course are lacking. From a developmental psychology perspective, *well-being* is a broad integrative concept reflecting health and positive physical, psychological, and behavioral functioning operating within a multilevel, dynamic developmental system (R. M. Lerner, Bornstein, & Smith, 2003). Although research on well-being in childhood and adolescence has emerged, the majority of studies on well-being involve college-age students or adults. In part, this may be due to measurement challenges in which assessing well-being relies on self-reports of subjective internal states (e.g., experiences of positive or negative affect) or psychological functioning in areas such as personal growth, purpose in life, or self-acceptance (Ryff & Singer, 2008).

DOI: 10.1037/14092-013
The Best Within Us: Positive Psychology Perspectives on Eudaimonia, Alan S. Waterman (Editor)
Copyright © 2013 by the American Psychological Association. All rights reserved.

249

Measurement along some of these dimensions may not be developmentally appropriate for children or adolescents. Similarly, the two predominant philosophical approaches to understanding well-being, hedonism and eudaimonism (see Chapter 1, this volume), often provide valuable guidance to studies of well-being in adulthood and emerging adulthood, but less about how these apply to child and youth development. Our view is that the developmental period of adolescence, with its multitude of physical, cognitive, and social changes and its archetypical developmental task of identity formation (Erikson, 1968), is an ideal period to study well-being and a eudaimonic approach in particular.

The literature on well-being in adolescence is scant. Historically, the period has been viewed from a deficit model focusing on the emergence of problem behaviors, rather than on well-being or the characteristics and attributes that help youth develop into healthy and contributing citizens of society. Despite the historical neglect, there are several important touch points between eudaimonist conceptions of well-being and the rapidly growing field of positive youth development (PYD; J. V. Lerner, Phelps, Forman, & Bowers, 2009).

In this chapter, we discuss how early developmental and conceptual models of functioning for children and youth have shaped our general understanding of wellness or well-being across the early periods of development. We emphasize how well-being is characterized within the PYD tradition and give special attention to emerging work around the concept of thriving. Next, we present results from our own program of research with adolescents that derives in part from a PYD perspective and incorporates eudaimonic identity theory (Waterman, 1993; see also Chapter 5, this volume). We end the chapter with some thoughts about the application of a eudaimonic perspective to helping youth find the best within themselves.

The element of eudaimonist philosophy that will track throughout this chapter is eudaimonic identity theory (see Chapter 5, this volume). In this theory, the processes of identity development are those of self-discovery and self-realization. Great moral and personal value is given to recognizing and understanding one's *daimon*, a metaphorical aspect of our being that represents our true self. In this regard, our theoretical perspective aligns most closely with the categorization of eudaimonia as self-realization, but with considerable connection to eudaimonia as happiness in the sense that it is through subjective experiences that one recognizes that the activities one is doing are consistent with one's true self (see Introduction, this volume). Eudaimonic identity theory is partially founded in Erikson's (1968) argument that the significance of an identity is not just its existence but also the quality of its existence. Waterman (2011) further described the developmental goal of identity formation as the discovery of personal possibilities, choosing one's purpose in living and finding opportunities to act on these potentials and purposes in living. Connection with the daimon is represented in objective and subjective terms. Objectively, it is seen in the choices we make about the activities we engage in, work, leisure, and activities of daily living. Many activities we do to survive as a human being, and others we pursue because they are in accord with our daimon, our true nature. Eudaimonic identity theory provides a framework that connects the growing literature on activity settings to identity development. During adolescence, youth sample many different activities in an active effort to understand who they are. These have been called *self-defining activities* (Coatsworth, et al., 2005) because they represent who adolescents believe they are at that point in development. Self-defining activities are often readily apparent to others too, and youth frequently categorize each other on the basis of their activities (e.g., jock, nerd; Eccles & Barber, 1999).

On one's journey of self-discovery, however, not all self-defining activities will be clear, objective representations of one's daimon. Some are not the best identity choices or good representations of our true selves. Better identity choices are those activities that connect with our daimon and that are distinguished by a corresponding set of subjective experiences that signal a special fit, what Waterman (1993) termed *feelings of personal expressiveness*. This psychological representation involves feelings that the activity is "right," reflects who one is, and leads to thoughts that "this is what I was meant to do" (Waterman, 1993). Personal expressiveness may be accompanied by the *flow* experience (Csikszentmihalyi, 1990), which signals that an individual is in harmony with his or her potential and keeps the individual engaged in the task in a way that builds skills and strengthens the connection to the daimon. A third set of experiences related to eudaimonic identity theory involves the creation and pursuit of personal identity goals. Goal-directed behaviors represent actions taken toward setting goals, making plans, and working toward establishing an identity (Gollwitzer & Kirchhof, 1998). That is, as individuals discover talents, abilities, and interests in self-defining activities, they also begin to more clearly define themselves in certain ways and seek opportunities, through goal setting, to behave in ways that reflect their emerging identity.

POSITIVE DEVELOPMENT IN CHILDHOOD AND ADOLESCENCE

Although some scholarly work focusing on the period of childhood has emphasized a strengths-based approach, it has not included a eudaimonic perspective. One concept that does focus attention on child and youth adaptation and wellness is that of competence (Masten, Burt, & Coatsworth, 2006). *Competence* refers to a set of constructs related to the effectiveness of individual adaptation in developmental context (Masten & Coatsworth, 1995). Competence is a judgment regarding the success of meeting standards for behavior related to adaptive functioning in society and suggests that individuals are "doing adequately well" in age-salient developmental tasks. Historically, models of competence have emerged from ego psychology (e.g., Hartmann, 1939/1958) and developmental task theory (Havighurst, 1972), among other theories, and have helped shift the focus of developmental research to children's health and well-being (Masten et al., 2006).

Similarly, PYD has emerged as a strengths-based and resource-focused approach, emphasizing explicit definitions of positive outcomes and embracing an optimistic view of adolescents (Damon, 2004). Two of the emerging models of PYD are (a) the five Cs framework, which references character, confidence, connections, caring, and competence as five positive areas of development (R. M. Lerner et al., 2005), and (b) the Search Institute's developmental assets framework, which points to building blocks essential for adolescent functioning and later adulthood (Scales, Benson, Leffert, & Blyth, 2000).

R. M. Lerner and his colleagues (e.g., R. M. Lerner et al., 2005; Theokas et al., 2005) found that the five dimensions relate strongly to a higher order latent construct (a sixth C) contribution, which is associated with indicators of how actively youth are engaged in their communities (Phelps, Zimmerman, Warren, Jelicic, von Eye, & Lerner, 2009). These authors also demonstrated that the five Cs model shows stability across early adolescence. Higher scores on the five Cs have been shown to have a protective effect for delinquency and drug/alcohol use (Phelps et al., 2009; Zimmerman, Phelps, & Lerner, 2008) and may delay initiation of alcohol, drugs, and sexual behaviors (Schwartz et al., 2010).

Developmental assets (Benson, 2003) are a set of interpersonal/intrapersonal and environmental strengths that are linked positively to better educational and health outcomes for youth (Scales et al., 2000) and negatively to involvement in high-risk behaviors (Leffert et al., 1998). Conceptually, the strengths are grouped into eight asset categories. Support, empowerment, boundaries and expectations, and constructive use of time make up a higher order grouping of *external assets*, whereas commitment to learning, positive values, social competencies, and positive identity make up a higher order set called *internal assets* (Benson, 2003). These internal and external assets are conceptualized as building blocks for youth healthy development.

Both the developmental assets model and the five Cs model provide objective criteria by which successful adaptation is being measured. But both propose another concept, *thriving,* that was absent in earlier conceptualizations of competence and adaptation. Thriving is more concerned with the optimal development of adolescents that is evident beyond the basic academic, social–emotional, and behavioral competencies that compose PYD models. As conceptualized by both R. M. Lerner and colleagues (2003) and by Benson and Scales (2009), thriving is a dynamic, developmental construct that represents an effective relationship between person and context. Of the concepts that have been proposed as part of the study of PYD, thriving most closely connects with a eudaimonic philosophy of well-being. In particular, the concept of thriving as discussed by Benson and Scales (2009) connects very closely to eudaimonic identity theory (see Chapter 5, this volume).

For example, Benson (2008) wrote that a central component of thriving is an element of level of self-knowledge that he referred to as identifying one's "spark," a self-identified core passion, interest, skill, or ability. A spark provides energy, joy, purpose, and direction in a youth's life. It is internally motivating to pursue this passion. Recognition of a spark should be followed by intrinsically motivated action that is intended to nurture and fully develop the interest or skill (Benson & Scales, 2009), and such action may be followed by affective experiences such as flow (Csikszentmihalyi, 1990) or initiative (Larson, 2000). This description is very similar to the discovery process described previously with respect to eudaimonic identity theory.

EUDAIMONIC IDENTITY THEORY AND ADOLESCENT DEVELOPMENT: A PROGRAM OF RESEARCH

In 2000, we sought to start a study of adolescent development that would investigate subjective experiences of personal expressiveness in diverse activities and how various characteristics of the activity, family, and community contributed to variability in those subjective experiences. Activity involvement is seen as a context for PYD (Dworkin, Larson, & Hansen, 2003), but there is a limited understanding of the specific mechanisms that operate in those contexts and how families and communities influence these processes. We believed that activity involvement provided a unique opportunity for adolescents to explore identities and discover what was best within them (Waterman, 1993). We saw a need for further research and model building to understand adolescent development in the context of self-defining and personally expressive activities, and for informing intervention work with youth. Moreover, we wanted to link the experiences of personal expressiveness that youth felt within particular activities to future orientation, another important adolescent developmental task. We believed that the experiences of personal expressiveness would provide adolescents with a strong sense of who they are and a sense of where they need to go. That is, adolescents who are truly thriving will report those exceptional experiences within a self-defining activity and see that those experiences have broader meaning about themselves and their future.

Measurement

For our studies, we adopted the Personally Expressive Activities Questionnaire (PEAQ; Waterman, 1998) to assess adolescent eudaimonic functioning, although it had not yet been used with participants younger than college age. In the PEAQ, participants self-report activities in which they participate and would use to describe themselves ("who they are" and "who they want to be"). We considered these self-defining activities (Coatsworth et al., 2005) to be an important part of the adolescent's identity, potentially. Participants rate the strength of a variety of subjective experiences with each listed activity. In consultation with Alan Waterman, we modified the PEAQ to focus on only three hypothesized dimensions of functioning associated with the identity formation process: personal expressiveness, flow experiences, and goal-directed behavior. Factor analyses revealed that these dimensions could be modeled in a three-factor structure and with a higher order single factor of expressive identity (Coatsworth et al., 2005).

Samples

We have used the PEAQ with three distinct samples of adolescents. One sample (Parenting for Adolescent Wellness; Coatsworth et al., 2006) consisted of 115 high school adolescents (M age = 16.5, 61% girls) from three communities in a northeastern state. According to the U.S. Census definitions, two communities could be characterized as urban areas within rural counties, and one community could be classified as urban fringe. All were characterized by above-average levels of poverty, unemployment, and youth problem behaviors. We recruited the adolescents from school and community youth organizations in their respective communities. Ninety-four percent of the participants identified as White, consistent with the demographics of these communities. A second sample (Activity Involvement & Youth Adaptation; Sharp & Coatsworth, 2012) consisted of 250 ninth-grade public school students (M age = 14.78) from a rural, low-income community in the Deep South. This sample represented 90% of all ninth-grade public school students from that community. This sample was slightly younger than the first and had a more even gender distribution (50%). The sample was also predominantly African American (82%) and poor, with 82% receiving free or reduced-cost lunch. The third was a cross-national sample of 572 high school students (Adolescent Rules Project; Coatsworth et al., 2005) drawn from three major cities in three different countries: (a) Santiago, Chile; (b) Milan, Italy; and (c) Miami, Florida. The sample included youth between the ages of 15 and 18 (M = 16.48, SD = 1.05) and included slightly more females (55% female).

Self-Defining Activities

One of the first questions addressed in our program of research was: "How many and what kinds of self-defining activities do adolescents report?" Regarding how many activities our participants listed, the results across studies were consistent with the vast majority (95% or more) of adolescents identifying at least one self-defining activity. This rate is identical to the percentage of youth in a national sample that indicated that they had a "spark" (Scales, Benson, & Roehlkepartain, 2011). The majority of adolescents in our studies reported multiple self-defining activities, with 80% listing the maximum number possible (two or four). These results indicate that adolescents can readily identify aspects of their leisure, work, or academic lives that strongly reflect their self-concept.

One attribute of the PEAQ is that it allows participants to report a broad range of self-defining activities, which allowed us to examine associations between activity type and identity experiences. To accomplish this we created a qualitative activity classification scheme. We started with existing schemes (Eccles & Barber, 1999; Hansen, Larson, & Dworkin, 2003) and modified as necessary. We ended up with eight distinct classes: (a) passive and risky activities (watching television, drinking alcohol); (b) socializing activities (spending time with friends); (c) instrumental activities (studying, housework, paid work); (d) sports, physical, and outdoor activities (running, skateboarding, fishing); (e) performing/fine arts, music; (f) literary (reading, writing); (g) religious and altruistic activities (youth group, tutoring children); and (h) other organized club (Scouts, 4H).

Results within and across studies indicate that the array of activities adolescents use to define themselves range from relatively common social interactions (e.g., being with friends) to time-consuming structured activities (e.g., acting in the school play) to community/school activism and leadership (e.g., school council). Most participants reported activities from several categories, suggesting that adolescents define themselves in a variety of ways. Across these studies, sports and physical activities were identified most often (34%–46%), far outdistancing performing and fine arts/music, the next most frequently reported activity (14%–17%). Literary activities were reported the least (2%–4%), with instrumental and passive/risk activities also being reported relatively less frequently (5%–10%). Differences across studies indicated some effect of context on activity availability or choice. For example, one study was conducted in a relatively context-rich and more religiously oriented community in the northeast United States, and the rates of reporting religious/altruistic and other organized clubs were significantly higher than in the other two samples. Socializing activities, although substantially represented across studies, were significantly higher in the international sample.

These findings are consistent with broader time-use studies that document sports participation as one of the most common uses of leisure time and also that adolescents spend a great deal of their free time hanging out with friends (Larson, 2001; Larson & Seepersad, 2003). Activities in which adolescents are spending the most time are also the activities that they select most often to define themselves. Gender differences also emerged, with girls more likely to list social, instrumental, and literary/arts activities as self-defining, whereas boys were more likely to report sports/physical activities as self-defining. These results are consistent with research indicating gender influences in the kinds of activities that youth choose to pursue (Eccles et al., 2003). The qualitative and gender differences across studies mirror those found across the three countries of the international sample (Sharp, Coatsworth, Darling, Cumsille, & Ranieri, 2007).

Expressiveness in Self-Defining Activities

A primary goal of our studies has been to examine youth subjective experiences in their self-chosen, self-defining activities. We predicated our studies on a eudaimonic belief that some identity choices would be better than others, the best within us, and that these better choices would be represented in youths' subjective experiences. We did not expect all individuals to report high levels of subjective identity experiences, nor did we expect all activities in which youth participate to provide the subjective experiences related to identity discovery or to provide insight into their talents and purposes. Our approach to studying this has been to use both a between-person (or between activity) and a within-person analytic strategy.

Our within-person approach has been represented in two ways. First, in our finding that when examining whether a self-defining activity was "personally expressive" on the basis of an established cutpoint (i.e., item mean of 6 or greater across items; Waterman, 2004), 34% of individuals listed zero, 34% listed one, and 31% listed more than one activity that met criteria across the three studies. These figures are comparable to the "thirds" found by Waterman in his college samples (Waterman, 2004). We also used multilevel modeling to demonstrate that there was 4 times as much variance between the different identity scores reported by an individual adolescent than across activity type (Coatsworth et al., 2006). This suggests that most adolescents are engaged in a variety of activities that they feel define themselves, but not all are yielding high levels of personal expressiveness and other positive subjective experiences associated with eudaimonic identity theory.

But we also expected differences in subjective identity experiences (e.g., personal expressiveness, flow experiences, identity-goal related behaviors) by activity type. For example, mandated activities such as school or a job are less likely to facilitate experiences related to eudaimonic identity than leisure activities because they provide less opportunity for self-direction and initiative (Larson, 2000). To examine adolescent subjective experiences across activity class, we selected the individual's activity with the highest personal expressiveness score. This avoided the methodological issue of dependence and different number of activities allowed across studies. Consistent with other studies that have shown that identity experiences differ across activity type (Hansen et al., 2003), results across our studies have generally demonstrated differences in eudaimonic-related subjective experiences at the activity level.

- *Performing arts and sports.* These two activity classes produced comparable profiles across the subjective reports of expressiveness, flow, and goal-directed behavior. Although there were no significant differences in personal expressiveness across any of the groups (recall that the activities were selected for high levels of expressiveness), youth who identified activities in these two classes reported relatively high levels of personal expressiveness compared with the other classes. These activities also had relatively high levels of flow but more moderate levels of goal-directed behavior.
- *Religious/altruistic and other organized clubs.* These two activity classes were characterized by the two highest mean scores on personal expressiveness. They also showed moderate levels of flow and high goal-directed behavior.
- *Instrumental.* Instrumental activities were associated with reports of relatively low expressiveness. Activities in this category comprised about 10% of the activities listed and had the lowest mean level of expressiveness, and although these were the highest rated personally expressive activity for some youth, the mean levels did not reach the cutpoint to classify them as personally expressive (Waterman, 2004). They also were associated with low flow experiences and modest goal-directed behavior. These results are similar to previous research that suggested that school and academic settings are generally not conducive to creating experiences of interest, concentration, initiative, and motivation in adolescence (Csikszentmihalyi, Rathunde, Whalen, & Wong, 1993; Larson, 2000).
- *Passive/risk and social.* The passive/risk and social categories were characterized by very low levels of goal-directed behavior. They were the two lowest categories on that dimension and were significantly different from all others except literary. Both also had below average levels of flow and although passive/risk

was associated with low levels of expressiveness, socializing had more moderate levels of personal expressiveness. In general, socializing activities tend to have negative or neutral developmental effects, but as noted, these are important aspects of adolescent development, and it may be that optimal development requires a balance of structured (e.g., school, sports, arts) and unstructured (e.g., socializing with peers) leisure activities. In contrast to studies that suggest neutral to negative effects of socializing and passive activities on development (Larson, 2000), our results indicate that expressiveness scores for socializing are comparable to other activities. These results are consistent with prior research demonstrating high levels of personal expressiveness within socializing activities (Waterman, 2004).

- *Literary.* Although a small category with just under 5% of individual activities classified here, reading and writing produced an unusual profile. This category was associated with relatively low expressiveness, very low goal-directed behavior (the lowest), and very high flow (the highest).

These patterns across activities were qualified somewhat by the different samples and the sample by activity interaction. For example, participants in the Parenting for Adolescent Wellness (Northeast) sample tended to report greater flow than the others, and youth from the Activity Participation and Youth Adaptation Study (Deep South) tended to report greater goal-directed behaviors. The relative frequency of reported activities also varied by sample. The picture that has emerged from our analyses across our studies is that adolescents are typically engaged in a wide range of activities that they can use to define themselves and that most adolescents are able to find the contexts that allow for discovery or creation of an expressive identity. This means that, consistent with eudaimonic identity theory (Waterman & Schwartz, this volume, Chapter 5), it is unlikely to be the activity type per se that promotes identity development, but the person–activity context fit. Youth are finding the activities that bring them in accord with their daimon.

Personal Expressiveness and Other Indicators of Adolescent Well-Being

Our studies were also designed to investigate how personal expressiveness is associated with other indicators of adolescent well-being. Our results begin to help explain the question of how activity participation is linked to adolescent well-being. We tested the relations between personal expressiveness and two indicators of adolescent well-being: (a) subjective well-being, computed from the Positive and Negative Affect Schedule (Watson, Clark, & Tellegen, 1988) and the Satisfaction With Life Scale (Diener, Emmons,

Larson, & Griffin, 1985) and (b) the Internal Assets (positive qualities possessed by adolescents themselves) composite from the Developmental Assets Checklist (Search Institute, 2001). A composite of the subjective experiences of eudaimonic identity was significantly associated with both adolescent well-being outcomes after controlling for demographic variables (e.g., sex, age, socioeconomic status), global levels of activity participation and number of self-defining activities (Coatsworth et al., 2006). Although activity participation was an important predictor, it did not appear to be the central feature linking to wellness; rather, the subjective experiences within activities appeared to be more important to one's level of subjective well-being. Mediation analyses indicate that experiences of expressive identity within activities accounted for the relations between activity participation and wellness.

This finding was corroborated by our person-centered analyses. On average, youth who reported more expressive activities were more likely to report higher levels of wellness, with differences most evident between the extreme groups (youth reporting zero and youth reporting three or four personally expressive activities). Our findings less clearly distinguished the groups in the middle (youth reporting one or two personally expressive activities) from either of the extreme groups. One of our guiding questions was whether youth would experience similar levels of well-being by being deeply involved in one personally expressive activity, or whether the breadth (number) of activities is equally important (see also Bohnert, Fredricks, & Randall, 2010). Consistent with findings from other studies that show that breadth of activities is uniquely related to successful adolescent development (cf. Busseri & Rose-Krasnor, 2010), our results suggest that youth require relatively high levels of expressiveness across multiple self-defining activities to garner the clearest information about their true interests and talents, a clearer vision of their identity, and greater wellness. Qualitative analyses of data from this sample suggest that for many youth, the variety of activities they list as self-defining reflect different aspects of their emerging self (i.e., personal identity, social identity, and relational identity; Coatsworth, Sharp, Palen, & Kohley, 2011).

Another set of analyses demonstrated that the subjective identity experiences were also related to self-reported delinquency but not to self-reported adolescent internalizing symptoms (Palen & Coatsworth, 2007). Moreover, goal-related identity experience was the strongest predictor of the three subjective experiences, and the only unique significant predictor. Learning how to set and achieve goals through activities may be one of the more useful identity-related experiences that adolescents can have. Emmons (1996) suggested that, broadly, setting and achieving goals is essential to meeting one's basic human needs. Goal-setting skills learned within an activity may generalize to other domains of adolescents' lives, allowing them to meet psychological needs that would be associated with increased well-being and lower incidence of problem behaviors.

Finally, we have conducted analyses to examine how eudaimonic identity experiences are related to four distinct but related dimensions of future orientation: (a) clarity of future goals and plans, (b) their importance, (c) optimism toward the future, and (d) preparation for the future (Sharp & Coatsworth, 2012). Personal expressiveness demonstrated a strong association with future perspective, but these relations were qualified by socioeconomic context such that relations were attenuated in our poor African American sample. This finding is consistent with theory that suggests that a developing sense of identity may be the necessary driving force behind individual motivation and action toward the future (Adams & Marshall, 1996; Larson, 2000). Larson (2000) argued that many adolescents go through their daily lives without feeling any excitement or energy but that adolescents' self-chosen activities have the potential to facilitate self-discovery and create personal excitement and investment in the future. Our results suggest that the affective experience of discovering one's personal interests, talents, and potentials in a self-defining activity may be a critical element of an adolescent's future orientation.

This series of studies, founded on eudaimonic identity theory and using the PEAQ, a measure specifically intended to assess subjective experiences hypothesized as aspects of eudaimonic well-being, is unique to the literature in its focus on adolescent experiences rather than those of adults or emerging adults. Results indicate that the measure is reliable with this age group and shows associations with aspects of adolescent functioning consistent with eudaimonic identity theory. It is surprising to us that these studies are among the few applications of eudaimonic identity theory with adolescents. Identity formation is considered adolescents' paradigmatic task and involves fitting self to context by reflecting on and integrating one's intrinsic nature (aptitudes, talents and inclinations) with the existing cultural context (Erikson, 1968). In postmodern society, extracurricular activities are often where adolescents consider identity alternatives, experiment with new interests or elaborate on existing ones, evaluate one's abilities in relation to those of others, receive recognition and feedback that reinforces or weakens identity commitments and discovers one's talents, and purposes of being. Expanded work on eudaimonic theories of well-being seem warranted for adolescents and youth.

One promising area for research is linking concepts from eudaimonic identity theory to other developmental processes—for example, future orientation (Sharp & Coatsworth, 2012). Identity experiences and the development of a well-organized future perspective are likely intertwined in a complex iterative developmental process (Luyckx, Lens, Smits, & Goossens, 2010). Longitudinal studies can help examine how subjective experiences of personal expressiveness, goal-directed behavior, and flow experiences in leisure activities may lead adolescents to become more focused on their futures and gain a stronger future orientation. In turn, a stronger future orientation may be necessary to drive adolescents to invest further to develop identity goals and begin to achieve a more comprehensive and coherent self-definition.

CONCLUSION: PROMOTING EUDAIMONIC IDENTITY EXPERIENCES

It is a substantial leap from studying associations between variables to understanding developmental processes to purposely intervening in those processes to promote healthy development. Yet, central to PYD is the promotion of human development through activities designed to facilitate health and wellness (Schwartz, Pantin, Coatsworth, & Szapocznik, 2007). There are several potential contexts for promoting eudaimonic well-being through identity exploration in adolescence. Two intervention projects demonstrate significant promise for altering youth activity involvement and enhancing their experiences of personal expressiveness.

Some individually focused leisure education programs designed to assist rural adolescents with selecting leisure activities that are personally meaningful show promising results in their ability to influence important hypothesized mediators of youth motivation and initiative (Caldwell, Baldwin, Walls, & Smith, 2004). *TimeWise: Taking Charge of Leisure Time* is a classroom-based intervention that, among other goals, seeks to increase middle school participants' awareness of personal interests and talents and link them to opportunities that are a good fit with these characteristics (Caldwell, 2004). Youth participating in this program become more involved in leisure and develop leisure-related skills and awareness (Caldwell et al., 2004). Results from our program of research indicate that expressive identity might also be an important mediator to examine. Promoting expressive identity and wellness in youth will most likely require significant individual focus and substantial flexibility in the processes and parameters of the intervention. Rather than applying a one-model-fits-all framework, programs will have to be intentionally designed so that adolescents can manipulate opportunities, activities, and the context to fit their emerging interests and developmental needs and to actively create these enhancing environments. To maximize the effect on wellness, these programs may have to extend to multiple activities for each youth.

The Changing Lives Program (CLP; Kurtines et al., 2008) is a positive youth developmental program focusing primarily on identity formation in adolescence and is directed toward working with high-risk youth in community settings. CLP is part of the Miami Youth Development Project and works with youth in an alternative high school. Conceptually, the intervention uses an empowerment approach fusing Erikson's (1968) identity theory with Elder's (1998) life course theory to engage youth in self-selected and self-directed transformative activities intended to build mastery, solve problems in their lives, and alter the meaning youth give to life experiences, including their own identity experiences (Montgomery et al., 2008). To evaluate the efficacy of the intervention, the designers selected the PEAQ as the most theoretically meaningful measure of positive identity (Eichas et al., 2010). Results indicated a positive intervention effect on changing youth-reported personal expressiveness, and that expressiveness may operate as a putative mediator of internalizing and externalizing symptoms. Those findings extend our own program of research, in particular our findings relating expressiveness to externalizing behaviors (Palen & Coatsworth, 2007).

Additional contexts for intervention might be intervening directly with parents and teachers. Both are identified as identity agents (Schachter & Ventura, 2008) and have considerable motivation and investment in assisting youth with exploring and examining alternate identity choices. Schachter and Ventura (2008) proposed that parents, as a primary socializing agent for their children, could also participate in a cocreation of identity. Although it will require a careful, nurturing, and more mindful approach to parenting (Duncan, Coatsworth & Greenberg, 2009), parents should work to limit their control over the choices the youth must necessarily make. Our own work has examined the role of parents in personally expressive activities, and we have developed a measure to assess parent involvement in their youth's identity exploration (Coatsworth, Palen, & Sharp, 2011). The two dimensions from this measure are (a) encouragement of exploration and independence and (b) pressure and intrusion, and both predicted personal expressiveness beyond typical measures of parenting practices (e.g., positive parenting, control). This idea is also consonant with the idea of helping parents promote their child's "sparks" (Benson, 2008). Although current parenting interventions are effective in changing parenting behaviors, these are primarily related to behavioral control or enhancing the relationship with their youth and are not focused on helping parents clearly see what is the best within their child—their child's interests, talents, and aptitudes—and construct opportunities to nurture those (Coatsworth, Duncan, Greenberg, & Nix, 2010).

It has also been proposed that well-trained teachers may serve as identity agents (Harrell-Levy & Kerpelman, 2010) by using transformative pedagogy that would allow youth to explore their interests and talents and perhaps increase the number of youth who discover their potentials. With these kinds of parent and teacher interventions, perhaps our society can move to transforming our educational systems to assist youth in making wise "life-shaping" decisions, finding what is best within them, and living a good life (Norton, 1995).

REFERENCES

Adams, G. R., & Marshall, S. K. (1996). A developmental social psychology of identity: Understanding the person-in-context. *Journal of Adolescence, 19,* 429–442.
doi:10.1006/jado.1996.0041

Benson, P. L. (2003). Developmental assets and asset building communities: Conceptual and empirical foundations. In R. M. Lerner & P. L. Benson (Eds.),
*Developmental assets and asset-building communities: Implications for research,
policy, and practice* (pp. 19–43). Norwell, MA: Kluwer Academic.

Benson, P. L. (2008). *Sparks: How parents can help ignite the hidden strengths of teenagers.* San Francisco, CA: Jossey-Bass.

Benson, P. L., & Scales, P. C. (2009). The definition and preliminary measurement of thriving in adolescence. *The Journal of Positive Psychology, 4,* 85–104.
doi:10.1080/17439760802399240

Bohnert, A., Fredricks, J., & Randall, E. (2010). Capturing unique dimensions of youth
organized activity involvement: Theoretical and methodological considerations.
Review of Educational Research, 80, 576–610. doi:10.3102/0034654310364533

Busseri, M. A., & Rose-Krasnor, L. (2010). Addressing three common issues in
research on youth activities: An integrative approach for operationalizing
and analyzing involvement. *Journal of Research on Adolescence, 20,* 583–615.
doi:10.1111/j.1532-7795.2010.00652.x

Caldwell, L. L. (2004). *TimeWise: Taking charge of leisure time curriculum for middle
school students.* Scotts Valley, CA: ETR Associates.

Caldwell, L. L., Baldwin, C. K., Walls, T., & Smith, E. A. (2004). Preliminary effects
of a leisure education program to promote healthy use of free time among middle
school adolescents. *Journal of Leisure Research, 36,* 310–335.

Coatsworth, J. D., Duncan, L. G., Greenberg, M. T., & Nix, R. L. (2010). Changing
parents' mindfulness, child management skills, and relationship quality with
their youth: Results from a randomized pilot intervention trial. *Journal of Child
and Family Studies, 19,* 203–217. doi:10.1007/s10826-009-9304-8

Coatsworth, J. D., Palen, L. A., & Sharp, E. H. (2011). *Parenting for adolescent identity
exploration: Development and properties of a new measure.* Unpublished manuscript, The Pennsylvania State University, University Park.

Coatsworth, J. D., Palen, L., Sharp, E. H., & Ferrer-Wreder, L. (2006). Self-defining
activities, expressive identity, and adolescent wellness. *Applied Developmental
Science, 10,* 157–170. doi:10.1207/s1532480xads1003_5

Coatsworth, J. D., Sharp, E. H., Palen, L. A., Darling, N., Cumsille, P., & Marta, M.
(2005). Exploring adolescent self-defining leisure activities and identity experiences across three countries. *International Journal of Behavioral Development, 29,*
361–370.

Coatsworth, J. D., Sharp, E. H., Palen, L., & Kohley, J. A. (2011). *A qualitative
examination of the identity-fostering leisure activities of adolescents.* Unpublished
manuscript, The Pennsylvania State University, University Park.

Csikszentmihalyi, M. (1990). *Flow: The psychology of optimal experience*. New York, NY: Harper & Row.

Csikszentmihalyi, M., Rathunde, K. R., Whalen, S., & Wong, M. (1993). *Talented teenagers: The roots of success and failure*. New York, NY: Cambridge University Press.

Damon, W. (2004). What is positive youth development? *The Annals of the American Academy of Political and Social Science, 591*, 13–24. doi:10.1177/0002716203260092

Diener, E., Emmons, R. A., Larson, R. J., & Griffin, S. (1985). The Satisfaction With Life Scale. *Journal of Personality Assessment, 49*, 71–75. doi:10.1207/s15327752jpa4901_13

Duncan, L. G., Coatsworth, J. D., & Greenberg, M. T. (2009). A model of mindful parenting: Implications for parent–child relationships and prevention research. *Clinical Child and Family Psychology Review, 12*, 255–270. doi:10.1007/s10567-009-0046-3

Dworkin, J. B., Larson, R., & Hansen, D. (2003). Adolescents' accounts of growth experiences in youth activities. *Journal of Youth and Adolescence, 32*, 17–26. doi:10.1023/A:1021076222321

Eccles, J. S., & Barber, B. L. (1999). Student council, volunteering, basketball, or marching band: What kind of extracurricular involvement matters? *Journal of Adolescent Research, 14*, 10–43. doi:10.1177/0743558499141003

Eccles, J. S., Barber, B. L., Stone, M., & Hunt, J. (2003). Extracurricular activities and adolescent development. *Journal of Social Issues, 59*, 865–889. doi:10.1046/j.0022-4537.2003.00095.x

Eichas, K., Albrecht, R. E., Garcia, A. J., Ritchie, R. A., Varela, A., Garcia, A., . . . Kurtines, W. M. (2010). Mediators of positive youth development intervention change: Promoting change in positive and problem outcomes? *Child & Youth Care Forum, 39*, 211–237. doi:10.1007/s10566-010-9103-9

Elder, G. H. (1998). The life course and human development. In R. M. Lerner (Ed.), *Handbook of child psychology: Vol. 1. Theoretical models of human development* (5th ed., pp. 939–991). New York, NY: Wiley.

Emmons, R. A. (1996). Striving and feeling: Personal goals and subjective well-being. In P. M. Gollwitzer & J. A. Bargh (Eds.), *The psychology of action: Linking cognition and motivation to behavior* (pp. 313–337). New York, NY: Guilford Press.

Erikson, E. H. (1968). *Identity: Youth and crisis*. New York, NY: Norton.

Gollwitzer, P. M., & Kirchhof, O. (1998). The willfull pursuit of identity. In J. Heckhausen & C. S. Dweck (Eds.), *Motivation and self-regulation across the life span* (pp. 389–423). New York, NY: Cambridge University Press. doi:10.1017/CBO9780511527869.017

Hansen, D. M., Larson, R. W., & Dworkin, J. B. (2003). What adolescents learn in organized youth activities: A survey of self-reported developmental experiences. *Journal of Research on Adolescence, 13*, 25–55. doi:10.1111/1532-7795.1301006

Harrell-Levy, M. K., & Kerpelman, J. L. (2010). Identity process and transformative pedagogy: Teachers as agents of identity formation. *Identity: An International Journal of Theory and Research, 10,* 76–91. doi:10.1080/15283481003711684

Hartmann, H. (1958). *Ego psychology and the problem of adaptation* (D. Rapaport, Trans.). New York, NY: International Universities Press. (Original work published 1939)

Havighurst, R. J. (1972). *Developmental tasks and education* (3rd ed.). New York, NY: David McKay.

Kurtines, W. M., Ferrer-Wreder, L., Berman, S. L., Lorente, C. C., Briones, E., Montgomery, M. J., . . . Arrufat, O. (2008). Promoting positive youth development: The Miami Youth Development Project (YDP). *Journal of Adolescent Research, 23,* 256–267. doi:10.1177/0743558408314375

Larson, R., & Seepersad, S. (2003). Adolescents' leisure time in the United States: Partying, sports, and the American experiment. *New Directions for Child and Adolescent Development, 2003*(99), 53–64. doi:10.1002/cd.66

Larson, R. W. (2000). Toward a psychology of positive youth development. *American Psychologist, 55,* 170–183. doi:10.1037/0003-066X.55.1.170

Larson, R. W. (2001). How U.S. children and adolescents spend time: What it does (and doesn't) tell us about their development. *Current Directions in Psychological Science, 10,* 160–164. doi:10.1111/1467-8721.00139

Leffert, N., Benson, P. L., Scales, P. C., Sharma, A. R., Drake, D. R., & Blyth, D. A. (1998). Developmental assets: Measurement and prediction of risk behaviors among adolescents. *Applied Developmental Science, 2,* 209–230. doi:10.1207/s1532480xads0204_4

Lerner, J. V., Phelps, E., Forman, Y., & Bowers, E. P. (2009). Positive youth development. In R. M. Lerner & L. Steinberg (Eds.), *Handbook of adolescent psychology: Vol. 1. Individual bases of adolescent development* (3rd ed., pp. 524–558). Hoboken, NJ: Wiley.

Lerner, R. M., Bornstein, M. H., & Smith, C. (2003). Child well-being: From elements to integrations. In M. H. Bornstein, L. Davidson, C. M. Keyes, K. Moore, & The Center for Child Well-Being (Eds.), *Well-being: Positive development across the life course* (pp. 501–523). Mahwah, NJ: Erlbaum.

Lerner, R. M., Lerner, J. V., Almerigi, J., Theokas, C., Phelps, E., Gestsdottir, S., . . . von Eye, A. (2005). Positive youth development, participation in community youth development programs, and community contributions of fifth grade adolescents: Findings from the first wave of the 4-H Study of Positive Youth Development. *The Journal of Early Adolescence, 25,* 17–71. doi:10.1177/0272431604272461

Luyckx, K., Lens, W., Smits, I., & Goossens, L. (2010). Time perspective and identity formation: Short-term longitudinal dynamics in college students. *International Journal of Behavioral Development, 34,* 238–247. doi:10.1177/0165025409350957

Masten, A. S., Burt, K., & Coatsworth, J. D. (2006). Competence and psychopathology. In D. Cicchetti & D. Cohen (Eds.), *Developmental psychopathology: Vol. 3. Risk, disorder and psychopathology* (2nd ed., pp. 696–738). New York, NY: Wiley.

Masten, A. S., & Coatsworth, J. D. (1995). Competence, resilience, and psychopathology. In D. Cicchetti & D. J. Cohen (Eds.), *Developmental psychopathology: Vol. 2. Risk, disorder, and adaptation* (pp. 715–752). New York, NY: Wiley.

Montgomery, M. J., Kurtines, W. M., Ferrer-Wreder, L., Berman, S. L., Lorente, C. C., Briones, E., . . . Eichas, K. (2008). A Developmental Intervention Science (DIS) outreach research approach to promoting youth development: Theoretical, methodological, and meta-theoretical challenges. *Journal of Adolescent Research, 23,* 268–290. doi:10.1177/0743558408314376

Norton, D. L. (1995). Education for self-knowledge and worthy living. In J. Howie & G. Schedler (Eds.), *Ethical issues in contemporary society* (pp. 155–176). Carbondale: Southern Illinois University Press.

Palen, L. A., & Coatsworth, J. D. (2007). Activity-based identity experiences and their relations to problem behavior and psychological well-being in adolescence. *Journal of Adolescence, 30,* 721–737. doi:10.1016/j.adolescence.2006.11.003

Phelps, E., Zimmerman, S., Warren, A. A., Jelicic, H., von Eye, A., & Lerner, R. M. (2009). The structure and developmental course of positive youth development (PYD) in early adolescence: Implications for theory and practice. *Journal of Applied Developmental Psychology, 30,* 571–584. doi:10.1016/j.appdev.2009.06.003

Ryff, C. D., & Singer, B. (2008). Know thyself and become what you are: A eudaimonic approach to psychological well-being. *Journal of Happiness Studies, 9,* 13–39. doi:10.1007/s10902-006-9019-0

Scales, P. C., Benson, P. L., Leffert, N., & Blyth, D. A. (2000). The contribution of developmental assets to the prediction of thriving among adolescents. *Applied Developmental Science, 4,* 27–46. doi:10.1207/S1532480XADS0401_3

Scales, P. C., Benson, P. L., & Roehlkepartain, E. C. (2011). Adolescent thriving: The role of sparks, relationships, and empowerment. *Journal of Youth and Adolescence, 40,* 263–277. doi:10.1007/s10964-010-9578-6

Schachter, E. P., & Ventura, J. J. (2008). Identity agents: Parents as active and reflective participants in their children's identity formation. *Journal of Research on Adolescence, 18,* 449–476. doi:10.1111/j.1532-7795.2008.00567.x

Schwartz, S. J., Pantin, H., Coatsworth, J. D., & Szapocznik, J. (2007). Addressing the challenges and opportunities of today's youth: Toward an integrative model and its implications for research and intervention. *The Journal of Primary Prevention, 28,* 117–144. doi:10.1007/s10935-007-0084-x

Schwartz, S. J., Phelps, E., Lerner, J. V., Huang, S., Brown, C. H., Lewin-Bizan, S., . . . Lerner, R. M. (2010). Promotion as prevention: Trajectories of positive youth development as protective against tobacco, alcohol, illicit drug, and sex initiation. *Applied Developmental Science, 14,* 197–211. doi:10.1080/10888691.2010.516186

Search Institute. (2001). *Developmental Assets profile: Preliminary user manual.* Minneapolis, MN: Author.

Sharp, E. H., & Coatsworth, J. D. (2012). The Future Perspective Questionnaire: Development, factor structure, reliability and validity. *Identity: An International Journal of Theory and Research, 12,* 129–156.

Sharp, E. H., Coatsworth, J. D., Darling, N., Cumsille, P., & Ranieri, S. (2007). Gender differences in the self-defining activities and identity experiences of adolescents and emerging adults. *Journal of Adolescence, 30,* 251–269. doi:10.1016/j.adolescence.2006.02.006

Theokas, C., Almerigi, J. B., Lerner, R. M., Dowling, E. M., Benson, P. L., Scales, P. C., & von Eye, A. (2005). Conceptualizing and modeling individual and ecological asset components of thriving in early adolescence. *The Journal of Early Adolescence, 25,* 113–143. doi:10.1177/0272431604272460

Waterman, A. S. (1993). Two conceptions of happiness: Contrasts of personal expressiveness (eudaimonia) and hedonic enjoyment. *Journal of Personality and Social Psychology, 64,* 678–691. doi:10.1037/0022-3514.64.4.678

Waterman, A. S. (1998). *The Personally Expressive Activities Questionnaire: A manual.* Unpublished manuscript.

Waterman, A. S. (2004). Finding someone to be: Studies on the role of intrinsic motivation in identity formation. *Identity: An International Journal of Theory and Research, 4,* 209–228. doi:10.1207/s1532706xid0403_1

Waterman, A. S. (2011). Eudaimonic identity theory: Identity as self-discovery. In S. J. Schwartz, K. Luyckx, & V. L. Vignoles (Eds.), *Handbook of identity theory and research* (pp. 357–379). New York, NY: Springer. doi:10.1007/978-1-4419-7988-9_16

Watson, D., Clark, L. A., & Tellegen, A. (1988). Development and validation of brief measures of positive and negative affect: The PANAS scales. *Journal of Personality and Social Psychology, 54,* 1063–1070. doi:10.1037/0022-3514.54.6.1063

Zimmerman, S. M., Phelps, E., & Lerner, R. M. (2008). Positive and negative developmental trajectories in US adolescents: Where in the PYD perspective meets the deficit model. *Research in Human Development, 5,* 153–165. doi:10.1080/15427600802274001

13

HUMAN STRENGTHS AND WELL-BEING: FINDING THE BEST WITHIN US AT THE INTERSECTION OF EUDAIMONIC PHILOSOPHY, HUMANISTIC PSYCHOLOGY, AND POSITIVE PSYCHOLOGY

P. ALEX LINLEY

In this chapter, my intention is to explore how human strengths—their use and development—can be understood within the context of subjective, psychological, and eudaimonic well-being. In doing so, I seek to integrate perspectives from eudaimonic philosophy, humanistic psychology, and recent developments in positive psychology, specifically strengths psychology. I consider relevant theory and review the extensive empirical literature linking strengths and well-being. I seek to integrate these into a holistic understanding of how our use of our human strengths reflects the best within us, enables us to develop in the ways that are right for us, helps us to realize our potentials, and enables us to flourish.

DOI: 10.1037/14092-014
The Best Within Us: Positive Psychology Perspectives on Eudaimonia, Alan S. Waterman (Editor)
Copyright © 2013 by the American Psychological Association. All rights reserved.

269

WELL-BEING WITHIN THE CONTEXT
OF POSITIVE PSYCHOLOGY

One of the big debates in positive psychology has centered on the nature of well-being, with positive psychology researchers often defining well-being through the lens of subjective well-being (e.g., Kashdan, Biswas-Diener, & King, 2008), rather than embracing definitions of well-being that include psychological well-being (Ryff & Keyes, 1995) and eudaimonic well-being (Waterman, 2008). This focus on subjective well-being has often been driven by the desire for a positive-focused science and epistemology that is seen as scientific and evidence based and therefore distinct from earlier humanistic psychology. The implied, and often explicit, contrasts with humanistic psychology despite often overlapping theoretical conceptualizations have drawn valid critiques from proponents of humanistic psychology (Taylor, 2001). Even as this happens, however, it is important to note that there are other voices within the positive psychology community who do not subscribe to this narrow view of well-being, including, for example, Delle Fave, Massimini, and Bassi (2010); Ryan and Deci (2000); and Vittersø (Vittersø, Oelmann, & Wang, 2009), among others.

There is increasing evidence, however, that this "either/or" debate may itself also be shifting to become more of a "both/and" consensus about the nature of different types of well-being and the role that these types of well-being all play in leading fulfilling lives. For example, Martin Seligman, the founder and leading proponent of the positive psychology movement, has shifted from talking about *authentic happiness* (Seligman, 2002) to focusing more specifically on *flourishing* as the definition of a life well lived (Seligman, 2011). This is an encouraging and most welcome shift. The chapters in the current volume will also likely play an important part in advancing the theory development, research base, and practical implications of a deeper, more multifaceted, and better nuanced understanding of well-being.

MY APPROACH TO WELL-BEING

Having explored the positive psychology perspective on well-being generally, I turn now to how I have approached and understood well-being in my own work. It has covered, at times, subjective well-being, psychological well-being, and elements of eudaimonic well-being. In reflecting on my approach to well-being, I have been able to identify five tenets that have served as the guideposts for my own thinking about well-being.

First, in my area of focus in relation to happiness and well-being, I am interested in the highest good—that which is good in and of itself, and for its own sake, something that is pursued as the end in itself, rather than as a means to an end. Aristotle described this as the *summum bonum*, the ultimate end or goal at which all human action is directed. As such, this is something that I also understand to be infinite and ongoing, something one cannot have "too much" of or reach a plateau that then begins to tail off, as can be the case with subjective well-being and the hedonic treadmill effect (Brickman & Campbell, 1971).

Second, the developmental trajectory of individual human beings is their life span, and for the human species as a whole, it is evolution (Tooby & Cosmides, 1992). As such, in my work I am interested in identifying something that is fitting and applicable across the life span and the course of human evolution and development.

Third, I am interested in deep explanations that have profound, rather than superficial, explanatory power. These deep explanations will reach the fundamentals of their premise, rather than merely skating over their surface. As such, they will be multifaceted in their explanatory power and will allow integration across a range of theories and empirical research.

Fourth, my interest is to find a way of living that is pragmatic and realistic, which fits with our lived experience of being in the world. If happiness really is the highest good, then why do people not always strive for "happiness" in a way that can be explained by theories of subjective well-being, but instead find great fulfillment in areas in which they are also experiencing significant challenge, such as parenting (e.g., Delle Fave & Massimini, 2004)?

Fifth, although these considerations led me to a focus on eudaimonic well-being as the highest human good and a focus on the development and deployment of strengths as my program for research and practice, I also acknowledge that I have often been "definition-agnostic." That is, I have not restricted my research attention to a particular paradigm, definition, or measure of well-being, but instead I have used measures of life satisfaction, positive and negative affect (and combining these to compute composite subjective well-being measures), psychological well-being, and such elements of eudaimonic well-being as organismic valuing and authenticity.

It is important to recognize that the tenets I use do not preclude a relationship among subjective well-being, psychological well-being, and eudaimonic well-being. Rather, they simply specify that the three constructs are independent but not necessarily orthogonal. Indeed, as Waterman (see Introduction, this volume) noted and as empirical work has attested (Keyes, Shmotkin, & Ryff, 2002; P. A. Linley, Maltby, Wood, Osborne, & Hurling, 2009), the constructs are typically highly correlated but are, nonetheless, distinct in terms of their antecedents and outcomes. Within the various definitions of well-being and their distinctions, I see human strengths being related to each and explained at the theoretical and epistemological level by the eudaimonic approach to well-being and human development.

Locating my thinking in the context of the frameworks laid out by Waterman (Introduction, this volume) and Tiberius (Chapter 1, this volume), I would argue that my theoretical viewpoint accords most closely with that of eudaimonia as self-realization—that is, I see eudaimonic well-being as being achieved through the development and fulfillment of one's potentials. From this, eudaimonia as happiness and eudaimonia as flourishing may follow as outcomes, but my fundamental theoretical position is that of eudaimonia as self-realization.

Following from this, the reader will not be surprised that my theoretical viewpoint is also most closely aligned to the nature-fulfillment theory of well-being that is outlined by Tiberius (Chapter 1, this volume) and specifically, the fulfillment of our nature as individuals, which is proposed by Haybron (2008). My view is that we develop our highest eudaimonic well-being through the development of our strengths and potentials in a way that is right for us, that is, in doing what is right for us as specific individuals, rather than of necessity what is right for all of us as generic members of the human species. As the chapter goes on to show, this is the theoretical framework that underpins how I see the development and deployment of our individual human strengths as a key pathway for our fulfillment and our development of eudaimonia as self-realization.

A EUDAIMONIC PERSPECTIVE ON HUMAN STRENGTHS

Two major approaches to strengths have emerged from the positive psychology tradition. The first is the Values in Action (VIA) Classification of Strengths, developed by Peterson and Seligman (2004), which seeks to provide a "manual of the sanities" documenting the strengths and virtues of human beings. It was developed in counterpoint to the *Diagnostic and Statistical Manual of Mental Disorders* (4th ed., text rev.; American Psychiatric Association, 2000). The second is the approach to strengths I have taken in my own work, beginning with a focus on the use of strengths (Govindji & Linley, 2007) and moving on to a fuller theoretical exposition of how strengths emerge, how they are developed, and how they lead to valued outcomes in terms of performance and well-being (A. Linley, 2008; A. Linley, Willars, & Biswas-Diener, 2010).

The VIA Classification of Strengths includes 24 character strengths (Peterson & Seligman, 2004), whereas the Strengths Use Scale (Govindji & Linley, 2007) is concerned with generic strengths use, and the Realise2 strengths assessment that was developed in part on the basis of this work includes 60 psychological strengths (A. Linley et al., 2010). Notably, these classifications and approaches are concerned with strengths defined as constructs that are authentic and energizing to the person using them, as distinct from more value-neutral personality constructs, and typically assess a range of strengths under an umbrella assessment. A focus on "strengths as strengths" (as distinct from more general and generic individual differences) is important because there is a wealth of research focused on specific individual difference characteristics, which may be considered as specific strengths, and to their relations with well-being. These include, for example, gratitude (Emmons & McCullough, 2003), hope and optimism (Bailey, Eng, Frisch, & Snyder, 2007), and curiosity (Kashdan & Steger, 2007), among others. In contrast to that research relating individual characteristics to well-being, in this chapter I focus exclusively on the broad conceptualization of strengths as these have been explicitly defined, assessed, and investigated in terms of their membership in the category of *strengths*.

In exploring the nature of a strength, we are able to shed light on the assumptions that provide a foundation for a potential eudaimonic theory of strengths. For example, Peterson and Seligman (2004) specified 10 criteria for a character strength, the first of which is that "a strength contributes to various fulfillments that constitute the good life, for oneself and for others" (p. 17). They go on to locate this thinking within the Aristotelian tradition of eudaimonia:

> What, then, is this contributory relationship of character strengths to fulfillments? Our thinking here has been guided by the Aristotelian notion of *eudaimonia*, which holds that well-being is not a consequence of virtuous action but rather an inherent aspect of such action. (p. 18)

Peterson and Seligman (2004) went on to list a number of criteria for what they called a *signature strength*, that is, one of the strengths that is most defining of an individual. These criteria include a sense of ownership and authenticity in relation to the strength, intrinsic motivation and a sense of yearning to use the strength, a feeling of excitement and engagement when doing so, and invigoration rather than exhaustion when using the strength (Peterson & Seligman, 2004). As is clear from these descriptions, one can readily understand the existence and use of character strengths as being linked to one's sense of the best within us and being guided by the organismic valuing process leading to eudaimonic fulfillment through using the strength—in Aristotelian terms, to the realization of one's daimon.

In a similar vein, P. A. Linley and Harrington (2006) argued that strengths are consistent with and can be linked to following one's organismic valuing process:

> Strengths are natural, they come from within, and we are urged to use them, develop them, and play to them by an inner, energising desire. Further, that when we use our strengths, we feel good about ourselves, we are better able to achieve things, and we are working toward fulfilling our potential. (p. 41)

Building on this definition, A. Linley (2008) defined strengths as "a pre-existing capacity for a particular way of behaving, thinking, or feeling, that is authentic and energising to the user, and enables optimal functioning, development and performance" (p. 9). Again, the links to a eudaimonic view of human functioning are clear.

STRENGTHS AND WELL-BEING: REVIEWING THE EVIDENCE

Having shown the theoretical basis for the role of strengths in enabling human well-being, a theory developed at the intersection of eudaimonic philosophy, humanistic psychology, and positive psychology, I turn next to the question of what the empirical evidence shows us about human strengths and their role and association with subjective well-being, psychological well-being, and eudaimonic well-being. In reviewing this evidence, it should be noted that there are three broad approaches to how research in this area has been conducted. First, there are simple correlations between "having" strengths and types of well-being, an approach that is typical of the VIA Inventory of Strengths paradigm. Second, there are examinations of the association of "using" strengths and types of well-being, the approach I have tended to adopt most frequently. Third, there are more experimental studies that are premised around the use of strengths in practice and the implications of this use for different types of well-being. I review the evidence for these three types of studies, considering them in relation to each of subjective well-being, psychological well-being, and eudaimonic well-being in turn.

Strengths and Subjective Well-Being

In their seminal paper on the VIA character strengths and happiness, Park, Peterson, and Seligman (2004) showed that of the 24 character strengths of the VIA classification, hope, zest, love, gratitude, and curiosity were robustly and consistently associated with life satisfaction (i.e., an element of subjective well-being). Associations with all 24 strengths were positive across three samples, and only six of 72 correlations between character strengths and life satisfaction were nonsignificant at $p < .002$.

Peterson, Ruch, Beermann, Park, and Seligman (2007) examined the associations between the 24 VIA character strengths, life satisfaction (as measured by the Satisfaction With Life Scale; Diener, Emmons, Larsen, & Griffin, 1985), and orientations to happiness. The Orientations to Happiness Scale (Peterson, Park, & Seligman, 2005) examines three orientations to happiness, namely pleasure (e.g., "Life is too short to postpone the pleasures it can provide"), engagement (e.g., "I am always very absorbed in what I do") and meaning (e.g., "I have a responsibility to make the world a better place"), which might be argued to equate loosely to the three dimensions of subjective well-being, psychological well-being, and eudaimonic well-being. Peterson and colleagues' results showed that zest and hope were the most consistently and highly correlated VIA strengths with life satisfaction and the pleasure, engagement, and meaning orientations to happiness. Love was also highly correlated to life satisfaction and the pleasure orientation. It was notable that the strengths most strongly and consistently associated with life satisfaction were also strongly correlated with all three orientations to happiness, leading the authors to make the case for the full life—a life of pleasure, engagement, and meaning—as distinct from an empty life that is devoid of one or more of these orientations.

Park and Peterson (2006) examined the associations between character strengths and happiness in 680 children (ages 3–9 years). The happiness variable was rated as "happiness," without specification as to subjective, psychological, or eudaimonic well-being—on which basis the term is judged to be reliably defined as referring to subjective well-being. In this analysis, the strengths of love ($r = 0.31$, $p < .002$), zest ($r = 0.31$, $p < .002$), and hope ($r = 0.12$, $p < .002$) were significantly associated with happiness.

In an experimental study, Seligman, Steen, Park, and Peterson (2005) showed that using signature strengths in new and different ways led to statistically significant decreases in depression as measured by the CES-D (Center for Epidemiologic Studies–Depression) Scale relative to a placebo control at posttest, 1 week, 1 month, 3 months, and 6 months. Further, the same intervention demonstrated statistically significant increases in happiness (as measured by the Steen Happiness Index [SHI]) relative to a placebo control at 1 month, 3 months, and 6 months. Interestingly, the SHI was designed to reflect the three types of happiness described by Seligman (2002), namely, the pleasant life (experiencing and savoring pleasures), the engaged life (losing the self in engaging activities), and the meaningful life (participating in meaningful activities). As such, the assessment of the three types of well-being within the SHI is confounded because the measure conflates what we might broadly equate to being the subjective (cf. pleasant life), psychological (cf. engaged life), and eudaimonic (cf. meaningful life) types of well-being.

These findings were extended by Seligman, Rashid, and Parks (2006), who showed that positive psychotherapy, one element of which was the strengths exercise described previously, led to decreases in depressive symptoms of groups with mild-to-moderate depression and higher remission rates among outpatients with major depressive disorder.

Proyer, Gander, Wyss, and Ruch (2011) examined the relation of past, present, and future life satisfaction with endorsement of the VIA character strengths in a sample of 1,087 women ages 19 to 73 years. The highest correlations with past life satisfaction were with love ($r = 0.22$) and hope ($r = 0.20$);

with present life satisfaction, they were with hope ($r = 0.47$), zest ($r = 0.43$), and love ($r = 0.38$); and with future life satisfaction, they were with hope ($r = 0.53$), zest ($r = 0.46$), gratitude ($r = 0.35$), and love and curiosity (both $r = 0.34$).

In a quasi-experimental, treatment-control study with a total of 638 adolescents ages 12–14 years, Proctor, Tsukayama, et al. (2011) showed that the Strengths Gym, a series of character-strengths development interventions, led to increased life satisfaction both over a 6-month time period with corresponding increases not observed in a nonintervention comparison group (made up of students at the same schools and in the same years, but not receiving the intervention).

The Strengths Gym is a series of activities constructed around the 24 character strengths described by Peterson and Seligman (2004). The aim of the Strengths Gym program was to encourage students to build their strengths, learn new strengths, and to recognize strengths in others. The included activities for students were called *strengths builders* and *strengths challenges*. For each lesson, there was a definition of the character strength being focused on, two strengths builders exercises for students to choose from, and a strengths challenge as follow-up activity.

Notably from this research, there were no significant differences for positive or negative affect, suggesting that strengths interventions may have differential effects on life satisfaction as distinct from affect, notwithstanding that each of life satisfaction, positive affect, and negative affect are typically combined as a composite measure for subjective well-being.

Proctor, Maltby, and Linley (2011) examined generic strengths use and its associations with subjective well-being and health-related quality of life in a sample of 135 undergraduate students. They found that strengths use was a unique predictor of subjective well-being but not health-related quality of life. Subjective well-being was calculated by standardizing scores for life satisfaction, positive affect, and negative affect and then subtracting negative affect from the sum of life satisfaction and positive affect (see also Govindji & Linley, 2007; and Sheldon & Elliot, 1999, for this approach to calculating subjective well-being). Endorsement of the VIA character strengths of hope and zest was significantly and positively correlated with life satisfaction.

Govindji and Linley (2007) developed the Strengths Use Scale, which assesses the generic use of strengths, or the things that we do best and enjoy doing. Strengths use was significantly and positively associated with subjective well-being ($r = 0.51$, $p < .001$) and also significantly predicted subjective well-being in a multiple regression model that also included self-esteem and organismic valuing as significant predictors, whereas strengths knowledge and self-efficacy were not.

P. A. Linley, Nielsen, Wood, Gillett, and Biswas-Diener (2010) examined the role of strengths use in goal attainment with a sample of 240 college students. They showed that strengths use was significantly and positively associated with goal progress, which in turn positively influenced need satisfaction and subjective well-being (calculated as the sum of life satisfaction and positive affect, subtracting negative affect), as demonstrated using confirmatory factor analysis with longitudinal data collected over a 3-month period. In another study, Minhas (2010) showed that participants who focused on developing their strengths reported higher levels of life satisfaction over a 4-week period.

Strengths and Psychological Well-Being

Wood, Linley, Maltby, Kashdan, and Hurling (2011) showed that strengths use predicted lower levels of stress and higher levels of self-esteem, vitality, and positive affect at both 3-month and 6-month follow-ups in a longitudinal study with a community sample of 207 participants. Notably, there were no significant effects for negative affect, partially consistent with the finding of Proctor, Tsukayama, et al. (2011), who found no associations with either positive or negative affect for their Strengths Gym strengths development intervention.

Govindji and Linley (2007) showed that strengths use was significantly and positively associated with psychological well-being ($r = 0.56$, $p < .001$), psychological well-being defined by Ryff's Scales of Psychological Well-Being (Ryff & Keyes, 1995), and also with subjective vitality ($r = 0.45$, $p < 0.001$), subjective vitality assessed by the Subjective Vitality Scale (Ryan & Frederick, 1997). Strengths use also significantly predicted psychological well-being in a multiple regression model that included self-esteem and organismic valuing as significant predictors, whereas strengths knowledge and self-efficacy did not. Further, Minhas (2010) showed that participants who focused on developing their strengths reported higher levels of psychological well-being and work engagement over a 4-week period.

Strengths and Eudaimonic Well-Being

Govindji and Linley (2007) showed that strengths use was significantly and positively associated with organismic valuing ($r = 0.60$, $p < .001$), which can be taken as indicative of eudaimonic functioning. As described by Sheldon and Elliot (1999), the organismic valuing process can be understood as an inner voice that guides us in the directions that are right and satisfying for us:

> Along with Rogers (1961), we believe that individuals have innate developmental trends and propensities that may be given voice by an organismic valuing process occurring within them. The voice can be very difficult to hear, but the current research suggests that the ability to hear it is of crucial importance for the pursuit of happiness. (p. 495)

Joseph and Linley (2005) developed an organismic valuing theory of growth through adversity, which posited that individuals have an intrinsic motivation toward growth (building from Rogers' ideas of the actualizing tendency; Rogers, 1963) and the organismic valuing process (Rogers, 1964). They showed how this intrinsic motivation toward growth explained the states of intrusion and avoidance that are characteristic of cognitive–emotional processing following traumatic events and how, with support from a positive social environment, the person would positively accommodate the new traumatic information, leading to growth through adversity. These positive changes are likely to include positive growth in self-image, as the person copes with the aftermath of the traumatic event and discovers new strengths and capabilities they did not know they had before.

This theory was lent indirect support in relation to character strengths because Peterson, Park, Pole, D'Andrea, and Seligman (2008) found small but positive associations between the number of traumatic events experienced and the endorsement of character strengths, as well as significant positive correlations between posttraumatic growth and all 24 of the VIA character strengths. The highest correlations with the Posttraumatic Growth Inventory (Tedeschi & Calhoun, 1996) and VIA character strengths were found for religiousness (partial $r = 0.35$), gratitude (partial $r = 0.33$), and kindness (partial $r = 0.30$). As such, there is at least tentative evidence to suggest that the development of strengths (even through traumatic events) may enable increases in eudaimonic well-being.

IN SUMMARY: STRENGTHS AND WELL-BEING

Taking this evidence for the links between strengths and well-being as a whole, several key themes emerge. Most notable is that by far the most empirical attention has been given to the relation of strengths with subjective well-being (defined as the sum of life satisfaction and positive affect, subtracting negative affect), followed by some evidence for the relation of strengths with psychological well-being (as defined by Ryff & Keyes, 1995), and very little research indeed that has examined the empirical links between strengths and eudaimonic well-being—although it is notable that there has been substantial theoretical development that provides a clear rationale for how strengths use and development are indicative of eudaimonic well-being (A. Linley, 2008; P. A. Linley & Harrington, 2006; Peterson & Seligman, 2004). Clearly, there is a significant research opportunity to further explore the links between strengths, strengths use, and eudaimonic well-being and to understand more about the pathways through which this may come about. It is likely that there may be several causal pathways through which strengths and strengths use enable well-being, with potential candidates including need satisfaction (P. A. Linley, Nielsen, et al., 2010; Sheldon, Elliot, Kim, & Kasser, 2001), organismic valuing (Govindji & Linley, 2007; Sheldon, Arndt, & Houser-Marko, 2003), authenticity (Wood et al., 2008), and psychological energy (A. Linley, 2008; A. Linley et al., 2010).

IMPLICATIONS FOR PRACTICE

As the evidence reviewed in the previous sections indicate, strengths and strengths use are consistently and reliably associated with higher levels of subjective, psychological, and eudaimonic well-being. This being the case, it is reasonable to question what this means for practice—particularly given the normative prescription used within eudaimonic philosophy that is concerned with how people ought to live. As someone who subscribes fundamentally to the view of the organismic valuing process and actualizing tendency described by Rogers (1963, 1964), I have an immediate instinctive reaction against prescriptions of *ought:* My fundamental philosophical position is that people should be enabled and empowered to make their own choices and choose their own directions in life and that social structures should be designed to enable and empower this choice.

As such, my interest in the final section of this chapter is how society and social structures might enable and empower the choice and self-direction of individuals to develop in the ways that are right for them and fulfilling of their daimon. There is an essential philosophical position that underpins these implications for practice, which may be summarized as follows:

1. The strengths approach focuses on what is right, what is working, and what is strong—as such, it is a perspective attuned naturally to the positive, while not denying or denigrating the negative.
2. Strengths are a human fundamental: Every person in the world has strengths, irrespective of his or her culture, background, education, or upbringing.
3. The use, enablement, and empowerment of our strengths create the conditions in which we will experience higher well-being, with respect to subjective, psychological, and eudaimonic well-being.
4. Through the identification, development, and expression of our strengths, we are realizing the inherent potential of the best within us and developing the potentialities of our inner daimon.

5. Ultimately, the development of our strengths is a manifestation of our intrinsic psychosocial development in the direction of our actualizing tendency and guided by our organismic valuing process. The highest manifestation of this development is the experience of fully eudaimonic functioning and well-being.

There are a number of sources that address the use of strengths-based approaches and the development of strengths across areas of application and practice. It is beyond the scope of this chapter to review these in any detail; instead, I direct the reader to further resources in each area. The development of strengths begins in childhood, and the interested reader is referred to research examining strong families from a strengths-based perspective (DeFrain & Asay, 2007), as well as strengths-based programs and their effects in schools (e.g., Fox Eades, 2008; Proctor, Tsukayama, et al., 2011). In the world of work, strengths-based approaches to organization are increasingly being used, given the double-win of benefits that they deliver for both individuals and organizations (e.g., Garcea & Linley, 2011). In yet broader perspective, one can see strengths approaches at work in community development (Kretzman & McKnight, 1993; P. A. Linley, Bhaduri, Sen Sharma, & Govindji, 2011), strengths-based social work practice (Saleebey, 2006), and strengths-based approaches to social policy (Hill, 2008; Maton, Schellenbach, Leadbeater, & Solarz, 2004).

As with any development that promotes a particular perspective, strengths-based approaches have not been without their critics. For example, Warren (2010) argued that the role of positive psychology and strengths approaches in work could be misused to promote organizational agendas over and above the needs of individuals. Kaiser (2009) argued that a strengths approach taken too far can lead to calamity when strengths become overplayed or the focus becomes excessively strengths-based. Other authors have taken a more nuanced approach to these arguments, relating their perspective back to Aristotelian theory and the role of *phronesis* (practical wisdom) in making good judgments about the use of strengths (e.g., Schwartz & Sharpe, 2006), or the golden mean in relation to how much of a strength to use and when (doing something to the right amount, in the right way, at the right time; A. Linley, 2008).

The Realise2 model, which my colleagues and I developed (e.g., A. Linley et al., 2010), addresses this criticism by defining strengths along three independent axes of energy, performance, and use. Scoring high on all three dimensions denotes a realized strength, whereas low use but high energy and performance denote an unrealized strength. High performance but low energy (with use being variable) equates to what is termed a *learned behavior*, whereas low performance and low energy (again with use being variable) denotes a weakness. In this way, the four quadrants of the Realise2 model provide a more holistic perspective on strengths and one which is supported by the advice of the 4M model—to marshal realized strengths (i.e., use them appropriately for the situation, being careful not to overplay them), to moderate learned behaviors (i.e., use them in moderation and only when needed), to minimize weaknesses (i.e., to find ways to stop using them altogether or use them less and, if this cannot be avoided, to minimize their impact on performance where necessary), and to maximize unrealized strengths (i.e., to find opportunities to use them more); see A. Linley et al. (2010) for further discussion of these concepts.

CONCLUSION

In this chapter, I have set out to demonstrate how human strengths can be understood in the context of a broader theory of eudaimonic human functioning and how the evidence supports the theoretical positioning of strengths within eudaimonic theory. There is an important distinction between having a strength and using a strength that sees the two constructs often conflated, and further research is needed to tease out these distinctions and their impact on well-being—across each well-being dimension of subjective, psychological, and eudaimonic well-being. Given the evidence for the impact of strengths on well-being, the implications for practice were briefly reviewed, and the core philosophical premise made that a genuinely strengths-based approach will always be premised on enabling and empowering individuals with choice and direction to make the decisions that are right for them.

In this chapter, we have seen the intersection of different lines of thought and inquiry from eudaimonic philosophy, humanistic psychology, and more recent developments in positive psychology and strengths psychology. Through the continued dialogue among and integration of these approaches, we are likely to discover ever more about how we might most effectively enable and empower the best within us.

REFERENCES

American Psychiatric Association. (2000). *Diagnostic and statistical manual of mental disorders* (4th ed., text rev.). Washington, DC: Author.

Bailey, T. C., Eng, W., Frisch, M. B., & Snyder, C. R. (2007). Hope and optimism as related to life satisfaction. *The Journal of Positive Psychology, 2,* 168–175. doi:10.1080/17439760701409546

Brickman, P., & Campbell, D. T. (1971). Hedonic relativism and planning the good society. In M. H. Appley (Ed.), *Adaptation-level theory: A symposium* (pp. 287–302). New York, NY: Academic Press.

DeFrain, J., & Asay, S. M. (2007). Family strengths and challenges in the USA. *Marriage & Family Review, 41*, 281–307. doi:10.1300/J002v41n03_04

Delle Fave, A., & Massimini, F. (2004). Parenthood and the quality of experience in daily life: A longitudinal study. *Social Indicators Research, 67*, 75–106. doi:10.1023/B:SOCI.0000007335.26602.59

Delle Fave, A., Massimini, F., & Bassi, M. (2010). *Psychological selection and optimal experience across cultures: Social empowerment through personal growth*. Dordrecht, the Netherlands: Springer.

Diener, E., Emmons, R. A., Larsen, R. J., & Griffin, S. (1985). The Satisfaction with Life Scale. *Journal of Personality Assessment, 49*, 71–75. doi:10.1207/s15327752jpa4901_13

Emmons, R. A., & McCullough, M. E. (2003). Counting blessings versus burdens: An experimental investigation of gratitude and subjective well-being in daily life. *Journal of Personality and Social Psychology, 84*, 377–389. doi:10.1037/0022-3514.84.2.377

Fox Eades, J. (2008). *Celebrating strengths: Building strengths-based schools*. Coventry, England: CAPP Press.

Garcea, N., & Linley, P. A. (2011). Creating positive social change through building positive organizations: Four levels of intervention. In R. Biswas-Diener (Ed.), *Positive psychology as social change* (pp. 159–174). Dordrecht, the Netherlands: Springer. doi:10.1007/978-90-481-9938-9_10

Govindji, R., & Linley, P. A. (2007). Strengths use, self-concordance and well-being: Implications for strengths coaching and coaching psychologists. *International Coaching Psychology Review, 2*, 143–153.

Haybron, D. (2008). *The pursuit of unhappiness*. Oxford, England: Oxford University Press.

Hill, K. (2008). A strengths-based framework for social policy: Barriers and possibilities. *Journal of Policy Practice, 7*, 106–121. doi:10.1080/15588740801937920

Joseph, S., & Linley, P. A. (2005). Positive adjustment to threatening events: An organismic valuing theory of growth through adversity. *Review of General Psychology, 9*, 262–280. doi:10.1037/1089-2680.9.3.262

Kaiser, R. B. (2009). The rest of what you need to know about strengths-based development. In R. B. Kaiser (Ed.), *The perils of accentuating the positive* (pp. 1–12). Tulsa, OH: Hogan Press.

Kashdan, T. B., Biswas-Diener, R., & King, L. A. (2008). Reconsidering happiness: The costs of distinguishing between hedonics and eudaimonia. *The Journal of Positive Psychology, 3*, 219–233. doi:10.1080/17439760802303044

Kashdan, T. B., & Steger, M. F. (2007). Curiosity and pathways to well-being and meaning in life: Traits, states, and everyday behaviors. *Motivation and Emotion, 31*, 159–173. doi:10.1007/s11031-007-9068-7

Keyes, C. L. M., Shmotkin, D., & Ryff, C. D. (2002). Optimizing well-being: The empirical encounter of two traditions. *Journal of Personality and Social Psychology, 82*, 1007–1022. doi:10.1037/0022-3514.82.6.1007

Kretzman, J., & McKnight, J. L. (1993). *Building communities from the inside out: Center for Urban Affairs and Policy Research.* Chicago, IL: ACTA Publications.

Linley, A. (2008). *Average to A+: Realising strengths in yourself and others.* Coventry, England: CAPP Press.

Linley, A., Willars, J., & Biswas-Diener, R. (2010). *The strengths book: Be confident, be successful, and enjoy better relationships by realising the best of you.* Coventry, England: Capp Press.

Linley, P. A., Bhaduri, A., Sen Sharma, D., & Govindji, R. (2011). Strengthening underprivileged communities: Strengths-based approaches as a force for positive social change in community development. In R. Biswas-Diener (Ed.), *Positive psychology as social change* (pp. 141–156). Dordrecht, the Netherlands: Springer. doi:10.1007/978-90-481-9938-9_9

Linley, P. A., & Harrington, S. (2006). Strengths coaching: A potential-guided approach to coaching psychology. *International Coaching Psychology Review, 1,* 37–46.

Linley, P. A., Maltby, J., Wood, A. M., Osborne, G., & Hurling, R. (2009). Measuring happiness: The higher order factor structure of subjective and psychological well-being measures. *Personality and Individual Differences, 47,* 878–884. doi:10.1016/j.paid.2009.07.010

Linley, P. A., Nielsen, K. M., Wood, A. M., Gillett, R., & Biswas-Diener, R. (2010). Using signature strengths in pursuit of goals: Effects on goal progress, need satisfaction, and well-being, and implications for coaching psychologists. *International Coaching Psychology Review, 5,* 6–15.

Maton, K. I., Schellenbach, C. J., Leadbeater, B. J., & Solarz, A. L. (Eds.). (2004). *Investing in children, youth, families, and communities: Strengths-based research and policy.* Washington, DC: American Psychological Association. doi:10.1037/10660-000

Minhas, G. (2010). Developing realised and unrealised strengths: Implications for engagement, self-esteem, life satisfaction and well-being. *Assessment & Development Matters, 2,* 12–16.

Park, N., & Peterson, C. (2006). Character strengths and happiness among young children: Content analysis of parental descriptions. *Journal of Happiness Studies, 7,* 323–341. doi:10.1007/s10902-005-3648-6

Park, N., Peterson, C., & Seligman, M. E. P. (2004). Strengths of character and well-being. *Journal of Social and Clinical Psychology, 23,* 603–619. doi:10.1521/jscp.23.5.603.50748

Peterson, C., Park, N., Pole, N., D'Andrea, W., & Seligman, M. E. P. (2008). Strengths of character and posttraumatic growth. *Journal of Traumatic Stress, 21,* 214–217. doi:10.1002/jts.20332

Peterson, C., Park, N., & Seligman, M. E. P. (2005). Orientations to happiness and life satisfaction: The full life versus the empty life. *Journal of Happiness Studies, 6,* 25–41. doi:10.1007/s10902-004-1278-z

Peterson, C., Ruch, W., Beermann, U., Park, N., & Seligman, M. E. P. (2007). Strengths of character, orientation to happiness, and life satisfaction. *The Journal of Positive Psychology, 2,* 149–156. doi:10.1080/17439760701228938

Peterson, C., & Seligman, M. E. P. (2004). *Character strengths and virtues: A handbook and classification*. New York, NY: Oxford University Press.

Proctor, C. L., Maltby, J., & Linley, P. A. (2011). Strengths use as a predictor of well-being and health-related quality of life. *Journal of Happiness Studies, 12*, 153–169. doi:10.1007/s10902-009-9181-2

Proctor, C. L., Tsukayama, E., Wood, A. M., Maltby, J., Fox Eades, J., & Linley, P. A. (2011). Strengths Gym: The impact of a character strengths-based intervention on the life satisfaction and well-being of adolescents. *The Journal of Positive Psychology, 6*, 377–388. doi:10.1080/17439760.2011.594079

Proyer, R. T., Gander, F., Wyss, T., & Ruch, W. (2011). The relation of character strengths to past, present and future life satisfaction among German-speaking women. *Applied Psychology: Health and Well-Being, 3*, 370–384. doi:10.1111/j.1758-0854.2011.01060.x

Rogers, C. R. (1961). *On becoming a person*. Boston, MA: Houghton Mifflin.

Rogers, C. R. (1963). The actualizing tendency in relation to "motives" and to consciousness. In M. R. Jones (Ed.), *Nebraska Symposium on Motivation: Vol. 11* (pp. 1–24). Lincoln: University of Nebraska Press.

Rogers, C. R. (1964). Toward a modern approach to values: The valuing process in the mature person. *The Journal of Abnormal and Social Psychology, 68*, 160–167. doi:10.1037/h0046419

Ryan, R. M., & Deci, E. L. (2000). Self-determination theory and the facilitation of intrinsic motivation, social development, and well-being. *American Psychologist, 55*, 68–78. doi:10.1037/0003-066X.55.1.68

Ryan, R. M., & Frederick, C. M. (1997). On energy, personality and health: Subjective vitality as a dynamic reflection of well-being. *Journal of Personality, 65*, 529–565. doi:10.1111/j.1467-6494.1997.tb00326.x

Ryff, C. D., & Keyes, C. L. (1995). The structure of psychological well-being revisited. *Journal of Personality and Social Psychology, 69*, 719–727. doi:10.1037/0022-3514.69.4.719

Saleebey, D. (Ed.). (2006). *The strengths perspective in social work practice* (4th ed.). Boston, MA: Allyn & Bacon.

Schwartz, B., & Sharpe, K. E. (2006). Practical wisdom: Aristotle meets positive psychology. *Journal of Happiness Studies, 7*, 377–395. doi:10.1007/s10902-005-3651-y

Seligman, M. E. P. (2002). *Authentic happiness*. New York, NY: Free Press.

Seligman, M. E. P. (2011). *Flourish: A new understanding of happiness and well-being—and how to achieve them*. London, England: Nicholas Brealey.

Seligman, M. E. P., Rashid, T., & Parks, A. C. (2006). Positive psychotherapy. *American Psychologist, 61*, 774–788. doi:10.1037/0003-066X.61.8.774

Seligman, M. E. P., Steen, T. A., Park, N., & Peterson, C. (2005). Positive psychology progress: Empirical validation of interventions. *American Psychologist, 60*, 410–421. doi:10.1037/0003-066X.60.5.410

Sheldon, K. M., Arndt, J., & Houser-Marko, L. (2003). In search of the organismic valuing process: The human tendency to move towards beneficial goal choices. *Journal of Personality, 71*, 835–869. doi:10.1111/1467-6494.7105006

Sheldon, K. M., & Elliot, A. J. (1999). Goal striving, need satisfaction, and longitudinal well-being: The self-concordance model. *Journal of Personality and Social Psychology, 76*, 482–497. doi:10.1037/0022-3514.76.3.482

Sheldon, K. M., Elliot, A. J., Kim, Y., & Kasser, T. (2001). What is satisfying about satisfying events? Testing 10 candidate psychological needs. *Journal of Personality and Social Psychology, 80*, 325–339. doi:10.1037/0022-3514.80.2.325

Taylor, E. (2001). Positive psychology and humanistic psychology: A reply to Seligman. *Journal of Humanistic Psychology, 41*, 13–29. doi:10.1177/0022167801411003

Tedeschi, R. G., & Calhoun, L. G. (1996). The Posttraumatic Growth Inventory: Measuring the positive legacy of trauma. *Journal of Traumatic Stress, 9*, 455–471. doi:10.1002/jts.2490090305

Tooby, J., & Cosmides, L. (1992). The psychological foundations of culture. In J. H. Barkow, L. Cosmides, & J. Tooby (Eds.), *The adapted mind: Evolutionary psychology and the generation of culture* (pp. 19–136). New York, NY: Oxford University Press.

Vitterso, J., Oelmann, H. I., & Wang, A. L. (2009). Life satisfaction is not a balanced estimator of the good life: Evidence from reaction time measures and self-reported emotions. *Journal of Happiness Studies, 10*, 1–17. doi:10.1007/s10902-007-9058-1

Warren, S. (2010). What's wrong with being positive? In P. A. Linley, S. Harrington, & N. Garcea (Eds.), *Oxford handbook of positive psychology and work* (pp. 313–322). New York, NY: Oxford University Press.

Waterman, A. S. (2008). Reconsidering happiness: A eudaimonist's perspective. *The Journal of Positive Psychology, 3*, 234–252. doi:10.1080/17439760802303002

Wood, A. M., Linley, P. A., Maltby, J., Baliousis, M., & Joseph, S. (2008). The authentic personality: A theoretical and empirical conceptualization, and the development of the Authenticity Scale. *Journal of Counseling Psychology, 55*, 385–399. doi:10.1037/0022-0167.55.3.385

Wood, A. M., Linley, P. A., Maltby, J., Kashdan, T. B., & Hurling, R. (2011). Using personal and psychological strengths leads to increases in well-being over time: A longitudinal study and the development of the strengths use questionnaire. *Personality and Individual Differences, 50*, 15–19. doi:10.1016/j.paid.2010.08.004

INDEX

Abstractionist approach, 229
Accommodation, 46
Achievement goals, 197
Actions, 7
Activities
    consistent with aptitudes, 7
    controlled internalization of, 186
    eudaimonic, 110–111
    eudaimonic and hedonic motives for,
        144–150
    and eudaimonic functioning,
        107–111, 113
    expressing potentialities, 58
    expressions of interest in, 105
    external influences on, 7
    hedonic, 110–111, 163, 168–169
    passionate. See Passion
    self-defining, 251, 255–258
    self-directed, 59–60
    and well-being, 162
Actualization, 6–7
    self-, 11
    in self-determination theory, 63–64
Acute identity experiences, 105
Adaptation, authentic happiness and, 24
Adolescence, 249–262
    competence in, 251–252
    developmental assets in, 252
    and eudaimonic identity theory,
        250–251, 253–261
    positive development in, 251–253
    promoting eudaimonic identity
        experiences in, 261–262
    thriving in, 252–253
Affective/emotional well-being, 42–43
Age
    biomarkers and reported well-being,
        86–87
    and dimensions of well-being, 84
    health changes with, 89
    and meaning in life, 171
Allport, G. W., 81, 82
Andersen, S. M., 209–212
Annas, J., 44
Anxiety
    in college students, 64

effects of yoga on, 194
and eudainomic identity function-
    ing, 113–114
and ruminative exploration, 112
in senior citizens, 189
well-being therapy for, 90
Approach behaviors, pleasure and, 45
Aptitudes, 7, 103
Aristippus of Cyrene, 4
Aristotle, 4–7, 27, 44, 140
    on confusing material goods with liv-
        ing well, 59
    on happiness, 103, 122, 161, 162
    on hedonic happiness, 163
    on highest good, 78–79, 271
    on intellectual potentialities, 59–60
    on self-reflection, 68
    on volition, 63–64
Arndt, J., 210
Arneson, R., 26
Arora, R., 64
"Art: Architects' furniture," 159–160
Arts, fulfilling potentialities
    through, 60
Aspirations, in self-determination
    theory, 65–67
Assessment tools, creating, 83–84
Assimilation, 46
Ataraxia, 30
Attention, to novel objects, 49–50
Attitudes, hereditability of, 103
Attitude view, attribute view vs., 41
Attitudinal processes, life satisfaction
    and, 43
Attitudinal theory of pleasure, 21
Attribute view, attitude view vs., 41
Authentic happiness, 24, 28, 270
Authenticity
    in authentic functioning, 211
    in close relationships, 212
    and eudaimonia, 104, 140, 148
    Haybron's theory of, 28
    in identity formation, 170–171
    as life goal, 12
    meaning and direction in life for, 81
    and optimal self-presentation, 130

Authenticity, *continued*
    and positive psychological function-
        ing, 210–211
    and relationship development, 212
    in self-concordance theory, 11
    and signature strength, 273
    in true self studies, 215
    and well-being, 271
Authentic life satisfaction, 32
Autobiographical reasoning, 171–172
Autonomy
    as core dimension of well-being,
        82–83
    as evolved need, 124
    and internalization, 62
    and intrinsic motivation, 62
    for optimal functioning, 61
    in self-determination theory, 64–65
    and well-being, 62–63
    and wellness, 64–65
Avoidance behaviors, pain and, 45
Awareness, 68–69

Baumeister, R. F., 214, 217
Baxter, D., 152
b-cognition, 9
Beermann, U., 152–153, 274
Behavior, authentic functioning and,
    210–211
Belaise, C., 90
Bellah, R. N., 214
Benson, P. L., 253
Bentham, Jeremy, 21, 40, 42
Bernstein, J. H., 63
Berzonsky, M. D., 112
Bias
    cultural, 228
    in measurement of subjective
        well-being, 123
Biswas-Diener, R., 58, 276–277
Blanchard, C., 196
Boundaries, in views of "the best," 164
Brain activation patterns, 87
Brewer, B. W., 193
Brombin, C., 90
Brown, K. W., 63, 68

Caffo, E., 90
Caldwell, L. L., 261
Capabilities, 47

Carbonneau, N., 194
Carefreeness, 147–148
Carver, C. S., 45
Caudroit, J., 193
Chairs, 159–160
Changing Lives Program (CLP),
    261–262
Character, as daimon, 102
Character strengths
    criteria for, 273
    exercise of virtues activities as, 44
Charness, N., 196–197
Childhood
    development of strengths in, 280
    positive development in, 251–253
Chirkov, V., 64
Citizenship, Aristotle's ideal of, 59
Clinton, Hillary, 133
CLP (Changing Lives Program),
    261–262
Cognitive–affective experience
    eudaimonia as, 104
    of flow, 105
Common good, self-realization consis-
    tent with, 59–60
Community welfare
    cultural comparisons of meaningful-
        ness of, 233–235, 241
    in OFIS model, 188
    passionate activities contributing to,
        198–199
Competence, 47–48
    in childhood and adolescence,
        251–252
    as evolved need, 124
    happiness vs., 48
    and internalization, 62
    and intrinsic motivation, 62
    for optimal functioning, 61
    and well-being, 62–63
Constructivist approach, 228
Content-free well-being. *See* Subjective
    well-being (SWB)
Contributions to society, passion and,
    198–200
Cooper, M. L., 128
Criterion of descriptive adequacy,
    35
Criterion of normative adequacy, 35

Cross-cultural perceptions of meaning
and goals, 227–244
context of individual well-being,
228–230
eudaimonic and hedonic happiness
investigation study, 230–242
family in, 237–239
individual pursuit of well-being, 230
and philosophies of well-being,
242–244
work in, 239–240
Csikszentmihalyi, M., 9, 105
Cultural information, internalizing/
integrating, 62

Daimon (true self), 207–218
during adolescence, 250, 251
beliefs about, 216–217
concept of, 6
defined, 101
defining, 208–209
and eudaimonia, 212–214
and identity choices, 103–105
in identity formation, 170–171
lay beliefs about, 208–209
and meaning in life, 214–217
as personal potentialities, 101–102
as philosophical and psychological
construct, 101–103
and psychological functioning,
209–212
psychological processes of, 6–7
qualities of, 6
and self-defining activities, 251
self-discovery of, 11
D'Andrea, W., 278
d-cognition, 9
Deci, E., 229
Deci, E. D., 9–10, 47
Deci, E. L., 10, 66, 129, 140, 162, 164
Decision making, true self in, 216
Deliberate practice, 49, 196–197
Depression
and eudaimonic identity, 113–114
and meaning in life, 167
and self-discovery, 210, 213
in senior citizens, 189
and signature strength, 275
well-being therapy for, 90
Deroche, T., 193
Descartes, René, 184

Descriptive adequacy, criterion of, 35
Design, 160
Desire-fulfillment theories, 22–24, 31
addition of idealizing conditions in,
25–26
and self-concordance model, 132–133
Developmental assets, 252
Developmental assets framework (PYD),
252
Diener, E., 42, 43, 58, 64, 120, 163
Donahue, E. G., 195
The Double Helix (J. Watson), 46
Dowd, J. J., 85
Dualistic model of passion, 185–186
Dunkel, C., 112

Education
autonomy in, 63–64
and dimensions of well-being, 85
and inflammatory marker IL-6, 88
Efficacy, and meaning in life, 173
Einstein, Albert, 39
Elevating experience, 145–146
Elitism, 33
Elliot, A. J., 124–125, 197, 277
Emmons, R. A., 259
Emotional-state theory of happiness, 28
Emotions, eudaimonic, 45–47
The empty life, 151
Environmental mastery
as core dimension of well-being, 82
and inflammatory marker IL-6, 88
Epicurus, 44
Ericson, M., 48
Ericsson, K. A., 196–197
Erikson, E. H., 81–82, 107, 250
Ethical theory, hedonism as, 4
Eudaimonia
definitions of, 140–141, 161
effects over time, 150
experiences of, 104–105
as flourishing, 5–6
functions of, 144–147
Greek philosophers' use of term, 19
as happiness, 5
hedonia vs., 105–106
Hedonic and Eudaimonic Motives
for Activities Scale, 141–142
and meaning in life, 163–165
as normative concept, 7–8

Eudaimonia, *continued*
  objective meaning of, 6
  and personal well-being, 151
  pursuing both hedonia and, 139
  relationship of hedonia and, 142–144
  as self-realization, 6–7
  subjective definition of, 5–6
  subjective vs. objective, 131
  and the true self, 212–214
  and well-being of other people, 139,
    151–152
Eudaimonically-oriented individuals,
    152–155
Eudaimonic feelings, 45–47
Eudaimonic functioning. *See also*
    individual constituents of functioning
  at level of activities, 109–111, 113
  at level of the person, 111–114
  motivation concepts in, 10
  multidimensional perspective on, 188
  nature of, 107–108
  nourishing and supporting, 133–134
  operational definitions of, 108–109
  promoting, 114–115
  self-concordant view of, 133–134
  studied as within-person variable, 107
  true self in, 212–214
Eudaimonic identity theory, 99–115
  and adolescent development,
    250–251, 253–261
  central questions in, 99–100
  and daimon as philosophical and
    psychological construct,
    101–103
  developing identity choices,
    106–107
  and eudaimonia vs. hedonia,
    105–106
  eudaimonic functioning at level of
    activities, 109–111
  eudaimonic functioning at level of
    the person, 111–113
  guidelines for promoting eudaimonic
    functioning, 114–115
  identity formation metaphors,
    100–101
  and nature of eudaimonic function-
    ing, 107–108
  operational definitions of eudaimonic
    functioning, 108–109

  recognizing identity choices,
    103–105
  research program based on,
    108–114
Eudaimonic well-being (EWB), 44–49,
    77–91
  broad and narrow meanings of, 12.
    See also Flourishing; Self-
    realization
  conceptualization of, 12
  core dimensions of, 80–83
  creating assessment tools for, 83–84
  de-ontological vs. consequentialist
    views of, 130–131
  empirical findings on, 84–86
  eudaimonic feelings in, 45–47
  and health, 77–78, 86–90
  hedonic well-being contrasted
    with, 10
  Hellenic perspectives on, 78–80
  and human strengths, 277–278
  meaning in life as indicator of,
    166–168
  normatively beneficial qualities
    constituting, 162
  optimal functioning in, 47–49
  and positive psychology, 10–13, 270
  self-realization as, 10–12
Eudaimonism, *xiii*, 4
Eudaimonist philosophy
  on consequences of actions, 7–8
  and general process approach to
    SWB, 130–133
Eudaimonist psychological research, 34
Evaluative/cognitive well-being, 42–43
Evolved needs, 124, 125
EWB. *See* Eudaimonic well-being
Excellence
  achieving, 48–49
  Aristotle on, 5–7, 60
  criticisms of, 151
  and eudaimonia, 101–102,
    144–145, 148
  and habitual hedonia, 147
  in Hedonic and Eudaimonic Motives
    for Activities Scale, 141
  in human nature, 140
  in Questionnaire for Eudaimonic
    Well-Being, 109
  studies of, 173, 198

and virtues activities, 44, 48–49,
103–104
Experience account, 21
Experience machine, 22, 31, 132
Experiences
acute identity, 105
cognitive–affective, 104, 105
elevating, 145–146
of eudaimonia, 104–106
flow, 9, 105, 111, 230, 251
of hedonia, 106
peak, 9, 105
External assets, 252
Externalist theory of pleasure, 21
Extrinsic aspirations, 65–67
Extrinsic goals, 129

Family
cultural comparisons of
meaningfulness of, 233–239
as long-term and proximal
commitment, 241
Fava, G. A., 90
Feelings of personal expressiveness, 251
Fiske, S. T., 48
Five Cs framework (PYD), 252
Flourishing, 57–70. *See also*
Psychological well-being
eudaimonia as, 5–6
eudaimonist conception of, 58
exercise of virtues activities for, 44
psychological well-being as, 9–10,
12–13
self-determination theory, 60–69
and self-realization consistent with
the common good, 59–60
Seligman's focus on, 270
in terms of human functional
capabilities, 27
theories of, 13
Flow experiences, 9, 105
cultural information units associated
with, 230
eudaimonic and hedonic activities
in, 111
and identity formation, 251
Forest, J., 200
Frankl, V. E., 81, 85, 165
Frede, D., 58–59
Frederick, C., 148

Fredrickson, B. L., 191, 195
Frijda, N. H., 41
Fromm, E., 101
Full-information theory, 23
The full life, 151
Function, 27
Functional well-being approach
(FWBA), 45–46
Functioning
meanings of term, 47
optimal, 47–49
FWBA (functional well-being
approach), 45–46

Gander, F., 275–276
Gaver, W. W., 46
Gender
and dimensions of well-being, 85
and self-defining activities in
adolescence, 256
General process model of SWB, 125–133
and eudaimonist philosophy,
130–133
research applying, 129–130
and self-concordance as deep person/
goal fit, 128–129
and self-concordance construct,
126–127
and universal need satisfaction,
127–128
Gergen, K. J., 208
Gewirth, A., 48
Gillett, R., 276–277
Goals
achievement, 197
cultural comparisons of, 233–237
identifying specific steps toward,
174–175
in identity formation, 251
intrinsic and extrinsic, 65–67, 129
in life-span developmental
theories, 81
and meaning in life, 174
of psychopaths, 133
purpose vs., 174
self-concordant, 11, 127–129, 174
in self-determination theory, 65–68
tasks in achieving, 106–107
wrong vs. right, 126
Goal-setting skills, 259–260

Goldman, B. M., 210, 211
Good
    highest, 78–79, 270–271
    right vs., 8
Good life
    autonomy in, 65
    eudaimonic predictions about, 58
    hedonic view of, 4–5
    ingredients of, 30–32
    limits and boundaries in, 164
    and means by which happiness is
        brought about, 5
    objective qualities of functioning
        for, 6
Govindji, R., 276, 277
Grape, C., 48
Greenfield, E. A., 84
Greenfield, S., 50
Growth
    life stories with themes of, 172
    personal. *See* Personal growth
Growth narrative, 172
Gunz, A., 211

Hansson, L.-O., 48
Happiness. *See also* Well-being
    Aristotle on, 79
    authentic, 24, 28, 270
    competence vs., 48
    and consistency of self-
        presentation, 130
    cultural interpretations of, 232
    definition of, 120
    differentiations in pursuit of, 58
    as element in a good life, 4
    emotional-state theory of, 28
    eudaimonia as, 5
    hedonic, 4
    meaningfulness vs., 240
    measurement of, 122–124
    need satisfaction vs., 125
    objective, 34
    operational definition of, 120
    psychological vs. philosophical
        studies of, 58
    subjective well-being as, 8–9, 12–13
    terms used for, 5
Harmonious passion, 185–189
    and contributions to society,
        199, 200

and interpersonal relationships,
    195, 196
and performance, 197–198
and physical health, 193–194
and psychological well-being,
    190–192
Harrington, S., 273
Hartr, J., 64
Haybron, D., 21, 28, 33, 36, 243, 272
Haybron, D. M., 6
Health
    cultural comparisons of meaningful-
        ness of, 234, 237
    eudaimonic well-being and, 77–78,
        86–90
Health care domain, autonomy in, 64
Hedonia
    definitions of, 140, 161
    effects over time, 150
    eudaimonia vs., 105–106
    functions of, 147–148
    Hedonic and Eudaimonic Motives
        for Activities Scale, 141–142
    and meaning in life, 163–165
    and personal well-being, 151
    pursuing both eudaimonia and, 139
    as pursuit of life of pleasure, 4–5
    relationship of eudaimonia and,
        142–144
    and well-being of other people, 151,
        152
Hedonic and Eudaimonic Motives
    for Activities (HEMA) Scale,
    141–142
Hedonic-oriented individuals
    characteristics of, 152–155
    eudaimonically-oriented individuals
        compared to, 152–155
Hedonic well-being (HWB), 40–42,
    168–169
Hedonism, 21–22
Hegel, Georg Wilhelm Friedrich, 184,
    196
HEMA (Hedonic and Eudaimonic
    Motives for Activities) Scale,
    141–142
Heraclitus, 6, 102
Hereditability of attitudes, 103
Hicks, J. A., 168
Highest good, 78–79, 270–271

Horney, K., 102
Houlfort, N., 189, 195
Humanism, objective good and subjective happiness in, 59
Humanistic psychology, 270
Human nature
    concept of, 103
    organismic perspective on, 123–124
    volitional helping, 67
Human nature-fulfillment theories, 27–28, 165. *See also* Nature-fulfillment theories of well-being
Human strengths, 269–281
    eudaimonic perspective on, 272–274
    and eudaimonic well-being, 277–278
    implications for practice, 279–281
    links between well-being and, 274–279
    and perspectives on well-being, 270–272
    and psychological well-being, 277
    and subjective well-being, 274–277
Huppert, F. A., 122, 188
Hurling, R., 277
Huta, V., 140, 151–153
Huta, V. A., 9–10
HWB (hedonic well-being), 40–42, 168–169

Idealized self, 102
Idealizing conditions, 25–26
Identity choices
    developing, 106–107
    recognizing, 103–105
Identity commitments, establishing, 111–112
Identity formation. *See also* Eudaimonic identity theory
    during adolescence, 250–251, 253–262
    cognitive aspect of, 171
    defined, 100
    and dualistic model of passion, 185–187
    and meaning in life, 170–173
    metaphors for, 100–101
    in postitive psychology, 3
    promoting, 170–173
    and self-realization, 11
Identity status, well-being and, 85

Individualistic approach, 229
Individual nature fulfillment, 140
Individual well-being, contextual factors in, 228–230
Inflammatory marker IL-6, 87, 88
Informed desire-fulfillment theories, 23–24, 132–133
Ingroup bias, 27
Intellectual potentialities, Aristotle on, 59–60
Intense pleasure, episodes of, 50
Interests
    in activities, expressions of, 105
    potentialities for assimilating knowledge/skills out of, 61
Internal assets, 252
Internalist view of pleasure, 21
Internalization
    of activities, 186
    and relatedness, 62
Internal locus of control, eudaimonic well-being and, 113–114
Internal perceived locus of causality (IPLOC), 62, 127
Interpersonal relationships
    cultural comparisons of meaningfulness of, 237
    as long-term and proximal commitment, 241
    passion and, 194–196
    positive. *See* Positive relations with others
    and the true self, 211–212
    well-being of other people, 139, 151–152
Intrinsic aspirations, 65–68
Intrinsic goals, 129
Intrinsic motivation, 7
    and link of true self and meaningfulness, 213–214
    in self-determination theory, 61–62
    and states of intrusion/avoidance, 278
Intrinsic self, 210
IPLOC (internal perceived locus of causality), 62, 127
Iran-Nejad, A., 46

Jahoda, M., 80–82
Joseph, S., 278

Jung, C. G., 80, 82
Justification, and meaning in life, 173

Kahneman, D., 30, 40, 42, 58
Kaiser, R. B., 280
Kaplan, U., 64
Kashdan, T. B., 58, 277
Kasser, T., 66, 124–125, 129, 133
Kernis, M. H., 210, 211
Keyes, C. L. M., 44, 121, 229
Kierkegaard, S., 210–211
Kim, Y., 64, 124–125
King, L. A., 58, 168
Kitayama, S., 121
Knowledge, pleasure in, 59
Kraut, R., 5
Kurtines, W. M., 171

Lafrenière, M.-A. K., 199
Laliberté, M.-L., 196
Larson, R. W., 260
Lavigne, G., 187, 195
Learned behaviors, 280
Lerner, R. M., 252, 253
Le Scanff, C., 193
Life balance, 129
Life goals, in self-determination theory,
    65–67
Life narratives, 172–173
Life satisfaction
    and attitudinal processes, 43–44
    authentic, 32
    and character strength, 274–277
    as cognitive and emotional, 43–44
    and dramatic arts, 197
    in eudaimonia and hedonia, 148, 151
    and eudaimonic well-being, 271
    as global life evaluation, 148–150
    as a good thing, 34
    happiness as, 24, 238t
    and health outcomes, 87
    in human nature, 243
    and meaning in life, 167, 213
    and meeting day-to-day life
        demands, 12–13
    and obsessive passion, 190
    pleasure and affective fulfillment
        vs., 164
    and positive psychological
        functioning, 3

research on, 120–121, 163
    in senior citizens, 189
    and subjective well-being, 8–9, 30,
        120, 143t, 145, 164
Life-satisfaction theories, 24–25
    addition of idealizing conditions in,
        25–26
    ingredients of well-being in, 31–33
Life-span theories, 81
Life story schema, 171
Life well lived. See also Good life
    nature of, 3
    objective qualities of functioning
        for, 6
Likeableness, 47
Limits, in views of "the best," 164
Linley, A., 274, 281
Linley, P. A., 273, 276–278
"Lower" pleasures/gratifications, 122–123

Madsen, R., 214
Mageau, G. A., 196
Maltby, J., 276, 277
Mandler, G., 46
Marks, N., 84
Maslow, A. H., 9, 81, 82, 105, 207
Massicotte, S., 194
Mastery goals, 197
Materialistic lifestyles, 59
May, R., 5
Meaning
    building sense of, 144–145
    cultural attributions of, 230. See also
        Cross-cultural perceptions of
        meaning and goals
    definitions of, 166
    and health, 86
    individuals' sources of, 173
    pleasure and, 49–51
    and well-being, 49–51
Meaningfulness, happiness vs., 240
Meaningful things in life, cultural
    comparisons of, 233–237
Meaning in life (meaningful life),
    159–175
    defined, 166
    defining, 160–161, 165–166
    and eudaimonic aspiring, 161–162
    as eudaimonic well-being indicator,
        166–168

as flagship indicator of well-being, 169
global judgments of, 213–216
and hedonic aspiring, 163
as hedonic well-being indicator, 168–169
promoting, 170
promoting comprehension and identity formation, 170–173
promoting purpose, 174–175
and the true self, 213–217
and views of eudaimonia and hedonia, 163–165
Measurement
of carefreeness, 147–148
of core dimensions of well-being, 83–86
of elevating experience, 145–146
of happiness, 123, 124
of ingredients of good life, 33–34
of meaning, 144–145
of self-connectedness, 146–147
of subjective well-being, 123
of well-being in childhood/adolescence, 249–250
Measures of well-being, 120–122
Mental health
and autonomy, 64
daily wellness indicators, 63
Jahoda's concepts of, 80–82
in Keyes' continuum theory, 229
and psychological well-being, 12–13
Mies van der Rohe, Ludwig, 160
Mill, J. S., 21, 40, 42, 80
Mindfulness, 68–69
Minhas, G., 277
Montgomery, M. J., 171
Motivation(s)
eudaimonic and hedonic, 144–150
for eudaimonic functioning, 10
Hedonic and Eudaimonic Motives for Activities Scale, 141–142
intrinsic, 7, 61–62, 278
in self-determination theory, 61

Na, J., 121
Narrative meaning making, 171–172
Nature fulfillment
in eudaimonia, 140
and eudaimonic well-being, 272

in psychology, 33
and self-expressiveness, 165
Tiberius's theory of, 119
Nature-fulfillment theories of well-being, 27–28, 31
ingredients of well-being in, 32
and self-concordance model, 133
Needs. *See also specific needs*
evolved, 124, 125
for optimal functioning, 61–63
psychological, 60
satisfaction of, 63–64, 125
universal. *See* Universal needs
Negative affect, subjective well-being and, 8–9, 120
Neugarten, B. L., 82
Ng, W., 64
Nichomachean Ethics (Aristotle), 4, 78–79
Nielsen, K. M., 276–277
Niemiec, C. P., 66, 68, 129
Normative
eudaimonia as, 7–8
well-being as, 34
Normative adequacy, criterion of, 35
Normative concept, 24
Normative conclusions, psychological fact vs., 33–34
Normative questions, in positive psychology, 3–4
Norton, D. L., 5, 6, 79, 81, 102, 103, 243
Nozick, R., 22, 31, 132
Ntoumanis, N., 196
Nussbaum, M., 27, 31

Objective-list theories of well-being, 26
Objective theories of well-being, 21, 28–29
ingredients of well-being in, 30–31
nature-fulfillment theories, 27–28
objective-list theories, 26
Obsessive passion, 185–189
and contributions to society, 199–200
and interpersonal relationships, 195, 196
and performance, 197–198
and physical health, 193–194

Obsessive passion, *continued*
    and psychological well-being,
        190–192
OH (Orientations to Happiness) scale,
        141, 274–275
Optimal functioning, 47–49
    fundamental needs for, 61
    and meaning in life, 167
Optimal functioning in society (OFIS),
        183–202
    components of, 188
    and passion, 188–200
    and psychology of passion, 184–188
Optimal self-presentation, 130
Organismic perspective, on subjective
        well-being, 123–124
Organismic thinking, in self-
        determination theory, 61
Organismic valuing, 277–278
Orientations to Happiness (OH) scale,
        141, 274–275

Papini, D., 112
Park, N., 141, 152–153, 274–275, 278
Parks, A. C., 275
Passion, 183–202
    and contributions to society,
        198–200
    defined, 185
    dualistic model of, 185–186
    and elements of OFIS, 188–189
    harmonious, 185–189
    and ill-being, 189
    initial research on, 187–188
    and interpersonal relationships,
        194–196
    obsessive, 185–189
    and performance, 196–198
    and physical health, 193–194
    and psychological well-being,
        189–193
    psychology of, 184–188
Passion Scale, 187, 189
Peak experiences, 9, 105
PEAQ. *See* Personally Expressive
        Activities Questionnaire
Peerson, C., 275
Pelletier, L. G., 152, 196
Perceived locus of causality (PLOC),
        126–127

Performance
    in OFIS model, 188
    passion and, 196–198
Performance-approach goals, 197
Performance-avoidance goals, 197
Personal Destinies (D. Norton), 79
Personal expressiveness
    in adolescents' self-defining
        activities, 256–258
    and adolescent well-being,
        258–261
    and eudaimonic functioning at
        activities level, 109–110
    feelings of, 105
    and identity formation, 251
    and link of true self and
        meaningfulness, 213–214
    other factors accompanying,
        164–165
    value of, 34
Personal growth
    as core dimension of well-being, 81
    cultural comparisons of
        meaningfulness of, 237
    and health, 86
    self-concordance view of, 133
Personally Expressive Activities
        Questionnaire (PEAQ),
        108–109, 254, 255
Person/goal fit, self-concordance as,
        128–129
Person level, eudaimonic functioning at,
        111–114
Peterson, C., 141, 151–153, 229,
        272–276, 278
Philipp, F. L., 187, 195
Philosophical foundations of psycho-
        logical theories, *xiii, xiv*
Philosophical psychological construct,
        daimon as, 101–103
Philosophies of well-being, 242–244
Phronesis, 280
Physical health. *See also* Health
    in OFIS model, 188
    passion and, 193–194
Physical well-being, and meaning in
        life, 167
Pleasure(s)
    as essential to welfare, 49
    functional role of, 49

in functional well-being approach,
45–46
in hedonic well-being, 40–42
in hedonism, 4, 32
kinds of, 41–42
"lower," 122–123
and meaning, 49–51
as proattitude, 41
in subjective well-being, 43–44
theories of, 21
in well-being, 49–51
PLOC (perceived locus of causality),
126–127
Pole, N., 278
Positive affect
as hedonic outcome, 60–61, 147
and inflammatory marker IL-6, 88
in passion–psychological well-being
relationship, 191–192
promoting, 34
and subjective well-being, 44, 120
Positive emotions
nonhedonic, 45, 46
and wellness, 58
Positive psychology
central premise in, 3
conceptualizations of well-being in,
8–13
constructivist approach in, 228
cultural bias in, 228
eudaimonic thinking in, 44
eudaimonic well-being in, 10–13
individualistic and approach
in, 229
normative questions in, 3–4
psychological well-being in, 9–10
research in, 229
subjective well-being in, 8–9
well-being in context of, 270
Positive relations with others
as core dimension of well-being,
80–81
and health changes with aging, 89
and inflammatory marker IL-6, 88
neurobiological correlates of, 87
in OFIS model, 188
Positive youth development (PYD),
250, 252–253
Potentialities
activities expressing, 58

for assimilating knowledge/skills out
of interest, 61
of the daimon, 101–102
discovering/attaining, 6–7
and feelings of personal
expressiveness, 105
fulfilled through the arts, 60
in human nature, 103
intellectual, 59–60
realization of, 79
self-concordance view of, 133
tasks in achieving, 106–107
Preference-satisfaction theories, 22, 23.
See also Desire-fulfillment theories
Prescriptive, normative and, 24
Present-desire theories, 23
Proattitudes, 41
Proctor, C. L., 276, 277
Proyer, R. T., 275–276
Psychological fact, normative
conclusions vs., 33–34
Psychological functioning
authenticity and, 210–211
and eudaimonic identity
functioning, 13
as flourishing, 9–10
self-concordant view of, 133–134
and the true self, 209–212
Psychological health, as ability to lead a
fulfilling, meaningful life, 3
Psychological needs
self-concordant view of, 134
universal, 60
Psychological processes, of the daimon,
6–7
Psychological states, empirical evidence
about, 26
Psychological well-being (PWB)
conceptualization of, 12
dimensions of, 10, 80–86, 121
and dramatic arts, 197
and eudaimonic identity
functioning, 13, 113–114
in eudaimonic well-being, 271
as flourishing, 9–10, 12–13
and health, 88
and human strengths, 277
and meaning in life, 167
in mental health therapy, 90
metrics of, 164

Psychological well-being, *continued*
 neurobiological correlates of, 86–88
 obsessive passion vs. harmonious,
  199–200
 in OFIS model, 188
 and optimal functioning, 47, 198
 passion and, 189–193
 and positive psychology, 270
 in positive psychology, 9–10
 research studies on, 121
Psychology
 etic/emic debate in, 244
 of passion, 184–188
Psychopaths, goals of, 133
Psychosocial qualities, 121
Purpose
 as core dimension of well-being, 81
 goals vs., 174
 and health, 86
 and health changes with aging, 89
 and inflammatory marker IL-6, 88
 and meaning in life, 173–175
 promoting, 174–175
 subjective vs. objective
  interpretations of, 33
PYD (positive youth development),
  250, 252–253

Questionnaire for Eudaimonic
 Well-Being (QEWB), 109

Rashid, T., 275
Rasmussen, D. B., 6
Realise2 model, 280–281
Real self, 102
Recognizing identity choices, 103–105
Reflective equilibrium, 35
Reflective volition, 64
Reich, Lily, 160
Relatedness
 as evolved need, 124
 and internalization, 62
 and intrinsic motivation, 62
 for optimal functioning, 61
 and well-being, 62–63
Resilience, 85
Richins, M. L., 153
Right
 good vs., 8
 individual, 272

Rogers, C., 47, 207, 213
Rogers, C. R., 81, 82, 279
Ross, L., 211–212
Rousseau, F. L., 191
Ruch, W., 152–153, 274–276
Ruini, C., 90
Rush Memory and Aging Project, 89
Russell, B., 80, 81
Ryan, R., 229
Ryan, R. M., 9–10, 47, 63, 64, 66–68,
  129, 140, 148, 151, 162–164
Ryff, C. D., 10, 113, 121, 162, 164, 229

Sandgren, M., 48
Sartre, J.-P., 81, 82, 101
Scales, P. C., 253
Schachter, E. P., 261–262
Schachtman, T. R., 211
Schimel, J., 210
Schuler, J., 128–129
Schwartz, B., 48
Schwartz, S. J., 113, 170, 171
Schwarz, N., 58
SDT. *See* Self-determination theory
Search Institute, 252
Sebire, S. J., 66
Séguin-Lévesque, C., 196
Self
 idealized, 102
 real, 102
Self-acceptance
 as core dimension of well-being, 82
 and inflammatory marker IL-6, 88
Self-actualization, theoretical discus-
  sions of, 11
Self-authorship, 172
Self-awareness, true, 210
Self-concordance theory/model,
  126–129
 construct, 126–127
 as deep person/goal fit, 128–129
 defined, 11
 eudaimonic well-being as, 12
 and self-determination theory, 11–12
Self-concordant goals, 174
Self-connectedness, 146–147
Self-consistency, 11
Self-creation/self-construction, identity
  as, 100–101
Self-defining activities, 251, 255–258

Self description, true, 215
Self-determination theory (SDT),
      60–69, 124
   autonomy and wellness in, 64–65
   and awareness, 68–69
   on life goals and aspirations, 65–67
   processes of actualization in, 63–64
   and self-concordance theory, 11–12
   true self in, 208
Self-directed activities, 59–60
Self-discovery
   identity as, 100, 101
   and self-concordance construct, 131
   of true self, 209–210
Self-esteem
   in children, 151–152
   in eudaimonia and hedonia, 143t,
      148–149
   and eudaimonic identity function-
      ing, 113–114
   and knowledge of true self, 209–210
   in life satisfaction, 238
   and meaning in life, 167
   and obsessive passion, 186
   and perceived true self-knowledge,
      216
   and self-acceptance, 82
   in subjective well-being, 276–277
   true, 211
Self-expression. *See* Personal
      expressiveness
Self-fulfillment
   definitions of, 48
   happiness as, 28
   and optional functioning, 48
Self-gratification, 169
Self-insight, 134
Self-knowledge, true, 209–210, 215–216
Self-presentation, optimal, 130
Self-realization
   activities related to, 11
   Aristotle on, 79
   consistent with the common good,
      59–60
   eudaimonia as, 6–7, 164
   in eudaimonic function, 109–115,
      183
   and eudaimonic functioning at
      activities level, 110
   in eudaimonic identity theory, 250

as eudaimonic well-being, 10–13, 272
and eudaimonist ethics, 104
exercise of virtues activities for, 44
and identity choices, 106–107
and individual daimon, 131–132
Norton's concept of, 243
and optimal functioning in society,
      201–202
and personal growth, 81, 162
and self-connectedness, 146–147
and self-transcendence, 173
societal benefits of, 77–78
studies of, 189
theoretical discussions of/research
      on, 11
and well-being/socioeconomic status,
      84–86
in well-being therapy, 90
Self-reflection, importance of, 68
Self-transcendence, 173
Self-worth, and meaning in life, 173
Seligman, M. E. P., 122, 141, 152–153,
      188, 229, 270, 272–276, 278
Shared family narratives, 172
Sharpe, K. E., 48
Sheldon, K. M., 11, 64, 124–125,
      128–130, 133, 164, 211, 214, 277
SHI (Steen Happiness Index), 275
Short-term gratification, 122–123
Signature strengths, 273
Simple preference-satisfaction
      theories, 23
Singer, B. H., 164
Sleep, and positive relations with
      others, 87
So, T. T. C., 122
Social character, true self vs., 211
Social–cognitive processes, in
      constructing life narratives, 172
Social goodness, 47–48, 67
Social information, internalizing/
      integrating, 62
Social institutions, "structural lag"
      problem and, 84
Social perception, 47
Social relationships, 233–235, 238. *See
      also* Interpersonal relationships
Society
   choice and self-direction empowered
      by, 279–280

Society, *continued*
    contributions to, 198–200
    cultural comparisons of
        meaningfulness of,
            233–235, 241
    proper aim of, 59
Socioeconomic variants
    in cross-cultural studies, 241
    and dimensions of well-being, 84–85
    and health, 88
Soenens, B., 112
Spirituality, 234, 242
Standage, M., 66
State level, relationship of hedonia and
    eudaimonia at, 142–144
Staudinger, U. M., 172
Steen, T. A., 275
Steen Happiness Index (SHI), 275
Steger, M. F., 166, 168–170, 172
Stephan, Y., 193
St-Louis, A., 199
Stoics, 44
Strengths Gym, 276
Strengths Use Scale, 272, 276
Stress, mindfulness and, 68
"Structural lag" problem, 84
Subjective experiences, 104–105
Subjective theories of well-being, 21,
    28–29
    desire-fulfillment theories, 22–24
    idealizing conditions in, 25–26
    ingredients of well-being in, 30–32
    life-satisfaction theory, 24–25
    values in, 25
Subjective well-being (SWB), 42–44
    of adolescents, 258–259
    components of, 145
    conceptualization of, 12
    Deiner's approach to, 163
    in eudaimonia, 140
    and eudaimonic identity
        functioning, 13, 113–114
    general process model of, 125–133
    as happiness, 8–9, 12–13
    high scores on measures of, 9
    and human strengths, 274–277
    mediation of idiographic goal effects
        by universal need satisfaction,
            127–128
    noneudaimonic measure of, 120–123

nonhedonic elements in, 40
operational definition of, 120
organismic perspective, 123–124
in positive psychology, 8–9, 270–271
and psychological/eudamaimonic
    well-being, 231
in psychology vs. philosophy, 243
self-concordance as deep person/goal
    fit, 128–129
and self-concordance construct,
    126–127
in self-determination theory, 61
and social character vs. true self, 211
terminology, 164
and three universal needs, 124–125
Sullivan, W. M., 214
Sumner, L., 33, 35, 243
Sumner, L. W., 21, 24, 42
SWB. *See* Subjective well-being
Swidler, A., 214

Telfer, E., 5, 106
Temperament, 103
Thagard, P., 46–47
Theorell, T., 48
Theories of well-being, 20–36. *See also*
    individual theories
    basic criteria for, 34–36
    desire-fulfillment theories, 22–24
    hedonism, 21–22
    idealizing conditions in, 25–26
    and importance of philosophical
        distinctions, 32–34
    ingredients of a good life in, 30–32
    life-satisfaction theory, 24–25
    and meta-theoretical
        assumptions, 231
    nature-fulfillment theories, 27–28
    objective, 21, 28–29
    objective-list theories, 26
    subjective, 21, 28–29
Thinking
    eudaimonic, 44, 58
    feeling and, 40
    organismic, 61
Thompson, A., 152
Thriving, 123, 252–253
Tiberius, V., 24, 130–133
Time magazine, 159–160
TimeWise (L. L. Caldwell), 261

Tipton, S. M., 214
Tocqueville, Alexis de, 198
Tomkins, S. S., 49–50
Trait level, relationship of hedonia and
        eudaimonia at, 142–144
True self. See Daimon (true self)
True self description, 215
True self-esteem, 211
Tsukayama, E., 276, 277
Turner, R. H., 211

Universal nature fulfillment, 140
Universal needs, 124–125
    individual perception of needs vs., 58
    mediation of idiographic goal effects
        by satisfaction of, 127–128
    psychological, 60
    in self-determination theory, 60

Vallerand, R. J., 185, 187, 189, 191,
        193–196, 199, 200
Value orientations
    intrinsic vs. extrinsic, 66–67
    and meaning in life, 173
Values
    in life-satisfaction theory, 24–25
    and objective-list theories, 26
    in subjective theories of
        well-being, 25
    in theories of well-being, 33
Values in Action (VIA) Classification
        of Strengths, 272–273
Van Hiel, A., 66
van Reekum, C. M., 87
Vansteenkiste, M., 66, 112
Ventura, J. J., 261–262
VIA (Values in Action) Classification
        of Strengths, 272–273
Virtue(s)
    Aristotle on, 79
    development of, 161–162
    eudaimonia as, 44
    intellectual, 60
Vitality, in eudaimonian and hedonia,
        148–149
Volition, in eudaimonic living, 63–64

Warren, S., 280
Waterman, A. S., 47, 100, 106, 108–112,
        151, 162–164, 208, 250–251, 256

Watson, J., 46
Wealth, 59
"Weekend effect," 63
Weinstein, N., 67
Well-being, 39–51. See also Happiness;
        individual aspects of well-being
    ancient Greek's conception of,
        30–31
    concept of, 8–13
    conceptualizations of, 12–13
    context of, 228–230
    definition of, 20, 120
    from developmental psychology
        perspective, 249
    eudaimonic. See Eudaimonic
        well-being
    eudaimonic ingredients of, 44
    fundamental needs for, 62–63
    hedonic, 40–42, 168–169
    individual pursuit of, 230
    links between human strengths and,
        274–279
    meaning in life as flagship indicator
        of, 169
    multifaceted measures of,
        120–122
    nature of, xiii–xiv
    as normative, 34
    operational definition of, 120
    of other people, 139, 151–152
    personal, 151
    pleasure and meaning in, 49–51
    psychological. See Psychological
        well-being
    and pursuit of both eudaimonia and
        hedonia, 139
    subjective. See Subjective
        well-being
    theories of. See Theories of
        well-being
    and well-doing, 49
Well-being research, importance of
        philosophical distinctions in,
        32–34
"Well-being therapy," 90
Well-doing, well-being and, 49
Well lived life, questions in defining,
        19–20. See also Good life
Wellness
    and autonomy, 64–65

Wellness, *continued*
    and positive emotions, 58
    self-determination theory viewpoint
        on, 61–69
    and volitional helping, 67
Whitehouse, H., 50
Williams, M., 209–210
Wisdom, 60
Women, biomarkers and reported
        well-being in, 86–87
Wood, A. M., 276–277

Work
    autonomy in, 63
    in cross-cultural perceptions of
        happiness, 239–240
    cultural comparisons of meaning-
        fulness of, 233–235, 237,
        239–240
    intrinsic aspirations in, 66
    as long-term and proximal
        commitment, 241
Wyss, T., 275–276

ABOUT THE EDITOR

Alan S. Waterman, PhD, is a personality and developmental psychologist. He received his doctorate in clinical psychology from the State University of New York at Buffalo in 1966. He is currently Professor Emeritus in Psychology at The College of New Jersey. He has served as president of the Society of Research in Identity Formation (SRIF) and is currently serving as editor of *Identity: An International Journal of Theory and Research*, a journal sponsored by SRIF. He is a fellow in Divisions 7 (Developmental Psychology) and 24 (Society for Theoretical and Philosophical Psychology) of the American Psychological Association. His interests include the philosophical foundations of personality theories and empirical research on identity formation; the quality of identity choices; and, more broadly, quality of life.